Developing Secure Applications with Visual Basic®

Davis Chapman

A Division of Macmillan USA
201 West 103rd St., Indianapolis, Indiana, 46290 USA

Developing Secure Applications with Visual Basic®

Copyright © 2000 by Sams Publishing

International Standard Book Number: 0-672-31836-9

Library of Congress Catalog Card Number: 99-66271

Printed in the United States of America

First Printing: May 2000

02   01   00   4   3   2   1

Trademarks

Warning and Disclaimer

ASSOCIATE PUBLISHER
Bradley L. Jones

EXECUTIVE EDITOR
Chris Webb

DEVELOPMENT EDITOR
Steve Rowe

MANAGING EDITOR
Charlotte Clapp

PROJECT EDITOR
Carol L. Bowers

COPY EDITORS
Barbara Hacha
Chuck Hutchinson

INDEXER
Kevin Fulcher

PROOFREADER
Jill Mazurczyk

TECHNICAL EDITOR
John Hooven

TEAM COORDINATOR
Meggo Barthlow

MEDIA DEVELOPER
Jason Haines

INTERIOR DESIGNER
Anne Jones

COVER DESIGNER
Anne Jones

COPY WRITER
Eric Bogert

Contents at a Glance

Contents

About the Author

Davis Chapman first began programming computers while working on his Masters Degree in Music Composition. While writing applications for computer music, he discovered that he enjoyed designing and developing computer software. It wasn't long before he came to the realization that he stood a much better chance of eating if he stuck with his new-found skill and demoted his hard-earned status as a "starving artist" to a part-time hobby. Since that time, Davis has focused on the art of software design and development, with a strong emphasis on the practical application of Client/Server and Web/Internet technologies. Davis was the lead author for *Sams Teach Yourself Visual C++ 6 in 21 Days*, *Web Development with Visual Basic 5,* and *Building Internet Applications with Delphi 2*. Davis was also a contributing author on *MFC Programming with Visual C++ 6 Unleashed*, *Special Edition Using Active Server Pages*, and *Running a Perfect Web Site, Second Edition*. He has been a consultant working and living in Dallas, Texas, for the past 10 years, and is currently with Rare Medium, an award-winning Web site and Web application design firm. Davis can be reached at davischa@onramp.net.

Dedication

As always, this is dedicated to my beautiful wife, Dore. I promise that next year I'll have the time to spend with you during the holidays, Valentines Day, your birthday...

Acknowledgments

Numerous people deserve a big thank you for all their help and support during the writing of this book. First, my wife, Dore, deserves a great big hug for allowing me to take the time necessary to write this book. It's been a long, difficult task to get this one finished. I also need to thank Chris Webb for carrying on within Macmillan, insisting that I was the one they needed to write this book. I also need to thank Chris, Steve Rowe, and the rest of the editorial team for putting up with me with a lot of patience and understanding through this project. John Hooven deserves special credit for doing a great job as a technical editor. He made sure and pointed out to me when I wasn't doing something in quite as pure a Visual Basic way as I could have, and he also let me know when I tried to get a little too fancy for my own good. I need to extend a big thank you to Loren, Pierre, and Bill for pitching in and helping me finish writing this book, and to Mickey for letting me adapt what he had written. I also have to thank John Banes at Microsoft for taking the time to answer my questions. Finally, I'd like to thank everyone at Rare Medium for providing me with a very enjoyable day job, and also for keeping me so busy that it added at least a couple of months onto the time it took for me to write this book. Last but not least, I'd like to thank you, the reader, for buying the books I write, so that Macmillan continues to allow me to write books on topics such as this. Thank you!

Tell Us What You Think!

As the reader of this book, *you* are our most important critic and commentator. We value your opinion and want to know what we're doing right, what we could do better, what areas you'd like to see us publish in, and any other words of wisdom you're willing to pass our way.

I welcome your comments. You can fax, email, or write me directly to let me know what you did or didn't like about this book—as well as what we can do to make our books stronger.

Please note that I cannot help you with technical problems related to the topic of this book, and that due to the high volume of mail I receive, I might not be able to reply to every message.

When you write, please be sure to include this book's title and author as well as your name and phone or fax number. I will carefully review your comments and share them with the author and editors who worked on the book.

Fax: 317-581-4770

E-mail: `adv_prog@mcp.com`

Mail: Bradley L. Jones
            Publisher
            Sams Publishing
            201 West 103rd Street
            Indianapolis, IN 46290 USA

Introduction

I know what you're thinking. You saw this book on the shelf and picked it up out of curiosity, thinking, "Encryption and Visual Basic? Security and Visual Basic? Aren't these topics normally reserved for the ranks of C/C++ developers?" Well, they used to be, but not anymore. Now you can perform these tasks within Visual Basic, without having to dip into any C/C++ code.

The next question on your mind probably is, "Do I have to be a super mathematician to do this? Doesn't encryption require you to do some heavy calculations?" The answers to these questions are, respectively, no and yes. Encryption does require some complex and heavy mathematical calculations, but you don't have to worry about those. You can continue to code your regular Visual Basic code, with a few new twists to add in some very advanced functionality.

Thanks to Microsoft, all the topics covered in this book are built in to the latest versions of its Windows and NT operating systems. This book shows you how to tap into these capabilities, enabling you to include this functionality in your applications. In short, you'll be letting the operating system do all the work for you.

However, just because the operating system is doing all the heavy lifting, it doesn't mean that you get out of all the work. You still need to write some code to control this functionality. Some of the code that you'll need to write may stretch your Visual Basic skills beyond what you've seen in most other programming situations. You'll also have to delve into areas of programming that Visual Basic normally tries to hide from you.

Take fair warning! This book is not for the Visual Basic beginner. If you just picked up Visual Basic for the first time last week, this is not the book for you (yet). This book is written with the assumption that you already know your way around Visual Basic and already have a bit of Visual Basic programming experience under your belt. However, if you've built several applications using Visual Basic and you pretty much know all the basics, you shouldn't have anything to fear.

How This Book Is Organized

I wrote this book to match the way that I read technical books. If you're like me, you aren't likely to read this book by starting on page 1 and reading straight through to the last page (not that anything is wrong with doing that). When I read a book like this, I skip around, reading just the chapters and sections that cover the specific topic that I want to learn. As a result, I'm as likely to start with Chapter 12 before I read Chapter 1. I'm also likely to read only one or two chapters to learn what I need right now, and then come back to this book several weeks or months later to read another couple of chapters on the next topic that I need to learn.

Therefore, this book is designed to be read in two ways. As is normal, this book is written and organized to be read from page 1 to the end. It is also designed for the skip-and-jump style reader, who reads only the chapters that cover what he or she needs to learn. Whenever a chapter covers a topic that requires you to have some knowledge that is found in a previous chapter, the topics are listed in a "Prerequisites" area. This enables you to glance over the background information that you need before reading a particular chapter, so that you can make the decision on whether you are ready to tackle that chapter or whether you need to back up and read an earlier chapter or two first.

This book is also organized around topic areas. The first portion of the book is concerned with encryption. The second portion of the book focuses on security programming. The third portion of the book covers some nonprogramming topics that you might need to be familiar with.

System Requirements

The ideal system for you to use for trying out the code in this book is a brand-new computer running Windows 2000 and Visual Basic 6 (with maximum memory and disk space, surround sound, DVD video, and so on. After all, I am talking about the ideal system). You also need to have ready access to a computer running Windows 2000 Server, with Certificate Services (Certificate Server) installed. You also should have access to the Administrator account on both of those computers.

Now, to reenter the real world, the preceding requirements are not realistic for all interested programmers. They are also not necessary for everything covered in this book. In reality, there are a variety of requirements for the different topics covered within these pages.

For most of the encryption topics, you'll need a base system of Windows 95 with Microsoft Internet Explorer 3.02 (or later) installed. It is preferable that you have at least Internet Explorer 4 installed. Some specific functions exist that require Windows 98 or Windows 2000, and some are available only on Windows 2000.

For the chapters dealing with certificates, you'll need access to a Certificate Authority (you can use Verisign, but unless you want to fork out some money, you may be limited to a temporary certificate). The ideal situation is to have Microsoft's Certificate Server installed on a nearby machine. Some of the COM objects used for interacting with the Certificate Authority are available only with the Windows 2000 version of Certificate Server. Microsoft's Certificate Server is available only on the Server (or later) versions of NT 4.0 and Windows 2000. You won't find it on NT 4.0 Workstation or Windows 2000 Professional.

For the section dealing with security, you need to work with NT 4.0 or Windows 2000. For a couple of the chapters in this section, you'll be limited to working with Windows 2000.

Conventions Used

Several conventions are used in this book. Some of these are illustrated here.

`Syntax`

```
Function declarations are presented in a very bland-looking type (my
editor wants me to describe it as a "computer type"). This distinguishes
them from the surrounding text. After all, I wouldn't want you to miss
something as important as function and type declarations by making them
blend into the rest of the page.
```

Listing 00.1   **THE FOLLOWING CODE IS A LISTING**

```
Actual code listings look very similar to the function and type
declarations. One difference is that code listings are preceded by a
listing number and a very short description of what is in the listing.
Also, code listings are usually a bit longer than function and type
declarations (but not always).
```

Term

Whenever a new term that you might not be familiar with is used, I provide a brief definition of the term. This is set apart from the rest of the text by making it look like what you are seeing here. This makes it easily recognizable so that if you already know the term and don't need to have it explained, you can skip the definition and continue on with your reading.

NOTE

Anything that I think is important for you to know, but that is outside of whatever is being discussed at the time, is set off from the main text by formatting it like this. It's a good idea to at least glance at these notes so that you are familiar with what they are trying to convey. Of course, there may be a time or two where I just felt like making some unimportant remark that really shouldn't be part of the main topic, so I'll mark those as notes, too.

> **CAUTION**
>
> Warning! Warning! Man the lifeboats! Oops, sorry—I got a little carried away. This is what warnings look like. It is important to pay attention to these. Warnings are usually the result of some scars that I acquired from doing what the warning tells you not to do. Don't be like my kids and do what I tell you not to do in these warnings.

Finally, some cute little icons let you know at a glance that whatever they are beside is available only on Windows 2000 or on Windows 98 and Windows 2000. When you see one of these, you'll know that what is beside them is of no use to you if you are still working with Windows 95 or NT 4.0.

Web Site

 A Web site containing source code and other items is also included with the book. You can access this book's Web site at www.samspublishing.com.

 If you're still reading this while standing in the aisle of the bookstore—enough already! It's time to make the decision either to buy this book or to put it back on the shelf. The reason I'm drawing the line here is because it's time to get busy and start the real portion of the book—learning how to add encryption and security functionality to your Visual Basic applications. If you've made the decision to buy this book, I thank you very much. Now turn the page and start learning the stuff that you bought this book to learn.

Thanks,

Davis Chapman

Understanding Encryption and Application Security

IN THIS CHAPTER

With the explosion of commerce and business applications on the Internet, whole areas of programming expertise have entered the limelight. Just a few short years ago, encryption and application security were areas of programming limited to academic and military programming, along with some Research and Development labs at various corporations. Now encryption and application security have become essential components of most applications over the past few years.

Until very recently, the areas of encryption and application security programming remained the exclusive realm of C/C++ programmers. Never would anyone have conceived of attempting any type of encryption or security using Visual Basic. These areas of programming required capabilities far beyond what was capable with other languages.

My, how times have changed! Now, it is possible to use Visual Basic to accomplish these tasks. This book is all about exploring how you can use Visual Basic to perform various encryption and application security tasks. These are exciting times for Visual Basic programmers!

Exploring Encryption

One of the key technologies involved with making secure communications possible, especially over the Internet, is encryption. At this point, almost every application that communicates over the Internet has some encryption capabilities. The use of encryption will only increase in the near future, and if you are building applications that will communicate over the Internet, you'll need to be able to include encryption capabilities.

When you're working with encryption, you need to be aware that numerous forms of encryption are available today. All these different forms of encryption have different strengths and weaknesses. You need to be aware of them and be able to weigh all the options as to which form of encryption to use, based on the specific needs of your application. Over the next few pages, you'll learn about several of the basic types of encryption in use today.

Encryption Algorithms and Standards

One of the key aspects of building secure encryption algorithms is making the algorithms public knowledge. At first, making the algorithms public sounds like the last thing you would want to do, but it actually leads to stronger encryption algorithms because many people are able to review the algorithms and find any weaknesses that would make them easy to "crack" or break.

Crack

When an encryption algorithm has been "cracked," it means that someone who is not supposed to be able to decrypt the message has broken the key to the message and is thus able to decrypt the message at will.

So, if the encryption algorithm is public knowledge, how do messages stay secure? The key to having secure encryption algorithms is the use of encryption keys. A key is a sequence of random values used to specify how messages are to be encrypted by the algorithm being used. The only way to decrypt a message is to use the key that was used to encrypt the message. If the encryption key is kept secret, then the message is kept secure, even if the algorithm is known.

CAUTION

Any encryption algorithm is only as secure as the key used to encrypt data. If an encryption key is easily available, any messages encrypted using that key can be easily decrypted. If you send an encrypted message to a friend, and have the encryption key freely available on a shared network drive, just about anyone who has access to that network drive will be able to decrypt the message. I cannot emphasize enough how important it is to keep encryption keys secure.

Another aspect of keeping encryption keys secure is when you use keys that are generated from passwords or other source material. It is important not to use words that are easily guessable. If you use the name of your spouse, child, or pet, then guessing the password to use is fairly trivial for any hacker using social hacking techniques.

Social Hacking

Also known as social engineering, this is a method commonly used by hackers to take advantage of common human behavior traits to extract passwords and other security information from people. It is easy to extract from someone the names of his or her spouse, children, and other people the person may be using as a password. It isn't difficult to engage anyone in conversation for a few minutes and extract these names, along with any hobbies the person enjoys, and the names of any people that the person admires and respects. Once you have this information, you have gone a long way toward being able to guess the person's password.

As computing power is rapidly increasing, so is the ease with which current encryption standards are able to be "cracked." The most common method of cracking a particular message is performing a brute-force generation of encryption keys, until the one that was used to encrypt the message is found.

Every encryption key can eventually be broken. The question is how long it will take to crack the key. For most purposes, cracking the encryption key will take long enough that the security of the message is no longer important. Almost every message that needs to be kept secure has a window of time in which the security needs to be maintained. Once that window is over, it no longer matters whether the message can be decrypted because the value of the message is gone.

Because of the increasing capacity to crack encryption keys, you need to be able to upgrade the encryption algorithms and key sizes you are using in your applications. One of the most basic ways of increasing the security of an encryption algorithm is to increase the size of the encryption key you use. The larger the key, the more possible combinations of random values, and the longer it will take to crack. The correlation between key length and number of possible combinations is an exponential curve (adding a single bit to an encryption key doubles the number of possible combinations, doubling the length of time necessary to crack the key), so doubling the length of the encryption key greatly increases the security of the algorithm.

Along with increasing the key length, new encryption algorithms are frequently being developed and introduced into the public marketplace for evaluation and possibly for adoption as a new standard. Therefore, you need to be able to occasionally update and add new algorithms to the capabilities supported by your applications.

Symmetric Encryption

There are two basic types of encryption algorithms. The first of these types is *symmetric encryption*. Symmetric encryption requires the same encryption key to be used for encrypting and decrypting a message, as illustrated in Figure 1.1. Therefore, both parties—the sender of the message and the receiver—need to have the same encryption key.

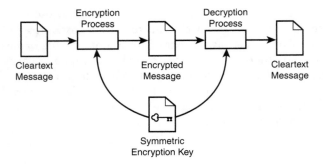

FIGURE 1.1
Symmetric encryption uses a single key.

One of the strengths of symmetric encryption is its speed. Symmetric encryption algorithms are among the fastest means of both encrypting and decrypting a message. One of the biggest weaknesses of symmetric encryption is that both parties need to have the same encryption key. The biggest problem surrounding the use of symmetric encryption is how to get the encryption key into the hands of both parties without it falling into the hands of a third party that should be prevented from decrypting the messages being passed between the first two parties.

Asymmetric Encryption

The second basic type of encryption algorithm is *asymmetric*, or public key, encryption. This form of encryption utilizes two keys: a public key that can be freely distributed and a private key that is kept secure. Anything encrypted using either of these two keys can only be decrypted using the other key. Usually, the sender encrypts a message using the public key of the message recipient. Only the recipient can decrypt the message using his or her private key.

In asymmetric encryption, both keys are derived from a single master encryption key, as illustrated in Figure 1.2. When the keys are derived from a common master key, the two keys are mathematically related, but neither key can be calculated from the other key. After the public and private keys have been derived, the master key is destroyed, thus removing any means of calculating either of the two keys at a later time.

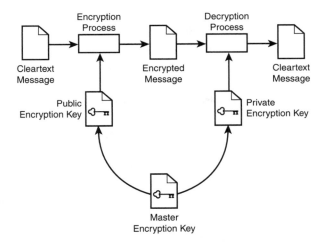

FIGURE 1.2
Asymmetric encryption uses two keys, derived from a single master key.

Because of the way asymmetric encryption works, it is ideal for use over a public network like the Internet. You can freely send out your public key, and anyone can use it to send you encrypted messages that only you can decrypt. As a result, you don't care if someone you don't want seeing messages intended for you intercepts your public key. All he or she can do is send you secure messages; this person cannot decrypt any of the messages.

One of the biggest problems with asymmetric encryption is that it is very slow in comparison with symmetric encryption. As a result, it is not suitable for encrypting large amounts of data in an interactive mode. As a result, what you'll often find in use is a combination of symmetric and asymmetric encryption. A symmetric encryption key is generated for use during the session; then this key is encrypted and exchanged using asymmetric encryption. When the session is over, the session key is destroyed.

Other Forms of Encryption

Symmetric and asymmetric encryption are not the only forms of encryption available. Several other forms of encryption can be used in special situations. Some of these other forms of encryption include exclusive OR (XOR), substitution and transposition, steganography, and one-time pads.

Exclusive OR (XOR)

Exclusive OR (XOR) is a simple form of symmetric encryption. XOR works on a bit level, combining two strings of bits, setting the bit in the resulting string to 1 if either one of the bits in the original strings happens to be set to 1, but setting the resulting bit to 0 if both original bits are either 1 or 0, as illustrated in Figure 1.3. After you have an encrypted string of bits, you can use XOR on it with either of the original strings of bits and get the second of the original strings of bits.

Original Message	**11010010**
	XOR
Encryption Key	**10111001**
	=
Encrypted Message	**01101011**
	XOR
Encryption Key	**10111001**
	=
Original Message	**11010010**

FIGURE 1.3

XOR combines two strings of bits to form a third string of bits.

Substitution and Transposition

Substitution and *transposition* are two of the oldest forms of encryption. These forms are also conceptually some of the easiest to understand. Basically, both of these forms of encryption replace every letter in a message with a different letter. The difference is in how the replacement letter is selected.

With a substitution algorithm, a table of substitutions is created, with letters randomly inserted into the table such that every letter and number in the alphabet, and likely every printable character or symbol, has a substitute character or symbol that is used in its place. The result is a message that looks like gobbledygook. To decrypt the message, an inverse substitution table is used.

With a transposition algorithm, a number is randomly chosen, and then each letter is transposed up or down the alphabet by that number of characters. The resulting message looks very similar to a substitution algorithm message. To decrypt the message, each letter is transposed the same number of characters in the opposite direction.

Steganography

Steganography is a type of encryption in which messages are passed in a form that is unrecognizable as a message. In this type of encryption, a message is embedded in something else, such as an image or another message. In one of the oldest forms of steganography a message contains a second, secret message. In this case, the first letter of each word or every fifth letter or some other repeating pattern is extracted from the host message to form a second, secret message.

One of the easiest ways to use this form of encryption with computers is to embed secret messages into images or other similar types of objects. In an image file, numerous bits are used to specify the color of each pixel in the image. If the least significant bit in each pixel color is modified to contain a message, there will be little, if any, noticeable difference in the image. The higher the resolution of the image, the easier it is to hide a message in it. A program that knows how the messages are encoded can easily extract these messages.

One-Time Pads

One-time pad is the only completely secure encryption method. It is basically a completely random, continuous stream of key values. As each character in the message is to be encrypted, the next key value is used to encrypt it, either by a *mod-26 method* or via XOR with electronic means. After a key value has been used, it is thrown away and never used again.

NOTE

It is widely believed that there is no completely secure form of encryption due to the dependence on encryption keys to tell the algorithm how to encrypt the data. Given enough time, anyone can create a duplicate key and be able to decrypt all messages encrypted with that particular key. This is often done by brute force, where every possible combination of numbers is tried until the correct combination is found. With increasingly powerful computers, the amount of time necessary to find the correct key is shrinking rapidly. Because of this, there is a constant movement to use longer and longer keys.

What makes the one-time pad method ultimately secure is that it has an infinite length key, with any number of possible combinations. Yes, you can fairly easily come up with a combination that decrypts a message in a way that makes sense. But as you'll see shortly, you can never be sure that you've decrypted the correct message. Any message encrypted using a one-time pad may be decrypted into an infinite number of messages.

As with all forms of key-based encryption, a one-time pad is only as secure as its key. If the key is kept in a readily accessible location, like on a shared network drive, then the encrypted message will not be very secure.

What makes this encryption scheme so secure is that an infinite number of possibilities exists for the key, each of which decrypts the message to a legible message. There is no way of knowing whether the message you've decrypted is the original message unless you possess the original key sequence. For instance, if you start with the message

ORIGINAL

and then encrypt using the key

BAYJFKID

you would come out with the following encrypted message:

QSHQOYJP

If you decrypt this word using the key

VAMVGSOD

you end up with the following message:

TRUTHFUL

How are you supposed to know whether you've decrypted the correct message? You don't!

Mod-26

Mod-26 is a character substitution method in which the sequential numbers from 0 to 25 are assigned to the letters of the alphabet (the number range is different for languages that have more or fewer characters than 26). Next, the numeric values of the original character and the key character are added. If the resulting value is less than 26, the corresponding character is substituted for the original character. If the number is equal to or more than 26, 26 is subtracted from the resulting number, and the corresponding character is used.

To decrypt, the key character values are subtracted from the encrypted character values. If the resulting value is negative, then 26 is added to the value to determine the correct substitution character. This method of encrypting has been used for years for performing one-time pad encryption by hand. For use with computers, an XOR method is much more practical and just as secure.

A few complicating factors with the one-time pad encryption method make it impractical for major use over the Internet. The first problem is that the key sequence needs to be truly random. The key cannot be pseudo-random. Computers are fully capable of generating pseudo-random numbers, but not truly random numbers. The random number generator that you have available to you in Visual Basic, or in any other programming language, is actually a mathematical formula that generates what appears to be random numbers. Because they are generated via a formula, they can be easily predicted, thus removing the security of the one-time pad key.

The next problem is the distribution of the key. The encryption key needs to be at least as long as the message being encrypted. The key also needs to be destroyed as it is used. The need to destroy the key eliminates the use of CDs or DVDs as a possible distribution method, although the use of CD-RWs begins to make this use a possibility (although it does restrict the hardware that can be used).

A third problem is keeping the keys perfectly in sync. If either key—the one being used to encrypt or decrypt the message—gets out of sync with the other, then the messages cannot be correctly decrypted. With the constant probability of transmission errors, keeping the keys in sync can be a very big problem with the use of one-time pads.

Using Certificates with Encryption

One of the biggest problems surrounding the use of public-key encryption algorithms is being able to verify that the public key you received is really from the person you want to send a secure message to. You need a method of verifying that the key is from the person you think it's from, and that it hasn't been modified or tampered with. This is the problem that *digital certificates* have been designed to solve.

A digital certificate packages a person's public key with a set of credentials to vouch for the person's identity. The entire package is digitally signed by a Certificate Authority (CA) to vouch for the identity of the owner of the certificate. The certificate also contains the Certificate Authority's credentials and the ID of the CA's own certificate that can be used to verify the signature in the certificate, as illustrated in Figure 1.4.

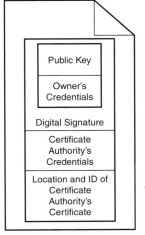

Digital Certificate

FIGURE 1.4

The packaging of a digital certificate.

Certificate Authorities

A Certificate Authority is a commonly agreed-upon authority whose verification of someone's identity is accepted by all parties. It can be a large, independent organization such as Verisign (www.verisign.com) or the security department within a corporation. The CA has the responsibility of verifying the identity of a certificate applicant and that the public key to be included in the certificate really belongs to the person applying for a certificate. After the CA has verified these items to its satisfaction, it packages the public key and credentials into a certificate and issues the certificate to the applicant.

Certificate Chains

When you're working with Certificate Authorities, you need to understand that you might have to navigate through multiple CAs to find a common CA. CAs can operate in a chain, each verified and certified by the next CA up the chain, until a common root CA is reached, as illustrated in Figure 1.5. This chain is called a *Chain of Trust*. If a CA low on the chain issues a certificate, you need to traverse the chain until you reach the root CA to verify the certificate. The idea is that, for each CA authorized by the root CA, that CA can be trusted to authorize the next level of CAs, and at each level, the CA can be trusted to issue certificates to individuals.

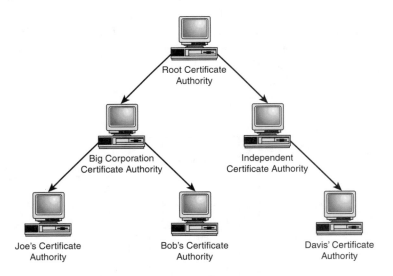

FIGURE 1.5
A Chain of Trust of Certificate Authorities.

Digital Signatures

One of the key technologies helping to make certificates work is *digital signatures*. A digital signature is basically a one-way hash of the message, or of whatever is being signed. This hash is then encrypted using the private key of the signer. The recipient of the message creates his or her own one-way hash of the message and then decrypts the signature hash and compares the two hashes. If the hashes match, the signature is valid, and the message hasn't been altered or tampered with since being signed. This process is illustrated in Figure 1.6.

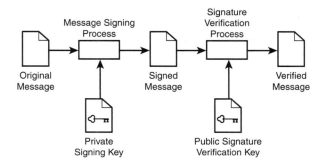

FIGURE 1.6
The digital signature process.

One-Way Hash

A *one-way hash* is like a fingerprint of a message or other object. Several algorithms can be used to generate a one-way hash, each producing a different hash value. If any change, no matter how small, is made to the original message, the resulting hash value will be different.

A key aspect of a one-way hash is that there is no way to re-create the message from the hash value. The hash algorithms are designed such that there is no possible way to re-create the original message from the hash value.

Digital signatures are used not only for validating digital messages, but they are also a key technology for verifying the sender of a message. For any message that needs to guarantee who sent the message, and that the message hasn't been modified or tampered with in any way, the use of digital signatures is crucial.

Message Enveloping

Combining digital signatures and encryption results in what is called *message enveloping*. An enveloped message is first signed using the sender's private signing key, and then the signed message is encrypted using the recipient's public key. When the recipient receives the message, the message is decrypted using the recipient's private key, and then verifies the message signature using the sender's public key, as shown in Figure 1.7.

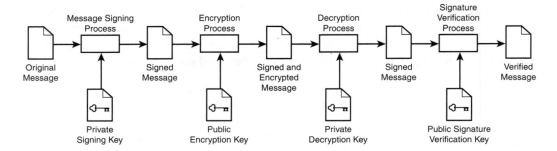

FIGURE 1.7
Combining digital signatures and encryption as message enveloping.

Message enveloping accomplishes two goals. When the inner message is signed by the sender, the contents of the message are verified to have come from the sender, without any modifications. By then encrypting the message and the signature, you are guaranteeing that only the intended recipient will be able to decrypt and read the message.

Secure Sockets Layer (SSL)

One of the most recognized technologies in use on the Internet is the Secure Sockets Layer (SSL) protocol. The reason for the notoriety is that this security protocol is used on the Web to secure the transfer of sensitive information. Every time you make a purchase over the Web, you see the SSL protocol at work, making sure that your credit card information is kept secure.

SSL is referred to as a *protocol* because that's exactly what it is. SSL uses a combination of the technologies that have already been described in this chapter to first establish the identity of the server and possibly the client (digital certificates), then to generate a session encryption key (symmetric encryption), and finally to securely exchange that session key using public/private keys (asymmetric encryption). After this process has been completed, the session key is used by both sides to securely encrypt and exchange data using the application protocol (HTTP, FTP, SMTP, and so on).

Security and Audit Logs

Changing subjects, let's look at a topic that is crucial to application security but will not be discussed elsewhere in this book (and is often overlooked in other books). If you are building a server application, one area of functionality, while not being one of the more glamorous areas of security programming, cannot be overlooked. This is the area of creating and writing security and audit logs. The creation of security and audit logs is crucial to the detection of security breaks and the pursuit of the guilty parties.

Why Do You Need Audit Logs?

Yes, writing security and audit logs is something that the operating system is already doing, so why do you need to concern yourself with building another audit log? If a user is interacting directly with your application, the operating system is not likely to recognize that a security breach has occurred. Only your application is in a position to recognize this situation and have the information necessary to identify what happened, who did it, and how it was done.

If a security breach occurs through your application, a security log can provide you with valuable information on how your application was compromised, so you can correct the problem and make your application more secure than it was. It can also provide key information for identifying and prosecuting the cracker who broke through your defenses, assuming that either damage was done or valuable information was stolen.

If your application accesses sensitive information, in a database or other information source, it is often important to maintain an audit log of who accessed what sensitive information and what information was accessed. This information will be important if sensitive information is revealed to someone who is not privy to the information, or if someone is abusing his or her access to this information. The information in the audit log will be used to determine who might be guilty of these indiscretions and what corrective action should be taken.

What Information Needs to Be Included?

In a security or audit log, you need to include as much information as you possibly can. For a security log, you need to include the IP address of the perpetrator, the login or username (if available), what was done or what command was issued, the data passed to the command that caused the error, the time and date, and any other relevant data (depending on your application).

For instance, if someone is trying to find a valid username/password combination for your application, you should record in the security log the IP address of the person, the username used, the date and time, and the fact that the login attempt failed. If subsequent attempts are made, you should include the number of failed attempts that have been made. It is debatable whether you should include the passwords tried in the log. Including the passwords tried in the log may enable you to tell whether the person is trying a brute-force method to find a valid password. At the same time, if someone is simply mistyping his or her password, recording the password in the log could compromise that user's account.

The information an audit log records is dependent on the particular situation. For controlling sensitive information in a database, an audit log would record the username of every user who accesses the sensitive information. The audit log would also record any changes made to this information, who made the change, and the before and after values for the information that was changed. As with security logs, the times and dates of all actions would be recorded in the audit log.

For instance, if someone were accessing and altering sensitive medical records, you would probably want to record the username, which records were accessed, what information was changed, and what the information was prior to being changed. You would also want to record the time and date the records were accessed and changed. Finally, if you have this information available, you would want to record how the user accessed the records, whether through an application screen or via some other known means.

Summary

In this chapter, you learned about several types of encryption and how they differ; you also read a high-level overview of how they work. You learned how, on a high-level, some of these encryption technologies are combined to form more-involved forms of encryption intended to solve multiple problems at one time, as with message enveloping and the Secure Socket Layer protocol. This description is as detailed as this book will get on any of these encryption algorithms. This book is not intended to teach you how to develop new encryption algorithms but instead how to use those that already exist and are available for your use as part of the Windows operating system. You need to understand, on a high-level, how these different types of encryption work, but you don't need to know the nitty-gritty details.

Also in this chapter, you looked briefly at the too-often-overlooked topic of security and audit logs. You learned why it is important to write and maintain these logs, along with what types of information you should be sure to record in them. You also learned under what circumstances you should record events in these logs.

In the next several chapters, you'll learn about the cryptographic extensions to the Windows API that Microsoft has been building into the operating system over the past few years. You'll see how you can use these API calls to build various cryptographic functions into your applications, all without knowing the nitty-gritty details of how the encryption is done. After the section on adding encryption capabilities into your applications, you'll find a series of chapters on interacting with the security infrastructure built into the Windows NT operating system, including some new security features in the Windows 2000 operating system. Finally, you'll find a few chapters on various related nonprogramming issues, such as an overview of Microsoft's Certificate Server application and an overview of the legal landscape surrounding encryption and security programming.

Anyway, you most likely didn't buy this book just to read about security and encryption on a high-level. You probably bought this book to learn how to program security and encryption into your applications, with actual code that you can get your hands around and play with. If this is the case, then let's get started with the next chapter. Get ready to start hacking some code!

Getting Started with the CryptoAPI

IN THIS CHAPTER

- CryptoAPI and Cryptographic Service Providers
- Listing CSPs and CSP Types

Many applications today incorporate some form of encryption into their functionality. Unfortunately, encryption is a realm of programming with which most programmers do not have much, if any, experience. So how are we supposed to add these capabilities to our applications without hiring a bunch of mathematicians who talk in numbers so that they sound like they're speaking a foreign language?

If you listen carefully, you'll hear the sound of Microsoft riding in from the northwest to save the day, like the hero in an old Clint Eastwood (or John Wayne) Western movie. It just so happens that Microsoft has been building cryptographic capabilities into the Windows operating systems for the past few years.

Microsoft began adding these capabilities to the operating system as an extension that would be installed with its Internet Explorer Web browser and with NT service packs, but now they come as part of the core operating system with Windows 2000. At this point in time, if you have Internet Explorer 3.02 or higher on any version of Windows, you've got these encryption capabilities. These capabilities make advanced encryption available to any programmer through a series of simple API calls. Nothing could be simpler. (Okay, I might be exaggerating a little here; many things are simpler, but this capability still makes adding encryption to your applications quite easy.)

In this chapter, you'll become familiar with some of the basics of the Microsoft CryptoAPI and build a couple of simple applications that use some of the capabilities of the CryptoAPI.

CryptoAPI and Cryptographic Service Providers

When the folks at Microsoft decided how they were going to build this cryptographic functionality into the operating system, they chose to make it very flexible and expandable. They realized that different applications would need different types and strengths of encryption. They also knew that new types of encryption would be released on a regular basis.

The question was how to make the API able to continuously expand and adapt as the state of the art for encryption changes, while not requiring constant changing and updating of all the applications that use the API. Microsoft's solution to this question was to make the API a front end that applications could use and call, while the back end was an open API for any encryption vendor to plug in its own encryption engine, as illustrated in Figure 2.1.

These plug-in encryption engines are called *Cryptographic Service Providers (CSPs)*. Windows is shipped with some default CSPs that serve most basic encryption needs. Even if your application needs require a CSP that is not shipped with Windows, you build your application no differently than if you could use a default one.

NOTE

The construction of Cryptographic Service Providers (CSP) is not covered in this book. This book covers only how to build applications that use the API.

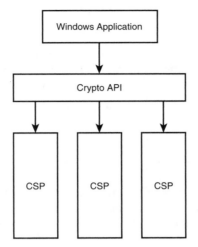

FIGURE 2.1
The CryptoAPI passes messages between applications and Cryptographic Service Providers.

With this design, the CryptoAPI does little more than pass messages back and forth between the applications using it and the CSPs being used by those applications. Consequently, all the responsibility for performing the encryption and decryption is placed on the CSP, not your application. You therefore can change what type of encryption you are using as the need arises. It also places the need to employ those number-speaking mathematicians on the vendors creating the CSPs.

Opening the CSP

One of the first steps that you have to take in an application that uses the CryptoAPI is to open a context handle to the appropriate CSP. The CSP context is opened with the `CryptAcquireContext` function. The declaration for the `CryptAcquireContext` function is as follows:

> ### Context Handle
>
> A *context handle* is an ID for a resource that has been opened and is being maintained by the operating system. A context handle is different from a pointer in that a pointer contains an actual memory address where the object can be found, whereas a handle contains an ID number that is used to identify the object. Context handles are typically used with resources that are made available for use by the operating system.

Syntax

```
Public Declare Function CryptAcquireContext Lib "advapi32.dll" _
    Alias "CryptAcquireContextA" (phProv As Long, _
    ByVal pszContainer As String, ByVal pszProvider As String, _
    ByVal dwProvType As Long, ByVal dwFlags As Long) As Long
```

NOTE

Microsoft has not packaged the CryptoAPI in an ActiveX or COM control (despite a lot of documentation from Microsoft mentioning such a control). As a result, all the function declarations in this book are given in the form of their API declarations so that Visual Basic can use the function.

TIP

In this and other function declarations that have string parameters, you have the option of declaring the alias with a trailing "W" instead of the trailing "A" if you know that you will be running on NT or Windows 2000. This will call the UNICODE versions of these functions, allowing you to use UNICODE strings. The other option that you have available to you is to declare all "ByVal String" parameters as "ByRef Byte" parameters, and pass in the first position in a byte array that you have copied the string into. If you will be working only with character sets that fit within the ANSI character set, or will be needing your applications to run on Windows 95/98, then leave all of the function alias declarations as they are specified in this book, using the ANSI version of the functions.

The first parameter to this function (phProv) is a long variable into which the handle for the CSP context will be placed. This variable will be used throughout your application.

The second variable (pszContainer) is the name of the key container to be opened. If you are using the default Microsoft CSP and pass a string consisting only of the NULL string (vbNullString), the CSP will use the login name of the current user for the name of the key container.

NOTE

If your application stores private key information in the key store, it is recommended that you do not use the default key store, no matter which CSP you are using. The reason for this is that it would be very easy for any other application to write over or otherwise alter the key information in the default key store. By creating an application-specific key store, you can store keys in it without worrying about other applications modifying them.

> ## Key Store
>
> A *key store* is a CSP-maintained database in which encryption keys are kept for use over multiple application sessions. Normally, session encryption keys are not kept in a key store, whereas public/private key pairs are usually kept in one. Some CSPs maintain their key store in the Registry database, whereas others maintain it in other locations, such as in Smart Cards or encrypted, hidden files.

2

The third variable (pszProvider) is the name of the CSP to be used. Constant definitions can be used for any of the Microsoft CSPs. These constants are listed in Table 2.1. If you pass the NULL string (vbNullString) as the provider name, the default provider for the specified CSP type (see the next parameter) will be used.

TABLE 2.1   Constant Definitions for Microsoft CSPs

Constant	Value
MS_DEF_PROV	Microsoft Base Cryptographic Provider v1.0
MS_ENHANCED_PROV	Microsoft Enhanced Cryptographic Provider v1.0
MS_DEF_RSA_SIG_PROV	Microsoft RSA Signature Cryptographic Provider
MS_DEF_RSA_SCHANNEL_PROV	Microsoft Base RSA SChannel Cryptographic Provider
MS_ENHANCED_RSA_SCHANNEL_PROV	Microsoft Enhanced RSA SChannel Cryptographic Provider
MS_DEF_DSS_PROV	Microsoft Base DSS Cryptographic Provider
MS_DEF_DSS_DH_PROV	Microsoft Base DSS and Diffie-Hellman Cryptographic Provider

The fourth parameter (dwProvType) is the provider type. A series of constants is defined for use with this parameter, as listed in Table 2.2. This list of types will expand as new encryption methods and formulas are introduced. It is important to choose a provider type that is supported by the provider selected in the previous parameter.

TABLE 2.2   Constant Definitions for Microsoft CSP Types

Constant	Value	Description
PROV_RSA_FULL	1	This general-purpose type supports both digital signatures and encryption.
PROV_RSA_SIG	2	A subset of the PROV_RSA_FULL type, this type is for hashes and digital signatures only.

continues

TABLE 2.2   Continued

Constant	Value	Description
PROV_DSS	3	This type implements the Digital Signature Algorithm (DSA) for hashes and digital signatures only.
PROV_FORTEZZA	4	This type implements a series of National Institute of Standards and Technology (NIST) algorithms.
PROV_MS_EXCHANGE	5	This provider type is designed for use with Microsoft Exchange and other MS Mail-compatible applications.
PROV_SSL	6	This provider type supports the Secure Sockets Layer (SSL) protocol.
PROV_RSA_SCHANNEL	12	This general-purpose type supports both the RSA and SChannel protocols.
PROV_DSS_DH	13	A superset of the PROV_DSS type, this type is for both digital signatures and encryption.

The fifth and final parameter (dwFlags) is used to specify options on how the CSP context needs to be opened. These options can be used to create a new key container or to prevent the application from having access to private keys. The available values that can be used in this flag are listed in Table 2.3. More often than not, you'll want to pass 0 for this parameter. Passing 0 signals that you want to open an existing keyset.

TABLE 2.3   CryptAcquireContext Flags

Flag	Value	Description
CRYPT_VERIFYCONTEXT	&HF0000000	This option is for use by applications that do not use private keys. When this option is used, the key container parameter (the second parameter) should be just the NULL character.
CRYPT_NEWKEYSET	&H8	A new key container will be created with the name in the key container parameter (the second parameter).
CRYPT_MACHINE_KEYSET	1&H20	This option tells the CSP that the key container is a machine container (the default is a user container, associated with the currently logged-on user). This option must be used if the application is running as a service.
CRYPT_DELETEKEYSET	&H10	The key container specified will be deleted. If the key container parameter is the NULL character, then the default key container will be deleted.
CRYPT_SILENT	&H40	The CSP will not display any user interface elements to the user.

WINDOWS
2000

The `CryptAcquireContext` function returns a C language Boolean, which you cast as a Visual Basic Boolean by using the `CBool` function. You can check the resulting Boolean value, as follows, to determine whether the function was successful:

```
Dim sContainer As String
Dim sProvider As String
Dim lHCryptProv as Long

'--- Prepare string buffers
sContainer = vbNullChar
sProvider = MS_DEF_PROV & vbNullChar

'--- Attempt to acquire a handle to the default key container.
If CBool(CryptAcquireContext(lHCryptProv, vbNullString, sProvider, _
        PROV_RSA_FULL, 0)) Then
    '--- We were successful, continue on...
```

Closing the CSP

After you have finished all the encryption that your application needs to do, you need to close the key container context by using the `CryptReleaseContext` function. This function is defined as follows:

Syntax

```
Public Declare Function CryptReleaseContext Lib "advapi32.dll" ( _
    ByVal hProv As Long, ByVal dwFlags As Long) As Long
```

Calling this function is simple because it has only one parameter of any importance. The first parameter (hProv) is the handle to the key context that you received in the `CryptAcquireContext` function (the first parameter in that function). This parameter tells the `CryptReleaseContext` function which key container context to close. The second parameter (dwFlags) is always zero (0). Therefore, you can call this function as you are closing your application, as in the following code:

```
Dim lResult As Long

'--- Do we have an open key context? If so, release it.
If (lHCryptProv <> 0) Then _
        lResult = CryptReleaseContext(lHCryptProv, 0)
```

The `CryptReleaseContext` function does return a Boolean result, but the only reason it might fail is if you pass it an invalid key container handle (or pass it something other than 0 for the second parameter).

Listing the Available CSPs

So what do you do if you need a particular CSP, and you don't know whether it's available on the user's computer? In this case, you can enumerate the CSPs on the system by using the `CryptEnumProviders` function. This function is defined as follows:

```
Public Declare Function CryptEnumProviders Lib "advapi32.dll" _
    Alias "CryptEnumProvidersA" (ByVal dwIndex As Long, _
    ByVal pdwReserved As Long, ByVal dwFlags As Long, _
    pdwProvType As Long, ByVal pszProvName As String, _
    pcbProvName As Long) As Long
```

The first parameter (dwIndex) to this function is the index number of the CSP to list. The index starts with zero (0) for the first CSP and increments from there. So, as you are looping through all the available CSPs, you need to have a counter variable that you can increment for each CSP you enumerate.

The second (pdwReserved) and third (dwFlags) parameters should always be zero (0). These parameters are "reserved for future use," so at some point, this use may change, but for now, just pass 0 for both of them.

The fourth parameter (pdwProvType) is a variable into which the provider type will be placed. For a list of the current provider types, see Table 2.2.

The fifth parameter (pszProvName) is a string variable into which the name of the provider will be placed. You can pass the NULL string (vbNullString) in this parameter to determine the length of the string needed to hold the provider name. The length of the provider name will be copied into the variable passed as the sixth parameter (pcbProvName). After you have sized the string for the fifth parameter, the sixth parameter should be populated with the length of the string being passed for the fifth parameter.

As with most CryptoAPI functions, this one returns a Boolean value that can be checked (after passing through the `CBool` function) to determine whether the function succeeded. You might use this function as follows:

```
Dim lResult As Long
Dim lIndex As Long
Dim sNameBuffer As String
Dim lNameLength As Long
Dim lProvType As Long

lIndex = 0
'--- Determine the size of the buffer needed
lResult = CryptEnumProviders(lIndex, 0, 0, lProvType, vbNullString, _
        lNameLength)
```

```
'--- We expect the preceding function call to fail, so we don't need to
'--- check the return value

'--- Prepare a string buffer for the CryptEncrypt function
sNameBuffer = String(lNameLength, vbNullChar)

'--- Get the provider name
If CBool(CryptEnumProviders(lIndex, 0, 0, lProvType, sNameBuffer, _
        lNameLength)) Then
    '--- Continue on
```

Listing the CSP Types

If you want to know what the available provider types are on a particular system, you can use the CryptEnumProviderTypes function. This function looks basically the same as the CryptEnumProviders function, as in the following definition:

```
Public Declare Function CryptEnumProviderTypes Lib "advapi32.dll" _
    Alias "CryptEnumProviderTypesA" (ByVal dwIndex As Long, _
    ByVal pdwReserved As Long, ByVal dwFlags As Long, _
    pdwProvType As Long, ByVal pszTypeName As String, _
    pcbTypeName As Long) As Long
```

The only difference between this function and the CryptEnumProviders function is that the name of the provider type is returned in the fifth parameter (pszTypeName). Otherwise, all the parameters are the same, and the two functions work the same.

Getting the Default CSP

When you want to determine which CSP is the default provider for a specific CSP type, you can use the CryptGetDefaultProvider function. This function is defined as follows:

 Syntax

```
Public Declare Function CryptGetDefaultProvider Lib "advapi32.dll" _
    Alias "CryptGetDefaultProviderA" (ByVal dwProvType As Long, _
    ByVal pdwReserved As Long, ByVal dwFlags As Long, _
    ByVal pszProvName As String, pcbProvName As Long) As Long
```

The first parameter (dwProvType) for this function is the CSP type for which you want to know the default CSP. These types are listed in Table 2.2. The second parameter (pdwReserved) is "reserved for future use" and should always be zero (0).

The third parameter (dwFlags) specifies whether to look up the user or machine default CSP. The available values are listed in Table 2.4.

TABLE 2.4   `CryptGetDefaultProvider` Flags

Flag	Value	Description
`CRYPT_MACHINE_DEFAULT`	&H1	Returns the computer default CSP for the specified CSP type
`CRYPT_USER_DEFAULT`	&H2	Returns the user default CSP for the specified CSP type

The fourth parameter (pszProvName) is a string into which the name of the default provider will be copied. The fifth parameter (pcbProvName) is the size of the string into which the name will be copied and the length of the CSP name after it is copied into the string.

As with most CryptoAPI functions, the `CryptGetDefaultProvider` function returns a Boolean value that you can check by using the `CBool` function.

Setting the Default CSP

To set the default CSP, you have two options, depending on which platform your application runs. The first option is the `CryptSetProvider` function, defined as follows:

Syntax

```
Public Declare Function CryptSetProvider Lib "advapi32.dll" _
    Alias "CryptSetProviderA" (ByVal pszProvName As String, _
    ByVal dwProvType As Long) As Long
```

This function takes two parameters. The first parameter (pszProvName) is the name of the CSP to be the default for the CSP type. The second parameter (dwProvType) is the CSP type for which to make the CSP specified as the default.

NOTE

Remember that if the NULL string is passed as the CSP name to the `CryptAcquireContext` function to open a CSP and key container, the default CSP is used.

The second option is the CryptSetProviderEx function, which is defined as follows:

 Syntax

```
Public Declare Function CryptSetProviderEx Lib "advapi32.dll" _
    Alias "CryptSetProviderExA" (ByVal pszProvName As String, _
    ByVal dwProvType As Long, ByVal pdwReserved As Long, _
    ByVal dwFlags As Long) As Long
```

In this version, the first two parameters are the same as with the CryptSetProvider version. The first (pszProvName) is the name of the CSP to be used, and the second (dwProvType) is the CSP type to make it the default. The third parameter (pdwReserved) is reserved and should always be zero (0).

The fourth parameter (dwFlags) is the real difference between these two versions. This parameter is used to specify whether you want to set the user or machine default CSP. You can also specify to delete (unset) the current default CSP for a particular type. The possible values for this parameter are listed in Table 2.5. You can use OR to combine these values to delete either the user or machine default.

TABLE 2.5   CryptSetProviderEx Flags

Flag	Value	Description
CRYPT_MACHINE_DEFAULT	&H1	Sets the computer default CSP for the specified CSP type
CRYPT_USER_DEFAULT	&H2	Sets the user default CSP for the specified CSP type
CRYPT_DELETE_DEFAULT	&H4	Deletes (unsets) the default CSP for the specified type

As usual, you can check the Boolean return value to determine whether these functions were successful by using the CBool function.

CSP Types and Encryption Algorithms

The various CSP types implement certain encryption algorithms for performing their various tasks. If you need to use a specific algorithm, you need to check which CSP type supports it. The current CSP types and the algorithms they support are listed in Table 2.6.

TABLE 2.6   CSP Types and the Algorithms Implemented

Type	Key Exchange	Signature	Encryption	Hashing
PROV_RSA_FULL	RSA	RSA	RC2 RC4	MD5 SHA
PROV_RSA_SIG		RSA		MD5 SHA
PROV_DSS		DSS		MD5 SHA
PROV_FORTEZZA	KEA	DSS	Skipjack	SHA
PROV_MS_EXCHANGE	RSA	RSA	CAST	MD5
PROV_SSL	RSA	RSA	Varies	Varies
PROV_RSA_SCHANNEL	RSA	RSA	CYLINK_MEK	MD5 SHA
PROV_DSS_DH	DH	DSS	CYLINK_MEK	MD5 SHA
PROV_DH_SCHANNEL	DH	DSS	RC2 RC4 CYLINK_MEK	MD5 SHA

NOTE

Not all the CSP types listed in Table 2.6 may be present, or have the same capabilities as listed, if you are working with an older version of the CryptoAPI. If you are working with the CryptoAPI 1.0 version, you might want to check the documentation to see which CSP types are supported, and what capabilities they have.

Listing CSPs and CSP Types

Now that you've looked at some of the basic functions that are necessary for managing the CSPs and key containers, you can get your hands dirty with some actual code. You'll build a simple application that displays the list of CSPs that are available on a computer, along with the list of CSP types.

Designing the Interface

For the user interface, you need two buttons to trigger the two lists, along with a third button to close the application. You also need a label control in which to display the lists of CSPs and types. Start a new standard Visual Basic project, and lay out the form as shown in Figure 2.2, setting the control properties as listed in Table 2.7.

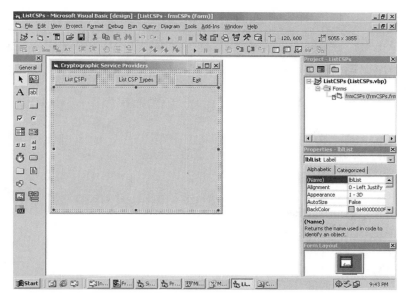

FIGURE 2.2
Application screen layout.

TABLE 2.7 Control Property Settings

Control	Property	Value
Command Button	Name	cmdListCSPs
	Caption	List &CSPs
Command Button	Name	cmdTypes
	Caption	List CSP &Types
Command Button	Name	cmdExit
	Caption	E&xit
Label	Name	lblList

Next, you need to add the CryptoAPI function declarations to be used. In this application, you need to use only the CryptEnumProviders and CryptEnumProviderTypes functions. Now add the function declarations as shown in Listing 2.1.

LISTING 2.1   API Function Declarations

```
Option Explicit

Private Declare Function CryptEnumProviderTypes Lib "advapi32.dll" _
    Alias "CryptEnumProviderTypesA" ( _
    ByVal dwIndex As Long, _
    ByVal pdwReserved As Long, _
    ByVal dwFlags As Long, _
    pdwProvType As Long, _
    ByVal pszTypeName As String, _
    pcbTypeName As Long) As Long

Private Declare Function CryptEnumProviders Lib "advapi32.dll" _
    Alias "CryptEnumProvidersA" ( _
    ByVal dwIndex As Long, _
    ByVal pdwReserved As Long, _
    ByVal dwFlags As Long, _
    pdwProvType As Long, _
    ByVal pszProvName As String, _
    pcbProvName As Long) As Long
```

One last piece of housekeeping that you need to take care of before you launch into the meat of this application is the exit code. Select the click event of the cmdExit button, and add code to close the application, as shown in Listing 2.2.

LISTING 2.2   The cmdExit_Click Subroutine

```
Private Sub cmdExit_Click()
    Unload Me
End Sub
```

Listing the CSPs

Now it's time to get to the code that you're building this application for. You need to get the size of the first CSP name and then size the string buffer appropriately. Next, you'll loop until the CryptEnumProviders function fails when retrieving the next CSP name. Within the loop, you'll add the current CSP name to the display label. Finally, you'll increment the index and get the size of the next CSP name, sizing the name buffer appropriately. To implement this functionality, add a private subroutine named EnumCSPs to your form. Add the code to this function shown in Listing 2.3.

LISTING 2.3   The EnumCSPs Subroutine

```
Private Sub EnumCSPs()
'****************************************************************
'* Written By: Davis Chapman
'* Date:        September 22, 1999
'*
'* Syntax:      EnumCSPs
'*
'* Parameters:  None
'*
'* Purpose: This subroutine loops through all of the CSPs
'*          installed on the system, listing them for the user.
'****************************************************************
    Dim lResult As Long
    Dim lIndex As Long
    Dim sNameBuffer As String
    Dim lNameLength As Long
    Dim lProvType As Long

    '--- Initialize the necessary variables
    lIndex = 0
    lblList.Caption = ""

    '--- Determine the size of the buffer needed
    lResult = CryptEnumProviders(lIndex, 0, 0, lProvType, _
            vbNullString, lNameLength)

    '--- Prepare a string buffer for the CryptEncrypt function
    sNameBuffer = String(lNameLength, vbNullChar)

    '--- Get the provider name, looping until all providers
    '--- have been listed
    While CBool(CryptEnumProviders(lIndex, 0, 0, lProvType, _
            sNameBuffer, lNameLength))

        '--- Add the current CSP to the display list
        If (lIndex > 0) Then lblList.Caption = lblList.Caption + vbCrLf
        lblList.Caption = lblList.Caption + sNameBuffer

        '--- Increment the index counter
        lIndex = lIndex + 1

        '--- Determine the size of the buffer needed
        lResult = CryptEnumProviders(lIndex, 0, 0, lProvType, _
                vbNullString, lNameLength)

        '--- Prepare a string buffer for the CryptEncrypt function
        sNameBuffer = String(lNameLength, vbNullChar)
    Wend
End Sub
```

Next, attach a subroutine to the `Click` event of the `cmdListCSPs` button. In this event subroutine, call the `EnumCSPs` subroutine, as shown in Listing 2.4.

LISTING 2.4   The `cmdListCSPs_Click` Subroutine

```
Private Sub cmdListCSPs_Click()
    EnumCSPs
End Sub
```

Now you should be able to run your application and get a list of the CSPs in your system, as shown in Figure 2.3.

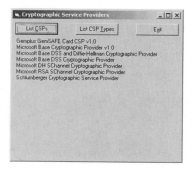

FIGURE 2.3
Listing the available CSPs.

Building a List of the CSP Types

Now you can do the same thing to get a list of the available CSP types. Create a private subroutine called `EnumTypes` on the form. Code this subroutine the same as for the `EnumCSPs` subroutine, using the `CryptEnumProviderTypes` function instead of the `CryptEnumProviders` function, as shown in Listing 2.5.

LISTING 2.5   The `EnumTypes` Subroutine

```
Private Sub EnumTypes()
'*****************************************************************
'* Written By: Davis Chapman
'* Date:       September 22, 1999
'*
'* Syntax:     EnumTypes
'*
'* Parameters: None
```

```
'*
'* Purpose: This subroutine loops through all of the CSP types
'*          installed on the system, listing them for the user.
'****************************************************************
    Dim lResult As Long
    Dim lIndex As Long
    Dim sNameBuffer As String
    Dim lNameLength As Long
    Dim lProvType As Long

    '--- Initialize the necessary variables
    lIndex = 0
    lblList.Caption = ""

    '--- Determine the size of the buffer needed
    lResult = CryptEnumProviderTypes(lIndex, 0, 0, lProvType, _
              vbNullChar, lNameLength)

    '--- Prepare a string buffer for the CryptEncrypt function
    lNameLength = lNameLength * 2
    sNameBuffer = String(lNameLength, vbNullChar)

    '--- Get the type name, looping until all types have been listed
    While CBool(CryptEnumProviderTypes(lIndex, 0, 0, lProvType, _
          sNameBuffer, lNameLength))

        '--- Add the current CSP to the display list
        If (lIndex > 0) Then lblList.Caption = lblList.Caption + vbCrLf
        lblList.Caption = lblList.Caption + sNameBuffer

        '--- Increment the index counter
        lIndex = lIndex + 1

        '--- Determine the size of the buffer needed
        lResult = CryptEnumProviderTypes(lIndex, 0, 0, lProvType, _
                  vbNullChar, lNameLength)

        '--- Prepare a string buffer for the CryptEncrypt function
        lNameLength = lNameLength * 2
        sNameBuffer = String(lNameLength, vbNullChar)
    Wend
End Sub
```

Finally, attach a subroutine to the Click event of the cmdTypes button. In this event subroutine, call the EnumTypes subroutine, as shown in Listing 2.6.

LISTING 2.6   The cmdTypes_Click Subroutine

```
Private Sub cmdTypes_Click()
    EnumTypes
End Sub
```

Now you should be able to run your application and get a list of the CSP types in your system, as illustrated in Figure 2.4.

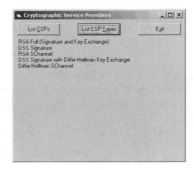

FIGURE 2.4
Listing the available CSP types.

Summary

In this chapter, you learned how the Microsoft CryptoAPI provides you with maximum encryption flexibility by allowing you to plug in any Cryptographic Service Provider (CSP) that you need. Doing so enables the CryptoAPI to support new encryption algorithms as they become available. You also learned how you can determine which CSPs are installed on a computer and which CSP types are available.

In the next chapter, you'll learn about the basics of encryption using the CryptoAPI. You'll learn how to generate and use hashes of messages and files. You'll also learn how to generate symmetric encryption keys and how to use those keys for encrypting and decrypting data. This next chapter will cover a lot of ground, so fasten your seatbelt and hang on.

Symmetric and Password Encryption

IN THIS CHAPTER

- Generating Hashes of Strings and Messages
- Generating Symmetric Keys
- Understanding Basic Encryption and Decryption
- Building a Simple Encryption Application
- Building a File Encryption/Decryption Utility

Knowing how to determine which encryption engines are available for your use is all well and good, but just knowing about them doesn't quite do the job when it comes to keeping data secure. To keep your data safe, you need to be able to take the next step and use the functionality of the CSPs on your system to actually encrypt something.

One of the original forms of key-based encryption is *symmetric encryption*, in which the same key is used to both encrypt and decrypt the data. To this day, symmetric encryption remains one of the most common, strongest, and fastest forms of encryption. In this chapter, you'll learn the basics of symmetric encryption and how you can use it to secure files that you want to maintain "for your eyes only." You'll also learn how you can use hashes to determine whether a message or file has been tampered with. One more thing that you'll learn is how to create symmetric encryption keys from passwords, so that a file may be password protected, without having to store the encryption key.

PREREQUISITES

Before reading this chapter, you need to make sure you have a good understanding of:

- Symmetric encryption and cryptographic hashes, as covered in Chapter 1.
- Opening and closing a key container and acquiring a handle to a CSP, as covered in Chapter 2.

Generating Hashes of Strings and Messages

When you're working with encryption, you'll often find yourself creating hashes. A hash is sort of like a fingerprint of a message or file. No two files or messages will produce hashes that are reliably the same, so the hashes can be used to determine whether a message or file has been modified or otherwise tampered with. You'll also use hashes generated from passwords or other sources to derive encryption keys.

Creating a Hash Object

Before you can do anything else, you have to create a hash object. This hash object will hold the hashes of data or session keys, or even combinations of hashes, depending on what your application needs might be. You create an empty hash object by using the `CryptCreateHash` function. This function is declared as follows:

Syntax

```
Public Declare Function CryptCreateHash Lib "advapi32.dll" ( _
    ByVal hProv As Long, ByVal Algid As Long, _
    ByVal hKey As Long, ByVal dwFlags As Long, _
    phHash As Long) As Long
```

The first parameter (hProv) for this function is the handle to the CSP that you created with the `CryptAcquireContext` function (covered in Chapter 2, "Getting Started with Crypto API").

The second parameter (Algid) is the ID of the hash algorithm to be used to create the hash. The available values are listed in Table 3.1. The values for these algorithm IDs consist of algorithm class ID, algorithm type ID, and algorithm sub-IDs that have all been combined using OR.

NOTE

When values are combined this way, it means they have been combined using a binary OR to produce a flag value that designates several values. The way this works is that you can have several options that use a single bit as an on/off indicator, as follows:

```
Const OPTION1 = &H1
Const OPTION2 = &H2
Const OPTION3 = &H4
Const OPTION4 = &H8
```

The desired combination of these options is built using the OR functionality, as follows:

```
Dim lFlag As Long
lFlag = OPTION1 Or OPTION3
```

Finally, to determine which of the options have been selected, the variable is compared with each of the option values using the AND functionality as follows:

```
If ((lFlag And OPTION1)> 0) Then
    '--- Option 1 was selected
End If
If ((lFlag And OPTION2)> 0) Then
    '--- Option 2 was selected
End If
'--- And so on
```

Combining option values in this way enables you to turn numerous options on and off using a single variable, reducing the number of parameters that need to be passed to a function.

3

SYMMETRIC AND PASSWORD ENCRYPTION

TABLE 3.1 Hash Algorithm IDs

Algorithm ID	Description
CALG_MD2	MD2 Hashing algorithm
CALG_MD4	MD4 Hashing algorithm
CALG_MD5	MD5 Hashing algorithm
CALG_SHA	US DSA Secure Hash Algorithm (SHA)
CALG_SHA1	SHA Hashing algorithm (same as CALG_SHA)
CALG_MAC	Message Authentication Code (MAC) keyed hash algorithm
CALG_SSL3_SHAMD5	SSL3 client authentication
CALG_HMAC	HMAC keyed hash algorithm

The third parameter (hKey) is the handle to the encryption key for use with keyed hash algorithms (CALG_MAC and CALG_HMAC). The handle to the key is created when you create a session key, which you'll learn about later in this chapter and the next chapter.

The fourth parameter (dwFlags) is "reserved for future use." So, for now, it must always be zero (0). The fifth and final parameter (phHash) is a long variable into which the handle of the hash object will be placed. You'll use this handle for all subsequent hash-related functions.

As with most Crypto API functions, this function returns a Boolean value (in a long variable) that you can check by using the CBool function to determine whether the function failed or succeeded.

Destroying a Hash Object

After you finish with a hash object, you need to destroy it to clean up after yourself. You do so by using the CryptDestroyHash function, which is defined as follows:

Syntax

```
Public Declare Function CryptDestroyHash Lib "advapi32.dll" ( _
    ByVal hHash As Long) As Long
```

The one and only parameter (hHash) passed to this function is the handle to the hash object that you created with the CryptCreateHash function. This function will destroy the hash object and release any resources that are being held by the hash object.

As usual, the CryptDestroyHash function returns a long Boolean value, which you can pass through the CBool function to determine the success of the function. A typical example of creating and destroying a hash object is as follows:

```
Dim lHash As Long
Dim lResult As Long

'--- Create an empty hash object.
If Not CBool(CryptCreateHash(m_lHCryptProv, CALG_MD5, 0, 0, lHash)) Then
    '--- Perform error handling here
End If
'--- Do whatever
.
.
.
'--- Destroy the hash object
If Not CBool(CryptDestroyHash(lHash)) Then
    '--- Perform error handling here
End If
```

Duplicating a Hash Object

On occasion, you might need to make an exact copy of a hash object—for instance, if you need to have two hash objects, and they both need to start with the hash of some common object. In these instances, you can use the `CryptDuplicateHash` function. This function is declared as follows:

Syntax

```
Public Declare Function CryptDuplicateHash Lib "advapi32.dll" ( _
    ByVal hHash As Long, pdwReserved As Long, _
    ByVal dwFlags As Long, phHash As Long) As Long
```

> **NOTE**
>
> You're probably wondering when and why you would want to duplicate a hash. One instance is when you have one set of data that you need to have a hash of. Now, if you have two different additions to the original data, you can duplicate the original hash, and just add the new data to each hash, resulting in two different hashes.

The first parameter (hHash) for this function is the handle for the original hash object that you want to copy. The copy is made of this hash object in its current state, with any hashes of data intact. The second (pdwReserved) and third (dwFlags) parameters are both reserved for future use, so you must pass zero (0) for both parameters.

3

SYMMETRIC AND PASSWORD ENCRYPTION

The fourth parameter (phHash) needs to be a long variable into which will be placed the handle to the new, copy hash. This hash is a copy and thus isn't affected by any changes to the original after this function is called (and vice versa). Also, because this function creates a second, independent hash object, you need to destroy both hash objects after you are finished with them.

Like with most other Crypto API functions, this one returns a long Boolean value that you can check by using the CBool function to determine whether it was successful.

Hashing Data

When you're ready to actually hash some data, you use the CryptHashData function. This function is declared as follows:

Syntax

```
Public Declare Function CryptHashData Lib "advapi32.dll" ( _
    ByVal hHash As Long, ByVal pbData As String, _
    ByVal dwDataLen As Long, ByVal dwFlags As Long) As Long
```

The first parameter (hHash) to this function is the handle of the hash object. This handle was created using either the CryptCreateHash or CryptDuplicateHash function.

The second parameter (pbData) is the data to be hashed. It is declared as a string in this instance, but it could be any textual or binary data. The third parameter (dwDataLen) is the length of the data to be hashed.

The fourth parameter (dwFlags) is a flag that determines how the hash is to be created. The only currently defined value for this flag is CRYPT_USERDATA (1). When this flag is used, the CSP prompts the user for the data to be hashed directly, without the application touching the data. This flag is often used to create hashes of passwords or personal identification numbers (PINs), in which the resulting hash is compared to previous hashes that have been stored in a database to determine whether the correct password or PIN has been entered. Many operating systems store hashes of user passwords instead of the actual passwords. This way, the operating system can verify user passwords by comparing hashes of the passwords. If you don't want to use this flag, pass a zero (0) for this parameter.

As usual, a long Boolean value is returned to state the success or failure of the function. Also, as usual, you need to use the CBool function to verify this value.

Hashing a Session Key

Often, in a distributed application, you need to make hashes of session keys being used. These session key hashes are exchanged so that all participants can verify the session key hasn't been tampered with, modified, or substituted. This process helps verify the security of the encryption key used to ensure the security of the data being exchanged.

To make a hash of the session key, you need to use the `CryptHashSessionKey` function. This function is defined as follows:

```
Public Declare Function CryptHashSessionKey Lib "advapi32.dll" ( _
    ByVal hHash As Long, ByVal hKey As Long, _
    ByVal dwFlags As Long) As Long
```

The first parameter (hHash) to this function is the hash object's handle created using either the `CryptCreateHash` or `CryptDuplicateHash` function. The second parameter (hKey) is the handle of the session key to be hashed (you'll learn about generated session keys later in this chapter).

The third parameter (dwFlags) is a flag that controls how the hash is created. Currently, the only defined flag value for this parameter is `CRYPT_LITTLE_ENDIAN` (1). This flag, when used, hashes the bytes of the session key in little endian form. If this flag is not used, and zero is passed in to this function, the bytes of the key are hashed in big endian form.

Endian

Endian refers to the byte order of numbers used by the processor in a computer. There are two forms of endian: big and little. In a big endian processor, the most significant byte in a multi-byte numeric value is on the left. In a little endian processor, the most significant byte is on the right.

3

SYMMETRIC AND PASSWORD ENCRYPTION

NOTE

The `CRYPT_LITTLE_ENDIAN` flag is available only with Internet Explorer 4 or higher, Windows 98, and Windows 2000.

As always, this function returns a long Boolean value. You can check it by using the `CBool` function.

Getting Hash Information

Sometimes you need to get information from a hash object. For example, you might need to retrieve the actual hash value. The function used for this purpose is called `CryptGetHashParam`. You might want to declare this function in two ways. The first way is as follows:

Syntax

```
Public Declare Function CryptGetHashParam Lib "advapi32.dll" ( _
    ByVal hHash As Long, ByVal dwParam As Long, _
    ByVal pbData As String, pdwDataLen As Long, _
    ByVal dwFlags As Long) As Long
```

The second way that you might want to declare it is to use an alias for this version, as follows:

Syntax

```
Public Declare Function CryptGetHashDWParam Lib "advapi32.dll" _
    Alias "CryptGetHashParam" (ByVal hHash As Long, _
    ByVal dwParam As Long, pbData As Long, _
    pdwDataLen As Long, ByVal dwFlags As Long) As Long
```

TIP

As an alternative to creating two declarations of this function, you can declare the third parameter (pbData) as "pbData As Any" and be able to pass any data type to this function. You need to be forewarned, however, that when you pass a string variable to this function, you need to specify when making the function call that the string is being passed "ByVal". The declaration for this version looks like this:

```
Public Declare Function CryptGetHashParam Lib "advapi32.dll" ( _
    ByVal hHash As Long, ByVal dwParam As Long, _
    pbData As Any, pdwDataLen As Long, _
    ByVal dwFlags As Long) As Long
```

The first parameter (hHash) to this function is the handle for the hash object. The second parameter (dwParam) is a value indicating what information you want to get from the hash object. The possible values for this parameter are listed in Table 3.2.

TABLE 3.2 CryptGetHashParam Parameter Values

Constant	Value	Description
HP_ALGID	&H1	Indicates that you want to retrieve the algorithm information from the hash object. This value was passed in as the second parameter in the CryptCreateHash function.
HP_HASHSIZE	&H4	Indicates that you want to retrieve the size of the actual hash value from the hash object.
HP_HASHVAL	&H2	Indicates that you want to retrieve the actual hash value from the hash object.

The third parameter (pbData) for this function is the variable into which the resulting value will be placed. The fourth parameter (pdwDataLen) is the size of the variable passed as the third parameter. With the CryptGetHashDWParam version of this function, the fourth parameter should be 4. The actual size of the returned value will be placed into this parameter, so it should always be a variable passed as this parameter, and never just the actual value.

> **CAUTION**
>
> After you retrieve the actual hash value, the hash object is marked as "finished," preventing you from adding any more data to the hash. This isn't a problem when dealing with small sets of data, but can be a concern when working with large sets of data in which you are making multiple calls to CryptHashData to create the hash.

The fifth parameter (dwFlags) is reserved for future use, so you should always pass zero (0) for this parameter.

The return value is a long Boolean value that you can check by using the CBool function.

Setting Hash Information

Just as you sometimes need to get information out of a hash object, you sometimes need to set information in a hash object. In one such circumstance, you might be creating a combination hash, such as the CALG_SSL3_SHAMD5 hash algorithm. In this circumstance, you create both of the individual hashes, extract the hash values by using the CryptGetHashParam function, concatenate them, and then use the CryptSetHashParam function to set the combination value into a new hash object that has the CALG_SSL3_SHAMD5 algorithm. The CryptSetHashParam function is declared as follows:

Syntax

```
Public Declare Function CryptSetHashParam Lib "advapi32.dll" ( _
    ByVal hHash As Long, ByVal dwParam As Long, _
    ByVal pbData As String, ByVal dwFlags As Long) As Long
```

The first parameter (hHash) is the handle to the hash object. The second parameter (dwParam) is an indicator of which aspect of the hash object is being set. The available values are listed in Table 3.3.

3

SYMMETRIC AND PASSWORD ENCRYPTION

TABLE 3.3   `CryptSetHashParam` Parameter Values

Constant	Value	Description
HP_HMAC_INFO	&H5	Indicates that you are passing in an HMAC_INFO type value to set the cryptographic algorithm and inner and outer strings to be used in the HMAC algorithm
HP_HASHVAL	&H2	Indicates that you want to set the actual hash value for the hash object

The third parameter (pbData) is the data to be set in the hash object. When you set the hash value, you pass it in as a string. If you set the hash algorithm using the HMAC_INFO type, you should declare a second version of the function using an alias, declaring the third parameter as a HMAC_INFO, passed by reference. The HMAC_INFO type is defined as follows:

Syntax

```
Type HMAC_INFO
    HashAlgid As Long
    pbInnerString As String
    cbInnerString As Long
    pbOuterString As String
    cbOuterString As Long
End Type
```

The fourth parameter (dwFlags) is reserved for future use, and thus is always zero (0). The return value is a long Boolean value that you can check by using the CBool function.

Generating Symmetric Keys

For most circumstances in which you'll be encrypting and decrypting data, you'll be using symmetric encryption, primarily because symmetric encryption is much faster than asymmetric encryption. This speed makes symmetric encryption much more practical for most applications today. After two applications have agreed on a symmetric encryption key, they can freely exchange encrypted messages with a minimum of overhead.

Symmetric encryption keys also are very practical for single application needs. A symmetric encryption key can be derived from a hash of any string or object. Thus, you can derive a symmetric key from the hash of a user password and use it to protect files or other sensitive files from other computer users.

Deriving a Key

When you derive a key from a base data value, such as the hash of a password, using the same CSP and algorithms, the resulting encryption key is always the same. You therefore can create an encryption key from a password, or other source data, and reliably re-create the same encryption key time and again. Thus, this method of creating an encryption key is an appropriate method for protecting files and other suitably sensitive data.

To derive a key from a base data value, you use the CryptDeriveKey function. This function is declared as follows:

Syntax

```
Public Declare Function CryptDeriveKey Lib "advapi32.dll" ( _
    ByVal hProv As Long, ByVal Algid As Long, _
    ByVal hBaseData As Long, ByVal dwFlags As Long, _
    phKey As Long) As Long
```

The first parameter (hProv) is the handle to the CSP that was created with the CryptAcquireContext function call. The second parameter (Algid) specifies the encryption algorithm for which the key is to be generated. The available encryption algorithms will be different, depending on which ones are available in the CSP that you are using. The symmetric encryption algorithms available in the Microsoft Base Cryptographic Provider are listed in Table 3.4. The values for these algorithm IDs consist of algorithm class ID, algorithm type ID, and algorithm sub-IDs that have all been combined using OR.

TABLE 3.4 Microsoft Base Cryptographic Provider Symmetric Algorithms

Algorithm ID	Description
CALG_RC2	RC2 block encryption algorithm
CALG_RC4	RC4 stream encryption algorithm

The third parameter (hBaseData) is the handle of the hash object used to hash the base data. So, to create a symmetric encryption key from a password you first create a hash object, use it to hash the password, and then derive the encryption key from the hash object.

The fourth parameter (dwFlags) to the CryptDeriveKey function is a flag value that dictates how the key is to be derived. The available options for this flag are listed in Table 3.5. These values can be combined using OR to create a combination flag value for specifying multiple options at one time.

TABLE 3.5 CryptDeriveKey Option Values

Option	Value	Description
CRYPT_EXPORTABLE	&H1	This flag allows the key to be exported. Exporting is necessary for any encryption key that needs to be used again or exchanged with another application or computer. If this flag is not set, the key that is created is available only for the duration of that application session.
CRYPT_USER_PROTECTED	&H2	If this flag is set, whenever certain actions are taken using the derived key, the user is notified either through a dialog box or by some other method. The method of this notification and the actions that trigger this notification are determined by the CSP being used. On Windows 2000, if the CRYPT_SILENT option is used when opening the CSP, this flag value causes this function to fail.
CRYPT_CREATE_SALT	&H4	This flag causes the CSP to generate salt values (random filler values) to cause the generated key to extend to the length of the hash value. If you export the key, you also need to get the salt value from the key by using the CryptKeyGetParam function (discussed in the next chapter) and keep the salt value with the exported key value.
CRYPT_UPDATE_KEY	&H8	Some CSPs allow you to create a key from multiple hash values. To create this key, you must call CryptDeriveKey multiple times, setting this flag each time (after the first call) this function is called. This flag value causes the key to be modified and updated by the new hash object, instead of a new key being generated.
CRYPT_NO_SALT	&H10	This flag specifies that no salt will be added to the generated key.

The fifth parameter (phKey) to this function is a long variable into which will be placed a handle to the generated key. You'll use this handle to pass to the subsequent functions for encrypting or decrypting data, exporting the key, and so on.

As usual, this function returns a Boolean value that you can check by using the CBool function to determine its success or failure.

Generating a Key

When you need to generate an encryption key, whether symmetric or asymmetric, and it doesn't need to be derived from any base data source, you can use the CryptGenKey function. This function is defined as follows:

Syntax

```
Public Declare Function CryptGenKey Lib "advapi32.dll" ( _
    ByVal hProv As Long, ByVal Algid As Long, _
    ByVal dwFlags As Long, phKey As Long) As Long
```

The first parameter (hProv) to this function is the handle to the CSP context created by the CryptAcquireContext function. The second parameter (Algid) is the algorithm ID with which this key will be used. The available values for this parameter vary depending on the CSP. With the Microsoft Base Cryptographic Provider, the available algorithms are listed in Table 3.6. If you are using a Diffie-Hellman Crypto Service Provider, you can use the algorithms listed in Table 3.7.

TABLE 3.6 Microsoft Base Cryptographic Provider Algorithms

Algorithm ID	Description
CALG_RC2	RC2 block encryption algorithm
CALG_RC4	RC4 stream encryption algorithm
AT_KEYEXCHANGE	Use this algorithm to generate a key exchange public/private key pair
AT_SIGNATURE	Use this algorithm to generate a signature public/private key pair

TABLE 3.7 Diffie-Hellman CSP Algorithms

Algorithm ID	Description
CALG_DH_EPHEM	An "ephemeral" Diffie-Hellman key
CALG_DH_SF	A "Store-and-Forward" Diffie-Hellman key

The third parameter (dwFlags) is an option flag, telling the CSP what options to use when creating the key. These option flags can be combined using OR to create a combination value. The available options are listed in Table 3.8.

TABLE 3.8 CryptGenKey Option Values

Option	Value	Description
CRYPT_EXPORTABLE	&H1	This flag allows the key to be exported. Exporting is necessary for any encryption key that needs to be used again or exchanged with another application or computer. If this flag is not set, the key that is created is available only for the duration of that application session.

continues

TABLE 3.8   Continued

Option	Value	Description
CRYPT_USER_PROTECTED	&H2	If this flag is set, whenever certain actions are taken using the derived key, the user is notified either through a dialog box or by some other method. The method of this notification and the actions that trigger this notification are determined by the CSP that is being used. On Windows 2000, if the CRYPT_SILENT option is used when opening the CSP, this flag value causes this function to fail.
CRYPT_CREATE_SALT	&H4	This flag causes the CSP to generate salt values (random filler values) to cause the generated key to extend to the length of just the key itself. If you export the key, you also need to get the salt value from the key by using the CryptKeyGetParam function (discussed in the next chapter) and keep the salt value with the exported key value.
CRYPT_NO_SALT	&H10	This flag specifies that no salt will be added to the generated key.
CRYPT_PREGEN	&H40	This flag specifies that an initial Diffie-Hellman or DSS key is being made. This flag is valid only with a Diffie-Hellman CSP.

The fourth parameter (phKey) is a variable into which the handle to the generated key will be placed. You should hang onto this handle until you have completed all encryptions or decryptions that you need to perform with this key.

As with most Crypto API functions, this one also returns a Boolean value in a long variable. And with this function, just like the other functions, you can use the CBool function to check its success or failure status.

Destroying a Key

After you finish using an encryption key, you need to destroy the key to release all the

Syntax

resources being held by the key. To do so, you use the CryptDestroyKey function, which is declared as follows:

```
Public Declare Function CryptDestroyKey Lib "advapi32.dll" ( _
    ByVal hKey As Long) As Long
```

The only parameter (hKey) to this function is the handle to the key object. As usual, this function returns a long variable that can be passed to the CBool function and treated as a Boolean.

To get an idea of how you might create and later destroy a key that is derived from a password, you might do something like the following:

```
Dim lHash As Long
Dim lResult As Long
Dim lHSessionKey As Long

'--- Create an empty hash object.
If Not CBool(CryptCreateHash(m_lHCryptProv, CALG_MD5, 0, 0, lHash)) Then
    '--- Do error handling
End If

'--- Hash the password string.
If Not CBool(CryptHashData(lHash, m_sPassword, Len(m_sPassword), 0)) Then
    '--- Do error handling
End If

'--- Create a derived block cipher session key.
If Not CBool(CryptDeriveKey(m_lHCryptProv, CALG_RC2, lHash, 0, _
        lHSessionKey)) Then
    '--- Do error handling
End If

'--- Destroy the hash object
If Not CBool(CryptDestroyHash(lHash)) Then
    '--- Do error handling
End If

'--- Do encryption/decryption processing
.
.
.

'--- Destroy the session key
If Not CBool(CryptDestroyKey(lHSessionKey)) Then
    '--- Do error handling
End If
```

In this code, notice that you destroy the hash object as soon as you're finished with it. You don't need to hold onto it during all the encryption/decryption processing, so why carry around unnecessary baggage?

Duplicating a Key

When you need to duplicate a key, you can use the CryptDuplicateKey function. This function, like its hash counterpart, makes an exact copy of the key object in its current state. From this point, you can make whatever changes are needed to the keys. The declaration for this function is as follows:

Syntax

```
Public Declare Function CryptDuplicateKey Lib "advapi32.dll" ( _
    ByVal hKey As Long, ByVal pdwReserved As Long, _
    ByVal dwFlags As Long, phKey As Long) As Long
```

This function is almost exactly like its hash counterpart. The first parameter (hKey) is the handle to the key object you need to copy . The second (pdwReserved) and third (dwFlags) parameters are both reserved for future use, and you should always pass zero (0) for those parameters. The fourth parameter (phKey) is a variable into which the handle to the newly created key will be placed.

As always, this function returns a long that you can pass to the CBool function to check its success or failure.

NOTE

By this point, you are probably thinking that all of the Crypto API functions return a Boolean success value in the form of a Long value. Although most of the Crypto API functions have this same return value, this is not always the case. Either way, you're probably tired of me stating this same thing for just about every API function. So, from here on, assume that every Crypto API function discussed has this same return value, unless otherwise stated.

Just as when you create a duplicate of a hash object, you need to be sure to destroy both the original and copy key objects after you finish using them.

Understanding Basic Encryption and Decryption

After you have a key, either derived or generated, you can use that key to encrypt or decrypt data. When you have your keys, your application will spend most of its time encrypting or decrypting. This is actually a simple matter of calling one of two functions.

Encrypting Data

You encrypt data by using the CryptEncrypt function. This function is declared as follows:

Syntax

```
Public Declare Function CryptEncrypt Lib "advapi32.dll" ( _
    ByVal hKey As Long, ByVal hHash As Long, _
    ByVal Final As Long, ByVal dwFlags As Long, _
    ByVal pbData As String, pdwDataLen As Long, _
    ByVal dwBufLen As Long) As Long
```

The first parameter (hKey) for this function is the handle of the encryption key to be used to encrypt the data. This handle was created either by the CryptDeriveKey or CryptGenKey function.

The second parameter (hHash) is optional. It is the handle to a hash object if the data needs to be hashed at the same time that it is encrypted. If you do not want the data to be hashed at the same time as being encrypted, pass a zero (0) for this parameter.

The third parameter (Final) is a C Boolean value (0 is FALSE, <> 0 is TRUE). This parameter indicates whether this is the last call to CryptEncrypt for a series of data being encrypted. If you decide to encrypt a file, or stream of data, in a series of blocks instead of all at once, this parameter needs to be zero (0) for all but the final block to be encrypted. If you are making only a single call to this function to encrypt the entire set of data at one time, this parameter should not be 0 (1 or -1 are often good values to pass).

The fourth parameter (dwFlags) is a flag value containing options for this function. Currently, only one possible option flag can be passed. You should use this option flag, CRYPT_OAEP (0x40), only when you're using the Microsoft Enhanced Provider and need to use PKCS #1 version 2 formatting with RSA encryption/decryption (only on Windows 2000). Otherwise, pass zero (0) for this parameter.

The fifth parameter (pbData) is the data to be encrypted. It needs to be copied into a string buffer that has been sized to hold the returned encrypted data, which will be returned in this same string parameter.

The sixth parameter (pdwDataLen) is a variable specifying the length of the data to be encrypted. The length of the encrypted data will be returned in this variable. If the string buffer passed in the fifth parameter is too small to hold the encrypted data, the size of buffer you need will be returned in this parameter. You can pass the NULL string (vbNullString) in place of the data to be encrypted to get the size of the buffer you need returned in this parameter.

The seventh parameter (dwBufLen) is the length of the string buffer holding the data to be encrypted.

NOTE

Another way that you can declare this function is to declare the fifth parameter as the "Any" data type, as follows:

```
Public Declare Function CryptEncrypt Lib "advapi32.dll" ( _
    ByVal hKey As Long, ByVal hHash As Long, _
    ByVal Final As Long, ByVal dwFlags As Long, _
    pbData As Any, pdwDataLen As Long, _
    ByVal dwBufLen As Long) As Long
```

The advantage to using this version of the declaration is that you can place the data to be encrypted into an array of bytes, enabling you to easily work with extended character sets.

Decrypting Data

When you need to decrypt data, you use the `CryptDecrypt` function. This function is very similar to the `CryptEncrypt` function, and it works basically the same. The declaration for this function is as follows:

Syntax

```
Public Declare Function CryptDecrypt Lib "advapi32.dll" ( _
    ByVal hKey As Long, ByVal hHash As Long, _
    ByVal Final As Long, ByVal dwFlags As Long, _
    ByVal pbData As String, pdwDataLen As Long) As Long
```

Just as with the `CryptEncrypt` function, the first parameter (hKey) is the handle to the encryption key.

The second parameter (hHash) is the handle to a hash object, assuming you want to get a hash of the decrypted data. This capability is often useful if you need to verify a digital signature.

The third parameter (Final) is a C Boolean value indicating whether this is the final block in a series of blocks being decrypted. If you are decrypting all your data at once, or if this is the last block in a series, this parameter should be 1.

The fourth parameter (dwFlags) is the option flag. It is normally zero (0), but under the same circumstances as with the `CryptEncrypt` function, you might need to pass the CRYPT_OAEP flag in this parameter.

The fifth parameter (pbData) is the data to be decrypted. The sixth parameter (pdwDataLen) is the length of the data being decrypted. There is no difference between the length of the data being decrypted and the size of the string buffer the data is in. The decrypted data is always at most the same length as the encrypted data, so there is no question about the buffer not being large enough to hold the decrypted data.

> **NOTE**
>
> Another way you can declare this function is to declare the fifth parameter as the "Any" data type, as follows:
>
> ```
> Public Declare Function CryptDecrypt Lib "advapi32.dll" ( _
>     ByVal hKey As Long, ByVal hHash As Long, _
>     ByVal Final As Long, ByVal dwFlags As Long, _
>     pbData As Any, pdwDataLen As Long) As Long
> ```
>
> The reasons for this are the same as for the `CryptEncrypt` function.

Building a Simple Encryption Application

At this point, to get some hands-on experience working with these functions, we'll take a look at two sample applications. Both of these applications will use the Crypto API functionality you've looked at. They both will use a symmetric key derived from a user-entered password. The first application will use this password to encrypt and then decrypt a message the user has entered. Following this exercise will give you a first-hand look at how encryption actually works.

As you are building these applications, you'll also start building an encryption class that encapsulates the Crypto API functionality. You will be able to take this class and use it in subsequent applications with minimal changes (most likely only additions for new functionality that you need).

> **NOTE**
>
> Encapsulating the entire Crypto API into a single class is not necessarily the only or best approach to this problem. Several people have encapsulated it into a series of classes, organizing the classes according to the type of functionality. Taking that approach, you might have one class that contains all the hashing functionality, another that contains all the key generation functionality, and yet a third that actually performs the encryptions and decryptions.

Declaring API Functions, Constants, and Variables

To start the first sample application, create a new Visual Basic project. It should be a standard EXE project. Name the project `SimpleEncryption`, and name the default form `frmSimpleEncrypt`.

3

SYMMETRIC AND PASSWORD ENCRYPTION

After you have created the initial project, create a new class by choosing Project, Add Class Module. Name this new class `clsCrypto` in the class properties. Finally, enter the constant, variable, and function declarations in Listing 3.1, found later in this chapter, into the class source code. (Yes, I know this is a lot to enter, but you'll have to enter this much code only one time.)

> **TIP**
>
> If you have Visual C++ installed on your computer or have access to a computer with Visual C++ installed, you can copy all the constant declarations from the WinCrypt.h header file and use Search and Replace to convert most of the constant declarations and comments. Unfortunately, that's about as far as you can take the automatic conversion; you'll have to do the rest by hand.

LISTING 3.1   Constant, API Function, and Class Variable Declarations for Class `clsCrypto`

```
Option Explicit
'***************************************************************
'* Written By: Davis Chapman
'* Date:        September 05, 1999
'*
'* Purpose: This class encapsulates a small amount of the
'*          Microsoft CryptoAPI functionality.
'*
'* Revisions
'*   Name          Date      Description
'*   ----------------------------------------------------------
'***************************************************************


' Algorithm IDs and Flags
'

' Algorithm classes
Private Const ALG_CLASS_ANY = 0
Private Const ALG_CLASS_SIGNATURE = 8192
Private Const ALG_CLASS_MSG_ENCRYPT = 16384
Private Const ALG_CLASS_DATA_ENCRYPT = 24576
Private Const ALG_CLASS_HASH = 32768
Private Const ALG_CLASS_KEY_EXCHANGE = 40960

' Algorithm types
Private Const ALG_TYPE_ANY = 0
Private Const ALG_TYPE_DSS = 512
Private Const ALG_TYPE_RSA = 1024
Private Const ALG_TYPE_BLOCK = 1536
Private Const ALG_TYPE_STREAM = 2048
```

```
Private Const ALG_TYPE_DH = 2560
Private Const ALG_TYPE_SECURECHANNEL = 3072

' RC2 sub-ids
Private Const ALG_SID_RC2 = 2

' Stream cipher sub-ids
Private Const ALG_SID_RC4 = 1
Private Const ALG_SID_SEAL = 2

' Diffie-Hellman sub-ids
Private Const ALG_SID_DH_SANDF = 1
Private Const ALG_SID_DH_EPHEM = 2
Private Const ALG_SID_AGREED_KEY_ANY = 3
Private Const ALG_SID_KEA = 4

' Hash sub ids
Private Const ALG_SID_MD2 = 1
Private Const ALG_SID_MD4 = 2
Private Const ALG_SID_MD5 = 3
Private Const ALG_SID_SHA = 4
Private Const ALG_SID_SHA1 = 4
Private Const ALG_SID_MAC = 5
Private Const ALG_SID_RIPEMD = 6
Private Const ALG_SID_RIPEMD160 = 7
Private Const ALG_SID_SSL3SHAMD5 = 8
Private Const ALG_SID_HMAC = 9

' algorithm identifier definitions
Private Const CALG_MD5 = ((ALG_CLASS_HASH Or ALG_TYPE_ANY) Or _
                          ALG_SID_MD5)
Private Const CALG_RC2 = ((ALG_CLASS_DATA_ENCRYPT Or ALG_TYPE_BLOCK) _
                          Or ALG_SID_RC2)

' dwFlags definitions for CryptAcquireContext
Private Const CRYPT_VERIFYCONTEXT = &HF0000000
Private Const CRYPT_NEWKEYSET = &H8
Private Const CRYPT_DELETEKEYSET = &H10
Private Const CRYPT_MACHINE_KEYSET = &H20

' dwFlag definitions for CryptGenKey
Private Const CRYPT_EXPORTABLE = &H1
Private Const CRYPT_USER_PROTECTED = &H2
Private Const CRYPT_CREATE_SALT = &H4
Private Const CRYPT_UPDATE_KEY = &H8
Private Const CRYPT_NO_SALT = &H10
Private Const CRYPT_PREGEN = &H40
```

3

SYMMETRIC AND PASSWORD ENCRYPTION

continues

LISTING 3.1   Continued

```
Private Const CRYPT_RECIPIENT = &H10
Private Const CRYPT_INITIATOR = &H40
Private Const CRYPT_ONLINE = &H80
Private Const CRYPT_SF = &H100
Private Const CRYPT_CREATE_IV = &H200
Private Const CRYPT_KEK = &H400
Private Const CRYPT_DATA_KEY = &H800

' dwFlags definitions for CryptDeriveKey
Private Const CRYPT_SERVER = &H400

Private Const KEY_LENGTH_MASK = &HFFFF0000

' dwFlag definitions for CryptSetProviderEx and CryptGetDefaultProvider
Private Const CRYPT_MACHINE_DEFAULT = &H1
Private Const CRYPT_USER_DEFAULT = &H2
Private Const CRYPT_DELETE_DEFAULT = &H4

'
' CryptSetProvParam
'
Private Const PROV_RSA_FULL = 1
Private Const PROV_RSA_SIG = 2
Private Const PROV_DSS = 3
Private Const PROV_FORTEZZA = 4
Private Const PROV_MS_EXCHANGE = 5
Private Const PROV_SSL = 6
Private Const PROV_RSA_SCHANNEL = 12
Private Const PROV_DSS_DH = 13
Private Const PROV_EC_ECDSA_SIG = 14
Private Const PROV_EC_ECNRA_SIG = 15
Private Const PROV_EC_ECDSA_FULL = 16
Private Const PROV_EC_ECNRA_FULL = 17
Private Const PROV_SPYRUS_LYNKS = 20

'
' Provider friendly names
'
Private Const MS_DEF_PROV = "Microsoft Base Cryptographic Provider v1.0"
Private Const MS_ENHANCED_PROV = _
              "Microsoft Enhanced Cryptographic Provider v1.0"
Private Const MS_DEF_RSA_SIG_PROV = _
              "Microsoft RSA Signature Cryptographic Provider"
Private Const MS_DEF_RSA_SCHANNEL_PROV = _
              "Microsoft Base RSA SChannel Cryptographic Provider"
Private Const MS_ENHANCED_RSA_SCHANNEL_PROV = _
              "Microsoft Enhanced RSA SChannel Cryptographic Provider"
```

```
Private Const MS_DEF_DSS_PROV = _
              "Microsoft Base DSS Cryptographic Provider"
Private Const MS_DEF_DSS_DH_PROV = _
            "Microsoft Base DSS and Diffie-Hellman Cryptographic Provider"

'--- WinCrypt API Declarations
Private Declare Function CryptAcquireContext Lib "advapi32.dll" _
    Alias "CryptAcquireContextA" (phProv As Long, _
    ByVal pszContainer As String, ByVal pszProvider As String, _
    ByVal dwProvType As Long, ByVal dwFlags As Long) As Long

Private Declare Function CryptReleaseContext Lib "advapi32.dll" ( _
    ByVal hProv As Long, ByVal dwFlags As Long) As Long

Private Declare Function CryptDeriveKey Lib "advapi32.dll" ( _
    ByVal hProv As Long, ByVal Algid As Long, _
    ByVal hBaseData As Long, ByVal dwFlags As Long, _
    phKey As Long) As Long

Private Declare Function CryptDestroyKey Lib "advapi32.dll" ( _
    ByVal hKey As Long) As Long

Private Declare Function CryptEncrypt Lib "advapi32.dll" ( _
    ByVal hKey As Long, ByVal hHash As Long, _
    ByVal Final As Long, ByVal dwFlags As Long, _
    ByVal pbData As String, pdwDataLen As Long, _
    ByVal dwBufLen As Long) As Long

Private Declare Function CryptDecrypt Lib "advapi32.dll" ( _
    ByVal hKey As Long, ByVal hHash As Long, _
    ByVal Final As Long, ByVal dwFlags As Long, _
    ByVal pbData As String, pdwDataLen As Long) As Long

Private Declare Function CryptCreateHash Lib "advapi32.dll" ( _
    ByVal hProv As Long, ByVal Algid As Long, _
    ByVal hKey As Long, ByVal dwFlags As Long, _
    phHash As Long) As Long

Private Declare Function CryptHashData Lib "advapi32.dll" ( _
    ByVal hHash As Long, ByVal pbData As String, _
    ByVal dwDataLen As Long, ByVal dwFlags As Long) As Long

Private Declare Function CryptDestroyHash Lib "advapi32.dll" ( _
    ByVal hHash As Long) As Long

'constants from WinErr.h
Private Const ERROR_INVALID_HANDLE As Long = 6
```

3

**SYMMETRIC AND
PASSWORD
ENCRYPTION**

continues

LISTING 3.1 Continued

```
Private Const ERROR_INVALID_PARAMETER As Long = 87
Private Const NTE_BAD_KEY As Long = &H80090003
Private Const NTE_BAD_UID As Long = &H80090001
Private Const NTE_NO_KEY As Long = &H8009000D
Private Const NTE_BAD_SIGNATURE As Long = &H80090006

' Private property buffers
Private m_sPassword As String    ' Password used to create encryption key

Private m_sInBuffer As String    ' Used as an input buffer for all
                                 ' data to be encrypted or decrypted

Private m_sOutBuffer As String   ' Used as an output buffer for all
                                 ' data that has been encrypted or decrypted

Private m_sErrorMsg As String    ' Error message string

' Private class-level variables
Private m_lHCryptProv As Long    ' Handle for the cryptographic
                                 ' service provider (CSP)

Private m_lHSessionKey As Long   ' Session key for encrypting and
                                 ' decrypting data
```

The first portion of this listing consists of constant values taken directly from the Crypto API declarations. The initial constants are used in the definition of algorithm IDs. They are followed by flags used by the various Crypto API functions that will be used in this application. Finally, you see the CSP types and name declarations.

Following the constant declarations are the declarations of the Crypto API functions you'll be using in this application. After the function declarations are a few constant declarations for error IDs. Finally, some class variables are declared, some of which will be exposed as properties and others that will be used internally.

Exposing Properties

The next step is to expose the properties for which you declared variables in the Listing 3.1. Two of the properties, the InBuffer and Password properties, are read-write. The other two properties, the OutBuffer and ErrorMsg properties, are read-only, and thus need only the Get property methods. To expose these properties, add the code in Listing 3.2 to the clsCrypto class.

LISTING 3.2 Exposed Properties for Class `clsCrypto`

```
Public Property Get InBuffer() As String
    InBuffer = m_sInBuffer
End Property

Public Property Let InBuffer(vNewValue As String)
    m_sInBuffer = vNewValue
End Property

Public Property Get OutBuffer() As String
    OutBuffer = m_sOutBuffer
End Property

Public Property Get ErrorMsg() As String
    ErrorMsg = m_sErrorMsg
End Property

Public Property Get Password() As String
    Password = m_sPassword
End Property

Public Property Let Password(ByVal sNewValue As String)
    m_sPassword = sNewValue
End Property
```

Acquiring a Handle for the CSP

At this point, you've done most of the necessary work on the encryption class, and it's time to get down to business. The first thing you'll add is the initialization of the CSP. To do so, add a function called `InitUser` to the encryption class. Then edit this function, adding the code in Listing 3.3.

LISTING 3.3 The `InitUser` Function

```
Private Function InitUser() As Boolean
'*************************************************************
'* Written By: Davis Chapman
'* Date:       September 06, 1999
'*
'* Syntax:     InitUser
'*
'* Parameters:  None
'*
'* Purpose: This function loads the default CSP (specified
'*          in the defined constant MS_DEF_PROV). If the key
```

continues

LISTING 3.3 Continued

```
'*            container does not exist, then this function
'*            creates it.
'*****************************************************************
On Error Resume Next
    InitUser = False

    Dim lDataSize As Long

    Dim lResult As Long
    Dim sResult As String
    Dim sContainer As String
    Dim sProvider As String

    '--- Prepare string buffers
    sContainer = vbNullChar
    sProvider = MS_DEF_PROV & vbNullChar

    '--- Attempt to acquire a handle to the default key container.
    If Not CBool(CryptAcquireContext(m_lHCryptProv, sContainer, _
                sProvider, PROV_RSA_FULL, 0)) Then

        '--- Create default key container.
        If Not CBool(CryptAcquireContext(m_lHCryptProv, sContainer, _
            sProvider, PROV_RSA_FULL, CRYPT_NEWKEYSET)) Then
            m_sErrorMsg = "Error creating key container - " & _
                    CStr(Err.LastDllError)
            MsgBox m_sErrorMsg, vbOKOnly, "VB Crypto"

            Exit Function
        End If

    End If

    '--- Didn't exit early, return TRUE
    InitUser = True
    Exit Function
End Function
```

In the `InitUser` function, you made two efforts to acquire a handle to the CSP. The first attempt was made by trying to open the default key container. If this attempt failed, you can assume that the default container doesn't exist yet. So, in the second attempt, you pass the flag `CRYPT_NEWKEYSET` to create the default key container.

> **NOTE**
>
> In the previous chapter, you were warned against using the default key container. This is a security precaution only, as the default key container is easily accessible to any user who has access to the computer. Despite this, you use the default container in this example, and will continue to use it in future examples.
>
> In this example, you are only working with a session key that is not stored in the key container, so there's no harm in using the default container.

Now, you need to call the `InitUser` function when the class is first initialized. You can then hold onto the CSP handle for the remainder of the life of this class, using it with the various Crypto API function calls that you will be making. To call this function in the class initialization, select the class `Initialize` event and add the code in Listing 3.4.

LISTING 3.4 The `clsCrypto` Class Initialization

```
Private Sub Class_Initialize()
'**************************************************************
'* Written By: Davis Chapman
'* Date:       September 06, 1999
'*
'* Syntax:     Class_Initialize
'*
'* Parameters: None
'*
'* Purpose: Calls the InitUser function to initialize the
'*          class. The initialization process loads the CSP.
'**************************************************************
    If Not InitUser Then
        m_sErrorMsg = "Unable to initialize CryptoAPI."
        MsgBox m_sErrorMsg, vbOKOnly, "VB Crypto"
    End If
End Sub
```

Finally, you need to close the key container when the class is destroyed. To add this functionality, select the class `Terminate` event and add the code in Listing 3.5.

LISTING 3.5 The `clsCrypto` Class Termination

```
Private Sub Class_Terminate()
'**************************************************************
'* Written By: Davis Chapman
```

continues

3

SYMMETRIC AND
PASSWORD
ENCRYPTION

LISTING 3.5   Continued

```
'* Date:        September 06, 1999
'*
'* Syntax:      Class_Terminate
'*
'* Parameters:  None
'*
'* Purpose: This is executed when this class is destroyed. This
'*          subroutine examines each of the class-level handles
'*          for the keys and keycontext, and destroys or
'*          releases them as is appropriate to clean up after
'*          oneself.
'**************************************************************
    Dim lResult As Long

    '--- Do we have an open key context? If so, release it.
    If (m_lHCryptProv <> 0) Then _
            lResult = CryptReleaseContext(m_lHCryptProv, 0)
End Sub
```

In this code, you first check to see whether you have a handle to a key container. If you do, then you release the handle, closing the key container.

Deriving a Password-Based Key

The next step is to add the functionality to create a password-derived key. To add this functionality, add a new public function called GeneratePasswordKey. Then edit this function, adding the functionality in Listing 3.6.

LISTING 3.6   The GeneratePasswordKey Function

```
Public Function GeneratePasswordKey() As Boolean
'**************************************************************
'* Written By: Davis Chapman
'* Date:        September 06, 1999
'*
'* Syntax:      GeneratePasswordKey
'*
'* Parameters:  None
'*
'* Purpose: This will generate a session key from a hash of
'*          the password entered by the user. The session key
'*          will be placed into a private class variable.
'**************************************************************
```

```
On Error Resume Next
    Dim lHash As Long
    Dim lResult As Long

    GeneratePasswordKey = False

    '--- Create an empty hash object.
    If Not CBool(CryptCreateHash(m_lHCryptProv, CALG_MD5, 0, 0, _
            lHash)) Then
        m_sErrorMsg = "Error " & CStr(Err.LastDllError) & _
                " during CryptCreateHash!"
        MsgBox m_sErrorMsg, vbOKOnly, "VB Crypto"
        Exit Function
    End If

    '--- Hash the password string.
    If Not CBool(CryptHashData(lHash, m_sPassword, _
            Len(m_sPassword), 0)) Then
        m_sErrorMsg = "Error " & CStr(Err.LastDllError) & _
                " during CryptHashData!"
        MsgBox m_sErrorMsg, vbOKOnly, "VB Crypto"
        Exit Function
    End If

    '--- Create a derived block cipher session key.
    If Not CBool(CryptDeriveKey(m_lHCryptProv, CALG_RC2, lHash, 0, _
                m_lHSessionKey)) Then
        m_sErrorMsg = "Error " & CStr(Err.LastDllError) & _
                " during CryptDeriveKey!"
        MsgBox m_sErrorMsg, vbOKOnly, "VB Crypto"
        Exit Function
    End If

    '--- Destroy the hash object
    If Not CBool(CryptDestroyHash(lHash)) Then
        m_sErrorMsg = "Error " & CStr(Err.LastDllError) & _
                " during CryptDestroyHash!"
        MsgBox m_sErrorMsg, vbOKOnly, "VB Crypto"

        Exit Function
    End If

    GeneratePasswordKey = True
End Function
```

This function assumes the password will be copied to the Password property exposed in Listing 3.2. The first thing you do in this function is create a hash object. The handle to the hash object is a local variable in this function because you won't need it after you've created your encryption key. Thus, you can create and destroy it all within this one function.

After you have a handle to a hash object, you use it to hash the password that was placed in the Password property. When you have a hash of the password, you use the hash object to derive a key. You place the handle to the key into a class level variable, as you'll use it in other class methods.

Finally, after you have derived the session key, you can destroy the hash object. At this point, you can set the return value to TRUE to indicate the success of your function.

Destroying a Password-Based Key

At some point, you'll need to destroy the encryption key you have created. To enable this functionality, add a new public function to the encryption class and name it DestroySessionKey. Edit this function by adding the code in Listing 3.7.

LISTING 3.7   The DestroySessionKey Function

```
Public Function DestroySessionKey() As Boolean
'**************************************************************
'* Written By: Davis Chapman
'* Date:       September 06, 1999
'*
'* Syntax:     DestroySessionKey
'*
'* Parameters:  None
'*
'* Purpose: This will destroy the session key.
'**************************************************************
    Dim lResult As Long

    DestroySessionKey = False

    '--- Destroy the session key
    If Not CBool(CryptDestroyKey(m_lHSessionKey)) Then
        m_sErrorMsg = "Error " & CStr(Err.LastDllError) & _
                    " during CryptDestroyKey!"
        MsgBox m_sErrorMsg, vbOKOnly, "VB Crypto"

        Exit Function
    End If

    DestroySessionKey = True
End Function
```

This function is very simple because all you do is destroy the session key.

Performing Data Encryption

Now is the moment that we've all been waiting for, the encryption of actual data. To add the capability to encrypt data to your encryption class, add a public function named `EncryptMessageData`. Then edit this function with the code in Listing 3.8.

LISTING 3.8 The `EncryptMessageData` Function

```
Public Function EncryptMessageData()
'*************************************************************
'* Written By: Davis Chapman
'* Date:       September 06, 1999
'*
'* Syntax:     EncryptMessageData
'*
'* Parameters: None
'*
'* Purpose: This function will take the data in the InBuffer property
'*          and encrypt it using the session key. The resulting
'*          encrypted data is placed in the OutBuffer property.
'*************************************************************
On Error Resume Next
    EncryptMessageData = False

    Dim lDataSize As Long
    Dim lResult As Long
    Dim sCryptBuffer As String
    Dim lCryptLength As Long
    Dim lCryptBufLen As Long

    '--- Determine the size of the buffer needed for encrypting the data
    '--- in the InBuffer property
    lCryptLength = Len(m_sInBuffer)
    lResult = CryptEncrypt(m_lHSessionKey, 0, 1, 0, vbNullString, _
                           lCryptLength, lCryptBufLen)

    '--- Prepare a string buffer for the CryptEncrypt function
    lCryptBufLen = lCryptLength * 2
    lCryptLength = Len(m_sInBuffer)
    sCryptBuffer = String(lCryptBufLen, vbNullChar)

    '--- Copy in the contents of the InBuffer property
    LSet sCryptBuffer = m_sInBuffer

    '--- Encrypt data
```

continues

3

**SYMMETRIC AND
PASSWORD
ENCRYPTION**

LISTING 3.8 Continued

```
    If Not CBool(CryptEncrypt(m_lHSessionKey, 0, 1, 0, sCryptBuffer, _
                            lCryptLength, lCryptBufLen)) Then

        m_sErrorMsg = "Error " & CStr(Err.LastDllError) & _
                            " during CryptEncrypt!"
        MsgBox m_sErrorMsg, vbOKOnly, "VB Crypto"

        Exit Function
    End If

    '--- Copy the encrypted data to the OutBuffer property
    m_sOutBuffer = Mid$(sCryptBuffer, 1, lCryptLength)

    EncryptMessageData = True
End Function
```

In this function, you start by making some curious moves. First, you initialize the message length variable with the size of the message in the InBuffer property. Next, you call the EncryptData function, passing a NULL string in place of the data to be encrypted, as follows:

```
    '--- Determine the size of the buffer needed for encrypting the data
    '--- in the InBuffer property
    lCryptLength = Len(m_sInBuffer)
    lResult = CryptEncrypt(m_lHSessionKey, 0, 1, 0, vbNullString, _
                            lCryptLength, lCryptBufLen)
```

This call returns in the message length variable the total length of the buffer needed to encrypt the message in the input buffer. Following this call, you can see where you are sizing the buffer to hold both the input message and the encrypted data, as well as the variables that specify the size of the buffer:

```
    '--- Prepare a string buffer for the CryptEncrypt function
    lCryptBufLen = lCryptLength * 2
    lCryptLength = Len(m_sInBuffer)
    sCryptBuffer = String(lCryptBufLen, vbNullChar)
```

When you initially sized the buffer, you filled it with NULL characters. Next, you copied the input message into the buffer that you just sized by using the LSet statement:

```
    '--- Copy in the contents of the InBuffer property
    LSet sCryptBuffer = m_sInBuffer
```

Finally, you call the CryptEncrypt function with the actual data to be encrypted:

```
    '--- Encrypt data
    If Not CBool(CryptEncrypt(m_lHSessionKey, 0, 1, 0, sCryptBuffer, _
                            lCryptLength, lCryptBufLen)) Then
```

Finally, to wrap up this function, you copy the encrypted data into the output buffer property. The user then can access the encrypted message.

Performing Data Decryption

When you have encrypted data, you need some way of decrypting that same data. To add this functionality, add one more public function called `DecryptMessageData` to the encryption class. Then edit this function, adding the code in Listing 3.9.

LISTING 3.9   The `DecryptMessageData` Function

```
Public Function DecryptMessageData() As Boolean
'****************************************************************
'* Written By: Davis Chapman
'* Date:       September 06, 1999
'*
'* Syntax:     DecryptMessageData
'*
'* Parameters: None
'*
'* Purpose: This will use the session key to decrypt the data in
'*          the InBuffer property. The decrypted data is then
'*          placed in the OutBuffer property.
'****************************************************************
On Error Resume Next
    DecryptMessageData = False

    Dim lDataSize As Long
    Dim lResult As Long
    Dim sCryptBuffer As String
    Dim lCryptLength As Long
    Dim lCryptBufLen As Long

    '--- Prepare sCryptBuffer for CryptDecrypt
    lCryptBufLen = Len(m_sInBuffer)
    sCryptBuffer = String(lCryptBufLen, vbNullChar)
    LSet sCryptBuffer = m_sInBuffer

    '--- Decrypt data
    If Not CBool(CryptDecrypt(m_lHSessionKey, 0, 1, 0, sCryptBuffer, _
                              lCryptBufLen)) Then
        m_sErrorMsg = "Error " & CStr(Err.LastDllError) & _
                          " during CryptDecrypt!"
        MsgBox m_sErrorMsg, vbOKOnly, "VB Crypto"

        Exit Function
    End If
```

continues

LISTING 3.9   Continued

```
    '--- Apply decrypted string from sCryptBuffer to private buffer
    '--- for OutBuffer property
    m_sOutBuffer = Mid$(sCryptBuffer, 1, lCryptBufLen)

    '--- Didn't exit early, return TRUE
    DecryptMessageData = True
End Function
```

In this function, you don't need to jump through the hoops that you did while encrypting the message to get the buffer size correct. You can size the buffer the same as the encrypted message in the input buffer and copy the encrypted message into this buffer. Also, you need to try to call the CryptDecrypt function only one time. If it fails, resizing the buffer won't make any difference. Finally, you copy the decrypted message into the output buffer so the user can access it.

Designing the User Interface

Now that you've fleshed out the encryption class, you need to turn your attention back to the form that will make up the user interface. You can lay out the form as in Figure 3.1, populating the control properties as in Table 3.9 (left to right, top to bottom).

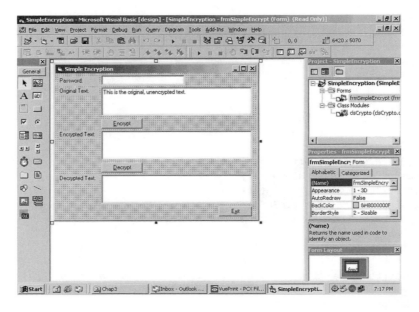

FIGURE 3.1

Application screen layout.

TABLE 3.9 Control Property Settings

Control	Property	Value
Label	Caption	Password:
TextBox	Name	txtPasswd
Label	Caption	Original Text:
TextBox	Name	txtOriginal
Command Button	Name	cmdEncrypt
	Caption	&Encrypt
Label	Caption	Encrypted Text:
TextBox	Name	txtEncrypted
Command Button	Name	cmdDecrypt
	Caption	&Decrypt
Label	Caption	Decrypted Text:
TextBox	Name	txtDecrypted
Command Button	Name	cmdExit
	Caption	E&xit

While we're wrapping up the user interface design, let's go ahead and add the application close functionality. To do so, add the code in Listing 3.10 to the `Click` event of the `cmdExit` button.

LISTING 3.10 The `cmdExit` Button `Click` Event

```
Private Sub cmdExit_Click()
    '-- Exit the application
    Unload Me
End Sub
```

Performing the Encryption

Now you need to perform the encryption on the message that the user has entered into the txtOriginal text box on the form. Because you built the encryption class such that each method does only one of the steps involved, and you didn't build any master methods that drive all the encryption functionality, you need to do that in the form. To add the function that will drive the encryption, add a new private subroutine called DoEncrypt to the form. Then edit this subroutine, adding the code in Listing 3.11.

3

SYMMETRIC AND
PASSWORD
ENCRYPTION

LISTING 3.11   The DoEncrypt Subroutine

```
Private Sub DoEncrypt()
'***************************************************************
'* Written By: Davis Chapman
'* Date:       September 06, 1999
'*
'* Syntax:     DoEncrypt
'*
'* Parameters: None
'*
'* Purpose: This subroutine creates an instance of the Crypto
'*          class, copies the password and message data to the
'*          password and input buffer properties of the class,
'*          and then performs the encryption in three steps.
'*          First, it creates a session key from the password.
'*          Second, it encrypts the message using the session
'*          key. Third, it destroys the session key. Finally,
'*          the encrypted message is copied from the output
'*          buffer property to the encrypted data control.
'***************************************************************
    '-- Create an instance of the encryption class
    Dim csCrypt As New clsCrypto

    '-- Set the password and input buffer properties
    csCrypt.Password = txtPasswd.Text
    csCrypt.InBuffer = txtOriginal.Text

    '-- Generate the password based session key
    If Not csCrypt.GeneratePasswordKey Then _
            Exit Sub

    '-- Encrypt the message data
    If Not csCrypt.EncryptMessageData Then _
            Exit Sub

    '-- Destroy the session key
    csCrypt.DestroySessionKey

    '-- Copy the encrypted data to the display control
    txtEncrypted.Text = csCrypt.OutBuffer
End Sub
```

In this subroutine, you create an instance of the encryption class and initialize the password and input buffer properties with the values that the user entered into the form. Next, you execute a sequence of encryption class methods. When one of the class methods returns FALSE, you exit the function.

To perform the encryption, you first need to generate a password-derived key. Next, you can encrypt the message that the user entered. Finally, you need to destroy the session key that was created. Don't forget that you are opening and closing the key container with the class initialization and termination events, so you don't need to worry about these steps in the code.

Finally, you can copy the encrypted message to the txtEncrypted text box so that the user can see the encrypted message. To trigger this method, you need to attach some code to the Click event of the cmdEncrypt button. Add the code in Listing 3.12 to this event.

LISTING 3.12   The cmdEncrypt Button Click Event

```
Private Sub cmdEncrypt_Click()
'*************************************************************
'* Written By: Davis Chapman
'* Date:       September 06, 1999
'*
'* Syntax:     cmdEncrypt_Click
'*
'* Parameters:  None
'*
'* Purpose: This function is called when the user clicks the
'*          Encrypt button. It checks to make sure that the
'*          user has entered a password and that there is
'*          message data to be encrypted. It then calls the
'*          DoEncrypt subroutine.
'*************************************************************
    '-- Do we have a password?
    If txtPasswd.Text = "" Then
        MsgBox _
        "You must provide a password to use for encrypting the message."
        txtPasswd.SetFocus

    '-- Do we have message data?
    ElseIf txtOriginal.Text = "" Then
        MsgBox "You must enter some text to be encrypted."
        txtOriginal.SetFocus

    '-- We can perform the encryption
    Else
        DoEncrypt
    End If
End Sub
```

In this event, you check to make sure that the user has entered both a password and a message to be encrypted. If both have been entered, you call the DoEncrypt subroutine, performing the encryption. At this point, you should be able to run this application and encrypt a message, as shown in Figure 3.2.

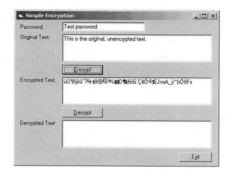

FIGURE 3.2
Encrypting a message.

Performing the Decryption

Now that you can encrypt a message, you need to decrypt that same message so that you can verify that the encryption is working correctly. To perform this action, add a new private subroutine called DoDecrypt to the form. Then edit this subroutine, adding the code in Listing 3.13.

LISTING 3.13   The DoDecrypt Subroutine

```
Private Sub DoDecrypt()
'*****************************************************************
'* Written By: Davis Chapman
'* Date:       September 06, 1999
'*
'* Syntax:     DoDecrypt
'*
'* Parameters: None
'*
'* Purpose: This subroutine creates an instance of the Crypto
'*          class, copies the password and encrypted data to the
'*          password and input buffer properties of the class,
'*          and then performs the decryption in three steps.
'*          First, it creates a session key from the password.
'*          Second, it decrypts the message using the session
'*          key. Third, it destroys the session key. Finally,
'*          the decrypted message is copied from the output
'*          buffer property to the decrypted data control.
'*****************************************************************
```

```
    '-- Create an instance of the encryption class
    Dim csCrypt As New clsCrypto

    '-- Set the password and input buffer properties
    csCrypt.Password = txtPasswd.Text
    csCrypt.InBuffer = txtEncrypted.Text

    '-- Generate the password based session key
    If Not csCrypt.GeneratePasswordKey Then _
        Exit Sub

    '-- Decrypt the message data
    If Not csCrypt.DecryptMessageData Then _
        Exit Sub

    '-- Destroy the session key
    csCrypt.DestroySessionKey

    '-- Copy the decrypted data to the display control
    txtDecrypted.Text = csCrypt.OutBuffer
End Sub
```

As with the DoEncrypt subroutine, in the DoDecrypt subroutine, you start by creating a new instance of the encryption class and copying the password, as well as the encrypted message to the password and input buffer properties of the encryption class. Next, you use the same Select Case flow control to call the encryption class methods in sequence.

The order in which you need to call the decryption methods is almost identical to the order in which you called the encryption methods. The only difference is that you call the DecryptMessageData method instead of the EncryptMessageData method. Finally, after you've decrypted the message, you copy the decrypted message from the encryption class output buffer to the txtDecrypted text box for the user to see.

Now, to wrap up, you need to trigger the DoDecrypt subroutine from the Click event of the cmdDecrypt button. To do so, attach this event method and edit it, adding the code in Listing 3.14.

LISTING 3.14 The cmdDecrypt Button Click Event

```
Private Sub cmdDecrypt_Click()
'*************************************************************
'* Written By: Davis Chapman
'* Date:       September 06, 1999
'*
'* Syntax:     cmdDecrypt_Click
'*
```

continues

3

SYMMETRIC AND
PASSWORD
ENCRYPTION

LISTING 3.14 Continued

```
'* Parameters:  None
'*
'* Purpose: This function is called when the user clicks the
'*          Decrypt button. It checks to make sure that the
'*          user has entered a password and that there is
'*          encrypted data to be decrypted. It then calls the
'*          DoDecrypt subroutine.
'*************************************************************
    '-- Do we have a password?
    If txtPasswd.Text = "" Then
        MsgBox _
        "You must provide a password to use for encrypting the message."
        txtPasswd.SetFocus

    '-- Do we have encrypted data?
    ElseIf txtEncrypted.Text = "" Then
        MsgBox "You must encrypt some text before decrypting."
        txtOriginal.SetFocus

    '-- We can perform the decryption
    Else
        DoDecrypt
    End If
End Sub
```

At this point, you should be able to run the application again and not only encrypt messages, but also decrypt those same messages, as shown in Figure 3.3.

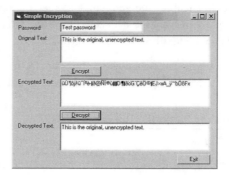

FIGURE 3.3

Decrypting the message.

Building a File Encryption/Decryption Utility

Now that you have a basic, functional ability to encrypt and decrypt messages, let's take this process one step further. For the next sample application, you'll build an application that encrypts and decrypts files. Not only will this application encrypt and decrypt files, but it will also include a hash of the decrypted file in the encrypted file, enabling the application to determine whether a file has been modified or tampered with since being encrypted.

Making Additional Declarations

To start this second sample application, start another standard EXE project. Name the project FileEncryption and the default form frmFileEncrypt. Just like with the last application, at this point, you can turn your attention to the encryption class and come back to the default form later.

To speed things along with this second application, you don't need to repeat what you did in the last sample application. Instead, you can copy the encryption class into the project directory for this new project and then include it in the new project that you've started (or if you're building this project in the same directory as the previous example, just include the class file in the project) by choosing Project, Add Class Module and then selecting the Existing tab on the New Class dialog.

After you've added the existing encryption class file to the project, open the file and edit the declaration section, adding the new declarations in Listing 3.15.

LISTING 3.15   New Constant, Function, and Variable Declarations

```
'--- New algorithm ID
Private Const CALG_SSL3_SHAMD5 = ((ALG_CLASS_HASH Or ALG_TYPE_ANY) _
                   Or ALG_SID_SSL3SHAMD5)

'--- New flag values
Private Const HP_ALGID = &H1            ' Hash algorithm
Private Const HP_HASHVAL = &H2          ' Hash value
Private Const HP_HASHSIZE = &H4         ' Hash value size
Private Const HP_HMAC_INFO = &H5        ' information for creating an HMAC

'--- New constants
Private Const CRYPT_FAILED = 0
Private Const CRYPT_SUCCEED = -1

'--- New API functions
Private Declare Function CryptGetHashParam Lib "advapi32.dll" ( _
    ByVal hHash As Long, ByVal dwParam As Long, _
```

continues

LISTING 3.15   Continued

```
    ByVal pbData As String, pdwDataLen As Long, _
    ByVal dwFlags As Long) As Long

Private Declare Function CryptGetHashDWParam Lib "advapi32.dll" _
    Alias "CryptGetHashParam" (ByVal hHash As Long, _
    ByVal dwParam As Long, pbData As Long, _
    pdwDataLen As Long, ByVal dwFlags As Long) As Long

'--- New class variables
Private m_sHashBuffer As String ' Used as a buffer for all the hash value

Private m_iHashLength As Long    ' Used to hold the hash length
```

These new declarations follow the same organization as the ones you added in the preceding example and can be divided and added in the appropriate sections of the declarations. Therefore, the constant declarations would be near the bottom of the existing constant declarations. The API function declarations would be with the other API function declarations, and the class variables would be at the bottom of the declaration section.

Hashing the Data File

After you've added the new constant, function, and variable declarations, you can turn your attention to the new functionality that you don't already have in the encryption class. The first functionality that you'll add is the function that hashes the plain text file. To add this functionality, add a new public function called HashFile and then edit it, adding the code in Listing 3.16.

LISTING 3.16   The HashFile Function

```
Public Function HashFile() As Boolean
'*****************************************************************
'* Written By: Davis Chapman
'* Date:       September 06, 1999
'*
'* Syntax:     HashFile
'*
'* Parameters: None
'*
'* Purpose: This function creates a hash value for the contents
'*          of the input buffer. The resulting hash value will
'*          be placed in the m_sHashBuffer variable for later
'*          use.
'*****************************************************************
On Error Resume Next
    Dim lHash As Long
    Dim lResult As Long
    Dim sCryptBuffer As String
```

```
Dim lCryptBufLen As Long
Dim lCryptHashSize As Long

HashFile = False

'--- Create an empty hash object.
If Not CBool(CryptCreateHash(m_lHCryptProv, CALG_MD5, 0, 0, _
                    lHash)) Then
    m_sErrorMsg = "Error " & CStr(Err.LastDllError) & _
            " during CryptCreateHash!"
    MsgBox m_sErrorMsg, vbOKOnly, "VB Crypto"
    Exit Function
End If

'--- Hash the password string.
If Not CBool(CryptHashData(lHash, m_sInBuffer, _
                    Len(m_sInBuffer), 0)) Then
    m_sErrorMsg = "Error " & CStr(Err.LastDllError) & _
            " during CryptHashData!"
    MsgBox m_sErrorMsg, vbOKOnly, "VB Crypto"
    Exit Function
End If

'--- Extract the hash value size.
lCryptBufLen = 4
If Not CBool(CryptGetHashDWParam(lHash, HP_HASHSIZE, _
            lCryptHashSize, lCryptBufLen, 0)) Then
    m_sErrorMsg = "Error " & CStr(Err.LastDllError) & _
            " during CryptGetHashParam!"
    MsgBox m_sErrorMsg, vbOKOnly, "VB Crypto"
    Exit Function
End If

'--- Prepare sCryptBuffer for CryptDecrypt
sCryptBuffer = String(lCryptHashSize, vbNullChar)
lCryptBufLen = lCryptHashSize

'--- Extract the hash value.
If Not CBool(CryptGetHashParam(lHash, HP_HASHVAL, sCryptBuffer, _
            lCryptBufLen, 0)) Then
    m_sErrorMsg = "Error " & CStr(Err.LastDllError) & _
            " during CryptGetHashParam!"
    MsgBox m_sErrorMsg, vbOKOnly, "VB Crypto"
    Exit Function
End If

'--- Destroy the Hash object
```

continues

LISTING 3.16 Continued

```
    If Not CBool(CryptDestroyHash(lHash)) Then
        m_sErrorMsg = "Error " & CStr(Err.LastDllError) & _
                " during CryptDestroyHash!"
        MsgBox m_sErrorMsg, vbOKOnly, "VB Crypto"
        Exit Function
    End If

    '--- Apply hash string from sCryptBuffer to private buffer for
    '--- HashBuffer variables
    m_sHashBuffer = Mid$(sCryptBuffer, 1, lCryptBufLen)
    m_iHashLength = lCryptBufLen

    '--- Didn't exit early, return TRUE
    HashFile = True
End Function
```

In this function, you first create the hash object. After you have the hash object, you use it to hash the input file (located in the input buffer). After hashing the input file, you use the alias of the CryptGetHashParam function (CryptGetHashDWParam) to get the size of the hash itself. You use this size to create a string buffer filled with NULL characters (vbNullChar). Finally, you extract the hash value and then destroy the hash object. After this, you copy the hash value into the class variable that you created to hold the hash value and length.

Encrypting the Data File

You already have functionality to encrypt a message built into the encryption class, but you don't have the functionality to encrypt a file, embedding the hash in the file. When adding this functionality, you can leverage the encryption functionality you already have by letting the existing functionality perform the actual encryption. Now all you have to do is wrap that functionality with the hashing and combining of the file and hash before encrypting. To add this functionality, add a new public function called EncryptFileData. Then edit this function, adding the code in Listing 3.17.

LISTING 3.17 The EncryptFileData Function

```
Public Function EncryptFileData() As Boolean
'**************************************************************
'* Written By: Davis Chapman
'* Date:       September 06, 1999
'*
'* Syntax:     EncryptFileData
'*
'* Parameters: None
'*
```

```
'* Purpose: This function places the hash of the original file
'*          at the front of the file (preceded by the hash
'*          length) and then calls EncryptMessageData to encrypt
'*          the whole thing.
'**************************************************************
    EncryptFileData = False

    Dim strInputData As String

    '--- Concatenate the length of the hash, the hash value, and the
    '--- original file contents
    strInputData = Trim(Str(m_iHashLength)) + m_sHashBuffer + m_sInBuffer

    '--- Copy the new string to the input buffer
    m_sInBuffer = strInputData

    '--- Call EncryptMessageData and return its return value
    EncryptFileData = EncryptMessageData
End Function
```

In this function, you can assume that you have already hashed the plain text file, so all you really need to do is concatenate the hash and the input file together. You also need to know (for decryption purposes) how long the hash is, so you will know how much to remove from the front of the file after you decrypt it. After you concatenate all these elements, you copy the entire thing back into the input buffer and call the EncryptMessageData function.

Decrypting the Data File

The last piece of missing functionality from the encryption class is the ability to decrypt the encrypted file. This function needs to be able to call the existing decryption functionality to decrypt the entire file and then strip off the original hash from the decrypted file, create a new hash of the decrypted file, and compare the two hashes to make sure that the file hasn't been modified. To add this functionality to the encryption class, add a new public function called DecryptFileData. Then edit this new function, adding the code in Listing 3.18.

LISTING 3.18 The DecryptFileData Function

```
Public Function DecryptFileData() As Boolean
'**************************************************************
'* Written By: Davis Chapman
'* Date:       September 06, 1999
'*
'* Syntax:     DecryptFileData
'*
'* Parameters: None
```

continues

3

LISTING 3.18   Continued

```
'*
'* Purpose: This function calls DecryptMessageData to decrypt
'*          the file contents. The original hash value is then
'*          stripped off the front of the decrypted data, and
'*          a new hash of the decrypted data is generated. If
'*          the two hash values match, the file has not been
'*          corrupted. If the two values don't match, the file
'*          has been corrupted.
'****************************************************************
    DecryptFileData = False

    Dim strInputData As String
    Dim strHash As String
    Dim strHashLength As String
    Dim lHashLength As Long

    '--- Decrypt the file data
    If Not DecryptMessageData Then Exit Function

    '--- Extract the original hash length
    strHashLength = Left(m_sOutBuffer, 2)
    lHashLength = CLng(strHashLength)

    '--- Extract the original hash value
    strHash = Mid(m_sOutBuffer, 3, lHashLength)

    '--- Extract the original file contents
    strInputData = Mid(m_sOutBuffer, (3 + lHashLength))

    '--- Copy the original file contents to the input buffer
    m_sInBuffer = strInputData

    '--- Hash the original file contents
    If Not HashFile Then Exit Function

    '--- Compare the original hash value to the new hash value
    If (strHash = m_sHashBuffer) Then
        '--- If they match, the file is unaltered, copy the original
        '--- file contents to the output buffer
        m_sOutBuffer = strInputData
    Else
        '--- The hash values don't match, the file has been corrupted
        MsgBox "File has been corrupted since original encryption."
        m_sOutBuffer = ""
        Exit Function
    End If
```

```
    '--- Didn't exit early, return TRUE
    DecryptFileData = True
End Function
```

In this function, you follow the steps outlined previously. You first decrypt the file using the `DecryptMessageData` function. Next, you extract the length of the hash from the front of the file. (This is always two characters; currently available hashes are usually either 16 or 24 bytes long.) When you have the length of the hash, you can strip the hash off the front of the decrypted file.

After you remove the hash from the decrypted file, you copy the file back to the input buffer and rehash the file. Then, when you have a new hash, you compare it with the original hash, determining whether the file is the same as it was before you encrypted it in the first place.

Designing the User Interface

Now that you've added the necessary functionality to the encryption class, you need to turn your attention back to the default form that you'll be using for this application.

Because you're dealing with files in this application, it would be desirable if you enabled the user to browse the file system for the file to be encrypted or decrypted. This requires that you add the Microsoft Common Dialog Control to your project. To add it, select Project, Components from the menu to open the Components dialog. Locate the Microsoft Common Dialog Control in the list of available controls, and select the check box beside the control, as shown in Figure 3.4. Click the OK or Apply button, and close the dialog. You should now see the Common Dialog Control on your toolbox.

3

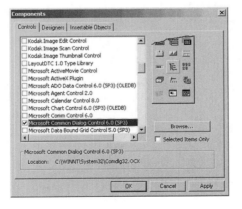

FIGURE 3.4
Including the Common Dialog Control.

Next, bring up the form layout designer, and place controls on the form, as shown in Figure 3.5. Set the appropriate properties on the controls as listed in Table 3.10.

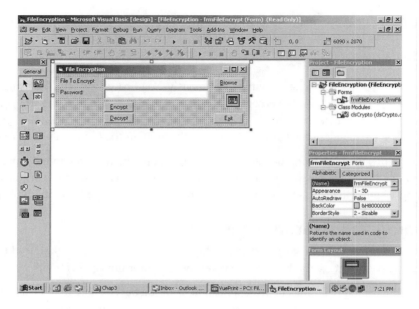

FIGURE 3.5

The second application screen layout.

TABLE 3.10   New Control Property Settings

Control	Property	Value
Label	Caption	File To Encrypt:
TextBox	Name	txtFileName
Command Button	Name	cmdBrowse
	Caption	&Browse
Label	Caption	Password:
TextBox	Name	txtPassword
Common Dialog	Name	cdFile
Command Button	Name	cmdEncrypt
	Caption	&Encrypt
Command Button	Name	cmdDecrypt
	Caption	&Decrypt
Command Button	Name	cmdExit
	Caption	E&xit

To take care of the miscellaneous form functionality, next attach an event subroutine to the `Click` event of the `cmdExit` button. Edit this event subroutine, adding the code in Listing 3.19 to close the application (the same as in the previous application).

LISTING 3.19   The `cmdExit` Button `Click` Event

```
Private Sub cmdExit_Click()
    '-- Exit the application
    Unload Me
End Sub
```

To wrap up the miscellaneous form functionality, attach the file browsing functionality to the `cmdBrowse` button. To do so, add the code in Listing 3.20 to the `Click` event for the `cmdBrowse` button.

LISTING 3.20   The `cmdBrowse` Button `Click` Event

```
Private Sub cmdBrowse_Click()
    cdFile.Filter = "Text File|*.txt|All Files|*.*"
    cdFile.ShowOpen
    txtFileName.Text = cdFile.FileName
End Sub
```

Performing the Data File Encryption

Now it's time to add the functionality to read in and encrypt the file. Add a new private subroutine named `DoEncrypt` to the form. Then edit this function with the code in Listing 3.21.

LISTING 3.21   The `DoEncrypt` Function

```
Private Sub DoEncrypt()
'***************************************************************
'* Written By: Davis Chapman
'* Date:       September 06, 1999
'*
'* Syntax:     DoEncrypt
'*
'* Parameters: None
'*
'* Purpose: This subroutine creates an instance of the Crypto
'*          class, copies the password and file data to the
'*          password and input buffer properties of the class,
'*          and then performs the encryption in three steps.
'*          First, it creates a session key from the password.
```

continues

LISTING 3.21 Continued

```
'*          Second, it encrypts the message using the session
'*          key. Third, it destroys the session key. Finally,
'*          the encrypted message is copied from the output
'*          buffer property to the original file.
'***************************************************************
    '-- Create an instance of the encryption class
    Dim csCrypt As New clsCrypto
    Dim strFile As String
    Dim lFileLength As Long

    '-- Get the length of the file to be decrypted
    lFileLength = FileLen(txtFileName.Text)

    '-- Allocate the string to hold the entire file
    strFile = String(lFileLength, vbNullChar)

    '-- Open the file in binary mode
    Open txtFileName.Text For Binary Access Read As #1

    '-- Read in the file
    Get 1, , strFile

    '-- Close the file
    Close #1

    '-- Set the password and input buffer properties
    csCrypt.Password = txtPassword.Text
    csCrypt.InBuffer = strFile

    '-- Generate a hash of the original file
    If Not csCrypt.HashFile Then _
        Exit Sub

    '-- Generate the password based session key
    If Not csCrypt.GeneratePasswordKey Then _
        Exit Sub

    '-- Encrypt the message data
    If Not csCrypt.EncryptFileData Then _
        Exit Sub

    '-- Destroy the session key
    csCrypt.DestroySessionKey

    '-- Do we have valid data to write back to the file?
    If csCrypt.OutBuffer <> "" Then
```

```
        '-- Delete the current file
        Kill txtFileName.Text

        '-- Open the file for writing in binary mode
        Open txtFileName.Text For Binary Access Write As #1

        '-- Write out the file
        Put 1, , csCrypt.OutBuffer

        '-- Close the file
        Close #1
    End If
End Sub
```

You start this subroutine by getting the size of the file to be encrypted. Next, you size the string that you are going to read the file into to be the size of the entire file. Then you open the file in binary mode and read the entire file in at once.

> **NOTE**
>
> Reading and writing the entire file at one time might not always be practical. This example is not designed to handle very large files; thus, reading the file in at one time is not a problem. If you need to be able to handle files too large to take this approach, you probably should check with one of the general-purpose books on Visual Basic programming that deals with reading and writing files.

After you read in the entire file, you copy the file to the input buffer of the encryption class and the password to the password property. Next, you use the Select Case flow control to step through the necessary encryption steps. First, you hash the file. Second, you derive the encryption key from the password. Third, you encrypt the file. Finally, you destroy the encryption key.

After you encrypt the file, you delete the original file by using the Kill statement. Then, after you delete the original file, you open a new version of the file in binary mode for writing and write the encrypted file to the disk.

Now you have to trigger all this functionality from the cmdEncrypt command button. To do so, attach a subroutine to the Click event of the cmdEncrypt button, and add the code in Listing 3.22.

LISTING 3.22 The cmdEncrypt Button Click Event (second application)

```
Private Sub cmdEncrypt_Click()
'****************************************************************
'* Written By: Davis Chapman
```

continues

LISTING 3.22   Continued

```
'* Date:         September 06, 1999
'*
'* Syntax:       cmdEncrypt_Click
'*
'* Parameters:  None
'*
'* Purpose: This function is called when the user clicks the
'*           Encrypt button. It checks to make sure that the
'*           user has entered a password and that there is
'*           message data to be encrypted. It then calls the
'*           DoEncrypt subroutine.
'***************************************************************
    '-- Do we have a password?
    If txtPassword.Text = "" Then
        MsgBox _
        "You must provide a password to use for encrypting the message."
        txtPassword.SetFocus

    '-- Do we have message data?
    ElseIf txtFileName.Text = "" Then
        MsgBox "You must specify a file to be encrypted."
        txtFileName.SetFocus

    '-- We can perform the encryption
    Else
        DoEncrypt
    End If
End Sub
```

In this event, you check to make sure that you have both a password and a filename. If you have both, you call the DoEncrypt function. You now should be able to run this application, as shown in Figure 3.6, and convert a plain text file, like the one shown in Figure 3.7, and convert it into an encrypted file, like the one in Figure 3.8.

FIGURE 3.6

Running the File Encryption application.

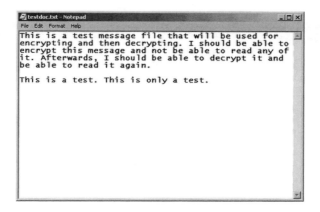

FIGURE 3.7

A plain text file before encrypting.

FIGURE 3.8

An encrypted file.

Performing the Data File Decryption

The last thing you need to add to your application is the capability to decrypt the file you just encrypted. An application that encrypts files isn't much use unless it can also decrypt those same files. To add this functionality, add a new private subroutine called DoDecrypt to the form. Then edit this subroutine, adding the code in Listing 3.23.

LISTING 3.23   The DoDecrypt Function

```
Private Sub DoDecrypt()
'****************************************************************
'* Written By: Davis Chapman
'* Date:       September 06, 1999
'*
'* Syntax:     DoDecrypt
'*
'* Parameters: None
'*
'* Purpose: This subroutine creates an instance of the Crypto
'*          class, copies the password and encrypted file to the
'*          password and input buffer properties of the class,
'*          and then performs the decryption in three steps.
'*          First, it creates a session key from the password.
'*          Second, it decrypts the message using the session
'*          key. Third, it destroys the session key. Finally,
'*          the decrypted message is copied from the output
'*          buffer property to the original file.
'****************************************************************
    '-- Create an instance of the encryption class
    Dim csCrypt As New clsCrypto
    Dim strFile As String
    Dim lFileLength As Long

    '-- Get the length of the file to be decrypted
    lFileLength = FileLen(txtFileName.Text)

    '-- Allocate the string to hold the entire file
    strFile = String(lFileLength, vbNullChar)

    '-- Open the file in binary mode
    Open txtFileName.Text For Binary Access Read As #1

    '-- Read in the file
    Get 1, , strFile

    '-- Close the file
    Close #1

    '-- Set the password and input buffer properties
    csCrypt.Password = txtPassword.Text
    csCrypt.InBuffer = strFile

    '-- Generate the password based session key
    If Not csCrypt.GeneratePasswordKey Then _
        Exit Sub
```

```
        '-- Decrypt the message data
        If Not csCrypt.DecryptFileData Then _
            Exit Sub

        '-- Destroy the session key
        csCrypt.DestroySessionKey

        '-- Do we have valid data to write back to the file?
        If csCrypt.OutBuffer <> "" Then

            '-- Delete the current file
            Kill txtFileName.Text

            '-- Open the file for writing in binary mode
            Open txtFileName.Text For Binary Access Write As #1

            '-- Write out the file
            Put 1, , csCrypt.OutBuffer

            '-- Close the file
            Close #1
        End If
End Sub
```

In this function, you deal with the file in the same way you did in the DoEncrypt subroutine. When it comes to actually decrypting the file, you take the encryption class methods in the following order: First, you derive the encryption key from the password; next, you decrypt the file, checking the hashes in the process; and finally, you destroy the encryption key.

Now you need to attach functionality to the Click event of the cmdDecrypt button. To do so, add the code in Listing 3.24 to this event.

LISTING 3.24   The cmdDecrypt Button Click Event (second application)

```
Private Sub cmdDecrypt_Click()
'*************************************************************
'* Written By: Davis Chapman
'* Date:       September 06, 1999
'*
'* Syntax:     cmdDecrypt_Click
'*
'* Parameters: None
'*
'* Purpose: This function is called when the user clicks the
'*          Decrypt button. It checks to make sure that the
'*          user has entered a password and that there is
```

continues

LISTING 3.24   Continued

```
'*           encrypted data to be decrypted. It then calls the
'*           DoDecrypt subroutine.
'**************************************************************
    '-- Do we have a password?
    If txtPassword.Text = "" Then
        MsgBox _
        "You must provide a password to use for encrypting the message."
        txtPassword.SetFocus

    '-- Do we have encrypted data?
    ElseIf txtFileName.Text = "" Then
        MsgBox "You must specify a file to be decrypted."
        txtFileName.SetFocus

    '-- We can perform the decryption
    Else
        DoDecrypt
    End If
End Sub
```

As you do with the `cmdEncrypt` button, you first check to make sure that you have a filename and a password before calling the `DoDecrypt` subroutine. At this point, you should be able to run the application again and decrypt the file that you previously encrypted, returning it to its former state (assuming you remembered the password you used in encrypting it).

Summary

This chapter covered a lot of ground. You learned how you can create hashes of messages and keys, and what you can do with those hashes. Next, you looked at how you can generate symmetric encryption keys by deriving them from some source data, such as a user-supplied password, as well as how to generate a random encryption key. Finally, you learned how you can use the keys that you've generated to both encrypt and decrypt data, and how you can use hashes of data to verify that the data hasn't been corrupted.

The next chapter will go further into the arena of key generation and encryption. You'll learn how to use public/private key pairs in conjunction with session keys. You'll also learn how to export and import keys, enabling you to exchange your public key and session keys with other applications or users. This information will provide you with a firm ground in the basics of encrypted and secure communications between applications and between computers.

Public/Private Key Communications

IN THIS CHAPTER

- Block Versus Stream Algorithms
- Generating, Saving, and Retrieving Public/Private Keys
- Exporting and Importing Keys
- Building a Secure Messaging Utility

Being able to protect files from snooping eyes by encrypting them with a password is all fine and good, but it doesn't do anything for those occasions when you need to exchange information with another user in a secure manner. You could give the other user the password to decrypt the messages you send, but then how do you send the password so that it is secure?

When you get right down to it, password-based key generation isn't good for much more than protecting files on your computer, or network, from people who shouldn't have access to them. However, a standard form of encryption is designed for use in securing communications between users or computers; it is known as *public/private key encryption.*

You already know how to generate a public/private key pair. You learned how to create this pair in the preceding chapter with the `CryptGenKey` function by using the `AT_KEYEXCHANGE` and `AT_SIGNATURE` algorithms (although you may not have realized it at the time). What you didn't learn in that chapter was how to *use* a key pair. Yes, you learned the basics of using a public/private key pair back in Chapter 1, but you didn't learn all the details that go into making this pair work. You also didn't learn details about the difference between block and stream algorithms, cryptographic salt, and cryptographic random number generation. That's some of what you're going to learn in this chapter.

PREREQUISITES

Before reading this chapter, you need to make sure you have a good understanding of the following:

- Symmetric encryption and cryptographic hashes, as covered in Chapter 1, "Understanding Encryption and Application Security"

- Opening and closing a key container and acquiring a handle to a CSP, as covered in Chapter 2, "Getting Started with the Crypto API"

- Hashing data, generating encryption keys, and encrypting and decrypting data, as covered in Chapter 3, "Symmetric and Password Encryption"

Block Versus Stream Algorithms

In the preceding chapter, where I described how to generate encryption keys, I mentioned some encryption algorithms that were labeled as either *block* or *stream* algorithms. You might be wondering what the difference is between these two types of encryption algorithms. Why would you want to use one over the other?

A block algorithm encrypts data in fixed size chunks. The block size is usually specified by the algorithm being used. Because these algorithms need to encrypt a block of data that is a specific size, the original data is often padded with additional random data. This additional data increases the amount of data so that it is the same size as the block size of the algorithm.

A stream algorithm encrypts data one byte at a time. The data is streamed through the encryption algorithm, each byte being encrypted as it passes through. Stream algorithms usually are much faster than block algorithms, but also are not as secure. Stream algorithms are also better at handling noise in the transfer of encrypted data. If one byte is garbled in the transfer, only one byte will be garbled when decrypted by a stream algorithm, whereas the entire block would be garbled when decrypted by a block algorithm.

So which type of algorithm is better? The answer depends on your specific needs. If you need encryption speed more than you need maximum security, you might prefer a stream algorithm. On the other hand, if you are trying to squeeze every last ounce of security from your encryption, you'll probably want to use a block algorithm.

Salt Values: What Are They and Why Use Them?

In the preceding chapter, when looking at the functions for deriving or generating encryption keys, you may have noticed some option flags for including or not including salt in the key. No, I'm not talking about seasoning some food; I'm talking about *cryptographic salt*.

Cryptographic salt is a string of random values added to the encryption key to create a longer key. With Microsoft's Base Cryptographic Provider, the generated session keys are 40 bits in length. The salt values it uses are 88 bits long, making a total key length of 128 bits.

So why use salt values? Salt values can be changed throughout a communication session, so any two identical blocks of information will not be encrypted the same. Having two identical encrypted blocks of data is often an indicator that the content is the same, thus making these blocks very attractive to someone trying to break the encryption. By changing the salt value, you can prevent this situation by making sure that no two blocks of identical data are encrypted into identical encrypted blocks.

The next question is how to use salt values. If they are part of the encryption key, how can you change them and still exchange encrypted data? Well, one of the key aspects of salt values is that they can be exchanged in cleartext without jeopardizing key security. So, you can generate a new salt value, use it to encrypt a block of data, and then send the salt value with the encrypted block of data to the recipient. The recipient can then take the new salt value and use it with the session key to decrypt the encrypted data.

Generating Salt Values

When you need to generate a salt value, or when you need to generate a new initialization value for use when generating a new key, you can use the CryptGenRandom function. This function is declared as follows:

Syntax

```
Public Declare Function CryptGenRandom Lib "advapi32.dll" ( _
    ByVal hProv As Long, ByVal dwLen As Long, _
    ByVal pbBuffer As String) As Long
```

The first parameter (hProv) for the CryptGenRandom function is the handle for the CSP. This handle was acquired with the CryptAcquireContext function. The second parameter (dwLen) is the number of bytes of salt, or initialization data, to be generated.

The third parameter (pbBuffer) is the string buffer into which the salt values will be placed. Just as with the encryption function, you need to allocate the string by using the String function to hold the random values generated.

NOTE

The CryptGenRandom function generates cryptographically random data. This type of data is different from normal random data that is generated from the Visual Basic Rnd function. The data generated by the Visual Basic Rnd function is not truly random but is generated by a formula in which the rest of the sequence can be predicted when any generated value is known. Cryptographically random data uses other sources of randomness. Sometimes this randomness comes from user input latency; other times, it comes from electronic "noise" or hardware-generated "jitter." Some researchers have even used lava lamps as sources of randomness for use in generating cryptographically random data. The method that is used to generate random data is dependent on the CSP being used.

You could use the CryptGenRandom function as in the following code:

```
Dim sSaltValue As String
Dim lDataSize As Long

lDataSize = 88
'--- Size the target string for the size specified, filling it with
'--- null characters
sSaltValue = String(lDataSize, vbNullChar)
```

```
'--- Generate the Salt Value
If Not CBool(CryptGenRandom(m_lHCryptProv, lDataSize, sSaltValue)) Then
    '--- Error Handling
End If
```

Extracting Salt Values from Session Keys

So, now you know how to generate salt values, either by themselves or as you are creating the encryption key. What you don't know yet, though, is how to extract the current salt value from the key or how to add a new salt value to the key. You can start by extracting the current salt value from the session key.

Among other things, you can get the salt value from a session key by using the CryptGetKeyParam function. This function is declared as follows:

Syntax

```
Public Declare Function CryptGetKeyParam Lib "advapi32.dll" ( _
    ByVal hKey As Long, ByVal dwParam As Long, _
    ByVal pbData As String, pdwDataLen As Long, _
    ByVal dwFlags As Long) As Long
```

An alternative declaration you might also want to use for getting numeric values is as follows:

Syntax

```
Public Declare Function CryptGetKeyDWParam Lib "advapi32.dll" _
    Alias "CryptGetKeyParam" (ByVal hKey As Long, _
    ByVal dwParam As Long, pbData As Long, _
    pdwDataLen As Long, ByVal dwFlags As Long) As Long
```

In this function, the first parameter (hKey) is the handle for an encryption key that was created using either CryptGenKey or CryptDeriveKey (both covered in the preceding chapter). The second parameter (dwParam) specifies what value you want to retrieve from the key object. The possible values for this parameter are listed in Table 4.1.

TABLE 4.1 CryptGetKeyParam Parameter Values

Key Type	Constant	Value	Function Version	Description
All	KP_SALT	2	1st	Indicates that you want to get the actual salt value currently being used by the key object.

continues

TABLE 4.1   Continued

Key Type	Constant	Value	Function Version	Description
All	KP_PERMISSIONS	6	2nd	Indicates that you want a long value containing the set of current permission flags. (The possible permission values are listed in Table 4.2.)
All	KP_ALGID	7	2nd	Indicates that you want to retrieve the algorithm information from the key object. This value was passed in as the second parameter in the CryptGenKey function.
All	KP_BLOCKLEN	8	2nd	Indicates that you want to retrieve the block length used by the encryption key. If the key handle is for a Stream algorithm, the resulting value is zero (0).
All	KP_KEYLEN	9	2nd	Indicates that you want the actual length of the key.
DSS	KP_P	11	1st	Indicates that you want the prime modulus P from the DSS key.
DSS	KP_Q	13	1st	Indicates that you want the prime Q from the DSS key.
DSS	KP_G	12	1st	Indicates that you want the generator G from the DSS key.
Block	KP_EFFECTIVE_KEYLEN	19	2nd	Indicates that you want the effective key length of an RC2 key.
Block	KP_IV	1	1st	Indicates that you want the current initialization vector.
Block	KP_PADDING	3	2nd	Indicates that you want to get the padding method being used by the key. The possible padding modes are listed in Table 4.3.
Block	KP_MODE	4	2nd	Indicates that you want to get the current cipher mode. The possible modes are listed in Table 4.4.
Block	KP_MODE_BITS	5	2nd	Indicates that you want the number of bits that are processed per cycle when the OFB or CFB modes are used.

> **NOTE**
>
> Key parameters labeled as All are available for use with all encryption keys. Parameters labeled as DSS are available only with DSS algorithms. Parameters labeled as Block are available with block algorithms only.

> ## DSS
>
> DSS stands for Digital Signature Standard. This is a standard that specifies the Digital Signature Algorithm (DSA) as it's signing algorithm, and the Secure Hash Algorithm (SHA-1) algorithm as it's message hash algorithm. This is a set of algorithms that can only be used for signing messages, and cannot be used for encrypting data.

The third parameter (pbData) is the variable into which the value requested will be placed. With the first version of the function, it is a string variable that you need to have sized prior to calling this function. If you are using the second version of this function, the variable is a long into which the value is placed. Depending on which parameter you passed in the second parameter (dwParam), the value returned in this parameter may be one of the values listed in Tables 4.2, 4.3, or 4.4.

The fourth parameter (pdwDataLen) is a long variable into which is placed the size of the value in the third parameter. Initially, it needs to be the length of the sized string for the first version of the function, and 4 for the second version.

The fifth parameter (dwFlags) is reserved for future use, so you should always pass zero (0) for this value.

As with most Crypto API functions, this one returns a long Boolean variable that you can check by using the CBool function. As I stated in the previous chapter, in order to keep from repeating myself ad nauseum, assume that all of these Crypto API functions return a C++ Boolean value, and I'll point out to you when they return something different.

TABLE 4.2   CryptGetKeyParam Permission Flags

Flag	Value	Description
CRYPT_ENCRYPT	&H1	Allows encryption
CRYPT_DECRYPT	&H2	Allows decryption
CRYPT_EXPORT	&H4	Allows a key to be exported

continues

TABLE 4.2 Continued

Flag	Value	Description
CRYPT_READ	&H8	Allows values to be read
CRYPT_WRITE	&H10	Allows values to be set
CRYPT_MAC	&H20	Allows MACs to be used with the key

TABLE 4.3 CryptGetKeyParam Padding Mode

Flag	Value	Description
PKCS5_PADDING	1	PKCS 5 (section 6.2) padding method
RANDOM_PADDING	2	Random padding method
ZERO_PADDING	3	No padding

TABLE 4.4 CryptGetKeyParam Cipher Modes

Flag	Value	Description
CRYPT_MODE_CBC	1	Cipher block chaining
CRYPT_MODE_ECB	2	Electronic codebook
CRYPT_MODE_OFB	3	Output feedback mode
CRYPT_MODE_CFB	4	Cipher feedback mode

Setting Salt Values in Session Keys

Now that you know how to get the current salt value, as well as a few other pieces of information from an encryption key, you probably want to know how to do the reverse and set some of these values (especially the salt value). You do so by using the CryptSetKeyParam function. This function is declared as follows:

Syntax

```
Public Declare Function CryptSetKeyParam Lib "advapi32.dll" ( _
    ByVal hKey As Long, ByVal dwParam As Long, _
    ByVal pbData As String, ByVal dwFlags As Long) As Long
```

As you can probably guess, a second way to declare this function is as follows:

Syntax

```
Public Declare Function CryptSetKeyDWParam Lib "advapi32.dll" _
    Alias "CryptSetKeyParam" (ByVal hKey As Long, _
    ByVal dwParam As Long, pbData As Long, _
    ByVal dwFlags As Long) As Long
```

Using this second version, you can set the numeric value and option flag parameters.

The first parameter (hKey) for this function is the handle to the encryption key object. The second parameter (dwParam) is a flag that specifies what aspect of the key is being set. The possible values are listed in Table 4.5.

TABLE 4.5 CryptSetKeyParam **Parameter Values**

Key Type	Constant	Value	Function Version	Description
All	KP_SALT	2	1st	Indicates that you are setting the salt value currently being used by the key object.
All	KP_ PERMISSIONS	6	2nd	Indicates that you are passing a new set of permission flags. (The possible permission values are listed in Table 4.2.)
All	KP_ALGID	7	2nd	Indicates that you are updating the algorithm for the key object. This constant is usually used only while in negotiation for an acceptable session key algorithm.
Block	KP_EFFECTIVE _KEYLEN	19	2nd	Indicates that you are setting the effective key length of an RC2 key.
Block	KP_IV	1	1st	Indicates that you are setting the initialization vector.
Block	KP_PADDING	3	2nd	Indicates that you are setting the padding method to be used by the key. The possible padding modes are listed in Table 4.3.
Block	KP_MODE	4	2nd	Indicates that you are setting the current cipher mode. The possible modes are listed in Table 4.4.
Block	KP_MODE_BITS	5	2nd	Indicates that you are setting the number of bits that are processed per cycle when the OFB or CFB modes are used.

4

PUBLIC/PRIVATE KEY COMMUNICATIONS

The third parameter (pbData) for this function is the value to be set. Depending on which version of the function you are using, it may be either a string or a long variable.

The fourth parameter (dwFlags) is a set of flags used if you are setting the KP_ALGID value for the key. The possible values for this flag are listed in Table 3.8 in the preceding chapter. Otherwise, you should pass zero (0) for this value.

You also can use another set of key parameter values. However, they don't lend themselves to use with Visual Basic because the parameter being set requires a third version of the CryptSetKeyParam function, as follows:

Syntax

```
Type CRYPT_INTEGER_BLOB
    cbData As Long
    pbData As Long
End Type

Public Declare Function CryptSetKeyBParam Lib "advapi32.dll" _
    Alias "CryptSetKeyParam" (ByVal hKey As Long, _
    ByVal dwParam As Long, pbData As CRYPT_INTEGER_BLOB, _
    ByVal dwFlags As Long) As Long
```

The pbData member of the CRYPT_INTEGER_BLOB type is a pointer to a string containing the value to be set. To use this version of the CryptSetKeyParam function, you need to build a C DLL that allows you to pass it a string variable and have it return the pointer value. The other member of the CRYPT_INTEGER_BLOB type, the cbData member, is the length of the string that is pointed to by the pbData member. The parameter values that require this version of the function are listed in Table 4.6.

TIP

If you really wanted to use this third version of this function, you could use the StrPtr function to get a string pointer to the string variable, but then you'd have problems with switching between ANSI and UNICODE strings. You'd be better off copying your string data into a byte array, and then passing a pointer to the first element in the array using the VarPtr function.

If you are unfamiliar with the StrPtr and VarPtr functions, it's because they are undocumented functions in Visual Basic. You'll get a good look at how to use these functions in a couple of chapters.

TABLE 4.6 `CryptSetKeyParam` Parameter Values

Key Type	Constant	Value	Description
All	`KP_SALT_EX`	10	Indicates that you are setting the salt value currently being used by the key object.
DSS	`KP_P`	11	Indicates that you are setting the prime modulus P for the DSS key.
DSS	`KP_Q`	13	Indicates that you are setting the prime Q for the DSS key.
DSS	`KP_G`	12	Indicates that you are setting the generator G for the DSS key.
DSS	`KP_X`	14	Indicates that you are setting the X value for the DSS key. The P, Q, and G values must already be set before you set this value.

Generating, Saving, and Retrieving Public/Private Keys

When I discussed generating encryption keys previously, I described only symmetric session keys. I haven't discussed working with public/private key pairs. So, now we need to turn our attention to how to generate, save, and retrieve public/private key pairs.

In the preceding chapter, you learned to generate key pairs by using the `AT_KEYEXCHANGE` and `AT_SIGNATURE` key algorithms, which were in the list for the `CryptGenKey` function. These algorithms are used to generate public/private key pairs.

NOTE

The two public/private key pair types, Key Exchange and Signature, generate a lot of confusion among newcomers to encryption. You might easily conclude that you need both types. However, all public/private key functions can be performed with either type of key.

It is advisable to use two different key pairs—one exclusively for encrypting data and the other exclusively for signing data. By relegating a key pair to a specific use, you stand much less chance of the key pair being compromised.

Now, as for the difference between the two types of key pairs, the Signature key pairs make use of algorithms that are better at signing data, whereas the Key Exchange pair uses algorithms that are stronger at encrypting data.

After you've generated a public/private key pair for use, you probably will want to be able to use the same key pair again later. The good news is that the key pair is automatically stored by the CSP in the key store that you opened with the `CryptAcquireContext` function.

So, how do you get an existing key pair from the key store? You call the `CryptGetUserKey` function. This function is declared as follows:

Syntax

```
Public Declare Function CryptGetUserKey Lib "advapi32.dll" ( _
    ByVal hProv As Long, ByVal dwKeySpec As Long, _
    phUserKey As Long) As Long
```

The first parameter (hProv) to this function is the handle to the CSP key context. It is the handle you received from the `CryptAcquireContext` function.

The second parameter (dwKeySpec) to this function specifies which key you want. The possible values for this parameter are AT_KEYEXCHANGE (1) or AT_SIGNATURE (2).

The third parameter (phUserKey) is a long variable into which the handle for the opened key object will be placed. This key handle is no different from the key object handle that you created using the `CryptGenKey` function, and it can be used in the same way, with all the same functions.

Exporting and Importing Keys

The last piece of information that you need to know before you can launch into building applications that use public/private key pairs is how to exchange encryption keys with another user. You need to be able to exchange both public and session keys. The key to exchanging is through exporting and importing keys.

When you export a key, it is translated into a series of ASCII-printable characters that are easily passed to another user. When these keys are imported, they are converted back into the binary series of numbers that make up the original key. In addition, keys can be encrypted during the export using the recipient's public key, ensuring that the recipient is the only user who can import the key. You therefore can exchange public and session keys with ease over a socket connection, or via files on floppy disk or other transport media.

Exporting Keys

When you need to export a key from a key object, you use the `CryptExportKey` function. This function is declared as follows:

Syntax

```
Public Declare Function CryptExportKey Lib "advapi32.dll" ( _
    ByVal hKey As Long, ByVal hExpKey As Long, _
    ByVal dwBlobType As Long, ByVal dwFlags As Long, _
    ByVal pbData As String, pdwDataLen As Long) As Long
```

The first parameter (hKey) to this function is the handle to the key that you want to export. It can be a public/private key pair or a session key.

The second parameter (hExpKey) is the handle for the recipient's key that is to be used to encrypt the exported key. If you are exporting your public key, this parameter must be zero (0). Usually, it is the handle of the recipient's public key. Occasionally, if the CSP supports it, this key might be the recipient's session key (Microsoft's Base and Enhanced Cryptographic Providers do not support using a session key). If you are exporting a private key, it usually has to be the handle to a session key that will be used to encrypt the private key.

The third parameter (dwBlobType) specifies the type of exported key blob you are creating. The possible values for this parameter are listed in Table 4.7.

Blob

The term *blob* is typically used to describe a large generic data object. It stands for Binary Large OBject. It can be used to describe any large data object, whether a long string or an image file, or any other large, unstructured object.

TABLE 4.7　Exported Key Blob Types

Constant	Value	Description
SIMPLEBLOB	&H1	A simple blob is used for transporting session keys.
PUBLICKEYBLOB	&H6	This blob type is used for transporting public keys.
PRIVATEKEYBLOB	&H7	This blob type is used for transporting public/private key pairs.
OPAQUEKEYBLOB	&H9	This blob type is used to store session keys in an SChannel CSP. This blob type can be imported only into the CSP that exported it. This type cannot be exchanged between computers.

The fourth parameter (dwFlags) is a flag value that specifies how the export is to be performed. The possible values for this parameter are listed in Table 4.8.

TABLE 4.8   CryptExportKey Option Flag Values

Constant	Value	Description
CRYPT_SSL2_FALLBACK	&H2	Causes the first eight bytes to be padded with &H03 instead of random data. This padding is to prevent version roll-back attacks and is discussed in the SSL3 specification. This flag is available for use only with SChannel CSPs.
CRYPT_DESTROYKEY	&H4	Causes the original key in the OPAQUEKEYBLOB to be destroyed. This flag is available for use only with SChannel CSPs.
CRYPT_OAEP	&H40	Causes the exported session key to be formatted as specified in the PKCS #1 version 2 specification.

The fifth parameter (pbData) is a string variable that will hold the exported key value. This string value must be sized to hold the key before calling this function. The sixth parameter (pdwDataLen) is a long variable that specifies the size of the string in the fifth parameter and, after calling this function, contains the size of the actual exported key. If a NULL string is passed in place of the fifth parameter, the sixth parameter will contain the size of the string that needs to be passed to hold the exported key.

A typical usage of this function might look like the following:

```
Dim lDataSize As Long
Dim lResult As Long

'--- Null the target string, so we can get the size of the string
'--- that will be exported
lDataSize = 0

'--- Call CryptExportKey with the nulled string. This will give us
'--- the required string size that will be needed to hold the exported
'--- key
lResult = CryptExportKey(m_lHCryptKey, 0, PUBLICKEYBLOB, 0, _
        vbNullString, lDataSize)

'--- Size the target string for the size specified, filling it with
'--- null characters
m_sExportKey = String(lDataSize, vbNullChar)

'--- Export the public key
If Not CBool(CryptExportKey(m_lHCryptKey, 0, PUBLICKEYBLOB, 0, _
        m_sExportKey, lDataSize)) Then
    '--- Perform error handling
```

Importing Keys

Next, you need to know how to import the keys that you just learned to export. As you can probably guess by now, you do so by using the CryptImportKey function. This function is declared as follows:

Syntax

```
Public Declare Function CryptImportKey Lib "advapi32.dll" ( _
    ByVal hProv As Long, ByVal pbData As String, _
    ByVal dwDataLen As Long, ByVal hPubKey As Long, _
    ByVal dwFlags As Long, phKey As Long) As Long
```

The first parameter (hProv) for this function is the handle to the CSP into which you want to import the key blob.

The second parameter (pbData) is the exported key string that was created using the CryptExportKey function. The third parameter (dwDataLen) is the size of the key blob in the second parameter.

The fourth parameter (hPubKey) is the handle to an existing key object. What this key is and how it is used depend on what type of key is being imported. If the key being imported is signed, then this parameter is the handle to the public key of the sender, which is to be used to verify the signature. If the key being imported is a session key that was encrypted using the recipient's public key, it is the handle of the recipient's public/private key pair to be used to decrypt the session key. If the key being imported is the public/private key pair, it is the handle to the session key to be used to decrypt the imported key pair. If the key being imported is a public key, or if it is an OPAQUEKEYBLOB type, this parameter must be zero (0).

The fifth parameter (dwFlags) is a series of option flags. The possible values for this parameter are listed in Table 4.9.

TABLE 4.9   CryptImportKey Option Flag Values

Constant	Value	Description
CRYPT_EXPORTABLE	&H1	Specifies that the key being imported may be re-exported. If this flag is not provided, any calls to CryptExportKey will fail. This flag is available only when you're importing public/private key pairs (PRIVATEKEYBLOB).
CRYPT_OAEP	&H40	Causes the imported session key formatting to be checked against the PKCS #1 version 2 specification. This flag is available only when you're importing session keys (SIMPLEKEYBLOB).
CRYPT_NO_SALT	&H10	Specifies that the session key being imported will be imported without salt. This flag is available only when you're importing session keys (SIMPLEKEYBLOB).

The sixth parameter (phKey) is a long variable into which the handle to the imported key will be placed. This key handle is no different from the key handles that are created using the `CryptGenKey` or `CryptDeriveKey` functions, and it can be used for any Crypto API functions that require key handles.

A typical use of this function is as follows:

```
Dim lDataSize As Long

'--- Get the size of the key being imported
lDataSize = Len(m_sImportKey)

'--- Import the key, storing it in the m_lHImportKey class variable
If Not CBool(CryptImportKey(m_lHCryptProv, m_sImportKey, _
        lDataSize, 0, 0, m_lHImportKey)) Then
    '--- Error handling
```

Building a Secure Messaging Utility

Now that you know how to export and import keys between users, it's time to see how you can make these processes work. To do so, you'll build a messaging application that can go through all the motions, performing the key creation, export, and import, all by itself, or with another copy of itself. To see this all working as it should, you will be able to run two copies of the application you are going to build on the same computer, but you really should run them on different machines connected over a network.

In the following sections, you'll learn how to do the following:

- Modify the crypto class that you started in the preceding chapter, adding the capability to open or generate a public/private key pair, and export and exchange public and session keys.

- Build an application form that can perform the key generation and exchange, both within itself and over a Winsock connection.

- Run the application in both modes (standalone and networked) to see how the key exchange works.

Creating the Initial Project

You start by creating a new Standard EXE Visual Basic project. Name the project `PubPrivKeys` and the default form `frmKeys`. Copy the clsCrypto.cls file from the project directory of the last application from the preceding chapter into the project directory of this project, and then include the file in the project by selecting Project|Add Class Module.

> **TIP**
>
> If you skipped reading the preceding chapter, you should create a new class named clsCrypto and go back to the Chapter 3 examples, adding the code to this class from the two sample applications you'll find there. I recommend this approach over copying the class from the Web (www.samspublishing.com). By creating the class yourself, you'll understand what functionality is already contained within.

Making Additional Declarations

The first step is to turn your attention to making the necessary additions and alterations to the encryption class. After you've made these changes, you can turn your attention back to the default form.

Before you do anything else, you need to add a few more constant, function, and variable declarations to the crypto class. These new additions are provided in Listing 4.1. Remember, they are additions to the constants, functions, and variables that you already have declared in this class, so you will probably want to place them close to the other declarations, as best makes sense. I recommend placing these constant declarations at the bottom of the existing constant declarations, the function declarations near the end of the existing function declarations, and the variable declarations at the end of the entire declaration section.

LISTING 4.1   New Constant, Function, and Variable Declarations

```
' exported key blob definitions
Private Const SIMPLEBLOB = &H1
Private Const PUBLICKEYBLOB = &H6
Private Const PRIVATEKEYBLOB = &H7
Private Const PLAINTEXTKEYBLOB = &H8

Private Const AT_KEYEXCHANGE = 1
Private Const AT_SIGNATURE = 2

'--- WinCrypt API Declarations
Private Declare Function CryptGenKey Lib "advapi32.dll" ( _
    ByVal hProv As Long, ByVal Algid As Long, _
    ByVal dwFlags As Long, phKey As Long) As Long

Private Declare Function CryptGetUserKey Lib "advapi32.dll" ( _
    ByVal hProv As Long, ByVal dwKeySpec As Long, _
    phUserKey As Long) As Long
```

continues

4

PUBLIC/PRIVATE KEY COMMUNICATIONS

LISTING 4.1   Continued

```
Private Declare Function CryptExportKey Lib "advapi32.dll" ( _
    ByVal hKey As Long, ByVal hExpKey As Long, _
    ByVal dwBlobType As Long, ByVal dwFlags As Long, _
    ByVal pbData As String, pdwDataLen As Long) As Long

Private Declare Function CryptImportKey Lib "advapi32.dll" ( _
    ByVal hProv As Long, ByVal pbData As String, _
    ByVal dwDataLen As Long, ByVal hPubKey As Long, _
    ByVal dwFlags As Long, phKey As Long) As Long

' Private property buffers
Private m_sExportKey As String     ' Used to publish the exported public
                                   ' key that can be sent to the other
                                   ' application that is to be sending
                                   ' encrypted data to this class

Private m_sImportKey As String     ' Used to import the public key of
                                   ' the other application to which this
                                   ' application will be sending encrypted
                                   ' data

Private m_sSessionKey As String    ' Used to publish and import the
                                   ' encrypted session key that is used
                                   ' to encrypt and decrypt the data to
                                   ' be passed between applications

' Private class-level variables
Private m_lHCryptKey As Long       ' Handle for the AT_KEYEXCHANGE
                                   ' (Public/Private) key for this
                                   ' application

Private m_lHImportKey As Long      ' Handle for the imported public
                                   ' key of the application to which
                                   ' this application will be sending
                                   ' data
```

Adding New Properties

Now you can add three new properties to the crypto class. They are properties for the import and export keys, as well as the session key. These properties will make the exchange of keys very accessible to the application form that will be performing the actual exchange of keys. To add these properties, add the code in Listing 4.2 to the crypto class.

LISTING 4.2 New Public Properties

```
Public Property Get ExportKey() As String
    ExportKey = m_sExportKey
End Property

Public Property Get SessionKey() As String
    SessionKey = m_sSessionKey
End Property

Public Property Let SessionKey(vNewValue As String)
    m_sSessionKey = vNewValue
End Property

Public Property Get ImportKey() As String
    ImportKey = m_sImportKey
End Property

Public Property Let ImportKey(vNewValue As String)
    m_sImportKey = vNewValue
End Property
```

Getting the User Public/Private Key Pair

The first piece of functionality that you need to add to the crypto class is the capability to open or generate a Key Exchange public/private key pair for the current user. To add this functionality, add the code in Listing 4.3 to the crypto class.

LISTING 4.3 The `GetExchangeKeypair` Function

```
Public Function GetExchangeKeypair() As Boolean
'***************************************************************
'* Written By: Davis Chapman
'* Date:       September 06, 1999
'*
'* Syntax:     GetExchangeKeypair
'*
'* Parameters:  None
'*
'* Purpose: This function loads the AT_KEYEXCHANGE keyset.
'*          If the keyset or key container does not exist,
'*          then this function creates them.
'***************************************************************
    Dim lResult As Long
    Dim sResult As String
```

continues

LISTING 4.3   Continued

```
GetExchangeKeypair = False

'--- Attempt to get handle to exchange key
If Not CBool(CryptGetUserKey(m_lHCryptProv, AT_KEYEXCHANGE, _
        m_lHCryptKey)) Then

    '--- Determine what the error was
    lResult = Err.LastDllError

    '--- If the problem is that there is no existing key,
    '--- generate one
    If ((lResult = NTE_NO_KEY) Or (lResult = 0)) Then
        If Not CBool(CryptGenKey(m_lHCryptProv, AT_KEYEXCHANGE, _
                0, m_lHCryptKey)) Then
            m_sErrorMsg = "Error during CryptGenKey - " & _
                    CStr(Err.LastDllError)
            MsgBox m_sErrorMsg, vbOKOnly, "VB Crypto"
            Exit Function
        End If
    Else

        '--- If there was another cause for the error, inform
        '--- the user what the problem is
        Select Case lResult
            Case ERROR_INVALID_HANDLE
                sResult = "Invalid handle"
            Case ERROR_INVALID_PARAMETER
                sResult = "Invalid parameter"
            Case NTE_BAD_KEY
                sResult = "Bad key"
            Case NTE_BAD_UID
                sResult = "Bad handle"
        End Select
        m_sErrorMsg = "Error during CryptGetUserKey - " + sResult
        MsgBox m_sErrorMsg, vbOKOnly, "VB Crypto"
        Exit Function
    End If
End If

'--- Didn't exit early, return TRUE
GetExchangeKeypair = True
End Function
```

In this function, you first try to open an existing key pair in the key store by using the
CryptGetUserKey function. If this function fails because no key exists, then you create the key
pair by using the CryptGenKey function.

> **TIP**
>
> In Listing 4.3, notice that the Crypto API error conditions are checked using the
> LastDLLError property of the Err object. This is the recommended way of checking
> for API function error conditions. Many VB programmers map the GetLastError API
> function to try to get the error condition codes. This approach is wrong because the
> VB runtime environment usually resets the error condition to ERROR_SUCCESS or
> NO_ERROR (both 0). VB does make the error condition code available through the
> LastDLLError property of the Err object, and this copy of the error code does not
> get reset, enabling you to check it to discover what went wrong.

Exporting the Public Key

The next piece of functionality you need to add is the capability to export the public key from
the Key Exchange key pair. The exported key will be made available through the ExportKey
property. To add this functionality to the crypt class, add the function in Listing 4.4.

LISTING 4.4 The ExportPublicKey Function

```
Public Function ExportPublicKey() As Boolean
'***************************************************************
'* Written By: Davis Chapman
'* Date:       September 06, 1999
'*
'* Syntax:     ExportPublicKey
'*
'* Parameters: None
'*
'* Purpose: This function exports the public key from the
'*          AT_KEYEXCHANGE keyset, placing the exported key
'*          into the ExportKey property
'***************************************************************
On Error Resume Next
    ExportPublicKey = False

    Dim lDataSize As Long
    Dim lResult As Long

    '--- Null the target string, so we can get the size of the string
    '--- that will be exported
    lDataSize = 0
```

continues

4

LISTING 4.4   Continued

```
'--- Call CryptExportKey with the nulled string. This will give us
'--- the required string size that will be needed to hold the ➡
'--- exported key
lResult = CryptExportKey(m_lHCryptKey, 0, PUBLICKEYBLOB, 0, _
        vbNullString, lDataSize)

'--- Size the target string for the size specified, filling it with
'--- null characters
m_sExportKey = String(lDataSize, vbNullChar)

'--- Export the public key
If Not CBool(CryptExportKey(m_lHCryptKey, 0, PUBLICKEYBLOB, 0, _
        m_sExportKey, lDataSize)) Then
    m_sErrorMsg = "Error during CryptExportKey - " & _
            CStr(Err.LastDllError) & Error$
    MsgBox m_sErrorMsg, vbOKOnly, "VB Crypto"
    Exit Function
End If

'--- Didn't exit early, return TRUE
ExportPublicKey = True
Exit Function
End Function
```

Here, you initially substituted a NULL string (vbNullString) for the export key property and set the size to zero (0) for the initial call to `CryptExportKey`. By doing so, you place the size of the string needed into the `lDataSize` variable. You can take that size and create the string buffer of the correct length before calling `CryptExportKey` a second time. You also export the public key directly to the `ExportKey` property variable.

Importing the Public Key

Next, you need to add the corresponding functionality to import the public key of the other user. In this function, you can assume that the exported key has been placed into the `ImportKey` property. You need to get the length of the exported key and then call the `CryptImportKey` function to import the key. Doing so gives you a handle to a key object containing the public key of the other user. To add this functionality to the crypto class, add the function in Listing 4.5.

LISTING 4.5   The *ImportPublicKey* Function

```
Public Function ImportPublicKey() As Boolean
'******************************************************************
'* Written By: Davis Chapman
'* Date:       September 06, 1999
'*
```

```
'* Syntax:      ImportPublicKey
'*
'* Parameters:  None
'*
'* Purpose: This will import the public key of the other
'*          application, taking it from the ImportKey property.
'*          The imported public key will be held in the
'*          m_lHImportKey class variable.
'***************************************************************
On Error Resume Next
    ImportPublicKey = False

    Dim lDataSize As Long

    '--- Get the size of the key being imported
    lDataSize = Len(m_sImportKey)

    '--- Import the key, storing it in the m_lHImportKey class variable
    If Not CBool(CryptImportKey(m_lHCryptProv, m_sImportKey, _
            lDataSize, 0, 0, m_lHImportKey)) Then
        m_sErrorMsg = "Error during CryptImportKey - " & _
                CStr(Err.LastDllError) & Error$
        MsgBox m_sErrorMsg, vbOKOnly, "VB Crypto"
        Exit Function
    End If

    '--- Didn't exit early, return TRUE
    ImportPublicKey = True
    Exit Function
End Function
```

Creating and Exporting the Session Key

Now that you can export and import a public key, you need to be able to create a session key
and export it, using the public key to encrypt it. To add this functionality, add the code in
Listing 4.6 to the crypto class.

LISTING 4.6   The CreateAndExportSessionKey Function

```
Public Function CreateAndExportSessionKey() As Boolean
'***************************************************************
'* Written By: Davis Chapman
'* Date:       September 07, 1999
'*
'* Syntax:     CreateAndExportSessionKey
```

4

PUBLIC/PRIVATE
KEY
COMMUNICATIONS

continues

LISTING 4.6 Continued

```
'*
'* Parameters:  None
'*
'* Purpose: This will generate a session key and export it,
'*          encrypting the exported key using the public key
'*          of the recipient. The exported session key will
'*          be placed in the SessionKey property.
'***************************************************************
On Error Resume Next
    CreateAndExportSessionKey = False

    Dim lDataSize As Long
    Dim lResult As Long
    Dim sCryptBuffer As String
    Dim lCryptLength As Long
    Dim lCryptBufLen As Long

    '--- Create a random block cipher session key.
    If Not CBool(CryptGenKey(m_lHCryptProv, CALG_RC2, _
            CRYPT_EXPORTABLE, m_lHSessionKey)) Then
        m_sErrorMsg = "Error " & CStr(Err.LastDllError) & _
                " during CryptGenKey!"
        MsgBox m_sErrorMsg, vbOKOnly, "VB Crypto"
        Exit Function
    End If

    '--- Determine the size of the key blob and allocate memory.
    lDataSize = 0
    lResult = CryptExportKey(m_lHSessionKey, m_lHImportKey, _
            SIMPLEBLOB, 0, vbNullString, lDataSize)
    m_sSessionKey = String(lDataSize, vbNullChar)

    '--- Export the session key, using the imported public key to ➥
    '--- encrypt it
    If Not CBool(CryptExportKey(m_lHSessionKey, m_lHImportKey, _
            SIMPLEBLOB, 0, m_sSessionKey, lDataSize)) Then
        m_sErrorMsg = "Error during CryptExportKey - " & _
                CStr(Err.LastDllError) & Error$
        MsgBox m_sErrorMsg, vbOKOnly, "VB Crypto"
        Exit Function
    End If

    '--- Didn't exit early, return TRUE
    CreateAndExportSessionKey = True
End Function
```

The first thing you do in this function is create an exportable session key. After you generate the session key, you substitute the NULL string (vbNullString) for the session key property and specify the length as zero (0). This way, you can call CryptExportKey, specifying to export the session key and to encrypt it using the public key, so that you can get the buffer size you need. When you have the correct buffer size, you size the session key property variable and call CryptExportKey again, using the same syntax, to actually export the encrypted session key directly to the session key property variable. You can now take the exported session key and send it to the recipient, knowing that the recipient is the only person who can decrypt and import the session key using his or her private key.

Importing the Session Key

Next, you need to be able to import the exported session key so that you can exchange encrypted messages with the other user. This process is almost like importing the public key; this time, though, you need to provide the handle to the public/private key pair so that the CSP knows to use the private key to decrypt the session key while importing it. To add this functionality to the crypto class, add the code in Listing 4.7.

LISTING 4.7   The ImportSessionKey Function

```
Public Function ImportSessionKey() As Boolean
'*****************************************************************
'* Written By: Davis Chapman
'* Date:       September 07, 1999
'*
'* Syntax:     ImportSessionKey
'*
'* Parameters: None
'*
'* Purpose: This will import the session key from the SessionKey
'*          property.
'*****************************************************************
On Error Resume Next
    ImportSessionKey = False

    Dim lDataSize As Long
    Dim lResult As Long
    Dim sCryptBuffer As String
    Dim lCryptLength As Long
    Dim lCryptBufLen As Long

    '--- Determine the size of the session key to be imported
    lDataSize = Len(m_sSessionKey)
```

continues

4

PUBLIC/PRIVATE KEY COMMUNICATIONS

LISTING 4.7   Continued

```
    '--- Import the session key. As it should have been encrypted using
    '--- our public key, the CAPI should use our private key to
    '--- decrypt the session key during the import
    If Not CBool(CryptImportKey(m_lHCryptProv, m_sSessionKey, _
            lDataSize, m_lHCryptKey, 0, m_lHSessionKey)) Then
        m_sErrorMsg = "Error during CryptImportKey - " & _
                CStr(Err.LastDllError) & Error$
        MsgBox m_sErrorMsg, vbOKOnly, "VB Crypto"
        Exit Function
    End If

    '--- Didn't exit early, return TRUE
    ImportSessionKey = True
End Function
```

Terminating the Class

The last update that you need to make to the crypto class is in the termination event of the
class. You may have multiple keys open when the class is terminated, so you need to check
each one to see whether you have a valid handle, and destroy each one for which you do have
a valid handle. Update the Class_Terminate event for the crypto class, adding the bolded code
shown in Listing 4.8.

LISTING 4.8   The Updated Class_Terminate Event

```
Private Sub Class_Terminate()
'****************************************************************
'* Written By: Davis Chapman
'* Date:       September 06, 1999
'*
'* Syntax:     Class_Terminate
'*
'* Parameters:  None
'*
'* Purpose: This is executed when this class is destroyed. This
'*          subroutine examines each of the class-level handles
'*          for the keys and keycontext, and destroys or
'*          releases them as is appropriate to clean up after
'*          oneself.
'****************************************************************
    Dim lResult As Long
```

```
'--- Do we have an imported key? If so, destroy it.
If (m_lHImportKey) Then lResult = CryptDestroyKey(m_lHImportKey)

'--- Do we have a Public/Private key pair? If so, destroy it
If (m_lHCryptKey) Then lResult = CryptDestroyKey(m_lHCryptKey)

'--- Do we have an open key context? If so, release it.
If (m_lHCryptProv) Then _
        lResult = CryptReleaseContext(m_lHCryptProv, 0)
End Sub
```

Designing the User Interface

Now, to make this a working application, you need to turn your attention back to the default form, adding the controls and code to make the whole thing work. Because this application will work over a network using the Winsock control, you need to add it to the project. To add the Winsock control, select Project, Components to open the Components dialog. Select the Microsoft Winsock Control from the list of controls, making sure that its check box is selected, as shown in Figure 4.1. Then click OK to add this control to your palette.

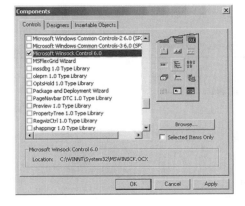

FIGURE 4.1

Including the Winsock control.

Now that you've added the Winsock control, add the various controls to the form as shown in Figure 4.2, setting the properties of the controls as listed in Table 4.10. The list of control settings in Table 4.10 are provided in left-to-right, top-to-bottom order (more or less).

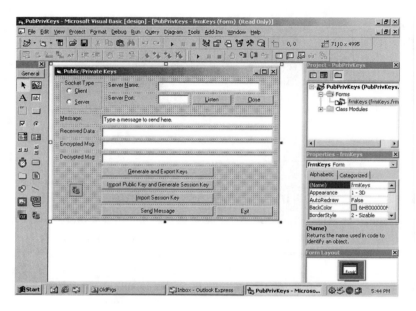

FIGURE 4.2

Application screen layout.

TABLE 4.10 Control Property Settings

Control	Property	Value
Frame (Group Box)	Name	frRole
	Caption	Socket Type
OptionButton	Name	optClient
	Caption	&Client
OptionButton	Name	optServer
	Caption	&Server
Label	Caption	Server &Name:
TextBox	Name	txtServerName
Label	Caption	Server &Port:
TextBox	Name	txtPort
Command Button	Name	cmdListen
	Caption	&Listen
Command Button	Name	cmdClose
	Caption	&Close
	Enabled	False

Control	Property	Value
Label	Caption	&Message:
TextBox	Name	txtMessage
Label	Caption	Received Data:
TextBox	Name	txtRecvdData
Label	Caption	Encrypted Msg:
TextBox	Name	txtEncryptMsg
Label	Caption	Decrypted Msg:
TextBox	Name	txtDecryptMsg
Winsock	Name	wsSocket
Command Button	Name	cmdGenKeys
	Caption	&Generate and Export Keys
Command Button	Name	cmdImportPublicKey
	Caption	I&mport Public
		Key and Generate
		Session Key
	Enabled	False
Command Button	Name	cmdImportSessionKey
	Caption	&Import
		Session Key
	Enabled	False
Command Button	Name	cmdSendMsg
	Caption	Sen&d Message
	Enabled	False
Command Button	Name	cmdExit
	Caption	E&xit

Performing Form Initialization, Cleanup, and Other Miscellaneous Functions

Before you get to the good stuff, you need to take care of some details. First, you need to declare a few form-level variables to use in your code. Add these variables to the form, as shown in Listing 4.9.

LISTING 4.9   Form Variable Declarations

```
Option Explicit

Private m_clsCrypto As clsCrypto
Private m_strPublicKey As String
Private m_strSessionKey As String
```

In the applications that you built in the preceding chapter, you used local variables for the crypto class object when you were performing the encryption or decryption. Because of the different nature of this application, you are going to have an instance of the crypto class object in existence for the entire life of the application. Therefore, you need to create an instance of the crypto class during the form loading and destroy it during the form unloading. To add this functionality, add the code in Listing 4.10 for the form Load and Unload events.

LISTING 4.10   Form Initialization and Cleanup

```
Private Sub Form_Load()
    '-- Create the instance of the crypto class
    Set m_clsCrypto = New clsCrypto
End Sub

Private Sub Form_Unload(Cancel As Integer)
    '-- Destroy the instance of the crypto class
    Set m_clsCrypto = Nothing
End Sub
```

Because this same application needs to operate in both Client and Server modes (when using Winsock for network communications), you provide the radio buttons for selecting which mode each instance is operating in. Each side needs to change what is done to initiate the connection between the two. Because of these differences in functionality, you can change the label on the button you will be using to make the connection to reflect that change. When the application is in Server mode, you can label the button "Listen," and when the application is in Client mode, you label the button "Connect." To add this functionality, add the code in Listing 4.11 to the Click events of the two radio buttons.

LISTING 4.11   Application Operation Mode Switching

```
Private Sub optClient_Click()
    '-- Client mode
    cmdListen.Caption = "Connec&t"
    Me.Caption = "Public/Private Keys - Client"
End Sub
```

```
Private Sub optServer_Click()
    '-- Server mode
    cmdListen.Caption = "&Listen"
    Me.Caption = "Public/Private Keys - Server"
End Sub
```

When you're closing the application, you need to check whether you have created a session key. If so, you need to destroy it before exiting. To add this functionality, add the code in Listing 4.12 to the Click event of the cmdExit button.

LISTING 4.12   The cmdExit_Click Event

```
Private Sub cmdExit_Click()
    '-- Did we create or receive a session key?
    If m_strSessionKey <> "" Then

        '-- If so, then destroy it
        m_clsCrypto.DestroySessionKey
    End If

    '-- Close the application
    Unload Me
End Sub
```

Yes, you could have just included the session key in the crypto class cleanup, but this is a more realistic way of handling the session cleanup. Whenever a session is ended, either by closing the connection or other means, the session key should be destroyed. You'll see later that you'll add this same functionality to the closing of the Winsock connection.

Performing the Initial Server Key Exchange

You can perform the key exchange in three steps. The first step is performed by the server, opening or creating the public/private key pair, exporting the public key, and sending it to the client. During the second step, the client imports the server's public key, generates a session key, and exports it using the server's public key to encrypt it. In the third and final step, the server imports the session key, decrypting it using the server's private key.

To start this process, you need to create a subroutine that controls the initial step of the process. To add this functionality, add the code in Listing 4.13 to the form.

LISTING 4.13 The `DoServerKeyExchange` Subroutine

```
Private Sub DoServerKeyExchange()
'*************************************************************
'* Written By: Davis Chapman
'* Date:       September 09, 1999
'*
'* Syntax:     DoServerKeyExchange
'*
'* Parameters:  None
'*
'* Purpose: The initial server portion of the key exchange
'*          consists of retrieving or creating a Public/Private
'*          key pair for the server. The public key is exported
'*          for sending to the client. Finally, the public key
'*          is sent to the client.
'*************************************************************
    '-- Continue until an error occurs
    '-- Generate or get the public/private key pair
    If Not m_clsCrypto.GetExchangeKeypair Then _
        Exit Sub

    '-- Export the public key
    If Not m_clsCrypto.ExportPublicKey Then _
        Exit Sub

        '-- Send the public key to the client
        m_strPublicKey = m_clsCrypto.ExportKey
        If wsSocket.State = sckConnected Then
            wsSocket.SendData m_strPublicKey
        Else
            cmdImportPublicKey.Enabled = True
        End If
        cmdGenKeys.Enabled = False
End Sub
```

In this subroutine, you either open or generate the Key Exchange key pair and then export the public key, saving it into the form-level variable. Finally, you check to see whether you have an active Winsock connection. If you do, you send the public key to the client. If you are not connected, you can assume that you are running in standalone mode and just need to enable the button to perform the next step in the key exchange.

To trigger this first step in the key exchange, you need to attach the code in Listing 4.14 to the Click event of the cmdGenKeys button. This button will be used to start the key exchange process when running in standalone mode.

LISTING 4.14   The cmdGenKeys_Click Event

```
Private Sub cmdGenKeys_Click()
    '-- Perform the initial server portion of the key exchange
    DoServerKeyExchange
End Sub
```

Performing the Client Key Exchange

For the second step in the key exchange, you need to copy the public key from the form variable to the ImportKey property of the crypto class and call the ImportPublicKey method. After you import the public key, you need to generate and export a session key. Finally, you need to check whether you have an open Winsock connection. If you do, you need to send the exported session key to the server. If not, you just need to enable the cmdImportSessionKey button to trigger the final step in the key exchange when in standalone mode. To add this functionality, add the subroutine in Listing 4.15 to the form.

LISTING 4.15   The DoClientKeyExchange Subroutine

```
Private Sub DoClientKeyExchange()
'******************************************************
'* Written By: Davis Chapman
'* Date:       September 09, 1999
'*
'* Syntax:     DoClientKeyExchange
'*
'* Parameters: None
'*
'* Purpose: The client portion of the key exchange starts by
'*          importing the server's public key. Next, a session
'*          key is generated, encrypted using the server's
'*          public key (ensuring that it can only be decrypted
'*          with the server's private key), and exported and
'*          sent to the server.
'******************************************************
    '-- Copy the public key to the Crypto object
    m_clsCrypto.ImportKey = m_strPublicKey

    '-- Continue until an error occurs
    '-- Import the server's public key
    If Not m_clsCrypto.ImportPublicKey Then _
        Exit Sub

    '-- Create and export a session key.
    '--- The session key is encrypted using the
```

continues

```
'--- server's public key during the export.
'--- This ensures that only the server can
'--- import and use this session key using
'--- its private key.
If Not m_clsCrypto.CreateAndExportSessionKey Then _
    Exit Sub

    '-- Send the session key to the client
    m_strSessionKey = m_clsCrypto.SessionKey
    If wsSocket.State = sckConnected Then
        wsSocket.SendData m_strSessionKey
        cmdSendMsg.Enabled = True
    Else
        cmdImportSessionKey.Enabled = True
    End If
    cmdImportPublicKey.Enabled = False
End Sub
```

Now you need to be able to trigger this second step. You can do so from the Click event of the cmdImportPublicKey button, as shown in Listing 4.16.

LISTING 4.16   The cmdImportPublicKey_Click Event

```
Private Sub cmdImportPublicKey_Click()
    '-- Perform the client portion of the key exchange
    DoClientKeyExchange
End Sub
```

Finishing the Server Key Exchange

To finish the key exchange, you need to import the session key into the crypto class object. At this point, you are ready to start exchanging messages. To add this functionality, add the subroutine in Listing 4.17 to the form.

LISTING 4.17   The FinishServerKeyExchange Subroutine

```
Private Sub FinishServerKeyExchange()
'**************************************************************
'* Written By: Davis Chapman
'* Date:       September 09, 1999
'*
'* Syntax:     FinishServerKeyExchange
'*
'* Parameters: None
'*
'* Purpose: The server completes the key exchange by importing
'*          and decrypting the session key. Once this is done,
```

```
'*          both applications are ready to start sending messages
'*          to each other.
'****************************************************************
    '-- Copy the session key to the Crypto object
    m_clsCrypto.SessionKey = m_strSessionKey

    '-- Import and decrypt the session key
    If m_clsCrypto.ImportSessionKey Then

        '-- We are now ready to send messages back and forth
        cmdSendMsg.Enabled = True
        cmdImportSessionKey.Enabled = False
    End If
End Sub
```

To trigger this last step while you're in standalone mode, call the subroutine you just created from the Click event of the cmdImportSessionKey button, as in Listing 4.18.

LISTING 4.18   The cmdImportSessionKey_Click Event

```
Private Sub cmdImportSessionKey_Click()
    '-- Perform the final server portion of the key exchange
    FinishServerKeyExchange
End Sub
```

Sending and Receiving Encrypted Messages

Now that you've completed the key exchange, you can send messages back and forth using the session key to encrypt and decrypt them. You send and receive messages much like you did in the applications that you built in the preceding chapter. First, you take the original message, copy it to the input buffer of the crypto object, encrypt the message, and then copy the encrypted message from the output buffer of the crypto object. At this point, if you have a Winsock connection, you send the encrypted message to the other user. If you are running in standalone mode, you can automatically trigger the message decryption process. To add this functionality, add the subroutine in Listing 4.19 to the form.

LISTING 4.19   The SendEncryptedMsg Subroutine

```
Private Sub SendEncryptedMsg()
'****************************************************************
'* Written By: Davis Chapman
'* Date:       September 09, 1999
'*
'* Syntax:     SendEncryptedMsg
'*
```

continues

LISTING 4.19   Continued

```
'* Parameters:  None
'*
'* Purpose: When sending a message, we need to encrypt it using
'*          the session key. Once the message has been encrypted,
'*          we can send it to the other application.
'****************************************************************
    '-- Copy the message to the Crypto object
    m_clsCrypto.InBuffer = txtMessage.Text

    '-- Encrypt the message using the session key
    If m_clsCrypto.EncryptMessageData Then

        '-- Display the encrypted message
        txtEncryptMsg.Text = m_clsCrypto.OutBuffer

        '-- Are we connected to another application?
        If wsSocket.State = sckConnected Then

            '-- Yes, so send the encrypted message
            wsSocket.SendData txtEncryptMsg.Text
        Else

            '-- No, Decrypt the message and display
            '-- the results
            ReceiveEncryptedMsg
        End If
    End If
End Sub
```

The message decryption functionality is basically the same as the encryption functionality. You copy the encrypted message to the input buffer of the crypto object, call the decryption method, and then copy the decrypted message from the output buffer of the crypto object. To add this functionality to the form, add the subroutine in Listing 4.20 to the form.

LISTING 4.20   The `ReceiveEncryptedMsg` Subroutine

```
Private Sub ReceiveEncryptedMsg()
'****************************************************************
'* Written By: Davis Chapman
'* Date:       September 09, 1999
'*
'* Syntax:     ReceiveEncryptedMsg
'*
'* Parameters:  None
'*
```

```
'* Purpose: When an encrypted message is received, it is
'*          decrypted using the session key.
'*************************************************************
    '-- Copy the encrypted message to the Crypto object
    m_clsCrypto.InBuffer = txtEncryptMsg.Text

    '-- Decrypt the message using the session key
    If m_clsCrypto.DecryptMessageData Then

        '-- Display the decrypted message
        txtDecryptMsg.Text = m_clsCrypto.OutBuffer
    End If
End Sub
```

Finally, you need to be able to trigger the message sending at will. To do so, you call the
SendEncryptedMsg subroutine from the Click event of the cmdSendMsg button, as in Listing
4.21.

LISTING 4.21   The cmdSendMsg_Click Event

```
Private Sub cmdSendMsg_Click()
    '-- Encrypt and send the message
    SendEncryptedMsg
End Sub
```

At this point, you should be able to run the sample application in standalone mode, using the
sequence of command buttons to walk through each step of the key exchange, and then encrypt
and decrypt messages using the session key, as shown in Figure 4.3.

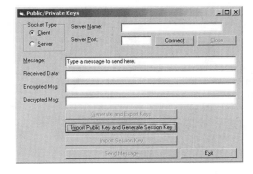

FIGURE 4.3
Stepping through the key exchange in standalone mode.

Listening for Connection Requests

Now that you have the standalone functionality working, you need to add the Winsock functionality to network-enable this application. You can start by placing the socket into Listen mode for the server functionality. Before placing the server socket into Listen mode, though, you need to set the port on which it needs to listen for connection requests. To add this functionality, add the subroutine in Listing 4.22 to the form.

> **NOTE**
>
> If you do not have experience working with Winsock communications, or don't understand how it works and want a thorough explanation of the topic, you might want to pick up *Sams Visual Basic 6 Unleashed*, which provides an in-depth look at Winsock and other Visual Basic topics.

LISTING 4.22   The StartListen Subroutine

```
Private Sub StartListen()
'****************************************************************
'* Written By: Davis Chapman
'* Date:       September 09, 1999
'*
'* Syntax:     StartListen
'*
'* Parameters: None
'*
'* Purpose: This subroutine checks to see that a number has
'*          been entered in the port text box. If one has, the
'*          socket is configured to use that port, and is placed
'*          in "Listen" mode.
'****************************************************************
    '-- Do we have a valid value for the port to listen on?
    If IsNumeric(txtPort) Then

        '-- Yes, don't allow the mode to be changed
        frRole.Enabled = False
        cmdListen.Enabled = False

        '-- Set the port on the socket
        wsSocket.LocalPort = CLng(txtPort)

        '-- Start the socket listening for connection requests
        wsSocket.Listen
    Else
```

```
        '-- No port specified, tell the user
        MsgBox "You must specify a port on which to listen."
    End If
End Sub
```

Connecting to the Server

You also need to add the client portion of the socket connection initialization. For this, you need to tell the Winsock control not just the port to connect to, but also the computer on which the server is running. After you set all this information on the Winsock control, you can call its Connect method to connect to the server. To add this functionality to the application, add the ConnectToServer subroutine in Listing 4.23 to the form.

LISTING 4.23   The ConnectToServer Subroutine

```
Private Sub ConnectToServer()
'**************************************************************
'* Written By: Davis Chapman
'* Date:       September 09, 1999
'*
'* Syntax:     ConnectToServer
'*
'* Parameters: None
'*
'* Purpose: This subroutine checks to see that a number has
'*          been entered in the port text box, and a server name
'*          has been entered in the server text box. If one has, the
'*          socket is configured to connect to that port and server,
'*          and the "Connect" method is called.
'**************************************************************
    '-- Do we have a server name to connect to?
    If txtServerName <> "" Then

        '-- Do we have a valid value for the port to connect to?
        If IsNumeric(txtPort) Then

            '-- Yes, don't allow the mode to be changed
            frRole.Enabled = False
            cmdListen.Enabled = False

            '-- Tell the socket what server and port to connect to
            wsSocket.RemotePort = CLng(txtPort)
            wsSocket.RemoteHost = txtServerName
            wsSocket.LocalPort = 0
```

continues

LISTING 4.23   Continued

```
        '-- Open the connection
        wsSocket.Connect
    Else

        '-- No port specified, tell the user
        MsgBox "You must specify a port to connect."
    End If
Else

    '-- No server specified, tell the user
    MsgBox "You must specify a server name or IP address."
End If
End Sub
```

Now that you've built the functionality to start the connection process for both the Server and Client modes, you need to trigger the appropriate set of functionality. You can do so from the Click event of the cmdListen button. You can check which mode you're running in and call the appropriate subroutine, as in Listing 4.24.

LISTING 4.24   The cmdListen_Click Event

```
Private Sub cmdListen_Click()
    '-- Are we in client or server mode?
    If optClient Then

        '-- Client mode, open a connection to the server
        ConnectToServer
    Else

        '-- Server mode, start listening for connection requests
        StartListen
    End If
End Sub
```

Receiving the Connection Request

You need to add one more step to complete the connection process. You need to add the code to complete the connection once the ConnectionRequest event is triggered on the server. First, you need to close the listening socket and then accept the incoming connection request. After you establish the connection, you can trigger the first part of the key exchange process. To add this functionality, add the code in Listing 4.25 to the ConnectionRequest event of the Winsock control.

LISTING 4.25   The wsSocket_ConnectionRequest Event

```
Private Sub wsSocket_ConnectionRequest(ByVal requestID As Long)
    '-- Close the socket from listen mode
    If wsSocket.State <> sckClosed Then wsSocket.Close

    '-- Accept the connection request
    wsSocket.Accept requestID

    '-- Connection established, set the socket connection buttons.
    cmdClose.Enabled = True

    '-- Perform the initial server portion of the key exchange
    DoServerKeyExchange
End Sub
```

After you make the connection, you need to do a little housekeeping on the client. On the Connect event of the Winsock control, add the code in Listing 4.26 to enable and disable the appropriate command buttons on the form.

LISTING 4.26   The wsSocket_Connect Event

```
Private Sub wsSocket_Connect()
    '-- Connection established, set the socket connection buttons.
    cmdListen.Enabled = False
    cmdClose.Enabled = True
End Sub
```

Handling Data Arrival

When you have an open Winsock connection, everything is triggered by the DataArrival event. As you receive data, you need to determine what data you are receiving and what you need to do with it. You can do so initially by checking the form variables to determine what you do and do not have. If you do not have anything in the public key variable, you can make the assumption that you are receiving the public key and that you need to trigger the second step in the key exchange process. If you don't have anything in the session key variable, you can assume that you are receiving the session key and need to trigger the final step in the key exchange. If you have something in both of these form variables, you must be receiving encrypted messages that you just need to decrypt and display for the user. To add this functionality to the form, add the code in Listing 4.27 to the DataArrival event of the Winsock control.

4

PUBLIC/PRIVATE
KEY
COMMUNICATIONS

LISTING 4.27   The wsSocket_DataArrival Event

```
Private Sub wsSocket_DataArrival(ByVal bytesTotal As Long)
'**************************************************************
'* Written By: Davis Chapman
'* Date:       September 09, 1999
'*
'* Event:      wsSocket_DataArrival
'*
'* Description: When data is received, we have to determine
'*              what the data might be, and what we need to
'*              do with it. Since this is implementing a very
'*              raw protocol, we can take a survey of what we
'*              have and have not received or generated to
'*              determine what we need to do with what we've
'*              received. If we have no public key, then we
'*              are the client and are receiving the public
'*              key for the server. If we have no session key
'*              then we must be the server receiving the client
'*              generated session key that has been encrypted
'*              using our public key. Otherwise, this is message
'*              data that just needs to be decrypted and displayed.
'**************************************************************
    Dim strData As String

    '-- Retrieve the data that has arrived
    wsSocket.GetData strData

    '-- Show it to the user
    txtRecvdData.Text = strData

    '-- Do we have a public key yet?
    If m_strPublicKey = "" Then

        '-- No, then this must be the public key of the
        '-- server that we are receiving
        m_strPublicKey = strData

        '-- Perform the client portion of the key exchange
        DoClientKeyExchange
        cmdGenKeys.Enabled = False
    Else
        '-- Do we have a session key yet?
        If m_strSessionKey = "" Then

            '-- No, then this must be the session key from the
            '-- client that we are receiving
            m_strSessionKey = strData
```

```
        '-- Perform the final server portion of the key exchange
        FinishServerKeyExchange

    Else

        '-- All keys have been exchanged, this is message data
        '-- that we are receiving
        txtEncryptMsg.Text = strData

        '-- Perform the message decryption
        ReceiveEncryptedMsg
    End If
    End If
End Sub
```

Closing the Socket Connection

To wrap up the application, you need to add the code to close the Winsock connection and to handle the closing of the Winsock connection. You can start with how the closing of the Winsock connection is triggered. When the user clicks the cmdClose button on either application, you should close the connection and clear out the session key. You also should reset the socket connection buttons so that the connection can be reinitialized. To add this functionality, add the code in Listing 4.28 to the Click event of the cmdClose button.

LISTING 4.28   The cmdClose_Click Event

```
Private Sub cmdClose_Click()
    '-- If the socket is not closed, close it
    If wsSocket.State <> sckClosed Then wsSocket.Close

    '-- Did we create or receive a session key?
    If m_strSessionKey <> "" Then

        '-- If so, then destroy it
        m_clsCrypto.DestroySessionKey
        m_strSessionKey = ""
    End If

    '-- Reset the socket connection buttons
    cmdListen.Enabled = True
    cmdClose.Enabled = False
End Sub
```

When one of the two applications closes the connection, the Close event is triggered in the other application. In this event, you need to perform the same steps as you did in the one that started the closing of the connection. To add this functionality, add the code in Listing 4.29 to the `Close` event of the Winsock control.

LISTING 4.29   The `wsSocket_Close` Event

```
Private Sub wsSocket_Close()
    '-- If the socket is not closed, close it
    If wsSocket.State <> sckClosed Then wsSocket.Close

    '-- Did we create or receive a session key?
    If m_strSessionKey <> "" Then

        '-- If so, then destroy it
        m_clsCrypto.DestroySessionKey
        m_strSessionKey = ""
    End If

    '-- Reset the socket connection buttons
    cmdListen.Enabled = True
    cmdClose.Enabled = False
End Sub
```

The last step is to add a single line of code to let the user know when a Winsock error occurs. Add the code in Listing 4.30 to the `Error` event of the Winsock control.

LISTING 4.30   The `wsSocket_Error` Event

```
Private Sub wsSocket_Error(ByVal Number As Integer, _
        Description As String, ByVal Scode As Long, _
        ByVal Source As String, ByVal HelpFile As String, _
        ByVal HelpContext As Long, CancelDisplay As Boolean)
    '-- Inform the user of the error
    MsgBox "WinSock Error: " + Str(Number) + " - " + Description
End Sub
```

At this point, your application is complete. However, you cannot just run it from the Visual Basic development environment. You need to be able to run two copies of this application. This means that you need to build an executable version before you can test all the Winsock functionality. After you build an executable, you can run the executable version and also run a debug version within the Visual Basic IDE. You can alternate which one is running in Server mode and which is in Client mode so that you can step through all the Winsock code in the debugger.

When you have a compiled executable, you can run two copies of this application, either on the same computer, as shown in Figure 4.4, or on two separate computers that are connected over a network. Remember that the copy running in Server mode needs to start listening for connection requests before the client tries to connect to it.

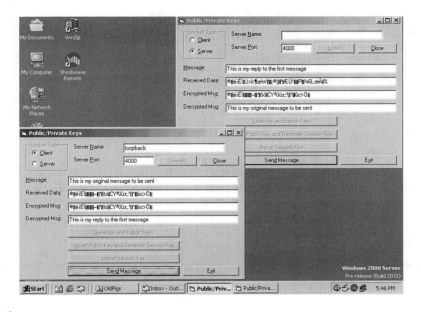

FIGURE 4.4

Exchanging messages between two instances of the application.

If you are running both copies of the application on the same computer, you can use the computer name `loopback` as the server name for the client to connect to. Otherwise, you need to specify the network name of the computer on which the server is running. For the port to use, I recommend using port numbers around 4000. There is a gap of port numbers that aren't commonly used by standard applications at this point in time.

4

PUBLIC/PRIVATE KEY COMMUNICATIONS

TIP

In order to run the example application, you'll need to have TCP/IP running on your computer. If you are not connected to a network and do not have a network card installed in your computer, you'll have to be connected to an ISP through a dial-up connection while running the example. The steps you follow to run this application are as follows:

- Start two copies of the application (you need to have compiled it to an EXE to do this).

- With the copy that will act as the Server, select the Server radio button, fill in a port to use (I suggest 4000), and click the Listen button.

continues

- With the copy that will act as the Client, select the Client radio button, fill in the name of the computer on which the Server copy is running (if the two copies are running on the same computer, use the name "loopback"), and then fill in the port number that you used on the Server copy. Click the Connect button to connect the two applications.

- After the two applications are connected, they should perform the key exchange automatically. If they do not connect, you might want to close both applications and try again, using a different port number.

- Type a message into the "Message" text box on either copy and click the Send Message button.

- Do the same on the other copy.

- After you are finished sending messages, click the Close button on either copy, and then click the Exit button on both copies.

Summary

Although this chapter didn't cover as much ground as the preceding chapter, it still covered quite a lot of material. You learned about the different aspects of encryption key types and how salt and padding are used within encryption to make encryption keys and encrypted data more secure. You also learned how you can generate new salt values, along with how to extract and replace the salt values that an encryption key is using. Finally, you learned how you can export and import encryption keys to exchange them with other users.

In the next chapter, you will look at digital certificates and the role they play in building secure communications. You'll learn how you can use a couple of Microsoft-provided controls to request and receive digital certificates from a certificate authority.

Requesting and Retrieving Certificates

IN THIS CHAPTER

- Digital Certificates Explained
- Acquiring Certificates
- Building a Certificate Request Utility

As you learned in the preceding chapter, public/private key encryption is a simple matter of exchanging public keys and using these keys to encrypt data that only the recipient can decrypt. In practice, this process is fairly straightforward. But how do you know that the public key you received is really from the person you think it is from? What if it was really some else's public key—someone you didn't want to receive the encrypted data? Not having some way of verifying the person a public key belongs to is a real problem.

Digital certificates were created to solve this problem with public/private key encryption. As the use of encryption spreads, a reliable means of guaranteeing that a particular public key does belong to a specific person, and that the person is who you think he is, is an important piece of the Internet infrastructure. Digital certificates provide this piece of the puzzle. In this chapter, you'll look at what digital certificates are and how they work. You'll also learn how to create certificate requests and get digital certificates you can use in your applications.

PREREQUISITES

Before reading this chapter, you need to make sure you have a good understanding of the following:

- Asymmetric encryption and digital certificates, as covered in Chapter 1, "Understanding Encryption and Application Security"

- Hashing data, generating encryption keys, and encrypting and decrypting data, as covered in Chapter 3, "Symmetric and Password Encryption"

- Using public/private encryption keys, as covered in Chapter 4, "Public/Private Key Communications"

Digital Certificates Explained

Digital certificates are the packaging of someone's public key with other identifying information that is signed by a Certificate Authority. A *Certificate Authority (CA)* is a third party that vouches for the identity of the person claiming to be the owner of the public key.

For this system to work, both parties have to trust the Certificate Authority and trust that the Certificate Authority has taken the appropriate steps to verify the identity of the owner of the public key. One of the most well-known Certificate Authorities is VeriSign (www.verisign.com), but almost anyone can be set up as a Certificate Authority by using Microsoft's Certificate Server. It is starting to become very common for corporate security departments to set themselves up as the corporate Certificate Authority, issuing certificates for use within a corporation.

Requesting a Certificate from a Certificate Authority

To request a certificate from a Certificate Authority, you need to generate a public/private key pair. You then need to package the public key with your name, email address, corporate identity, and other identifying information; format it in what is known as a PKCS #10 format, and then export this PKCS #10 certificate request in Base64 encoded format.

> **NOTE**
>
> The PKCS #10 format is specified in a document available from RSA Security, Inc. (www.rsasecurity.com). PKCS stands for Public-Key Cryptography Standard. When Public-Key standards are discussed, you'll often hear about PKCS with some number. This number refers to a particular standard that is outlined in the PKCS document with that particular number. All the PKCS standard documents are available through the RSA Web site.

> **Base-64**
>
> The base-64 encoding scheme translates mostly binary data into ASCII text. The scheme divides every three bytes into four six-bit characters, and then uses a cross-reference table to represent these as printable ASCII characters.

After you create the certificate request, it is sent to the Certificate Authority. The Certificate Authority then takes the steps necessary to verify the information you provided with the certificate request, depending on what type of certificate you have requested.

Different classes of certificates specify how thoroughly the information you've provided has been verified. The lowest class of certificates verifies only an email address and requires the CA to verify only that the email address provided does exist. For the higher classes of certificates, very detailed information must be provided, and might even require you to appear in person either at the CA or before a notary public to verify your identity.

After the Certificate Authority has approved your certificate request and has created a digital certificate from your certificate request, you can retrieve the certificate from the CA. After you retrieve the certificate, which is formatted in a PKCS #7 format, you put it into your certificate store with the private key that is associated with the public key in the certificate. This whole process of getting a digital certificate is illustrated in Figure 5.1.

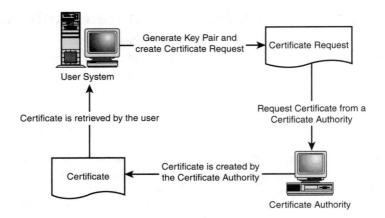

FIGURE 5.1

Getting a digital certificate from a Certificate Authority.

Verifying the Key Owner's Identity

When you receive a certificate from someone, how do you verify that it really is from who you think it is? Every certificate includes the ID and URL of the Certificate Authority that created the certificate and verified the identity of the owner. If you already have the certificate of the Certificate Authority installed on your computer, you can use it to verify the signature on the certificate you received. If the signature verifies correctly, you can safely assume that the certificate is really from the person you think it's from.

If you do not have the certificate of the Certificate Authority installed on your computer, you have to take a few additional steps to verify the certificate you received. First, you retrieve the CA's certificate from the URL included in the certificate you received. You can use this certificate to verify the certificate you received. The CA's certificate should contain the ID and URL of the CA that issued its certificate. Next, you can continue to follow the chain of CA certificates until either you reach the root of the chain or you reach a certificate that you already have and trust. This chain, known as a *chain of trust*, is illustrated in Figure 5.2.

The idea behind this organization is that, if you trust the CA at any point in the chain, you can trust any of the CAs that were verified by the CA you trust. This doesn't always mean that everyone down the chain is as reliable and trustworthy as the CA you originally trusted. As a result, certificates can be revoked by the Certificate Authority that issued the certificate. Each Certificate Authority maintains a list of certificate IDs it issued that have since been revoked. Because the CA has no means of taking the certificate back after it has been issued, it is the responsibility of the user who receives a certificate from someone to verify that it is not on the certificate revocation list of the CA that issued it. This goes for all the CAs in the chain of trust as well. One revoked certificate in the chain invalidates all the certificates that were issued by the CA with the revoked certificate.

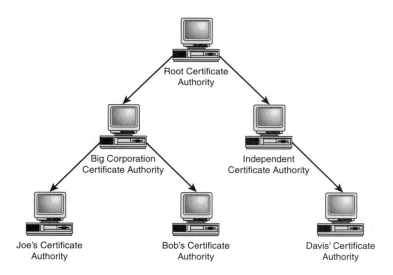

FIGURE 5.2
A Certificate Authority chain of trust.

Acquiring Certificates

Now that you have a basic understanding of how the process of acquiring and using certificates works, it's time to learn how to actually perform some of these tasks yourself. The first task is to request and retrieve a certificate from a Certificate Authority. Luckily, Microsoft has made this task fairly simple to perform, thanks to a couple of COM objects that are available for use.

> **NOTE**
>
> The remaining portion of this chapter requires that you have installed Windows 2000 Server or NT Server 4.0 with the Windows NT 4 Option Pack.

Generating a Certificate Request

Included with the latest version of Microsoft's Certificate Server is a COM object that can be used to generate certificate requests. It is also used to process and store the request, keys, and certificate in the appropriate certificate store. This object is the Certificate Enrollment Control; you can find it in xenroll.dll in the system32 directory. This control, which is a wrapper for Crypto API functions, simplifies the act of creating and processing a certificate request. It performs all the steps involved with requesting and retrieving a certificate, including generating the public/private key pair, except for the actual communication with the Certificate Authority.

When using the Certificate Enrollment Control, you do not include the reference to the control's type library. Instead, you declare a variable as an object and then use the `CreateObject` function as in the following code:

```
Dim m_objXen As Object

Set m_objXen = CreateObject("CEnroll.CEnroll.1")
```

NOTE

The xenroll.dll type library uses some variant types not available in Visual Basic, and thus cannot be used by including the type library in a Visual Basic project. As long as you use late binding, as previously shown, you can easily use most of the methods and properties of this object.

The Certificate Enrollment Control has several properties that can be set to control how it performs its tasks. They are listed in Table 5.1.

TABLE 5.1 Certificate Enrollment Control Properties

Property	Data Type	Description
CAStoreFlags	Long	Passed directly to the `CertOpenStore` function (which you'll look at in the next chapter), controlling how the certificate store is opened.
CAStoreName	String	Specifies the name of the certificate store for all non-ROOT and non-MY certificates to be stored.
CAStoreType	String	Specifies the type of certificate store to use for the store specified in the `CAStoreName` property.
ContainerName	String	Specifies the name of the key container to use.
DeleteRequestCert	Boolean	Deletes the dummy certificate that is created to hold the place of the requested certificate until the certificate is issued.
GenKeyFlags	Long	Passed directly to the `CryptGenKey` function to control how the keys are generated.
HashAlgorithm	String	Specifies the preferred hash algorithm to use for signing the PKCS #10 certificate request.
KeySpec	Long	Specifies the key type to be generated.

Property	Data Type	Description
MyStoreFlags	Long	Passed directly to the CertOpenStore function, controlling how the MY certificate store is opened.
MyStoreName	String	Specifies where certificates with linked private keys are kept.
MyStoreType	String	Specifies the type of store to use for the store specified in the MyStoreName property.
ProviderFlags	Long	The use of this property is controlled by the CSP used for generating the certificate request.
ProviderName	String	Specifies the CSP to use.
ProviderType	String	The use of this property is controlled by the CSP used for generating the certificate request.
PVKFileName	String	Specifies that the private key is to be generated as an exportable key and is to be stored in the file specified by this property.
RequestStoreFlags	Long	Passed directly to the CertOpenStore function, controlling how the REQUEST certificate store is opened.
RequestStoreName	String	Specifies the certificate store in which the dummy certificate is to be stored while waiting for the certificate to be issued.
RequestStoreType	String	Specifies the type of store to use for the store specified in the RequestStoreName property.
RootStoreFlags	Long	Passed directly to the CertOpenStore function, controlling how the ROOT certificate store is opened.
RootStoreName	String	Specifies where all trusted, self-signed ROOT certificates are kept.
RootStoreType	String	Specifies the type of store to use for the store specified in the RootStoreName property.
SPCFileName	String	Specifies a file to which the PKCS #7 certificate response is written.
UseExistingKeySet	Boolean	Specifies that an existing key set is to be used, instead of generating a new one.
WriteCertToCSP	Boolean	Specifies whether a certificate should be written to the CSP.

5

REQUESTING AND RETRIEVING CERTIFICATES

Creating a Certificate Request

You can create a certificate request by using one of two methods. The first of these two methods, `createPKCS10`, returns a string value that contains the certificate request. The syntax for this method is as follows:

Syntax

```
createPKCS10(DNName as String, Usage as String) as String
```

The first parameter (`DNName`) to this method is a string containing a series of identifying information. The elements in this string are in the format of one- or two-character codes, followed by an equal sign, and the value, with each element separated from the others by a comma. This string looks like the following:

```
CN=Davis Chapman,OU=Bullfrog Unit,O=The Frog
➥Pond,L=Dallas,S=TX,C=US,E=davischa@onramp.net
```

The possible elements that are available for including in this string are listed in Table 5.2.

TABLE 5.2   X.500 Distinguished Name Fields

Code	Description
CN	Common Name—The user's name, or if this is a request for a certificate for a server, the fully qualified hostname or URL.
O	Organization—The name of the organization or company for which the certificate is being requested. It should be the legal name for the company or organization.
OU	Organizational Unit—This name is used to differentiate different divisions within an organization or company. It can also be used to specify a DBA (Doing Business As) name for the certificate.
L	Locality—The city in which the organization or person resides.
S	State—The state in which the organization or person resides.
C	Country—The country in which the organization or person resides. The X.500 naming scheme limits this field to a two-character country code. For example, the code for the United States is US, and the code for Canada is CA.
E	Email Address—The email address for the person requesting the certificate (this element is optional).

The second parameter (Usage) is the OID (Object Identifier) that identifies the purpose of the certificate being generated. Some of the standard OIDs are listed in Table 5.3.

OID

An *Object Identifier (OID)* is a series of integers separated by periods. The organization of these numbers is similar to the organization of TCP/IP addresses. It is always treated as a string value when passing to functions.

TABLE 5.3   Certificate Purpose OIDs

Certificate Purpose	OID
Base Key OID	1.3.6.1.5.5.7.3
Server Authentication	1.3.6.1.5.5.7.3.1
Client Authentication	1.3.6.1.5.5.7.3.2
Code Signing	1.3.6.1.5.5.7.3.3
Email Protection	1.3.6.1.5.5.7.3.4

The return value from this function is a string containing the certificate request. A typical use of this function is as follows:

```
Dim strDN As String
Dim strReq As String

'--- Specify the certificate usage
m_strKeyUsage = "1.3.6.1.5.5.7.3.2"

'--- Build the distinguished name string
strDN = "CN=" + m_strUserName _
        + ",OU=" + m_strUnit _
        + ",O=" + m_strOrganization _
        + ",L=" + m_strCity _
        + ",S=" + m_strState _
        + ",C=" + m_strCountry

'--- Specify the key type
m_objXen.KeySpec = AT_KEYEXCHANGE

'--- Create the PKCS #10 request
strReq = m_objXen.createPKCS10(strDN, m_strKeyUsage)
```

The second method available for creating a certificate request is the `createFilePKCS10` function. This function takes the same two parameters and has a third parameter (PKCSFileName)

5

that is the name of the file to write the certificate request into. The syntax for this function is as follows:

Syntax

```
createFilePKCS10(DNName as String, Usage as String, _
        PKCSFileName as String)
```

This version writes the certificate request to a file that can be read in by the user and pasted into a Web form when submitting to the Certificate Authority.

Accepting a Certificate

When you are issued a certificate from the Certificate Authority, you need to retrieve the certificate and import it into your certificate store. The certificate is returned in a PKCS #7 format, so the function to import the certificate into the certificate store is called `acceptPKCS7`. It takes one parameter (`NewCert`), the certificate that was retrieved from the CA. The syntax for this function is as follows:

Syntax

```
acceptPKCS7(NewCert as String)
```

As with the methods for creating the certificate request, two methods are available for importing the certificate. The second version reads the certificate in from a file. This method, `acceptFilePKCS7`, takes the filename as its only parameter (`NewCertFileName`). The syntax for this method is as follows:

Syntax

```
acceptFilePKCS7(NewCertFileName as String)
```

Enumerating Containers

If you need to see what all the available certificate containers for the current CSP are, you can use the `enumContainers` method. This method takes a single parameter (`Index`), the container number to return, and returns a string containing the name of the container. The syntax for this function is as follows:

Syntax

```
enumContainers(Index as Long) as String
```

The container index number starts with zero (0) for the first container. After the last container has been passed, either the ERROR_NO_MORE_ITEMS or the ERROR_NO_MORE_DATA error is thrown. You might use this method as follows:

```
Public Const ERROR_NO_MORE_ITEMS = 259&
Public Const ERROR_NO_MORE_DATA = &H80070103
Dim strContainer as String
Dim lIndex as Long

'--- Set up the error handling
On Error GoTo EnumContainerErr

'--- Initialize the index
lIndex = 0
strContainer = ""

'--- Get the first container
strContainer = m_objXen.enumContainers(lIndex)

'--- Loop until out of containers
While (strContainer <> "")

    '--- Do whatever with the container name
    .
    .
    .
    '--- Increment the index
    lIndex = lIndex + 1
    strContainer = ""

    '--- Get the next container
    strContainer = m_objXen.enumContainers(lIndex)
Wend
'--- Perform Error Handling
EnumContainerErr:
'--- Have we run out of containers?
If Err.Number = ERROR_NO_MORE_ITEMS Then Resume Next
If Err.Number = ERROR_NO_MORE_DATA Then Resume Next
```

Enumerating Providers

When you need to determine which CSPs are available on a system for a particular provider type, you can use the enumProviders method. This method works virtually the same as the enumContainers method. The syntax for this function is as follows:

Syntax

```
enumProviders(Index as Long, Flags as Long) as String
```

This method has two parameters. The first parameter (`Index`) is the provider index, just as with the `enumContainers` method. This index starts at zero (`0`) for the first provider and can be incremented to loop through each provider. The second parameter (`Flags`) is passed to the flags parameter of the `CryptEnumProviders` function, so it should always be passed zero (`0`).

This method returns a string variable containing the name of the current CSP. Just like with the `enumContainers` method, after all the CSPs of the current provider type have been passed, either the `ERROR_NO_MORE_ITEMS` or the `ERROR_NO_MORE_DATA` error is thrown. You might use this method as follows:

```
Public Const ERROR_NO_MORE_ITEMS = 259&
Public Const ERROR_NO_MORE_DATA = &H80070103
Dim strProvider as String
Dim lIndex as Long

'--- Set up the error handling
On Error GoTo EnumProviderErr

'--- Initialize the index
lIndex = 0
strProvider = ""

'--- Get the first provider
strProvider = m_objXen.enumProviders(lIndex, 0)

'--- Loop until out of providers
While (strProvider <> "")

    '--- Do whatever with the provider name
    .
    .
    .
    '--- Increment the index
    lIndex = lIndex + 1
    strProvider = ""

    '--- Get the next provider
    strProvider = m_objXen.enumProviders(lIndex, 0)
Wend
'--- Perform Error Handling
EnumProviderErr:
'--- Have we run out of providers?
If Err.Number = ERROR_NO_MORE_ITEMS Then Resume Next
If Err.Number = ERROR_NO_MORE_DATA Then Resume Next
```

Retrieving Certificates

Now that you know how to generate certificate requests and accept issued certificates, the other piece of the puzzle is interacting with the Certificate Authority. If the Certificate Authority happens to be running Microsoft's Certificate Server, this interaction can be performed through another COM object. If the Certificate Authority is running a different Certificate Server, you'll probably have to paste the certificate into a Web form and retrieve the issued certificate either through an email message or another Web form.

For the remainder of this chapter, I'll assume that you are interacting with a Microsoft Certificate Server, so I'll describe the CCertRequest COM object. You can find this object in the CertCli type library in the CertCli.DLL. You can include this object in your Visual Basic project through the Project References dialog.

Submitting the Certificate Request

When you have the certificate request ready to send to the Certificate Authority, you can use the Submit method of the CCertRequest object to send it. This method submits the certificate request to a Microsoft Certificate Server CA. The syntax for this method is as follows:

Syntax

```
Submit(Flags as Long, strRequest as String, strAttributes as String, _
       strConfig as String) as Long
```

The first parameter (Flags) to this method is a combination of flags that specify the certificate request format. Three sets of flag values can be combined. The first set of flag values is listed in Table 5.4. These flag values specify how the certificate request is encoded.

TABLE 5.4 Submit Encoding Flag Values

Flag	Value	Description
CR_IN_BASE64HEADER	0	The request is encoded in Base64 encoding with begin/end markers.
CR_IN_BASE64	&H1	The request is encoded in Base64 encoding with no begin/end markers.
CR_IN_BINARY	&H2	The request is in binary form.

The second set of flag values is used to specify the request format. These flag values are specified in Table 5.5.

5

REQUESTING AND RETRIEVING CERTIFICATES

TABLE 5.5   Submit Format Flag Values

Flag	Value	Description
CR_IN_PKCS10	&H100	The request is in PKCS #10 format.
CR_IN_KEYGEN	&H200	The request is in keygen (Netscape) format.

The third set of flag values is used to specify any encrypting of the request that has been performed. These possible values are listed in Table 5.6.

TABLE 5.6   Submit Encryption Flag Values

Flag	Value	Description
CR_IN_ENCRYPTED_REQUEST	&H10000	The request is encrypted using the CA's public key.
CR_IN_ENCRYPTED_ATTRIBUTES	&H20000	The request attributes are encrypted.

The second parameter (strRequest) is the certificate request. It can be the string value that was returned by the Certificate Enrollment Control.

The third parameter (strAttributes) is a string of additional attributes to be included in the certificate request. These extra attributes are in name/value pairs, with a colon separating the name from the value, and each pair separated by the newline character (vbLf). A sample is as follows:

```
"Name1:Value1" + vbLf + "Name2:Value2"
```

The fourth parameter (strConfig) is a combination of the name of the computer on which the Certificate Authority is running and the name of the Certificate Authority. These names are separated by a backslash character, as follows:

```
"caserver.ca.com\My Certificate Authority"
```

The return value from the Submit method is a long value that indicates the status of the certificate request. The possible status codes are listed in Table 5.7.

TABLE 5.7   Certificate Request Status Codes

Status Code	Value	Description
CR_DISP_INCOMPLETE	0	The request was not complete or didn't complete.
CR_DISP_ERROR	&H1	The request failed, was corrupt, or otherwise had a problem.
CR_DISP_DENIED	&H2	The request was denied.

Status Code	Value	Description
CR_DISP_ISSUED	&H3	The certificate has been issued.
CR_DISP_ISSUED_OUT_OF_BAND	&H4	The certificate was issued separately.
CR_DISP_UNDER_SUBMISSION	&H5	The request is being processed.

A typical use of this method is as follows:

```
Dim lDisp As Long

'--- Submit the request to the CA
lDisp = m_objReq.Submit(CR_IN_BASE64 Or CR_IN_PKCS10, _
                        strReq, "", m_strServer + "\" + m_strCA)
```

Obtaining the Request ID

After you submit the certificate request to the CA, you need to get the request ID. You can use it to make subsequent requests to the CA to get updates of the status of your request and eventually retrieve the certificate once it's been issued. You do so by using the GetRequestId method.

The GetRequestId method takes no parameters and returns a long value that is the ID of your certificate request. This method should probably be called shortly after submitting the certificate request because the certificate may be issued much later. A typical use of this method is as follows:

```
Dim lReqID As Long

'--- Get the request ID
lReqID = m_objReq.GetRequestId
```

Obtaining the Request Status

Two methods are useful for determining the current status of a certificate request and for providing a readable status message for the user. The first of these methods is the RetrievePending method, which gets the current status of a certificate request from the CA. The syntax for this method is as follows:

Syntax

```
RetrievePending(RequestID as Long, strConfig as String) as Long
```

The first parameter (RequestID) this method takes is the request ID returned from the GetRequestId method. The second parameter (strConfig) is the machine name/Certificate Authority name combination used in the Submit method to specify the CA to submit the certificate request to.

The return value from this method is the current status code of the request. For a list of the possible status codes, refer to Table 5.7.

If you want to provide your users with a more readable status message, you can use the `GetDispositionMessage` method. This method, which doesn't take any parameters, returns a string containing the current status of the request in a readable form. A typical use of these two methods might be as follows:

```
Dim lDisp As Long
Dim strMsg As String

'--- Retrieve the current status of our request
lDisp = m_objReq.RetrievePending(m_lReqID, m_strServer + "\" + m_strCA)

'--- Get the textual description of the request status
strMsg = m_objReq.GetDispositionMessage
'--- Display it for the user
MsgBox strMsg, vbOKOnly, "Certificate Request"
```

If you want to get the status code from the last time you checked, you can use the `GetLastStatus` method to retrieve the last status code that was returned. This status code is one of the codes listed in Table 5.7.

Retrieving the Certificate

After the certificate has been issued, you can retrieve it by using the `GetCertificate` method. The syntax for this method is as follows:

Syntax

```
GetCertificate(Flags as Long) as String
```

The only parameter (`Flags`) for this method is a flag that specifies how the certificate should be retrieved. The first set of flag values specifies the certificate encoding. The possible values for this flag value are listed in Table 5.8.

TABLE 5.8   `GetCertificate` Encoding Flag Values

Flag	Value	Description
CR_OUT_BASE64HEADER	0	The certificate is encoded in Base64 encoding with begin/end markers.
CR_OUT_BASE64	&H1	The certificate is encoded in Base64 encoding with no begin/end markers.
CR_OUT_BINARY	&H2	The certificate is in binary form.

If the CA is using Microsoft Certificate Server 2.0 (released with Windows 2000), you can also use a second flag value to retrieve the entire certificate chain, including all the CA certificates in the chain of trust. To do so, you can use the flag value in Table 5.9.

TABLE 5.9 GetCertificate Certificate Chain Flag Values

Flag	Value	Description
CR_OUT_CHAIN	&H100	The complete certificate chain is returned in PKCS #7 format.

The return value is the certificate that was retrieved from the CA. You can take this returned certificate and import it into the certificate store by using the acceptPKCS7 method of the Certificate Enrollment Control.

Retrieving the CA's Certificate

When you need to retrieve the Certificate Authority's certificate, you can use the GetCACertificate method. This method's syntax is as follows:

Syntax

```
GetCACertificate(fExchangeCert as Long, strConfig as String, _
    Flags as Long) as String
```

The first parameter (fExchangeCert) is a Boolean value (0 is FALSE, <>0 is TRUE) that specifies whether to get the CA's Signature certificate or Key Exchange certificate. You can use the Key Exchange certificate to encrypt certificate requests that you are sending to the CA, whereas you can use the Signature certificate only to verify the signatures on the certificates issued by this CA. This parameter is used only with the version of Certificate Server that is included with NT 4 Option Pack. For the version of Certificate Server shipped with Windows 2000, this parameter must be zero (0), limiting you to only retrieving the CA's Signature certificate.

The second parameter (strConfig) is the machine name/CA name combination that you used in the Submit method. The third parameter (Flags) is the option flags that you used to retrieve your certificate with the GetCertificate method. The possible values for this flag are given in Table 5.8 and Table 5.9. The return value from this method is the certificate for the CA.

Building a Certificate Request Utility

To get a better understanding of how these two COM objects work, you'll build a Certificate Request utility. This utility will perform the following steps:

1. Collect identification information from the user
2. Allow the user to specify how the certificate will be used

3. Build the certificate request and send it to the CA

4. Allow the user to check the status of the request

5. After the certificate has been issued, retrieve the certificate and accept it into the certificate store

---

TIP

Because of the nature of this example, trying this utility against a local copy of Microsoft's Certificate Server would be a good idea. This way, you can issue and deny certificate requests that are generated by this utility.

Creating the Certificate Request Class

You start your project by creating a new, standard executable Visual Basic project. After you've created the application shell and default form, you can turn your attention to the Certificate Request functionality. First, though, you need to include a reference to the `CertCli` Type Library in the Project, References dialog, as shown in Figure 5.3.

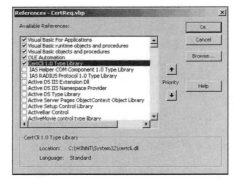

FIGURE 5.3

Including the Certificate Request object in the project.

Next, instead of extending the `crypto` class that you have been building over the last few chapters, you'll create a new class with just certificate request functionality in it. To get started, create a new class, name it `clsCertRequest`, and add the constant and type declarations in Listing 5.1.

LISTING 5.1   The `clsCertRequest` Class Declarations

```
Option Explicit

'--- Certificate Request Format
Const CR_IN_BASE64HEADER = 0
```

```
Const CR_IN_BASE64 = &H1
Const CR_IN_BINARY = &H2
Const CR_IN_ENCODEMASK = &HFF
Const CR_IN_PKCS10 = &H100
Const CR_IN_KEYGEN = &H200
Const CR_IN_FORMATMASK = &HFF00
Const CR_IN_ENCRYPTED_REQUEST = &H10000
Const CR_IN_ENCRYPTED_ATTRIBUTES = &H20000

'--- Certificate Request Status
Const CR_DISP_INCOMPLETE = 0
Const CR_DISP_ERROR = &H1
Const CR_DISP_DENIED = &H2
Const CR_DISP_ISSUED = &H3
Const CR_DISP_ISSUED_OUT_OF_BAND = &H4
Const CR_DISP_UNDER_SUBMISSION = &H5

'--- Issued Certificate Format
Const CR_OUT_BASE64HEADER = 0
Const CR_OUT_BASE64 = &H1
Const CR_OUT_BINARY = &H2
Const CR_OUT_ENCODEMASK = &HFF
Const CR_OUT_CHAIN = &H100

'--- Key Types
Const AT_KEYEXCHANGE = 1
Const AT_SIGNATURE = 2

Public Enum enmKeyType
    KT_KeyExchange = AT_KEYEXCHANGE
    KT_Signature = AT_SIGNATURE
End Enum

'----------------------------------------------------------------------
'  Enhanced Key Usage (Purpose) Object Identifiers
'----------------------------------------------------------------------
Const szOID_PKIX_KP = "1.3.6.1.5.5.7.3"

'--- Consistent key usage bits: DIGITAL_SIGNATURE, KEY_ENCIPHERMENT
'--- or KEY_AGREEMENT
Const szOID_PKIX_KP_SERVER_AUTH = "1.3.6.1.5.5.7.3.1"

'--- Consistent key usage bits: DIGITAL_SIGNATURE
Const szOID_PKIX_KP_CLIENT_AUTH = "1.3.6.1.5.5.7.3.2"

'--- Consistent key usage bits: DIGITAL_SIGNATURE
Const szOID_PKIX_KP_CODE_SIGNING = "1.3.6.1.5.5.7.3.3"
```

5

REQUESTING AND RETRIEVING CERTIFICATES

continues

LISTING 5.1 Continued

```
'--- Consistent key usage bits: DIGITAL_SIGNATURE, NON_REPUDIATION
'--- and/or (KEY_ENCIPHERMENT or KEY_AGREEMENT)
Const szOID_PKIX_KP_EMAIL_PROTECTION = "1.3.6.1.5.5.7.3.4"

Public Enum enmKeyUsage
    KU_ClientAuthentication = 0
    KU_EMailProtection = 1
    KU_ServerAuthentication = 2
    KU_CodeSigning = 3
End Enum

'-----------------------------------------------------------------
'  Microsoft Enhanced Key Usage (Purpose) Object Identifiers
'-----------------------------------------------------------------

'--- Signer of CTLs
Const szOID_KP_CTL_USAGE_SIGNING = "1.3.6.1.4.1.311.10.3.1"

'--- Signer of TimeStamps
Const szOID_KP_TIME_STAMP_SIGNING = "1.3.6.1.4.1.311.10.3.2"

'-----------------------------------------------------------------
'  Microsoft Attribute Object Identifiers
'-----------------------------------------------------------------
Const szOID_YESNO_TRUST_ATTR = "1.3.6.1.4.1.311.10.4.1"

'-- Properties
Private m_strUserName As String
Private m_strUnit As String
Private m_strOrganization As String
Private m_strCity As String
Private m_strState As String
Private m_strCountry As String
Private m_lReqID As Long
Private m_strServer As String
Private m_strCA As String
Private m_strEMail As String
Private m_lKeySpec As enmKeyType
Private m_strKeyUsage As String
Private m_lKeyUsage As enmKeyUsage

'-- Objects for Enrollment and Request controls
Private m_objXen As Object
Private m_objReq As CCertRequest
```

Creating the Class Properties

While going through all the class declarations, you might have noticed a whole string of property variables. They hold pieces of information you need to include with the certificate request and hold the request ID. Next, you need to expose all these properties, as in Listing 5.2.

LISTING 5.2 clsCertRequest Class Properties

```
Public Property Get UserName() As String
    UserName = m_strUserName
End Property

Public Property Let UserName(ByVal sNewValue As String)
    m_strUserName = sNewValue
End Property

Public Property Get EMail() As String
    EMail = m_strEMail
End Property

Public Property Let EMail(ByVal sNewValue As String)
    m_strEMail = sNewValue
End Property

Public Property Get Unit() As String
    Unit = m_strUnit
End Property

Public Property Let Unit(ByVal sNewValue As String)
    m_strUnit = sNewValue
End Property

Public Property Get Organization() As String
    Organization = m_strOrganization
End Property

Public Property Let Organization(ByVal sNewValue As String)
    m_strOrganization = sNewValue
End Property

Public Property Get City() As String
    City = m_strCity
End Property

Public Property Let City(ByVal sNewValue As String)
    m_strCity = sNewValue
End Property
```

continues

5

REQUESTING AND
RETRIEVING
CERTIFICATES

LISTING 5.2   Continued

```
Public Property Get State() As String
    State = m_strState
End Property

Public Property Let State(ByVal sNewValue As String)
    m_strState = sNewValue
End Property

Public Property Get Country() As String
    Country = m_strCountry
End Property

Public Property Let Country(ByVal sNewValue As String)
    m_strCountry = sNewValue
End Property

Public Property Get RequestID() As Long
    RequestID = m_lReqID
End Property

Public Property Get Server() As String
    Server = m_strServer
End Property

Public Property Let Server(ByVal sNewValue As String)
    m_strServer = sNewValue
End Property

Public Property Get CertificateAuthority() As String
    CertificateAuthority = m_strCA
End Property

Public Property Let CertificateAuthority(ByVal sNewValue As String)
    m_strCA = sNewValue
End Property

Public Property Get KeySpec() As enmKeyType
    KeySpec = m_lKeySpec
End Property

Public Property Let KeySpec(ByVal lNewValue As enmKeyType)
    m_lKeySpec = lNewValue
End Property

Public Property Get KeyUsage() As enmKeyUsage
    KeyUsage = m_lKeyUsage
End Property
```

```
Public Property Let KeyUsage(ByVal lNewValue As enmKeyUsage)
    '--- Set the key usage value
    m_lKeyUsage = lNewValue

    '--- Set the Key Usage OID to the appropriate string
    Select Case m_lKeyUsage
        Case KU_ClientAuthentication
            m_strKeyUsage = szOID_PKIX_KP_CLIENT_AUTH
        Case KU_EMailProtection
            m_strKeyUsage = szOID_PKIX_KP_EMAIL_PROTECTION
        Case KU_ServerAuthentication
            m_strKeyUsage = szOID_PKIX_KP_SERVER_AUTH
        Case KU_CodeSigning
            m_strKeyUsage = szOID_PKIX_KP_CODE_SIGNING
    End Select
End Property
```

In the KeyUsage property in Listing 5.2, notice that you set not only the variable holding the enumerated value, but also a string value to the OID associated with the specified key usage. You use constants that you declared in Listing 5.1 for these OID values. It's important that these OID values are correct, so it doesn't hurt to go back and review them for correctness.

Class Initialization and Termination

Upon creating this class, you need to create an instance of both the Certificate Enrollment Control and the Certificate Request object. You can keep these instances alive for the life of the class. You create the Certificate Enrollment Control by using the CreateObject function, whereas the Certificate Request object can be instantiated with the New keyword, as in Listing 5.3.

LISTING 5.3   clsCertRequest Class Initialization

```
Private Sub Class_Initialize()
'*************************************************************
'* Written By: Davis Chapman
'* Date:       September 12, 1999
'*
'* Syntax:     Class_Initialize
'*
'* Parameters: None
'*
'* Purpose: During the class initialization, the instances of
'*          the Certificate Enroll and Certificate Request
'*          objects are created.
'*************************************************************
    On Error GoTo InitErr
```

5

REQUESTING AND
RETRIEVING
CERTIFICATES

continues

LISTING 5.3 Continued

```
    m_lReqID = 0

    '--- Instantiate the certificate enrollment object
    Set m_objXen = CreateObject("CEnroll.CEnroll.1")

    '--- Instantiate the certificate request object
    Set m_objReq = New CCertRequest

    Exit Sub
InitErr:
    '--- Tell the user about the error
    MsgBox "Error creating request objects - " + Str(Err.Number) + _
           " - " + Err.Description
End Sub
```

When the class is being terminated, you'll want to free both of these resources by setting their variables to Nothing, as in Listing 5.4.

LISTING 5.4 clsCertRequest Class Termination

```
Private Sub Class_Terminate()
    '--- Free the objects
    Set m_objXen = Nothing
    Set m_objReq = Nothing
End Sub
```

Requesting Certificates

Now it's time to get down to action. The first real piece of meaty functionality that you can add to the class is the part that creates and submits the certificate request. In this functionality, you can build the distinguished names string from the information the user provides. Next, you can specify the key type that you want to generate and create a certificate request. When you have a certificate request, you can submit it to the CA and display the request status for the user. Once the request has been submitted, you can get the request ID for use at a later time. Finally, just for good measure, you can add some code that, if by some slim chance, the certificate was issued immediately, you can go ahead and get the certificate. To add all this functionality, add the code in Listing 5.5.

LISTING 5.5   The DoCertRequest Function

```
Public Function DoCertRequest() As Boolean
'***************************************************************
'* Written By: Davis Chapman
'* Date:       September 12, 1999
'*
'* Syntax:     DoCertRequest
'*
'* Parameters: None
'*
'* Purpose: This function builds the distinguished name string
'*          and then calls the XEnroll control to generate a
'*          public/private key pair and export the public key
'*          in the form of a certificate request. The certificate
'*          request is then submitted to the Certificate Authority
'*          using the Certificate Request control.
'***************************************************************
    DoCertRequest = False

    Dim strDN As String
    Dim strReq As String
    Dim lDisp As Long
    Dim strMsg As String

    On Error GoTo DoCertReqErr

    '--- Build the distinguished name string
    strDN = "CN=" + m_strUserName _
        + ",OU=" + m_strUnit _
        + ",O=" + m_strOrganization _
        + ",L=" + m_strCity _
        + ",S=" + m_strState _
        + ",C=" + m_strCountry

    '--- Do we have an E-Mail address?
    If (m_strEMail <> "") Then
        '--- Yes, so include it also
        strDN = strDN + ",E=" + m_strEMail
    End If

    '--- Specify the key type
    m_objXen.KeySpec = m_lKeySpec

    '--- Create the PKCS #10 request
    strReq = m_objXen.createPKCS10(strDN, m_strKeyUsage)
```

continues

LISTING 5.5 Continued

```
'--- Submit the request to the CA
lDisp = m_objReq.Submit(CR_IN_BASE64 Or CR_IN_PKCS10, _
                        strReq, _
                        "", _
                        m_strServer + "\" + m_strCA)

'--- Get the textual description of the request status
strMsg = m_objReq.GetDispositionMessage
'--- Display it for the user
MsgBox strMsg, vbOKOnly, "Certificate Request"

'--- Did we fail? If so, then exit early
If ((lDisp = CR_DISP_INCOMPLETE) Or _
    (lDisp = CR_DISP_ERROR) Or _
    (lDisp = CR_DISP_DENIED)) Then Exit Function

'--- Get the request ID
m_lReqID = m_objReq.GetRequestId

'--- If the certificate has already been issued,
'--- then get the certificate
If (lDisp = CR_DISP_ISSUED) Or _
      (lDisp = CR_DISP_ISSUED_OUT_OF_BAND) Then
    If Not GetCert Then Exit Function
End If

'--- Didn't exit early, return TRUE
DoCertRequest = True
Exit Function

DoCertReqErr:
    '--- Tell the user about the error
    MsgBox "Error - " + Str(Err.Number) + " - " + Err.Description

End Function
```

Retrieving Certificates

The next piece of functionality that you can add to your class is the retrieval of the issued certificate. In this function, you'll get the certificate from the server and then accept it into the certificate store. To add this functionality, add the code in Listing 5.6 to the clsCertRequest class.

LISTING 5.6   The GetCert Function

```
Public Function GetCert() As Boolean
'****************************************************************
'* Written By: Davis Chapman
'* Date:       September 12, 1999
'*
'* Syntax:     GetCert
'*
'* Parameters:  None
'*
'* Purpose: This function retrieves the issued certificate from
'*          the CA using the Certificate Request control. Next,
'*          the Certificate Enroll control is used to accept the
'*          certificate and to place it into the certificate
'*          store.
'****************************************************************
    On Error GoTo GetCertErr
    Dim strCert As String

    '--- Initialize the return value
    GetCert = False

    '--- Get the certificate
    strCert = m_objReq.GetCertificate(CR_OUT_BINARY Or CR_OUT_CHAIN)

    '--- Accept the certificate into the certificate store
    m_objXen.acceptPKCS7 strCert

    '--- Didn't exit early, return TRUE
    GetCert = True

    Exit Function

GetCertErr:
    '--- Tell the user about the error
    MsgBox "Error - " + Str(Err.Number) + " - " + Err.Description
End Function
```

Checking on Request Status

The final piece of functionality to be added to the clsCertRequest class is the checking of the request status. In this function, you'll need to retrieve the current status from the CA and display it for the user. If the certificate has already been issued, you'll call the GetCert function to retrieve the certificate. To add this functionality to the clsCertRequest class, add the code in Listing 5.7.

5

LISTING 5.7   The GetReqStatus Function

```
Public Function GetReqStatus() As Long
'***************************************************************
'* Written By: Davis Chapman
'* Date:       September 12, 1999
'*
'* Syntax:     GetReqStatus
'*
'* Parameters:  None
'*
'* Purpose: This function checks the current status of the
'*          current outstanding certificate request. If the
'*          request has been issued, then the certificate is
'*          retrieved.
'***************************************************************
    Dim lDisp As Long
    Dim strMsg As String

    '--- Retrieve the current status of our request
    lDisp = m_objReq.RetrievePending(m_lReqID, _
            m_strServer + "\" + m_strCA)

    '--- Get the textual description of the request status
    strMsg = m_objReq.GetDispositionMessage
    '--- Display it for the user
    MsgBox strMsg, vbOKOnly, "Certificate Request"

    '--- Set the status code to the return value
    GetReqStatus = lDisp

    '--- If the certificate has already been issued,
    '--- then get the certificate
    If (lDisp = CR_DISP_ISSUED) Or _
            (lDisp = CR_DISP_ISSUED_OUT_OF_BAND) Then
        If Not GetCert Then Exit Function
    End If
End Function
```

Designing the Form

Now it's time to turn your attention back to the application form. You need to gather a lot of information from the user of this utility, so you can add controls to the form as shown in Figure 5.4, setting their properties as specified in Table 5.10.

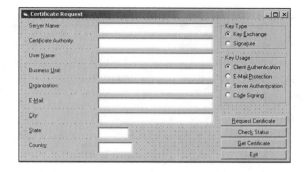

FIGURE 5.4
Designing the application form.

TABLE 5.10 Control Property Settings

Control	Property	Value
Label	Caption	Ser&ver Name:
TextBox	Name	txtServer
Label	Caption	Certi&ficate Authority:
TextBox	Name	txtCA
Label	Caption	User &Name:
TextBox	Name	txtUserName
Label	Caption	Business &Unit:
TextBox	Name	txtUnit
Label	Caption	&Organization:
TextBox	Name	txtOrganization
Label	Caption	E-&Mail:
TextBox	Name	txtEMail
Label	Caption	&City:
TextBox	Name	txtCity
Label	Caption	&State:
TextBox	Name	txtState
Label	Caption	Countr&y:
TextBox	Name	txtCountry
Frame (Group Box)	Caption	Key Type
OptionButton	Name	optKeyExchange
	Caption	Key &Exchange

continues

TABLE 5.10   Continued

Control	Property	Value
OptionButton	Name	optSignature
	Caption	Signa&ture
Frame (Group Box)	Caption	Key Usage
OptionButton	Name	optCliAuth
	Caption	Client &Authentication
OptionButton	Name	optEMailProt
	Caption	E-Mail &Protection
OptionButton	Name	optServAuth
	Caption	Server Authent&ication
OptionButton	Name	optCodeSign
	Caption	Co&de Signing
Command Button	Name	cmdReqCert
	Caption	&Request Certificate
Command Button	Name	cmdCheckStat
	Caption	Chec&k Status
Command Button	Name	cmdGetCert
	Caption	&Get Certificate
Command Button	Name	cmdExit
	Caption	E&xit

Form Initialization and Shutdown

In this application, it is easiest if you create a form-level instance of the Certificate Request class. To do so, add the code in Listing 5.8 to the form declaration section.

LISTING 5.8   Form Declarations

```
Option Explicit

Private crRequest As clsCertRequest
```

So that this instance of the Certificate Request class will be available throughout the life of the application, create it in the form load event, as in Listing 5.9.

LISTING 5.9   The Form Load Event

```
Private Sub Form_Load()
    '--- Create the Certificate Request object
    Set crRequest = New clsCertRequest
End Sub
```

To clean up after yourself, you should destroy the Certificate Request class during the form unload event, as in Listing 5.10.

LISTING 5.10   Form Termination

```
Private Sub Form_Unload(Cancel As Integer)
    '--- Destroy the Certificate Request object
    Set crRequest = Nothing
End Sub
```

To add the final piece of housekeeping code for the form, you need to close the application from the Exit button. To do so, add the code in Listing 5.11 to the Click event of the cmdExit button.

LISTING 5.11   The cmdExit Click Event

```
Private Sub cmdExit_Click()
    '--- Close this application
    Unload Me
End Sub
```

Performing the Certificate Request

Now you're ready to make the application submit a certificate request. You need to copy all the information the user has entered to the appropriate properties of the Certificate Request class. After all the information has been copied, you can call the class' DoCertRequest method, as in Listing 5.12.

LISTING 5.12   The DoCertReq Subroutine

```
Private Sub DoCertReq()
'*****************************************************************
'* Written By: Davis Chapman
'* Date:       September 12, 1999
'*
'* Syntax:     DoCertReq
'*
'* Parameters: None
```

5

continues

LISTING 5.12   Continued

```
'*
'* Purpose: This subroutine sets the values entered by the user
'*          to the appropriate properties on the Certificate
'*          Request object. Next, it calls the DoCertRequest
'*          method in the class to make the certificate request.
'**************************************************************

    '--- Set the certificate properties
    crRequest.UserName = txtUserName
    crRequest.Unit = txtUnit
    crRequest.Organization = txtOrganization
    crRequest.City = txtCity
    crRequest.State = txtState
    crRequest.Country = txtCountry
    crRequest.EMail = txtEMail

    '--- Specify what Certificate Authority to use
    crRequest.Server = txtServer
    crRequest.CertificateAuthority = txtCA

    '--- Specify how the certificate and key will be used
    If optSignature Then
        crRequest.KeySpec = KT_Signature
    Else
        crRequest.KeySpec = KT_KeyExchange
    End If
    Select Case True
        Case optCliAuth
            crRequest.KeyUsage = KU_ClientAuthentication
        Case optEMailProt
            crRequest.KeyUsage = KU_EMailProtection
        Case optServAuth
            crRequest.KeyUsage = KU_ServerAuthentication
        Case optCodeSign
            crRequest.KeyUsage = KU_CodeSigning
    End Select

    '--- Request the certificate
    If crRequest.DoCertRequest Then
    End If
End Sub
```

Now that you have the functionality to request the certificate, you need to trigger it from the Click event of the cmdReqCert button. To do so, add the code in Listing 5.13 to this event.

LISTING 5.13   The cmdReqCert Click Event

```
Private Sub cmdReqCert_Click()
    '--- Request a certificate
    DoCertReq
End Sub
```

Checking the Status and Getting the Certificate

The rest of the form functionality is fairly straightforward. You need to check the status of the request from the Click event of the cmdCheckStat button. This is a simple matter of calling the Certificate Request class' GetReqStatus method, as in Listing 5.14.

LISTING 5.14   The cmdCheckStat Click Event

```
Private Sub cmdCheckStat_Click()
    '--- Check the status of our certificate request
    crRequest.GetReqStatus
End Sub
```

The final piece of functionality is to retrieve the certificate from the cmdGetCert button. Here, you need to call the class' GetCert method from the Click event, as in Listing 5.15.

LISTING 5.15   The cmdGetCert Click Event

```
Private Sub cmdGetCert_Click()
    '--- Get the certificate
    crRequest.GetCert
End Sub
```

Running the Sample Application

Running this sample application requires having access to Certificate Server. You need to be able to issue the certificate fairly quickly because you didn't build in any functionality to maintain the certificate request ID across sessions. Therefore, you have to keep the application running until the certificate has been issued.

When you first start the application, you should fill in all the information on the form. Remember that the country code can be only two characters long. In the first text box, you enter the network name of the computer that has Certificate Server running on it. The second text box is the name of the Certificate Authority as configured in Certificate Server. Fill in the rest of the information as you see fit, as shown in Figure 5.5.

5

REQUESTING AND
RETRIEVING
CERTIFICATES

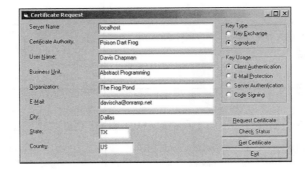

FIGURE 5.5
Running the sample application.

After you submit the certificate request to the server (assuming that you encountered no errors), you need to open the Certification Authority utility on the Certificate Server machine. This utility manages the certificates issued by Certificate Server. In this utility, there should be a folder containing certificate requests, and your certificate request should be located in this list. Find it and approve it (this process is also known as *resubmitting* it), as shown in Figure 5.6. In Certificate Server 2 (shipped with Windows 2000), you can resubmit it by right-clicking over your certificate and selecting Resubmit from the list of tasks.

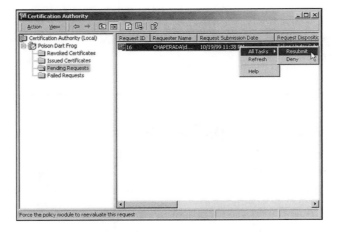

FIGURE 5.6
Issuing the certificate.

After the certificate has been issued, you can go back to your application and check the current status of the certificate. This action should automatically retrieve the certificate, placing it into your certificate store. To check, you can open the Properties dialog for Internet Explorer and then open the Certificates dialog from the Content tab. In the Certificates dialog, you should be able to find your new certificate in the Personal Certificates folder, as shown in Figure 5.7.

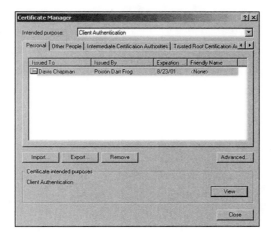

FIGURE 5.7
Viewing the certificate.

Summary

The topics covered in this chapter are key for building applications that communicate securely. To be able to establish the identity of the various parties that you are communicating with so that you know only the person you intend to read your messages is indeed the person you are sending them to, you need to use certificates. To be able to use certificates, you need the ability to request and retrieve certificates. Although part of what you learned in this chapter can only be used with Microsoft's Certificate Server, the process of actually creating the certificate requests can be used with any Certificate Authority, regardless of which Certificate Server they might be running.

In the next chapter, you'll dig into the certificate store and see how you can build applications to find certificates and to manage the certificates in your certificate store. This will be another key element to building complete and secure messaging applications.

Working with Certificates

IN THIS CHAPTER

- Managing Certificate Stores
- Managing Certificates and Certificate Contexts
- Getting Information from Certificates
- Building a Certificate Maintenance Utility

Now that you can issue certificate requests and retrieve issued certificates from the Certificate Authority, you need to know how to manage the certificates in your certificate store. You need to be able to find a particular certificate when you need it and remove old or expired certificates when you no longer need or want them.

In this chapter, you'll look at the Crypto API functionality that is used to manage the certificates you have stored on your computer. Although this is not one of the glamorous aspects of building encryption into your applications, it is still a very necessary aspect. Without the ability to manage your certificates, you cannot be sure that you are using the correct certificate for the purpose you're using it.

PREREQUISITES

Before reading this chapter, you need to make sure that you have a good understanding of the following:

- Asymmetric encryption and digital certificates, as covered in Chapter 1, "Understanding Encryption and Application Security"
- Selecting and opening Cryptographic Service Providers (CSP), as covered in Chapter 2, "Getting Started with the CryptoAPI"
- Hashing data, generating encryption keys, and encrypting and decrypting data, as covered in Chapter 3, "Symmetric and Password Encryption"
- Using public/private encryption keys, as covered in Chapter 4, "Public/Private Key Communications"
- Requesting and retrieving digital certificates, as covered in Chapter 5, "Requesting and Retrieving Certificates"

Managing Certificate Stores

The management of certificates is a very extensive area of functionality in the Crypto API. You can find functions for managing the certificate stores, managing the certificates, working with properties of certificates, and managing lists of trusted and revoked certificates. Some of this functionality can be used in Visual Basic, and some of it can't.

NOTE

This area of functionality uses many pointers to structures, a topic that would normally require diving into building DLLs with C or C++. However, with a lot of the functionality, you'll never need to touch any of the structures or the values they contain. As a result, you can often use a long variable for holding and passing around the pointers themselves. Holding pointers in long variables opens up a lot of functionality to the pure Visual Basic programmer.

The first area of functionality to look at is certificate store management. This area consists primarily of using functions for opening and closing certificate stores. Some other functions, such as those for enumerating the available certificate stores, don't work well within a pure Visual Basic programming idiom.

Opening Certificate Stores

The primary function for opening certificate stores is `CertOpenSystemStore`. When you use this function, it opens several related physical stores. You can use another function, `CertOpenStore`, to open a specific physical store, but it doesn't work well in Visual Basic. The syntax for the `CertOpenSystemStore` function is as follows:

Syntax

```
Public Declare Function CertOpenSystemStore Lib "Crypt32.dll" _
    Alias "CertOpenSystemStoreA" (ByVal hProv As Long, _
    ByVal szSubsystemProtocol As String) As Long
```

NOTE

`CertOpenStore` isn't easily used with Visual Basic because one of the parameters is a pointer to a pointer (a pointer passed by reference). You need to be able to use this pointer to point to various variable types, depending on how the function is being used. Although this is all possible in Visual Basic, it involves creating pointers to variables, and it's not essential for accomplishing what you need these functions to do. In a later chapter, you'll learn how to create pointers to variables without leaving Visual Basic.

The first parameter (`hProv`) to this function is the handle to the CSP. It must be a handle created by calling the `CryptAcquireContext` function. If a NULL value (0) is passed in, the default CSP is used.

The second parameter (`szSubsystemProtocol`) to this function is the name of the system certificate store to be opened. Some of the available system store names are listed in Table 6.1.

TABLE 6.1   System Certificate Store Names

Name	Description
CA	Certificate Authority certificates
MY	"My" certificates with their associated private keys
ROOT	Root certificates
SPC	Software Publisher Certificates

The return value from this function is a handle to the certificate store that has been opened. This handle will be used on subsequent calls to certificate store operations.

Closing Certificate Stores

After you finish working with the certificate store, you need to be sure to close it. You do so by using the CertCloseStore function. This function's syntax is as follows:

Syntax

```
Public Declare Function CertCloseStore Lib "Crypt32.dll" ( _
    ByVal hCertStore As Long, ByVal dwFlags As Long) As Long
```

The first parameter (hCertStore) to this function is the handle for the certificate store. This handle was returned from the CertOpenSystemStore function. The second parameter (dwFlags) is a flag that controls how the certificate store should be closed. By default, this parameter should be zero (0), but you can also use the values listed in Table 6.2.

TABLE 6.2   CertCloseStore Flag Values

Constant	Value	Description
CERT_CLOSE_STORE_CHECK_FLAG	&H2	Checks for Certificate, Certificate Trust List (CTL), and Certificate Revocation List (CRL) handles that have not been freed. This flag should be used only during development for testing purposes.
CERT_CLOSE_STORE_FORCE_FLAG	&H1	Forces the release of any Certificate, Certificate Trust List (CTL), or Certificate Revocation List (CRL) handles that have not been freed.

Duplicating the Store Handle

When you need to make a copy of a certificate store handle, you can use the CertDuplicateStore function. This function increments the store's reference count; therefore, you have to be sure to close both handles to the certificate store. The syntax for this function is as follows:

Syntax

```
Public Declare Function CertDuplicateStore Lib "Crypt32.dll" ( _
    hCertStore As Long) As Long
```

The parameter (hCertStore) to this function is the handle to the certificate store. This handle was returned from the CertOpenSystemStore function. The return value from this function is a second handle to the same certificate store.

Managing Certificates and Certificate Contexts

When you're working with certificates, you usually are actually working with a certificate context. In reality, you are working with a pointer to a certificate context. This normally makes this entire area of functionality a problem for Visual Basic programmers. However, rarely do you need to manipulate anything in the certificate context structure. You therefore can treat the pointer to the context structure as a long variable and just pass this variable value around. Using the pointer this way frees up a lot of certificate functionality so that it can be used with Visual Basic.

Creating a Certificate Context

When you have an encoded certificate, like the certificate retrieved from the Certificate Authority in the preceding chapter, you can convert it directly into a certificate context by using the CertCreateCertificateContext function. This function converts the encoded certificate into a certificate context, allowing you to use the certificate to verify signatures or to encrypt data using the public key enclosed, without storing the certificate in the certificate store. The syntax for this function is as follows:

Syntax

```
Public Declare Function CertCreateCertificateContext Lib "Crypt32.dll" ( _
    ByVal dwCertEncodingType As Long, ByVal pbCertEncoded As String, _
    ByVal cbCertEncoded As Long) As Long
```

The first parameter (dwCertEncodingType) is a flag that specifies the encoding and formatting used on the certificate. The currently defined encoding types, listed in Table 6.3, are often combined using a binary OR.

TABLE 6.3   Encoding Type Flag Values

Constant	Value	Description
X509_ASN_ENCODING	&H1	X.509 Encoding
PKCS_7_ASN_ENCODING	&H10000	PKCS #7 Message Formatting

The second parameter (pbCertEncoded) is a string containing the encoded certificate. The third parameter (cbCertEncoded) is the size of the certificate string passed in the second parameter.

The return value is a long value that is really a pointer to the certificate context. If the function fails, zero (0) is returned.

Duplicating a Certificate Context

When you need to duplicate a certificate, or in this case a certificate context (by incrementing the reference count), you can use the CertDuplicateCertificateContext function. The syntax for this function is as follows:

Syntax

```
Public Declare Function CertDuplicateCertificateContext _
    Lib "Crypt32.dll" (ByVal pCertContext As Long) As Long
```

> ### Reference Count
>
> A reference count is where various objects keep track of how many times they are being used. All COM objects do this. One of the reasons for this is so that the object can know when it's safe for it to be unloaded from memory. If an object has a reference count greater than zero, it is still being used and cannot be unloaded.

The one parameter (pCertContext) to this function is the certificate context pointer that you want to duplicate. The return value is a new pointer to the same certificate context.

Finding a Certificate

When you need to find a specific certificate in a certificate store, you can use the CertFindCertificateInStore function. You can use this function repeatedly to find all the certificates that match the search criteria. The syntax for this function is as follows:

Syntax

```
Public Declare Function CertFindCertificateInStore Lib "Crypt32.dll" ( _
    ByVal hCertStore As Long, ByVal dwCertEncodingType As Long, _
    ByVal dwFindFlags As Long, ByVal dwFindType As Long, _
    ByVal pvFindPara As String, ByVal pPrevCertContext As Long) As Long
```

An alternate declaration for this function is as follows:

Syntax

```
Public Declare Function CertDWFindCertificateInStore Lib "Crypt32.dll" _
    Alias "CertFindCertificateInStore" (ByVal hCertStore As Long, _
    ByVal dwCertEncodingType As Long, ByVal dwFindFlags As Long, _
    ByVal dwFindType As Long, ByRef pvFindPara As Long, _
    ByVal pPrevCertContext As Long) As Long
```

TIP

You can make a single declaration for this function specifying the fifth parameter (pvFindPara) as the Any data type, passing it by reference. If you do this, you'll need to be careful to pass any strings by value. The declaration for this version are as follows:

```
Public Declare Function CertFindCertificateInStore Lib "Crypt32.dll" ( _
    ByVal hCertStore As Long, ByVal dwCertEncodingType As Long, _
    ByVal dwFindFlags As Long, ByVal dwFindType As Long, _
    pvFindPara As Any, ByVal pPrevCertContext As Long) As Long
```

The first parameter (hCertStore) to this function is the handle to the certificate store. This same handle was returned from the CertOpenSystemStore function. The second parameter (dwCertEncodingType) specifies the encoding type of the certificate. These same encoding types were available for the CertCreateCertificateContext function, listed in Table 6.3.

The third parameter (dwFindFlags) is a flag value used to modify how certain searches are performed. The types of searches this value is used with do not lend themselves to use with Visual Basic, so for your purposes, this parameter should always be zero (0).

The fourth parameter (dwFindType) specifies how the find is being performed and what value the find is looking at. The practical (for Visual Basic) values for this parameter are listed in Table 6.4.

NOTE

The majority of find types require a pointer to a type structure to be passed in for the value to match. Most of these type structures contain pointers to other values that you would need to manipulate to specify the find criteria. As a result, these find types are not easily performed in pure Visual Basic without your dipping into a bit of C/C++ code. You are welcome to try your hand at using them, looking up the type codes and the type structures in the WinCrypt.h C/C++ header file and building your own DLL to perform the pointer manipulation. This approach will not be explored in this book.

TABLE 6.4   Certificate Find Type Values

Constant	Value	Description
CERT_FIND_ANY	&H0	Returns each certificate in the certificate store
CERT_FIND_EXISTING	&HD0000	Finds the certificate that is an exact match for the certificate context passed into this function.
CERT_FIND_ISSUER_OF	&HC0000	Finds a certificate that matches the issuer of the certificate context that is passed into this function
CERT_FIND_ISSUER_STR	&H70004	Finds a certificate that the issuer name matches the string passed into this function
CERT_FIND_KEY_SPEC	&H90000	Finds a certificate having the same key specification as the one passed in to this function
CERT_FIND_PROPERTY	&H50000	Finds a certificate with the property specified by the property identifier passed in to this function
CERT_FIND_SUBJECT_STR	&H70007	Finds a certificate containing the specified subject name string

The fifth parameter (pvFindPara) to this function is the value to be searched for. For the two string criteria (CERT_FIND_ISSUER_STR and CERT_FIND_SUBJECT_STR), the first version of the function (CertFindCertificateInStore) is used. For the rest, the second version of the function (CertDWFindCertificateInStore) is used.

The sixth parameter (pPrevCertContext) is the last certificate context returned by this function. On the first call to this function, this parameter should be zero (0).

The return value from this function is a pointer to a certificate context. As with any other certificate context pointer, this one should be freed using the CertFreeCertificateContext function that you'll be looking at later.

NOTE

In this and other functions that take the previously returned certificate context pointers, the CertFreeCertificateContext function is automatically called on the previous certificate context pointer that is passed in. This action occurs even if the function is unsuccessful at returning a new certificate context pointer.

Enumerating Certificates

When you need to loop through all the certificates in a particular certificate store, you can use the CertEnumCertificatesInStore function. The syntax for this function is as follows:

Syntax

```
Public Declare Function CertEnumCertificatesInStore Lib "Crypt32.dll" ( _
    ByVal hCertStore As Long, ByVal pPrevCertContext As Long) As Long
```

The first parameter (hCertStore) to this function is the handle to the certificate store. The second parameter (pPrevCertContext) is the pointer to the previous certificate context returned by this function. The first time this function is called, the second parameter should be zero (0). The return value from this function is a pointer to a new certificate context.

Getting an Issuer Certificate

When you want to retrieve the certificate of the issuer of a certificate from the certificate store, you can use the CertGetIssuerCertificateFromStore function. The syntax for this function is as follows:

Syntax

```
Public Declare Function CertGetIssuerCertificateFromStore _
    Lib "Crypt32.dll" (ByVal hCertStore As Long, _
    ByVal pSubjectContext As Long, ByVal pPrevIssuerContext As Long, _
    ByRef pdwFlags As Long) As Long
```

The first parameter (hCertStore) to this function is the handle to the certificate store. The second parameter (pSubjectContext) is the pointer to the certificate for which you want to retrieve the issuer certificates.

The third parameter (pPrevIssuerContext) is the pointer to the previous issuer certificate. On the first call to this function, this parameter must be zero (0).

NOTE

Certificate Authorities can often have multiple certificates, especially when close to the expiration date of one of their certificates.

The fourth parameter (pdwFlags) is a long variable in which a flag value is passed and returned. This flag can be passed through a bitwise AND to determine the various flag values that have been set on return. You can use a bitwise OR to combine values for controlling how the search is performed. The possible values are listed in Table 6.5.

TABLE 6.5   Certificate Issuer Retrieval Status Flags

Constant	Value	Description
CERT_STORE_NO_CRL_FLAG	&H10000	No matching CRL was found.
CERT_STORE_NO_ISSUER_FLAG	&H20000	No issuer certificate was found.
CERT_STORE_REVOCATION_FLAG	&H4	Checks to see whether the subject certificate is on the issuer's revocation list.
CERT_STORE_SIGNATURE_FLAG	&H1	Checks to see whether the signature of the subject certificate is valid using the issuer's public key.
CERT_STORE_TIME_VALIDITY_FLAG	&H2	Checks to see whether the subject certificate's validity period has expired.

For the last three of the flags in Table 6.5, if the verification check is successful, the flag is set to zero (0), so you do need to perform the bitwise check to verify the flag values after the function returns.

The return value from this function is a pointer to the certificate context of the issuer certificate. If no certificate is found, the return value is zero (0).

Serializing a Certificate

When you need to be able to store a certificate on a disk or other storage media, possibly even send it to another application, you can serialize the certificate, along with its properties, by using the CertSerializeCertificateStoreElement function. This function places the certificate and its properties into a string variable. The syntax for this function is as follows:

`Syntax`

```
Public Declare Function CertSerializeCertificateStoreElement _
    Lib "Crypt32.dll" (ByVal pCertContext As Long, _
    ByVal dwFlags As Long, ByVal pbElement As String, _
    pcbElement As Long) As Long
```

The first parameter (pCertContext) to this function is the pointer to the certificate context. This same long value was returned by the function used to retrieve the certificate from the certificate store. The second parameter (dwFlags) is reserved for future use and must always by zero (0).

The third parameter (pbElement) is the string variable into which the certificate will be placed. This variable must be sized to hold the certificate prior to calling this function. If the NULL string (vbNullString) is passed in this variable, the fourth parameter (pcbElement) will return the size of the string needed to hold the certificate and its properties.

The fourth parameter (pcbElement) is a long variable that specifies the size of the string variable passed in the third parameter. After the function has completed, this variable will contain the actual size of the certificate in the string variable.

You might use this function as follows:

```
Dim lCertSize As Long
Dim lResult As Long
Dim sCert as String

'--- Null the target string, so we can get the size of the string
'--- that will be exported
lCertSize = 0

'--- Call CertSerializeCertificateStoreElement with the nulled string.
'--- This will give us the required string size that will be needed to
'--- hold the exported key
lResult = CertSerializeCertificateStoreElement (m_lCertContext, 0, _
        vbNullString, lCertSize)

'--- Size the target string for the size specified, filling it with
'--- null characters
sCert = String(lCertSize, vbNullChar)

'--- Serialize the certificate
If Not CBool(CertSerializeCertificateStoreElement (m_lCertContext, 0, _
        sCert, lCertSize)) Then
    '--- Perform error handling
```

Verifying a Certificate

When you need to verify that a certificate is still valid, you can use the `CertVerifySubject`
➥`CertificateContext` function. This function checks the aspects of the certificate that you
specify, which are the same aspects that can be verified with the `CertGetIssuerCertificate`
➥`FromStore` function. The syntax for this function is as follows:

Syntax

```
Public Declare Function CertVerifySubjectCertificateContext _
    Lib "Crypt32.dll" (ByVal pSubject As Long, _
    ByVal pIssuer As Long, pdwFlags As Long) As Long
```

The first parameter (`pSubject`) for this function is the pointer to the certificate context of the
certificate to be verified. The second parameter (`pIssuer`) is the pointer to the certificate context of the issuer's certificate. This parameter can be zero (`0`) if the only aspect being checked
is to verify that the certificate isn't past its expiration date.

The third parameter (`pdwFlags`) is a set of flags that specify which aspects of the certificate to
check. These flags can be set using the `OR` statement and verified using an `AND`. When the certificate passes one of the checks, that flag is set to zero (`0`). The available flags are listed in
Table 6.6.

TABLE 6.6   Certificate Verification Status Flags

Constant	Value	Description
CERT_STORE_REVOCATION_FLAG	&H4	Checks to see whether the subject certificate is on the issuer's revocation list
CERT_STORE_SIGNATURE_FLAG	&H1	Checks to see whether the signature of the subject certificate is valid using the issuer's public key
CERT_STORE_TIME_VALIDITY_FLAG	&H2	Checks to see whether the subject certificate's validity period has expired

Deleting a Certificate

When you want to delete a particular certificate from a certificate store, you can use the
`CertDeleteCertificateFromStore` function. The syntax for this function is as follows:

Syntax

```
Public Declare Function CertDeleteCertificateFromStore _
    Lib "Crypt32.dll" (ByVal pCertContext As Long) As Long
```

The only parameter (pCertContext) to this function is the pointer to the certificate context.

NOTE

The CertDeleteCertificateFromStore function deletes the certificate from the certificate store and frees the certificate context being pointed at by the parameter passed in. However, if you have duplicate certificate contexts, you still need to free all of them to release the resources being held by the contexts.

Freeing a Certificate Context

After you have finished with a particular certificate context, you need to be sure to release the resources being held by the certificate context by calling the CertFreeCertificateContext function. The syntax for this function is as follows:

Syntax

```
Public Declare Function CertFreeCertificateContext _
    Lib "Crypt32.dll" (ByVal pCertContext As Long) As Long
```

The only parameter (pCertContext) to this function is the pointer to the certificate context.

TIP

Remember that functions that replace a passed-in context with a new context automatically delete the passed-in context, even if the function call fails. So be sure that you only use the CertFreeCertificateContext function to delete contexts that are still valid.

Getting Information from Certificates

Getting information from a certificate isn't an easy prospect when you're working with Visual Basic. The Certificate Context type structure includes a pointer to a Certificate Information type structure that contains most of the information you would want about the certificate. This information includes the certificate serial number, the issuer, the subject, the valid date range for the certificate, and other information. Unfortunately, this information is off-limits unless you dip into a little bit of C/C++ code in a DLL. (Actually, this information isn't as off-limits as you might think, as you'll discover in another chapter.)

Although building a DLL to access those properties is tempting, this is a Visual Basic book, so let's look at what's available without leaving the language. In fact, a couple of functions can be used with Visual Basic to get a lot of this information from the certificate context. Although you might not be able to get everything, you can still get a lot of information and most of what you really need.

Enumerating Certificate Properties

Not all the available certificate properties are included in every certificate. Some properties depend on the type of certificate and how the certificate is to be used. Therefore, it is a good idea to enumerate the properties of a certificate to determine which properties are available and which ones aren't. To do so, you use the CertEnumCertificateContextProperties function. The syntax for this function is as follows:

Syntax

```
Private Declare Function CertEnumCertificateContextProperties _
    Lib "Crypt32.dll" (ByVal pCertContext As Long, _
    ByVal dwPropId As Long) As Long
```

The first parameter (pCertContext) to this function is the pointer to the certificate context. The second parameter (dwPropId) is the ID of the last property returned by this function. The first time this function is called, this parameter should be zero (0).

The return value is the ID of the current property. This function should be called in a loop until the return value is zero (0). The possible properties are listed in Table 6.7.

TABLE 6.7   Certificate Property IDs

Property ID	Value	Description
CERT_ACCESS_STATE_PROP_ID	14	A long value that can be passed through the CBool function to determine whether changes to the certificate will be preserved.
CERT_AUTO_ENROLL_PROP_ID	21	A string that names the certificate type for which this certificate has been auto enrolled.
CERT_DESCRIPTION_PROP_ID	13	A description of the certificate's usage.
CERT_ENHKEY_USAGE_PROP_ID	9	An array of bytes that contain an ASN.1-encoded CERT_ENHKEY_USAGE type structure.

Property ID	Value	Description
CERT_FRIENDLY_NAME_PROP_ID	11	A string containing the friendly name for the certificate.
CERT_HASH_PROP_ID	3	The SHA1 hash of the certificate.
CERT_KEY_CONTEXT_PROP_ID	5	A CERT_KEY_CONTEXT type structure containing certain information about the certificate.
CERT_KEY_IDENTIFIER_PROP_ID	20	An identifier for the public key information.
CERT_KEY_PROV_HANDLE_PROP_ID	1	The provider handle from the CERT_KEY_CONTEXT type structure from the CERT_KEY_CONTEXT_PROP_ID property.
CERT_KEY_PROV_INFO_PROP_ID	2	A CRYPT_KEY_PROV_INFO type structure containing certain information about the certificate.
CERT_KEY_SPEC_PROP_ID	6	A long value specifying the private key from the CERT_KEY_CONTEXT type structure from the CERT_KEY_CONTEXT_PROP_ID property, if it exists. If that property doesn't exist, this property is derived from the CRYPT_KEY_PROV_INFO type structure from the CERT_KEY_PROV_INFO_PROP_ID property.
CERT_MD5_HASH_PROP_ID	4	The MD5 hash of the certificate.
CERT_PVK_FILE_PROP_ID	12	The filename containing the private key associated with the public key in the certificate.
CERT_SIGNATURE_HASH_PROP_ID	15	The signature hash.

Getting Property Values

Although you can use the CertEnumCertificateContextProperties function to determine which properties exist for a certificate, it doesn't provide you with the value of those properties. To find the values, you need to use the CertGetCertificateContextProperty function. You should declare at least two—if not three or four—versions of this function to be able to retrieve all the different properties from the certificate. The basic declaration for this function is as follows:

Syntax

```
Private Declare Function CertGetCertificateContextProperty _
    Lib "Crypt32.dll" (ByVal pCertContext As Long, _
    ByVal dwPropId As Long, ByVal pvData As String, _
    ByRef pcbData As Long) As Long
```

Because some of the properties are long values, you also should declare a second version as follows:

Syntax

```
Private Declare Function CertGetCertificateContextDWProperty _
    Lib "Crypt32.dll" Alias "CertGetCertificateContextProperty" ( _
    ByVal pCertContext As Long, ByVal dwPropId As Long, _
    ByRef pvData As Long, ByRef pcbData As Long) As Long
```

Because one property has a value that is a CERT_KEY_CONTEXT type structure, you might want to declare a third version along with the type definition for this structure as follows:

Syntax

```
Private Type CERT_KEY_CONTEXT
    cbSize As Long              ' size of CERT_KEY_CONTEXT
    hCryptProv As Long          ' handle of the CSP
    dwKeySpec As Long           ' Key Specification (e.g. Signature
                                ' or Key Exchange)
End Type

Private Declare Function CertGetCertificateContextKCProperty _
    Lib "Crypt32.dll" Alias "CertGetCertificateContextProperty" ( _
    ByVal pCertContext As Long, ByVal dwPropId As Long, _
    ByRef pvData As CERT_KEY_CONTEXT, ByRef pcbData As Long) As Long
```

And because another property has a value that is a CRYPT_KEY_PROV_INFO type structure, you can declare a fourth version of this function as follows:

Syntax

```
Type CRYPT_KEY_PROV_INFO
    pwszContainerName As Long   ' Pointer to the container name string
    pwszProvName As Long        ' Pointer to the CSP name
    dwProvType As Long          ' The provider type
    dwFlags As Long             ' Flags indicating whether a key
                                ' container is to be destroyed
    cProvParam As Long          ' Number of elements in the Key Prov
                                ' Param array
    rgProvParam As Long         ' Pointer to an array of
                                ' CRYPT_KEY_PROV_PARAM types
    dwKeySpec As Long           ' The key specification
                                ' (e.g. Signature or Key Exchange)
End Type
```

```
Private Declare Function CertGetCertificateContextKPIProperty _
    Lib "Crypt32.dll" Alias "CertGetCertificateContextProperty" ( _
    ByVal pCertContext As Long, ByVal dwPropId As Long, _
    ByRef pvData As CRYPT_KEY_PROV_INFO, ByRef pcbData As Long) As Long
```

> **TIP**
>
> For reasons that will be explained in the sample application, you will more likely use the original version of this function instead of the fourth version in your applications. It is advisable to be familiar with the CRYPT_KEY_PROV_INFO type structure so that you can understand how values are extracted from the string that is returned in the first version of the CertGetCertificateContextProperty function.

> **TIP**
>
> As with other functions that require multiple data types for a single parameter, you can make a single declaration for this function specifying the third parameter (pvData) as the Any data type, passing it by reference. If you do this, you'll need to be careful to pass any strings by value. The declaration for this version is as follows:
>
> ```
> Private Declare Function CertGetCertificateContextProperty _
>     Lib "Crypt32.dll" (ByVal pCertContext As Long, _
>     ByVal dwPropId As Long, pvData As Any, _
>     pcbData As Long) As Long
> ```

The first parameter (pCertContext) for this function is the pointer to the certificate context. The second parameter (dwPropId) is the property ID to be retrieved. The available property IDs and their values are listed in Table 6.7. Table 6.8 contains the list of the property IDs and identifies which version of the CertGetCertificateContextProperty function should be used.

TABLE 6.8 Certificate Property IDs and the Function Version to Use

Property ID	Function Version
CERT_ACCESS_STATE_PROP_ID	2
CERT_ARCHIVED_PROP_ID	2
CERT_AUTO_ENROLL_PROP_ID	1
CERT_DESCRIPTION_PROP_ID	1
CERT_ENHKEY_USAGE_PROP_ID	1
CERT_FRIENDLY_NAME_PROP_ID	1

continues

TABLE 6.8   Continued

Property ID	Function Version
CERT_HASH_PROP_ID	1
CERT_KEY_CONTEXT_PROP_ID	3
CERT_KEY_IDENTIFIER_PROP_ID	1
CERT_KEY_PROV_HANDLE_PROP_ID	2
CERT_KEY_PROV_INFO_PROP_ID	1 (4)
CERT_KEY_SPEC_PROP_ID	2
CERT_MD5_HASH_PROP_ID	1
CERT_PVK_FILE_PROP_ID	1
CERT_SIGNATURE_HASH_PROP_ID	1

The third parameter (pvData) is a variable into which will be placed the value of the property being requested. The fourth parameter (pcbData) is a long variable containing the size of the third parameter. If the variable in the third parameter is not large enough to hold the property value, the necessary size is returned in the fourth parameter variable. Therefore, you can pass the NULL string (vbNullString) in the string variable for the third parameter and zero (0) in the long variable for the fourth parameter to the first version of the function to get the size of string necessary to hold the property value.

Setting Certificate Properties

Although most of the certificate properties are technically updateable, most of them cannot be easily updated using Visual Basic because of all the pointers in the various type structures being passed about. A few properties can be easily set using Visual Basic, however. You set these properties by using the CertSetCertificateContextProperty function. The syntax for this function is as follows:

Syntax

```
Public Declare Function CertSetCertificateContextProperty _
    Lib "Crypt32.dll" (ByVal pCertContext As Long, _
    ByVal dwPropId As Long, ByVal dwFlags As Long, _
    ByRef pvData As Any) As Long
```

The first parameter (pCertContext) to this function is the pointer to the certificate context. The second parameter (dwPropId) is the property ID for the property being set. The properties available for updating with a purely Visual Basic approach are listed in Table 6.9.

TABLE 6.9   Updateable Certificate Property IDs and the Data Type to Use

Property ID	Variable Data Type
CERT_ARCHIVED_PROP_ID	Long (value must be 0)
CERT_KEY_CONTEXT_PROP_ID	CERT_KEY_CONTEXT
CERT_KEY_PROV_HANDLE_PROP_ID	Long (CSP handle for the private key)
CERT_KEY_SPEC_PROP_ID	Long (key spec for the private key)

The third parameter (dwFlags) is a flag that specifies how the property is to be updated. Usually, it is zero (0), but for the CERT_KEY_CONTEXT_PROP_ID and CERT_KEY_PROV_HANDLE_PROP_ID properties, this value can be set to the CERT_STORE_NO_CRYPT_RELEASE_FLAG (0x1) flag, which indicates that the CSP handle acquired in performing this function should not be released upon completion of the function.

The fourth parameter (pvData) is a variable holding the new value for the specified certificate property.

Getting the Subject Name

When you need to retrieve the subject name of a certificate, you can avoid going the properties route completely by using the CertGetNameString function. This function can be used to retrieve the subject name, email address, or other aspects of the certificate name. The syntax for this function is as follows:

Syntax

```
Private Declare Function CertGetNameString Lib "Crypt32.dll" _
    Alias "CertGetNameStringA" (ByVal pCertContext As Long, _
    ByVal dwType As Long, ByVal dwFlags As Long, _
    ByRef pvTypePara As Any, ByVal pszNameString As String, _
    ByVal cchNameString As Long) As Long
```

The first parameter (pCertContext) for this function is the pointer to the certificate context. The second parameter (dwType) is the type of name that you want to retrieve for the certificate specified. The available name types are listed in Table 6.10.

TABLE 6.10   Certificate Name Types

Name Type	Value	Description
CERT_NAME_EMAIL_TYPE	1	Returns this name if the certificate has an email address attached to it
CERT_NAME_ATTR_TYPE	3	Returns the name attribute specified by the OID passed in the fourth parameter
CERT_NAME_SIMPLE_DISPLAY_TYPE	4	Returns the first of either the common name, organizational unit name, organization name, or email address that is found

The third parameter (dwFlags) is a flag value that specifies how the name is returned. Usually, you should pass zero (0) for this parameter. The available flag values that you can pass are listed in Table 6.11.

TABLE 6.11   Certificate Name Flags

Name Type	Value	Description
CERT_NAME_ISSUER_FLAG	&H1	Returns the issuer's name instead of the subject name
CERT_NAME_DISABLE_IE4_UTF8_FLAG	&H10000	Decodes the name as 8-bit characters

The fourth parameter (pvTypePara) is used to specify which name attribute is returned if the name type is the CERT_NAME_ATTR_TYPE type. Otherwise, this parameter should always be zero (0). For the CERT_NAME_ATTR_TYPE, the available OID values are listed in Table 6.12.

TABLE 6.12   Certificate Name Attribute OIDs

Name Attribute	Value
szOID_COMMON_NAME	2.5.4.3
szOID_COUNTRY_NAME	2.5.4.6
szOID_LOCALITY_NAME	2.5.4.7
szOID_STATE_OR_PROVINCE_NAME	2.5.4.8
szOID_ORGANIZATION_NAME	2.5.4.10
szOID_ORGANIZATIONAL_UNIT_NAME	2.5.4.11

> **NOTE**
>
> The certificate name attribute OIDs provided in Table 6.12 are the common attributes that you are likely to find in most certificates. However, this list is not complete. Many more name attribute OIDs are defined in the WinCrypt.h C++ header file; you can declare them if you want to be able to retrieve all possible certificate name attributes.

The fifth parameter (pszNameString) is a string variable into which the name will be placed. This string must already have been sized prior to calling this function. The sixth parameter (cchNameString) is a long variable that contains the size of the string variable in the fifth parameter when calling this function.

The return value is the length of the name string returned. If the string is empty, the return value is the size of string required to hold the certificate name requested.

Building a Certificate Maintenance Utility

Now, to see how some of this certificate management functionality works, you'll build a utility that lists the certificates and all the properties that can be enumerated. This utility will provide a combo box that lists the primary stock certificate stores from which the user can select. After the user has selected a certificate store, the utility will open the specified certificate store and enumerate all the certificates in that store. It will enumerate all the properties of each certificate. For each property, it will get the current value of the property and display all the information in a big list for the user to see.

Creating the Project

To start this new project, start a new standard EXE project in Visual Basic. Copy the clsCrypto.cls file from the example you built for Chapter 4 into the project directory for this project, and add the file to the project. Next, add the new constants, types, and API function declarations to the clsCrytpo class that are given in Listing 6.1. You can split them up so that the constants are with the other constants, the types are after the constants, and the API function declarations are with the other API function declarations.

LISTING 6.1 New Constant, Function, and Variable Declarations

```
'+--------------------------------------------------------------
'   Certificate name types
'-----------------------------------------------------------------
Private Const CERT_NAME_EMAIL_TYPE = 1
Private Const CERT_NAME_RDN_TYPE = 2
```

continues

LISTING 6.1   Continued

```
Private Const CERT_NAME_ATTR_TYPE = 3
Private Const CERT_NAME_SIMPLE_DISPLAY_TYPE = 4
Private Const CERT_NAME_FRIENDLY_DISPLAY_TYPE = 5

Private Const CERT_SYSTEM_STORE_MASK = &HFFFF0000


'+--------------------------------------------------------------------------
'  Certificate, CRL and CTL property IDs
'
'  See CertSetCertificateContextProperty
'  or CertGetCertificateContextProperty
'  for usage information.
'--------------------------------------------------------------------------
Private Const CERT_KEY_PROV_HANDLE_PROP_ID = 1
Private Const CERT_KEY_PROV_INFO_PROP_ID = 2
Private Const CERT_SHA1_HASH_PROP_ID = 3
Private Const CERT_MD5_HASH_PROP_ID = 4
Private Const CERT_HASH_PROP_ID = CERT_SHA1_HASH_PROP_ID
Private Const CERT_KEY_CONTEXT_PROP_ID = 5
Private Const CERT_KEY_SPEC_PROP_ID = 6
Private Const CERT_IE30_RESERVED_PROP_ID = 7
Private Const CERT_PUBKEY_HASH_RESERVED_PROP_ID = 8
Private Const CERT_ENHKEY_USAGE_PROP_ID = 9
Private Const CERT_CTL_USAGE_PROP_ID = CERT_ENHKEY_USAGE_PROP_ID
Private Const CERT_NEXT_UPDATE_LOCATION_PROP_ID = 10
Private Const CERT_FRIENDLY_NAME_PROP_ID = 11
Private Const CERT_PVK_FILE_PROP_ID = 12
Private Const CERT_DESCRIPTION_PROP_ID = 13
Private Const CERT_ACCESS_STATE_PROP_ID = 14
Private Const CERT_SIGNATURE_HASH_PROP_ID = 15
Private Const CERT_SMART_CARD_DATA_PROP_ID = 16
Private Const CERT_EFS_PROP_ID = 17
Private Const CERT_FORTEZZA_DATA_PROP_ID = 18
Private Const CERT_ARCHIVED_PROP_ID = 19
Private Const CERT_KEY_IDENTIFIER_PROP_ID = 20
Private Const CERT_AUTO_ENROLL_PROP_ID = 21
Private Const CERT_PUBKEY_ALG_PARA_PROP_ID = 22

Private Const CERT_FIRST_RESERVED_PROP_ID = 23
' Note, 32 - 35 are reserved for the CERT, CRL, CTL and
' KeyId file element IDs.

Private Const CERT_LAST_RESERVED_PROP_ID = &H7FFF
Private Const CERT_FIRST_USER_PROP_ID = &H8000
Private Const CERT_LAST_USER_PROP_ID = &HFFFF
```

```
Private Type CRYPT_KEY_PROV_PARAM
    dwParam As Long
    pbData As Long
    cbData As Long
    dwFlags As Long
End Type

Private Type CRYPT_KEY_PROV_INFO
    pwszContainerName As Long
    pwszProvName As Long
    dwProvType As Long
    dwFlags As Long
    cProvParam As Long
    rgProvParam As Long
    dwKeySpec As Long
End Type

Private Type CERT_KEY_CONTEXT
    cbSize As Long                ' sizeof(CERT_KEY_CONTEXT)
    hCryptProv As Long
    dwKeySpec As Long
End Type

Private Declare Function CertOpenSystemStore Lib "Crypt32.dll" _
    Alias "CertOpenSystemStoreA" (ByVal hProv As Long, _
    ByVal szSubsystemProtocol As String) As Long

Private Declare Function CertEnumCertificatesInStore _
    Lib "Crypt32.dll" ( _
    ByVal hCertStore As Long, ByVal pPrevCertContext As Long) As Long

Private Declare Function CertEnumCertificateContextProperties _
    Lib "Crypt32.dll" (ByVal pCertContext As Long, _
    ByVal dwPropId As Long) As Long

Private Declare Function CertGetCertificateContextProperty _
    Lib "Crypt32.dll" (ByVal pCertContext As Long, _
    ByVal dwPropId As Long, ByVal pvData As String, _
    ByRef pcbData As Long) As Long

Private Declare Function CertGetCertificateContextDWProperty _
    Lib "Crypt32.dll" Alias "CertGetCertificateContextProperty" ( _
    ByVal pCertContext As Long, ByVal dwPropId As Long, _
    ByRef pvData As Long, ByRef pcbData As Long) As Long

Private Declare Function CertGetCertificateContextKCProperty _
    Lib "Crypt32.dll" Alias "CertGetCertificateContextProperty" ( _
```

continues

LISTING 6.1   Continued

```
    ByVal pCertContext As Long, ByVal dwPropId As Long, _
    ByRef pvData As CERT_KEY_CONTEXT, ByRef pcbData As Long) As Long

Private Declare Function CertGetCertificateContextKPIProperty _
    Lib "Crypt32.dll" Alias "CertGetCertificateContextProperty" ( _
    ByVal pCertContext As Long, ByVal dwPropId As Long, _
    ByRef pvData As CRYPT_KEY_PROV_INFO, ByRef pcbData As Long) As Long

Private Declare Function CertFreeCertificateContext Lib "Crypt32.dll" ( _
    ByVal pCertContext As Long) As Long

Private Declare Function CertCloseStore Lib "Crypt32.dll" ( _
    ByVal hCertStore As Long, ByVal dwFlags As Long) As Long

Private Declare Function CertGetNameString Lib "Crypt32.dll" _
    Alias "CertGetNameStringA" (ByVal pCertContext As Long, _
    ByVal dwType As Long, ByVal dwFlags As Long, _
    ByRef pvTypePara As Long, ByVal pszNameString As String, _
    ByVal cchNameString As Long) As Long
```

Listing the Certificates

Next, you'll add a rather oversized function that lists the certificates and their properties to the crypto class. This function will call a few functions that you'll define after you have hashed out the basic function. This function will first open the specified certificate store. Next, it will enumerate all the certificates in a loop. Within that loop, it will enumerate all the certificate properties within a second loop. Within the second loop, it will determine which version of the CertGetCertificateContextProperty function to use and then use it to get the current value of the property. To add all this functionality, add the ListCerts function in Listing 6.2 to the crypto class.

LISTING 6.2   The ListCerts Function

```
Public Function ListCerts(pszStoreName As String) As String
'****************************************************************
'* Written By: Davis Chapman
'* Date:       October 12, 1999
'*
'* Syntax:     ListCerts(pszStoreName)
'*
'* Parameters: pszStoreName As String
'*
'* Purpose: This will loop through all of the certificates in
```

```
'*          the specified store, listing the available
'*          properties of each in turn. It builds this
'*          information as a large text string that is returned
'*          to the calling function to be displayed to the user.
'**************************************************************

    On Error GoTo ListCertsErr

    Dim hCertStore As Long
    Dim pszNameString As String * 256
    Dim pvData As String
    Dim dwData As Long
    Dim kcData As CERT_KEY_CONTEXT
    Dim kpiData As CRYPT_KEY_PROV_INFO
    Dim cbData As Long
    Dim dwPropId As Long
    Dim strMsg As String
    Dim lpCertContext As Long
    Dim szStoreName As String
    Dim szRtnMsg As String
    Dim iPos As Integer
    Dim iVerToUse As Integer

    szRtnMsg = ""
    dwPropId = 0

    '--- Open a system certificate store.
    hCertStore = CertOpenSystemStore(0, pszStoreName)

    '--- Did we open a store?
    If (hCertStore <> 0) Then
        szRtnMsg = "The " + pszStoreName + " store has been opened." +

➥vbCrLf
    Else
        m_sErrorMsg = "Error during CertOpenSystemStore - " & _
            CStr(Err.LastDllError) & Error$
        MsgBox m_sErrorMsg, vbOKOnly, "VB Crypto"
        Exit Function
    End If

    '--- Use CertEnumCertificatesInStore to get the certificates
    '--- from the open store.
    lpCertContext = CertEnumCertificatesInStore(hCertStore, 0)

    '--- Loop until all certificates have been retrieved
    While (lpCertContext <> 0)
```

continues

LISTING 6.2   Continued

```
'--- A certificate was retrieved.
'--- Get the name from the certificate.
If (CertGetNameString(lpCertContext, _
        CERT_NAME_SIMPLE_DISPLAY_TYPE, _
        0, 0, pszNameString, 128)) Then

    '--- Find the end of the name
    iPos = InStr(1, pszNameString, vbNullChar, vbBinaryCompare)
    '--- Strip off the remaining NULL characters
    If iPos> 0 Then
            ➡pszNameString = Left(pszNameString, (iPos - 1))
    '--- Tell the user the name of the certificate
    szRtnMsg = szRtnMsg + vbCrLf + "Certificate for " + _
        Trim$(pszNameString) + vbCrLf
Else
    m_sErrorMsg = "Error during CertGetNameString - " & _
        CStr(Err.LastDllError) & Error$
    MsgBox m_sErrorMsg, vbOKOnly, "VB Crypto"
End If

'--- Loop to find all of the property identifiers for the
'--- specified certificate. The loop continues until
'--- CertEnumCertificateContextProperties returns zero.
dwPropId = CertEnumCertificateContextProperties( _
        lpCertContext, dwPropId)
While (dwPropId <> 0)

    '--- When the loop is executed, a property identifier has
    '--- been found, print the property number.
    strMsg = "Property # " + Str(dwPropId) + " found -> "

    '--- Initialize the property data type indicator
    iVerToUse = 1

    '---  Indicate the kind of property found.
    Select Case dwPropId
        Case CERT_FRIENDLY_NAME_PROP_ID
            strMsg = strMsg + "Friendly name: "
            iVerToUse = 5
        Case CERT_SIGNATURE_HASH_PROP_ID
            strMsg = strMsg + "Signature hash identifier "
        Case CERT_KEY_PROV_HANDLE_PROP_ID
            strMsg = strMsg + "KEY PROVE HANDLE "
            iVerToUse = 2
        Case CERT_KEY_PROV_INFO_PROP_ID
```

```
            strMsg = strMsg + "KEY PROV INFO PROP ID "
            iVerToUse = 4
    Case CERT_SHA1_HASH_PROP_ID
            strMsg = strMsg + "SHA1 HASH identifier "
    Case CERT_MD5_HASH_PROP_ID
            strMsg = strMsg + "md5 hash identifier "
    Case CERT_KEY_CONTEXT_PROP_ID
            strMsg = strMsg + "KEY CONTEXT PROP identifier "
    Case CERT_KEY_SPEC_PROP_ID
            strMsg = strMsg + "KEY SPEC PROP identifier "
            iVerToUse = 2
    Case CERT_ENHKEY_USAGE_PROP_ID
            strMsg = strMsg + "ENHKEY USAGE PROP identifier "
    Case CERT_NEXT_UPDATE_LOCATION_PROP_ID
            strMsg = strMsg + _
                    ➥"NEXT UPDATE LOCATION PROP identifier "
    Case CERT_PVK_FILE_PROP_ID
            strMsg = strMsg + "PVK FILE PROP identifier "
    Case CERT_DESCRIPTION_PROP_ID
            strMsg = strMsg + "DESCRIPTION PROP identifier "
            iVerToUse = 5
    Case CERT_ACCESS_STATE_PROP_ID
            strMsg = strMsg + "ACCESS STATE PROP identifier "
            iVerToUse = 2
    Case CERT_SMART_CARD_DATA_PROP_ID
            strMsg = strMsg + "SMART_CARD DATA PROP identifier "
    Case CERT_EFS_PROP_ID
            strMsg = strMsg + "EFS PROP identifier "
    Case CERT_FORTEZZA_DATA_PROP_ID
            strMsg = strMsg + "FORTEZZA DATA PROP identifier "
    Case CERT_ARCHIVED_PROP_ID
            strMsg = strMsg + "ARCHIVED PROP identifier "
            iVerToUse = 2
    Case CERT_KEY_IDENTIFIER_PROP_ID
            strMsg = strMsg + "KEY IDENTIFIER PROP identifier "
    Case CERT_AUTO_ENROLL_PROP_ID
            strMsg = strMsg + "AUTO ENROLL identifier. "
End Select

'--- Determine how to retrieve the property value based on the
'--- property type
Select Case iVerToUse
    Case 2
        '--- Set the value size
        cbData = 4
        '--- Retrieve the property value
        If (Not CBool(CertGetCertificateContextDWProperty( _
```

continues

LISTING 6.2   Continued

```
                    lpCertContext, dwPropId, _
                    dwData, cbData))) Then
            '--- Unable to retrieve the property value
            m_sErrorMsg = "Error during " & _
                "CertGetCertificateContextDWProperty - " & _
                CStr(Err.LastDllError) & Error$
            MsgBox m_sErrorMsg, vbOKOnly, "VB Crypto"
        End If

        '--- Show the results.
        strMsg = strMsg + vbCrLf + _
            "The Property Content is " + Str(dwData)

    Case 3
        '--- Set the value size
        cbData = 12
        '--- Retrieve the property value
        If (Not CBool(CertGetCertificateContextKCProperty( _
                lpCertContext, dwPropId, _
                kcData, cbData))) Then
            '--- Unable to retrieve the property value
            m_sErrorMsg = "Error during " & _
                "CertGetCertificateContextKCProperty - " & _
                CStr(Err.LastDllError) & Error$
            MsgBox m_sErrorMsg, vbOKOnly, "VB Crypto"
        End If
        '--- Show the results.
        strMsg = strMsg + vbCrLf + _
            "The Property Content is " + _
            Str(kcData.dwKeySpec)

    Case 4
        '--- Set the value size
        cbData = 28
        '--- Retrieve the property value
        If (CBool(CertGetCertificateContextKPIProperty( _
                lpCertContext, dwPropId, _
                kpiData, cbData))) Then
        End If

        '--- The call didn't succeed. Use the size to
        '--- allocate memory for the property.
        pvData = String(cbData, vbNullChar)

        '--- Allocation succeeded. Retrieve the property data
```

```vb
    If (Not CBool(CertGetCertificateContextProperty( _
            lpCertContext, dwPropId, _
            pvData, cbData))) Then
        '--- Unable to retrieve the property value
        m_sErrorMsg = "Error during " & _
            "CertGetCertificateContextProperty - " & _
            CStr(Err.LastDllError) & Error$
        MsgBox m_sErrorMsg, vbOKOnly, "VB Crypto"
    End If

    '--- Show the results.
    If cbData = 28 Then
        '--- We retrieved the type structure
        strMsg = strMsg + vbCrLf + _
            "The Property Content is " + _
            Str(kpiData.dwProvType)
    Else
        '--- We received a byte array
        strMsg = strMsg + vbCrLf + _
            "The Container Name is " + _
            GetContainerNameFromKPI(pvData)
        strMsg = strMsg + vbCrLf + "The CSP is " + _
            GetCSPFromKPI(pvData)
        strMsg = strMsg + vbCrLf + _
            "The Provider Type is " + _
            GetProvTypeFromKPI(pvData)
        strMsg = strMsg + vbCrLf + _
        "The Key Type is " + certificates>
            GetKeySpecFromKPI(pvData)
    End If
Case Else
    '--- Retrieve information on the property by first
    '--- getting the size
    '--- of the property size.
    cbData = 0
    If CBool(CertGetCertificateContextProperty( _
            lpCertContext, dwPropId, _
            vbNullString, cbData)) Then
    End If

    '--- The call succeeded. Use the size to allocate
    '--- memory for the property.
    pvData = String(cbData, vbNullChar)

    '--- Allocation succeeded. Retrieve the property data
    If (Not CBool(CertGetCertificateContextProperty( _
            lpCertContext, dwPropId, _
```

continues

LISTING 6.2   Continued

```
                           pvData, cbData))) Then
            m_sErrorMsg = "Error during " & _
                "CertGetCertificateContextProperty - " & _
                CStr(Err.LastDllError) & Error$
            MsgBox m_sErrorMsg, vbOKOnly, "VB Crypto"
        End If

        '--- Show the results.
        If iVerToUse = 5 Then
            '--- The value is a string, extract it from
            '--- the Byte array
            strMsg = strMsg + vbCrLf + _
                "The Property Content is " + _
                ConvertBytesToString(pvData)
        Else
            '--- A byte array, display the ASCII value of
            '--- the first character
            strMsg = strMsg + vbCrLf + _
                "The Property Content is " + Str(Asc(pvData))
        End If
    End Select

    '--- Add the value to the return string
    szRtnMsg = szRtnMsg + strMsg + vbCrLf

    '--- Get the next property
    dwPropId = CertEnumCertificateContextProperties( _
        lpCertContext, _
        dwPropId)
    Wend

    '--- Get the next certificate
    lpCertContext = CertEnumCertificatesInStore( _
        hCertStore, _
        lpCertContext)
Wend

'--- Clean up.
'--- If we have a current certificate, then release it
If lpCertContext <> 0 Then
    CertFreeCertificateContext lpCertContext
End If
'--- Close the Certificate store
CertCloseStore hCertStore, 0
szRtnMsg = szRtnMsg + vbCrLf + "The function completed successfully."
ListCerts = szRtnMsg
```

```
    Exit Function

ListCertsErr:
    MsgBox "Error: " + Str(Err.Number) + " - " + Err.Description
End Function
```

In this function, you first open the certificate store specified in the function parameter:

```
'--- Open a system certificate store.
hCertStore = CertOpenSystemStore(0, pszStoreName)
```

By passing zero (0) for the first parameter, you specify that the default CSP should be used for the certificate store.

Next, you start enumerating the certificates in the store, looping until all certificates have been retrieved through the following code:

```
'--- Use CertEnumCertificatesInStore to get the certificates
'--- from the open store.
lpCertContext = CertEnumCertificatesInStore(hCertStore, 0)

'--- Loop until all certificates have been retrieved
While (lpCertContext <> 0)
    .
    .

    .
    '--- Get the next certificate
    lpCertContext = CertEnumCertificatesInStore( _
        hCertStore, lpCertContext)
Wend
```

For each certificate that you retrieve, you also retrieve the common subject name by using the `CertGetNameString` function call:

```
'--- A certificate was retrieved. Get the name from the certificate.
If (CertGetNameString(lpCertContext, CERT_NAME_SIMPLE_DISPLAY_TYPE, _
        0, 0, pszNameString, 128)) Then
```

Next, you loop while enumerating all the properties from the certificate by using the following code:

```
'--- Loop to find all of the property identifiers for the specified
'--- certificate. The loop continues until
'--- CertEnumCertificateContextProperties returns zero.
dwPropId = CertEnumCertificateContextProperties( _
    lpCertContext, dwPropId)
While (dwPropId <> 0)
    .
    .
```

continues

LISTING 6.2 Continued

```
    '--- Get the next property
    dwPropId = CertEnumCertificateContextProperties( _
        lpCertContext, dwPropId)
Wend
```

Within this loop, you use a `Select Case` statement to determine which property you are getting and which version of the `CertGetCertificateContextProperty` function to use. The versions of this function are numbered in order, with string properties (for example, names) using a fifth version for reasons that will be discussed next.

At this point, you use another `Select Case` statement to control which version of the `CertGetCertificateContextProperty` function is used. Here, you might have noticed an interesting use of the fourth version, which returns a `CRYPT_KEY_PROV_INFO` type structure, as follows:

```
'--- Set the value size
cbData = 28
'--- Retrieve the property value
If (CBool(CertGetCertificateContextKPIProperty( _
    lpCertContext, dwPropId, _
    kpiData, cbData))) Then
End If

'--- The call didn't succeed. Use the size to
'--- allocate memory for the property.
pvData = String(cbData, vbNullChar)

'--- Allocation succeeded. Retrieve the property data.
If (Not CBool(CertGetCertificateContextProperty( _
    lpCertContext, dwPropId, _
    pvData, cbData))) Then
```

If you look back at the type declaration for the `CRYPT_KEY_PROV_INFO` type, you'll notice that the first two elements in this type structure are pointers to strings. The strings are placed in memory just after the end of the type structure. As a result, you have to allocate a string buffer large enough to hold both the type structure and the strings that are pointed at by the first two elements in the type structure. You'll learn how you can extract these strings without using pointer manipulation a little later.

After you have looped through all the certificates, you free any certificate context that you might still have open as follows:

```
'--- If we have a current certificate, then release it
If lpCertContext <> 0 Then
```

```
    CertFreeCertificateContext lpCertContext
End If
```

Finally, you close the certificate store by using the following code:

```
'--- Close the Certificate store
CertCloseStore hCertStore, 0
```

Converting Strings

While typing in the ListCerts function, you probably noticed that whenever you were working with a string property of a certificate, you called a function called ConvertBytesToString. You call this function because the string values are returned in Unicode strings, not ASCII strings. As a result, you need to perform a conversion on them. Visual Basic normally does this conversion automatically, but when strings are returned as byte arrays, as is the case in these functions, the strings remain in Unicode.

You can convert the strings from Unicode to ASCII by using the StrConv function. However, because the string variables have been sized larger than the Unicode strings, you might still need to trim some extraneous characters off the end. You can find them by searching for any NULL characters in the string. If a NULL character is found, you can trim the string just shy of the NULL character. You can add all this functionality to your application by entering the ConvertBytesToString function to the crypto class, as in Listing 6.3.

LISTING 6.3   The ConvertBytesToString Function

```
Private Function ConvertBytesToString(sbOrg As String) As String
'*************************************************************
'* Written By: Davis Chapman
'* Date:       October 12, 1999
'*
'* Syntax:     ConvertBytesToString(sbOrg)
'*
'* Parameters: sbOrg As String
'*
'* Purpose: This will convert a byte array value to a string
'*          value by skipping every other character (byte) in
'*          the original string.
'*************************************************************
    Dim strNew As String
    Dim iCurPos As Integer

    '--- Convert the string from Unicode
    strNew = StrConv(sbOrg, vbFromUnicode)
    '--- Find any NULL characters in the string
    iCurPos = InStr(1, strNew, vbNullChar, vbBinaryCompare)
```

continues

LISTING 6.3   Continued

```
    '--- If any NULL characters were found, trim the string
    '--- one character shy of the NULL character
    If (iCurPos> 0) Then strNew = Left(strNew, (iCurPos - 1))
    '--- Return the extracted string
    ConvertBytesToString = strNew
End Function
```

Extracting the Key Spec

Now that you can convert the string properties to a readable form, you need to turn your attention to interpreting other properties. The first one to look at is the KeySpec property. It can be determined by examining the KeySpec element in the CRYPT_KEY_PROV_INFO type structure. However, because you are retrieving this type as a string, and not as the type itself, you have to convert the four bytes into a long value.

Converting the four bytes into a long variable seems simple enough: You just convert each character into its ASCII value and add them all together one at a time, multiplying the leftmost values by 16 before adding the next byte to the right. The twist to all of this is that this number is stored in *little endian* format. This means that the bytes go from right to left, not left to right, as you might normally expect. As a result, you have to start with the last character and work your way backward. When you have the numeric value, you can determine which key spec type the certificate is and return a string specifying the type. To build this functionality, add the function in Listing 6.4 to the crypto class.

LISTING 6.4   The GetKeySpecFromKPI Function

```
Private Function GetKeySpecFromKPI(sbOrg As String) As String
'**************************************************************
'* Written By: Davis Chapman
'* Date:       October 12, 1999
'*
'* Syntax:     GetKeySpecFromKPI(sbOrg)
'*
'* Parameters: sbOrg As String
'*
'* Purpose: This will extract the key spec from the
'*          CRYPT_KEY_PROV_INFO type structure.
'**************************************************************
    Dim strCur As String
    Dim strChar As String
    Dim strRtn As String
    Dim iCurPos As Integer
    Dim iRelPos As Integer
```

6

```
    Dim lKeySpec As Long

    '--- Extract the key spec, starting at the
    '--- appropriate offset
    lKeySpec = Asc(Mid(sbOrg, 28, 1))
    lKeySpec = (lKeySpec * 16) + Asc(Mid(sbOrg, 27, 1))
    lKeySpec = (lKeySpec * 16) + Asc(Mid(sbOrg, 26, 1))
    lKeySpec = (lKeySpec * 16) + Asc(Mid(sbOrg, 25, 1))
    '--- Determine the key spec
    Select Case lKeySpec
        Case AT_KEYEXCHANGE
            strRtn = "AT_KEYEXCHANGE"
        Case AT_SIGNATURE
            strRtn = "AT_SIGNATURE"
    End Select
    '--- Return the key spec
    GetKeySpecFromKPI = strRtn
End Function
```

Extracting the Provider Type

Next, you'll add a function to extract the CSP provider type from the `CRYPT_KEY_PROV_INFO`
type structure. This works the same as how you extracted the key spec from the string that contains this type structure. After the provider type value has been extracted and converted, you
can determine which provider type it is and return a string description to the calling routine. To
add this functionality, add the code in Listing 6.5 to the `crypto` class.

LISTING 6.5 The `GetProvTypeFromKPI` Function

```
Private Function GetProvTypeFromKPI(sbOrg As String) As String
'***********************************************************
'* Written By: Davis Chapman
'* Date:       October 12, 1999
'*
'* Syntax:     GetProvTypeFromKPI(sbOrg)
'*
'* Parameters: sbOrg As String
'*
'* Purpose: This will extract the provider type from the
'*          CRYPT_KEY_PROV_INFO type structure.
'***********************************************************
    Dim strCur As String
    Dim strChar As String
    Dim strRtn As String
    Dim iCurPos As Integer
```

continues

LISTING 6.5   Continued

```
    Dim iRelPos As Integer
    Dim lProvType As Long

    '--- Extract the provider type, starting at the
    '--- appropriate offset
    lProvType = Asc(Mid(sbOrg, 12, 1))
    lProvType = (lProvType * 16) + Asc(Mid(sbOrg, 11, 1))
    lProvType = (lProvType * 16) + Asc(Mid(sbOrg, 10, 1))
    lProvType = (lProvType * 16) + Asc(Mid(sbOrg, 9, 1))
    '--- Determine the provider type
    Select Case lProvType
        Case PROV_RSA_FULL
            strRtn = "PROV_RSA_FULL"
        Case PROV_RSA_SIG
            strRtn = "PROV_RSA_SIG"
        Case PROV_DSS
            strRtn = "PROV_DSS"
        Case PROV_FORTEZZA
            strRtn = "PROV_FORTEZZA"
        Case PROV_MS_EXCHANGE
            strRtn = "PROV_MS_EXCHANGE"
        Case PROV_SSL
            strRtn = "PROV_SSL"
        Case PROV_RSA_SCHANNEL
            strRtn = "PROV_RSA_SCHANNEL"
        Case PROV_DSS_DH
            strRtn = "PROV_DSS_DH"
    End Select
    '--- Return the provider type
    GetProvTypeFromKPI = strRtn
End Function
```

Extracting the Container Name

Now it's time to turn your attention back to extracting the string values from the
CRYPT_KEY_PROV_INFO type structure. Because these values are included in the return string,
just after the type structure, you can extract them from that point on. The first string that you'll
extract is the container name. It starts just after the type structure. Because the
CRYPT_KEY_PROV_INFO type structure is 28 bytes long, you can extract everything from the
twenty-ninth character on and pass it to the ConvertBytesToString function to extract the
container name. You do so by adding the code in Listing 6.6 to the crypto class.

LISTING 6.6   The `GetContainerNameFromKPI` Function

```
Private Function GetContainerNameFromKPI(sbOrg As String) As String
'****************************************************************
'* Written By: Davis Chapman
'* Date:        October 12, 1999
'*
'* Syntax:      GetContainerNameFromKPI(sbOrg)
'*
'* Parameters:  sbOrg As String
'*
'* Purpose: This will extract the container name from the
'*          CRYPT_KEY_PROV_INFO type structure.
'****************************************************************
    Dim strCur As String
    Dim strChar As String
    Dim strRtn As String
    Dim iCurPos As Integer
    Dim iRelPos As Integer

    '--- Extract the container name, starting at the
    '--- appropriate offset
    strRtn = ConvertBytesToString(Mid(sbOrg, 29))
    '--- Return the container name
    GetContainerNameFromKPI = strRtn
End Function
```

Extracting the CSP Name

Extracting the CSP name is a little more complicated. First, it is after the container name in the string buffer returned with the `CRYPT_KEY_PROV_INFO` type structure. Plus, four extra bytes are inserted between the two strings (which convert to two extra characters after converting from Unicode). As a result, you can't just pass the string to the `ConvertBytesToString` function, but instead you must perform the conversion yourself.

After you have converted the entire string section from Unicode to ASCII, you can find the end of the container name by searching for the first NULL character. When you find this point, trim off everything through two more characters from the first of the string. This leaves you at the start of the CSP name. Now you can search for any additional NULL characters that mark the end of the CSP name and trim the end of the string at that point. To add this functionality, add the code in Listing 6.7 to the crypto class.

LISTING 6.7   The GetCSPFromKPI Function

```
Private Function GetCSPFromKPI(sbOrg As String) As String
'***************************************************************
'* Written By: Davis Chapman
'* Date:       October 12, 1999
'*
'* Syntax:     GetCSPFromKPI(sbOrg)
'*
'* Parameters: sbOrg As String
'*
'* Purpose: This will extract the CSP from the CRYPT_KEY_PROV_INFO
'*          type structure.
'***************************************************************
    Dim strChar As String
    Dim strRtn As String
    Dim iCurPos As Integer

    '--- Initialize the starting position
    iCurPos = 29
    '--- Trim off the CRYPT_KEY_PROV_INFO structure
    strChar = Mid(sbOrg, iCurPos)
    '--- Convert the string
    strRtn = StrConv(strChar, vbFromUnicode)
    '--- Find the end of the first string
    iCurPos = InStr(1, strRtn, vbNullChar, vbBinaryCompare)
    '--- Trim off the first string
    If (iCurPos> 0) Then strRtn = Mid(strRtn, (iCurPos + 3))
    '--- Find the end of the second string
    iCurPos = InStr(1, strRtn, vbNullChar, vbBinaryCompare)
    '--- Trim the string one character shy of the NULL character
    If (iCurPos> 0) Then strRtn = Left(strRtn, (iCurPos - 1))
    '--- Return the CSP name
    GetCSPFromKPI = strRtn
End Function
```

Designing the Form

At this point, you've added all the necessary new functionality to the crypto class, so it's time to turn your attention back to the form portion of the application. Add controls to the default form as shown in Figure 6.1, setting their properties as specified in Table 6.13.

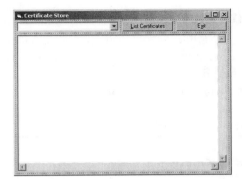

FIGURE 6.1
Designing the application form.

TABLE 6.13   Control Property Settings

Control	Property	Value
Combo Box	Name	cboStore
	List	MY
		ROOT
		CA
		SPC
		TRUST
Command Button	Name	cmdList
	Caption	&List Certificates
Command Button	Name	cmdExit
	Caption	E&xit
TextBox	Name	txtCerts
	Multiline	True

Next, attach the code in Listing 6.8 to the Click event of the Exit button to close the application.

LISTING 6.8   The cmdExit Click Event

```
Private Sub cmdExit_Click()
    '--- Exit the application
    Unload Me
End Sub
```

Listing the Certificates

Now, to perform the listing of certificates and their properties, call the ListCerts function of the crypto class with the name of the certificate store that the user has selected from the combo box, passing the returned string to the text box for the user to view. Do this in the Click event of the cmdList command button, as in Listing 6.9.

LISTING 6.9   The cmdList Click Event

```
Private Sub cmdList_Click()
    Dim csCrypt As New clsCrypto

    '--- Retrieve and display the list of certificates
    txtCerts = csCrypt.ListCerts(cboStore)
End Sub
```

At this point, you should be able to run this application on your system, viewing the certificates you have stored on your computer, as shown in Figure 6.2.

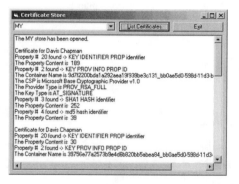

FIGURE 6.2
Viewing certificate properties.

Summary

In this chapter, you learned the basics of managing and working with certificates and certificate stores. You learned how to find and list the certificates in the various certificate stores on your computer. You also learned how to view the properties set on the certificates. You now know how to find the certificate that you need and to check any properties for which you want the value.

Although you learned a bit about working with certificates in this chapter and how to request certificates from a Certificate Authority in the preceding chapter, you're still not through. In the next chapter, you'll dive into the topic of maintaining Certificate Revocation Lists (CRL) and Certificate Trust Lists (CTL). These two mechanisms are widely used for maintaining which certificates to trust and which to reject as invalid.

Working with Certificate Revocation Lists

IN THIS CHAPTER

- Verifying Certificates Against a CA
- Building and Maintaining a Certificate Revocation List
- Managing a Certificate Revocation List

When you receive a certificate from someone or retrieve it from a directory, you can verify its signature by using the Certificate Authority's certificate, and you can verify that the certificate hasn't expired, but how do you verify that the certificate hasn't been revoked? The only thing you can do is go to the CA and check against its list of revoked certificates.

You can go about this task in a couple of ways. The first is to use another COM object that is available for use with Certificate Authorities running Microsoft's Certificate Server. This way, you can check a single certificate to make sure that it is still valid. The second way is to download the Certificate Revocation List (CRL) from the CA, store it in your certificate store, and verify the certificate against the CRL. You will examine this procedure in this chapter.

PREREQUISITES

Before reading this chapter, you need to make sure that you have a good understanding of the following:

- Asymmetric encryption and digital certificates, as covered in Chapter 1, "Understanding Encryption and Application Security"
- Selecting and opening Cryptographic Service Providers (CSP), as covered in Chapter 2, "Getting Started with the CryptoAPI"
- Hashing data, generating encryption keys, and encrypting and decrypting data, as covered in Chapter 3, "Symmetric and Password Encryption"
- Using public/private encryption keys, as covered in Chapter 4, "Public/Private Key Communications"
- Requesting and retrieving digital certificates, as covered in Chapter 5, "Requesting and Retrieving Certificates"
- Managing digital certificates in a certificate store, as covered in Chapter 6, "Working with Certificates"

Verifying Certificates Against a CA

If the CA that issued a particular certificate is running Microsoft's Certificate Server, Windows 2000 Server (also NT4 Server with the Option Pack installed) provides you with a COM object you can use to check the status of a particular certificate. You also can use this COM object to administer the certificate services of the CA, assuming that you have the appropriate permissions to do so.

Extracting a Certificate Serial Number

Before you can verify a certificate's validity, you need to be able to get the certificate's serial number. This piece of information is available through the CERT_INFO type structure. The definition for this type structure is as follows:

Syntax

```
Type CERT_INFO
    dwVersion As Long      ' Certificate's version number
    SerialNumber As CRYPT_INTEGER_BLOB
    SignatureAlgorithm As CRYPT_ALGORITHM_IDENTIFIER
    Issuer As CRYPT_INTEGER_BLOB
    NotBefore As FILETIME    ' Validity start date
    NotAfter As FILETIME     ' Validity end date
    Subject As CRYPT_INTEGER_BLOB
    SubjectPublicKeyInfo As CERT_PUBLIC_KEY_INFO
    IssuerUniqueId As CRYPT_BIT_BLOB
    SubjectUniqueId As CRYPT_BIT_BLOB
    cExtension As Long       ' Number of certificate extensions
    rgExtension As Long      ' Pointer to CERT_EXTENSION
End Type
```

Several elements in this type structure are other type structures. The one that you are concerned with right now is the CRYPT_INTEGER_BLOB type structure. The definition for this type structure is as follows:

Syntax

```
Type CRYPT_INTEGER_BLOB
    cbData As Long  ' Length of the Byte Array
    pbData As Long  ' Pointer to Byte Array
End Type
```

The first member of the CRYPT_INTEGER_BLOB type structure, cbData, is a long value specifying the length of the value pointed to by the second member, pbData. This pointer is pointing to the value you are looking for, the Certificate's serial number. Now, all you need is some way to perform pointer manipulation in Visual Basic.

Actually, you can easily perform pointer manipulation in Visual Basic, at least for the type of pointer manipulation you need in this situation. You can redefine the Windows API function CopyMemory so that you can pass in a pointer, and it will copy what the pointer is pointing at into a variable that you have declared and allocated. To do so, you can declare the CopyMemory function as follows:

```
Public Declare Sub CopyMemory Lib "kernel32" Alias "RtlMoveMemory" ( _
    Destination As Any, ByVal Source As Long, ByVal Length As Long)
```

The first parameter (Destination) to this function is the variable into which the value will be copied. For a string, you need to have already allocated the space for this value. You can size it as follows:

```
Dim crtInfo As CERT_INFO
Dim strSn As String

'--- Size the serial number string to hold the certificate serial number
strSn = String(crtInfo.SerialNumber.cbData, vbNullChar)
'--- Copy the certificate serial number into the string
CopyMemory ByVal strSn, crtInfo.SerialNumber.pbData, _
    crtInfo.SerialNumber.cbData
```

The second parameter (Source) is the pointer that is pointing at the data that you want to copy. The third parameter (Length) is the amount or length of data to copy.

Now the question is how to retrieve the CERT_INFO type structure from the certificate. In this case, one of the elements in the CERT_CONTEXT type structure is a pointer to the CERT_INFO type structure. The CERT_CONTEXT type structure is defined as follows:

```
Type CERT_CONTEXT
    dwCertEncodingType As Long   ' Encoding type
    pbCertEncoded As Long        ' Pointer to Byte Array
    cbCertEncoded As Long        ' Length of the byte array
    pCertInfo As Long            ' Pointer to CERT_INFO
    hCertStore As Long           ' Handle for the certificate store
End Type
```

As you might remember from the preceding chapter, you are primarily working with a pointer to the CERT_CONTEXT type structure as you work with and manage certificates. All you need to do is get the actual CERT_CONTEXT type structure, and from it, you can get the CERT_INFO type structure. You do so by using the same definition of the CopyMemory function you used to extract the certificate serial number, as follows:

```
Dim ccTx As CERT_CONTEXT
Dim crtInfo As CERT_INFO

'--- Get the CERT_CONTEXT type structure from the pointer
'--- to the CERT_CONTEXT type structure (lCertCtx)
```

```
CopyMemory ccTx, lCertCtx, 20
'--- Get the CERT_INFO type structure
CopyMemory crtInfo, ccTx.pCertInfo, 112
```

Before you can put these procedures to use, you need to take a quick look at the other type structures that are part of the CERT_INFO type structure. You've already looked at the CRYPT_INTEGER_BLOB type structure, which is used for holding not just the serial number, but also the CA's information and the certificate subject information. The next type structure is the CRYPT_ALGORITHM_IDENTIFIER, which holds the ID of the hashing algorithm used to sign the certificate. This type structure is defined as follows:

Syntax

```
Type CRYPT_ALGORITHM_IDENTIFIER
    pszObjId As Long      ' Pointer to String
    Parameters As CRYPT_INTEGER_BLOB
End Type
```

The next type structure used in the CERT_INFO type structure is the FILETIME type. This native Windows type structure is used to specify dates and times as a pair of long numbers. The declaration of this type structure is as follows:

Syntax

```
Type FILETIME
        dwLowDateTime As Long
        dwHighDateTime As Long
End Type
```

You can skip the next type used in the CERT_INFO type for a moment and move on to the CRYPT_BIT_BLOB. This type structure is similar to the CRYPT_INTEGER_BLOB, but it has one additional element that specifies the number of unused bits in the byte array. It is used for the IDs of the certificate's subject and issuer. Its definition is as follows:

Syntax

```
Type CRYPT_BIT_BLOB
    cbData As Long       ' Length of Byte Array
    pbData As Long       ' Pointer to Byte Array
    cUnusedBits As Long  ' Number of unused bits
End Type
```

7

WORKING WITH CERTIFICATE REVOCATION LISTS

The final type you need to define is the CERT_PUBLIC_KEY_INFO type structure. This type is used to hold the public key of the certificate owner. The definition of this type structure is as follows:

Syntax

```
Type CERT_PUBLIC_KEY_INFO
    Algorithm As CRYPT_ALGORITHM_IDENTIFIER
    PublicKey As CRYPT_BIT_BLOB
End Type
```

As you can see, this type structure consists of two of the type structures you have already defined. The CRYPT_ALGORITHM_IDENTIFIER type specifies which encryption algorithm the public key uses, and the CRYPT_BIT_BLOB type holds the actual public encryption key.

Formatting the Serial Number

Now that you know how to extract the serial number from the certificate, you're ready to start verifying certificates with the CAs that issued the certificates, right? Not yet. First, you have to reformat the serial number before trying to pass it to the CA for verification. Most CAs require that certificate serial numbers be converted into a string of hex values before they will accept and recognize them. Unfortunately, the serial number is in a binary format when you extract it from the certificate. Converting to hex should be a simple matter of looping through all the bytes in the serial number, getting their hex values, and building a string of the values. For example, you might use the following:

```
Dim strRtn As String
Dim lPos As Long
Dim strChr As String

'--- Initialize the return string
strRtn = ""
'--- Loop through the bytes
For lPos = 1 To Len(sbSN)
    '--- Get the current character's hex value
    '--- Append the hex value to the hex string
    strRtn = strRtn + Hex(Asc(Mid(sbSN, lPos, 1)))
Next
```

Unfortunately, this process is not quite so simple. The first problem is that any bytes with a hex value in which the first digit is zero (0) will come out as a single character. As a result, you need to be sure to pad those hex values that come out as one character long. Also, the bytes are encoded in reverse order. Therefore, you need to loop through the bytes in reverse order. The resulting conversion looks more like the following:

```
Dim strRtn As String
Dim lPos As Long
Dim strChr As String

'--- Initialize the return string
strRtn = ""
'--- Loop through the bytes in reverse order
For lPos = Len(sbSN) To 1 Step -1
    '--- Get the current character's hex value
    strChr = Hex(Asc(Mid(sbSN, lPos, 1)))
    '--- Do we need to pad it?
    If Len(strChr) < 2 Then
        '--- Pad the hex value so that it is 2 characters long
        If Len(strChr) = 1 Then
            strChr = "0" + strChr
        Else
            strChr = "00"
        End If
    End If
    '--- Append the hex value to the hex string
    strRtn = strRtn + strChr
Next
```

The `CertAdmin` COM Object

WINDOWS **2000** On Windows 2000 Server systems, or NT 4.0 Server systems that have the NT Option Pack installed, you can use a Certificate Services COM object to control the Certificate Server running on any NT machine. To be able to use this COM object, though, you need to have the appropriate security permissions to be able to administer the certificate services. If this is the case, you can use this COM object to easily verify certificates issued by this CA.

To use this object in a Visual Basic application, you need to include the `certadm` type library in the project references. You can do so by locating the certadm.dll in the System32 subdirectory. After you include this DLL in the project references, you can declare a variable as a `CCertAdmin` type, as follows:

```
Dim cAdm As New CCertAdmin
```

At this point, all the methods of this object become available for your use in the scope within which you've declared this object.

Verifying a Certificate

When you have the `CertAdmin` object, you can use it to verify any certificate that was issued by a CA running Microsoft's Certificate Server on which you have administrative rights. You do so by calling the `IsValidCertificate` method of the `CertAdmin` object. The definition of this method is as follows:

Syntax

```
IsValidCertificate(strConfig As String, strSerialNumber As String) as Long
```

The first parameter (`strConfig`) to this method is a string specifying both the server on which the CA is running and the name of the CA itself. You used the same combination with the Certificate Request object back in Chapter 5, "Requesting and Retrieving Certificates." The format of this string is the server name, a backslash character, and the Certificate Authority name. If the CA is located on a machine named `mycertauth.mydomain.com`, and the CA is named `My Certificate Authority`, this string would look like `"mycertauth.mydomain.com\My Certificate Authority"`.

The second parameter (`strSerialNumber`) to this method is the serial number of the certificate to be verified. This serial number needs to be in the form of a string of hex values, formatted as you learned a short while ago.

The return value from this method is an indicator of the status of the certificate queried. The possible values are listed in Table 7.1.

TABLE 7.1   `IsValidCertificate` Return Values

Constant	Value	Description
CA_DISP_INCOMPLETE	0	The call to verify the certificate was not complete.
CA_DISP_ERROR	&H1	An error occurred during the call to verify the certificate.
CA_DISP_REVOKED	&H2	The certificate has been revoked.
CA_DISP_VALID	&H3	The certificate is still valid.
CA_DISP_INVALID	&H4	The certificate has never been issued (or at least not by this CA).
CA_DISP_UNDER_SUBMISSION	&H5	The certificate is pending and has not been issued yet.

If the certificate you are checking on has been revoked, you can call a second method to determine the reason the certificate has been revoked. This method, called `GetRevocationReason`, is defined as follows:

Syntax

```
GetRevocationReason as Long
```

This method does not take any parameters. The return value is a code that specifies the reason the certificate has been revoked. The possible values are listed in Table 7.2.

CAUTION

Because it doesn't take any parameters, the only way that the GetRevocationReason method knows which certificate to check is by calling IsValidCertificate first. If the IsValidCertificate method is not called first, then the behavior of the GetRevocationReason method will be unpredictable.

TABLE 7.2 GetRevocationReason Return Values

Constant	Value	Description
CRL_REASON_UNSPECIFIED	0	The reason the certificate was revoked was not specified.
CRL_REASON_KEY_COMPROMISE	1	The private key associated with this certificate was compromised.
CRL_REASON_CA_COMPROMISE	2	The private key for the CA certificate used to sign the certificate was compromised.
CRL_REASON_AFFILIATION_CHANGED	3	The certificate owner's affiliation with the issuing organization has changed.
CRL_REASON_SUPERSEDED	4	The certificate has been superseded by another certificate.
CRL_REASON_CESSATION_OF_OPERATION	5	The owner of the certificate, or the Certificate Authority, has ceased operation.
CRL_REASON_CERTIFICATE_HOLD	6	The certificate has been placed on hold.

NOTE

Several more methods are available through the CertAdmin object, but they all center around the administration of Certificate Server. You'll find methods for issuing and rejecting certificate requests and for revoking certificates. You'll also find methods for setting certificate extensions and request attributes. They are all beyond the scope of what I'm discussing in this chapter. For more information on the other methods associated with this object, see the interface documentation on the Microsoft Developer Network CDs or Web site.

Building and Maintaining a Certificate Revocation List

Verifying each certificate against the CA programmatically is not always practical. First, you are not likely to have the administrative privileges necessary to use the CertAdmin object. Second, not all CAs are going to be running Microsoft's Certificate Server for their CA. If either of these conditions exist, you have a problem. If you don't verify a certificate you receive against the CA, you have no way of knowing whether the certificate is still valid or if it might have been revoked.

You can take another approach to solving this problem: You can use Certificate Revocation Lists (CRLs). Every CA publishes a CRL listing every certificate it has issued that has been revoked. These lists are freely available from the CA through the CA's Web site.

After you retrieve the CRL from a CA, you can create a CA context from it or import it into a certificate store. When you have a CRL context, you can use it to verify the validity of certificates issued by the CA that published the CRL.

Creating a CRL Context

When you have the CRL from the CA, whether you downloaded it through the Web site or programmatically through whatever interface the CA has made available, you can create a CRL context from it by calling the CertCreateCRLContext function. The syntax for this function is as follows:

Syntax

```
Public Declare Function CertCreateCRLContext Lib "Crypt32.dll" ( _
    ByVal dwCertEncodingType As Long, ByVal pbCrlEncoded As String, _
    ByVal cbCrlEncoded As Long) As Long
```

The first parameter (dwCertEncodingType) is a flag that specifies the encoding and formatting used on the CRL. The currently defined encoding types, listed in Table 7.3, are often combined using a binary OR.

TABLE 7.3   Encoding Type Flag Values

Constant	Value	Description
X509_ASN_ENCODING	&H1	X.509 Encoding
PKCS_7_ASN_ENCODING	&H10000	PKCS #7 Message Formatting

The second parameter (pbCrlEncoded) is a string containing the encoded CRL. The third parameter (cbCrlEncoded) is the size of the CRL string being passed in the second parameter.

The return value is a long value that is really a pointer to the CRL context. If the function fails, zero (0) is returned.

Adding a CRL to a Certificate Store

Unless you really want to retrieve a new CRL list from the Certificate Authority every time you need to validate a certificate, you'll probably want to be able to place the CRL list into a certificate store so that you will have it next time you need it. When you have a pointer to a CRL_CONTEXT type structure, you can add it to a certificate store by using the CertAddCRLContextToStore function. The definition of this function is as follows:

Syntax

```
Public Declare Function CertAddCRLContextToStore Lib "Crypt32.dll" ( _
    ByVal hCertStore As Long, ByVal pCrlContext As Long, _
    ByVal dwAddDisposition As Long, ByVal ppStoreContext As Long) As Long
```

The first parameter (hCertStore) to this function is a handle to the certificate store to which the CRL is to be saved. This parameter is the same value returned from the CertOpenSystemStore function you looked at in the preceding chapter.

The second parameter (pCrlContext) is the pointer to the CRL_CONTEXT returned by the CertCreateCRLContext function. This CRL will be added to the certificate store.

The third parameter (dwAddDisposition) is a flag value that will control how the CRL is added to the certificate store. The possible values for this flag are listed in Table 7.4.

TABLE 7.4 Add CRL to Store Flag Values

Constant	Value	Description
CERT_STORE_ADD_ALWAYS	4	A new CRL is always added to the certificate store. No check is made for any matching CRLs already existing in the store.
CERT_STORE_ADD_NEW	1	If a matching CRL already exists in the certificate store, the new CRL is not added.
CERT_STORE_ADD_NEWER	6	If a matching CRL already exists in the certificate store, the two CRLs are compared to determine which one is newer. The newer CRL is kept in the certificate store.

continues

7

WORKING WITH CERTIFICATE REVOCATION LISTS

TABLE 7.4   Continued

Constant	Value	Description
CERT_STORE_ADD_NEWER_ INHERIT_PROPERTIES	7	This flag is the same as the CERT_STORE_ADD_NEWER flag, except that any properties on the existing CRL are transferred to the new CRL. The result will be the new CRL in the certificate store with all the properties from the existing CRL, regardless of which CRL was the existing one.
CERT_STORE_ADD_ REPLACE_EXISTING	3	If a matching CRL is found, it is replaced with the new CRL.
CERT_STORE_ADD_REPLACE_ EXISTING_INHERIT_ PROPERTIES	5	This flag is the same as the CERT_STORE_ADD_ REPLACE_EXISTING flag, except that any properties on the existing CRL are transferred to the new CRL. The result will be the new CRL in the certificate store with all of the properties from the old CRL.
CERT_STORE_ADD_USE_ EXISTING	2	If an existing CRL is found, it is kept and any properties on the new CRL are added to the existing CRL. The new CRL is added only if no matching CRL is found.

The fourth parameter (ppStoreContext) is a pointer to a new CRL_CONTEXT that is returned with the CRL_CONTEXT referencing the certificate store in which it is stored. You can pass a zero (0) in this parameter and use the CRL_CONTEXT you passed in to the function. If you want to get this new CRL_CONTEXT, you need to redeclare this function, with the fourth parameter being passed by reference (ByRef) instead of by value (ByVal), and pass a long variable into which the pointer will be placed.

Another way you can add a CRL to a certificate store is to use the CertAddEncodedCRLToStore function. This function does in one place what the previous two do in concert. This function takes the encoded CRL as it was received from the CA and puts it into the certificate store. The syntax for this function is as follows:

Syntax

```
Public Declare Function CertAddEncodedCRLToStore Lib "Crypt32.dll" ( _
    ByVal hCertStore As Long, ByVal dwCertEncodingType As Long, _
    ByVal pbCrlEncoded As String, ByVal cbCrlEncoded As Long, _
    ByVal dwAddDisposition As Long, ppCrlContext As Long) As Long
```

The parameters for this function are a combination of the parameters of the previous two functions. The first parameter (hCertStore) is the handle to the certificate store into which the CRL will be added.

Working with Certificate Revocation Lists

CHAPTER 7

229

7

WORKING WITH
CERTIFICATE
REVOCATION LISTS

The second parameter (dwCertEncodingType) is the flag specifying the encoding type of the CRL list. You can find the possible values for this parameter back in Table 7.3.

The third parameter (pbCrlEncoded) is the encoded CRL retrieved from the CA. The fourth parameter (cbCrlEncoded) is a long value specifying the size of the encoded CRL in the third parameter.

The fifth parameter (dwAddDisposition) is a flag that specifies how the CRL should be added to the certificate store. The possible values for this flag are listed back in Table 7.4.

The sixth parameter (ppCrlContext) to this function is a long variable into which will be placed a pointer to the CRL_CONTEXT created when the CRL is added to the certificate store.

Duplicating a CRL

When you need to duplicate a CRL, you can use the CertDuplicateCRLContext function. The syntax for this function is as follows:

Syntax

```
Public Declare Function CertDuplicateCRLContext Lib "Crypt32.dll" ( _
    ByVal pCrlContext As Long) As Long
```

The only parameter (pCrlContext) to this function is the pointer to the CRL you want to duplicate. The return value from this function is a pointer to the duplicate of the CRL_CONTEXT. You need to free both of these pointers using the CertFreeCRLContext function you'll look at next.

Freeing a CRL Context

After you finish working with a CRL Context, you need to release all the resources associated with it by calling the CertFreeCRLContext function. The syntax for this function is as follows:

Syntax

```
Public Declare Function CertFreeCRLContext Lib "Crypt32.dll" ( _
    ByVal pCrlContext As Long) As Long
```

The only parameter (pCrlContext) to this function is the pointer to the CRL_CONTEXT that is to be freed.

Deleting a CRL

When you need to delete a CRL from the certificate store, you can use the CertDeleteCRLFromStore function. The syntax for this function is as follows:

Syntax

```
Public Declare Function CertDeleteCRLFromStore Lib "Crypt32.dll" ( _
    ByVal pCrlContext As Long) As Long
```

The only parameter (pCrlContext) to this function is the pointer to the CRL_CONTEXT of the CRL you want to delete from the certificate store.

Getting a CRL from a Certificate Store

Over the past few pages, you learned how you can save a CRL in a certificate store, enabling you to hold onto it for later use. Well, it's not much use to be able to store CRLs in the certificate store if you can't get them back out when you need them. You can get a CRL from a certificate store in a couple of ways. The first way is to enumerate all the CRLs in the store. You do so by using the CertEnumCRLsInStore function. The syntax for this function is as follows:

Syntax

```
Public Declare Function CertEnumCRLsInStore Lib "Crypt32.dll" ( _
    ByVal hCertStore As Long, ByVal pPrevCrlContext As Long) As Long
```

The first parameter (hCertStore) to this function is the handle to the certificate store from which you want to enumerate the CRLs. The second parameter (pPrevCrlContext) is a pointer to the previous CRL returned from this function. The first time this function is called, this parameter should be zero (0).

The return value from this function is a pointer to the next CRL in the certificate store. If no more CRLs are in the store, the return value will be zero (0).

A second method for getting a CRL from a certificate store is to use the CertGetCRLFromStore function. This second method enables you a little more control over which CRLs are retrieved from the certificate store. The syntax for this function is as follows:

Syntax

```
Public Declare Function CertGetCRLFromStore Lib "Crypt32.dll" ( _
    ByVal hCertStore As Long, ByVal pIssuerContext As Long, _
    ByVal pPrevCrlContext As Long, pdwFlags As Long) As Long
```

The first parameter (hCertStore) to this function is the handle of the certificate store from which the CRL should be retrieved.

The second parameter (pIssuerContext) is a pointer to a CERT_CONTEXT for a certificate of the issuer of the CRL to be retrieved. This certificate does not have to be from the same certificate store from which you are retrieving the CRL. If you pass zero (0) for this value, all the CRLs in the store will be retrieved.

The third parameter (pPrevCrlContext) is a pointer to the previous CRL_CONTEXT retrieved from the certificate store by this function. It points to the previous CRL_CONTEXT because a CA can have multiple CRLs in a certificate store. This parameter must be zero (0) the first time this function is called.

The fourth parameter (pdwFlags) is a flag that specifies how the CRLs should be found and retrieved. The possible values for this parameter are listed in Table 7.5. These values can be combined using the OR statement.

TABLE 7.5 Get CRL Flag Values

Constant	Value	Description
CERT_STORE_SIGNATURE_FLAG	&H1	Uses the issuer's certificate in the second parameter to verify the signature on the CRL
CERT_STORE_TIME_VALIDITY_FLAG	&H2	Verifies that the CRL list is still within its valid time and has not expired

The return value from this function is a pointer to a CRL_CONTEXT. If no CRL is found, this function returns zero (0).

Verifying Certificates Against a CRL

When you want to verify a certificate against a CRL, you can use the CertVerifyCRLRevocation function. The definition for this function is as follows:

Syntax

```
Public Declare Function CertVerifyCRLRevocation Lib "Crypt32.dll" ( _
    ByVal dwCertEncodingType As Long, ByVal pCertId As Long, _
    ByVal cCrlInfo As Long, ByRef rgpCrlInfo As Any) As Long
```

The first parameter (dwCertEncodingType) in this function is a flag specifying the encoding of the certificate being validated. The values for this flag can be combined using the OR statement. The possible values you can use for this flag are provided in Table 7.6.

TABLE 7.6   Encoding Type Flag Values

Constant	Value	Description
X509_ASN_ENCODING	&H1	X.509 Encoding
PKCS_7_ASN_ENCODING	&H10000	PKCS #7 Message Formatting

The second parameter (`pCertId`) is a pointer to the `CERT_INFO` type structure of the certificate being validated. You can pass the `pCertInfo` member of the `CERT_CONTEXT` type structure for this value. You learned how to get the actual `CERT_CONTEXT` type structure from the pointer earlier in this chapter.

The third parameter (`cCrlInfo`) to this function is the number of CRL lists being passed in the fourth parameter. The fourth parameter (`rgpCrlInfo`) is an array of pointers to `CRL_INFO` type structures. The values for these pointers can be copied directly from the `pCrlInfo` member of the `CRL_CONTEXT` type structures. The `CRL_CONTEXT` type structures are defined as follows:

Syntax

```
Type CRL_CONTEXT
    dwCertEncodingType As Long  ' Encoding type
    pbCrlEncoded As Long        ' Pointer to Byte Array
    cbCrlEncoded As Long        ' Length of the byte array
    pCrlInfo As Long            ' Pointer to CRL_INFO
    hCertStore As Long          ' Handle for the certificate store
End Type
```

You can get this type structure from the pointer to it by using the `CopyMemory` function as follows:

```
Dim cCrlTx As CRL_CONTEXT
Dim larrCrlInfos(1) As Long

'--- Get the CRL_CONTEXT type structure
CopyMemory cCrlTx, m_lCRLPointer, 20
'--- Put the pointer to the CRL_INFO type into an array
larrCrlInfos(0) = cCrlTx.pCrlInfo
```

For example, you might use this function as follows:

```
'--- Check the validity of the certificate
If CBool(CertVerifyCRLRevocation( _
      X509_ASN_ENCODING Or PKCS_7_ASN_ENCODING, _
      ccTx.pCertInfo, 1, larrCrlInfos(0))) Then
    strMsg = "Certificate is Valid"
Else
    strMsg = "Certificate is NOT Valid!!!"
End If
```

Managing a Certificate Revocation List

For the sample application you'll build in this chapter, you'll modify the certificate listing utility that you built in the preceding chapter. This time, as it prepares to list all the properties of each certificate, it will first check the validity of the certificate. You'll use two methods to check the validity of the certificates. One will check with the Certificate Authority using the CertAdmin object, and the other will compare the certificates against a CRL downloaded from the Certificate Authority.

Creating the Project

To create the project for this application, copy the crypto class, form, and project files from the application that you built in the preceding chapter into a new project directory. Open this project in Visual Basic. After you open the project, add a reference to the CertAdmin object in the Project References dialog, as shown in Figure 7.1.

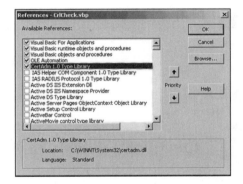

FIGURE 7.1

Adding a reference to the CertAdmin *object to the project.*

Before you get started coding, you also need to add the Microsoft Common Dialog Control to the project components through the Components dialog, as shown in Figure 7.2.

Now that you're ready to start modifying code, you can add some new declarations and API function calls to the crypto class. Just add the constant, function API calls, and variable declarations to the crypto class as in Listing 7.1, spreading the various declarations around to the appropriate locations within the declaration section.

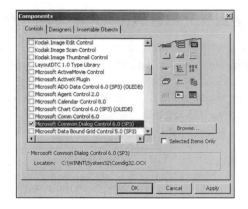

FIGURE 7.2

Adding the Microsoft Common Dialog Control to the project.

LISTING 7.1   Modifications to the Crypto Class Declarations

```
'
' Certificate Status
'
Const CA_DISP_INCOMPLETE = 0
Const CA_DISP_ERROR = &H1
Const CA_DISP_REVOKED = &H2
Const CA_DISP_VALID = &H3
Const CA_DISP_INVALID = &H4
Const CA_DISP_UNDER_SUBMISSION = &H5


'+------------------------------------------------------------------------
'   X509_CRL_REASON_CODE
'   szOID_CRL_REASON_CODE
'
'   pvStructInfo points to an int which can be set to one of the following
'   enumerated values:
'-------------------------------------------------------------------------
Const CRL_REASON_UNSPECIFIED = 0
Const CRL_REASON_KEY_COMPROMISE = 1
Const CRL_REASON_CA_COMPROMISE = 2
Const CRL_REASON_AFFILIATION_CHANGED = 3
Const CRL_REASON_SUPERSEDED = 4
Const CRL_REASON_CESSATION_OF_OPERATION = 5
Const CRL_REASON_CERTIFICATE_HOLD = 6
Const CRL_REASON_REMOVE_FROM_CRL = 8


'
```

```
' Issued Certificate Format
'
Const CR_OUT_BASE64HEADER = 0
Const CR_OUT_BASE64 = &H1
Const CR_OUT_BINARY = &H2
Const CR_OUT_ENCODEMASK = &HFF
Const CR_OUT_CHAIN = &H100


Const CRYPT_ASN_ENCODING = &H1
Const CRYPT_NDR_ENCODING = &H2
Const X509_ASN_ENCODING = &H1
Const X509_NDR_ENCODING = &H2
Const PKCS_7_ASN_ENCODING = &H10000
Const PKCS_7_NDR_ENCODING = &H20000


'+-------------------------------------------------------------------
' Add certificate/CRL, encoded, context or element disposition values.
'-------------------------------------------------------------------
Const CERT_STORE_ADD_NEW = 1
Const CERT_STORE_ADD_USE_EXISTING = 2
Const CERT_STORE_ADD_REPLACE_EXISTING = 3
Const CERT_STORE_ADD_ALWAYS = 4
Const CERT_STORE_ADD_REPLACE_EXISTING_INHERIT_PROPERTIES = 5
Const CERT_STORE_ADD_NEWER = 6
Const CERT_STORE_ADD_NEWER_INHERIT_PROPERTIES = 7


Private Type FILETIME
        dwLowDateTime As Long
        dwHighDateTime As Long
End Type


Private Type CRYPT_INTEGER_BLOB
    cbData As Long
    pbData As Long   ' Pointer to Byte Array
End Type


Private Type CRYPT_ALGORITHM_IDENTIFIER
    pszObjId As Long     ' Pointer to String
    Parameters As CRYPT_INTEGER_BLOB
End Type


Private Type CRYPT_BIT_BLOB
    cbData As Long
    pbData As Long   ' Pointer to Byte Array
    cUnusedBits As Long
End Type
```

continues

LISTING 7.1   Continued

```
Private Type CERT_PUBLIC_KEY_INFO
    Algorithm As CRYPT_ALGORITHM_IDENTIFIER
    PublicKey As CRYPT_BIT_BLOB
End Type

Private Type CERT_INFO
    dwVersion As Long
    SerialNumber As CRYPT_INTEGER_BLOB
    SignatureAlgorithm As CRYPT_ALGORITHM_IDENTIFIER
    Issuer As CRYPT_INTEGER_BLOB
    NotBefore As FILETIME
    NotAfter As FILETIME
    Subject As CRYPT_INTEGER_BLOB
    SubjectPublicKeyInfo As CERT_PUBLIC_KEY_INFO
    IssuerUniqueId As CRYPT_BIT_BLOB
    SubjectUniqueId As CRYPT_BIT_BLOB
    cExtension As Long
    rgExtension As Long      ' Pointer to CERT_EXTENSION
End Type

Private Type CERT_CONTEXT
    dwCertEncodingType As Long
    pbCertEncoded As Long     ' Pointer to Byte Array
    cbCertEncoded As Long
    pCertInfo As Long         ' Pointer to CERT_INFO
    hCertStore As Long
End Type

Private Type CRL_CONTEXT
    dwCertEncodingType As Long
    pbCrlEncoded As Long
    cbCrlEncoded As Long
    pCrlInfo As Long          ' Pointer to CRL_INFO
    hCertStore As Long
End Type

Private Declare Sub CopyMemory Lib "kernel32" Alias "RtlMoveMemory" ( _
    Destination As Any, ByVal Source As Long, _
    ByVal Length As Long)

Private Declare Function CertAddEncodedCRLToStore Lib "Crypt32.dll" ( _
    ByVal hCertStore As Long, ByVal dwCertEncodingType As Long, _
    ByVal pbCrlEncoded As String, ByVal cbCrlEncoded As Long, _
    ByVal dwAddDisposition As Long, ByVal ppCrlContext As Long) As Long
```

```
Private Declare Function CertCreateCRLContext Lib "Crypt32.dll" ( _
    ByVal dwCertEncodingType As Long, ByVal pbCrlEncoded As String, _
    ByVal cbCrlEncoded As Long) As Long

Private Declare Function CertVerifyCRLRevocation Lib "Crypt32.dll" ( _
    ByVal dwCertEncodingType As Long, ByVal pCertId As Long, _
    ByVal cCrlInfo As Long, ByRef rgpCrlInfo As Any) As Long

Private Declare Function CertFreeCRLContext Lib "Crypt32.dll" ( _
    ByVal pCrlContext As Long) As Long

Private Const CRYPT_E_EXISTS As Long = &H80092005
Private Const CRYPT_E_OSS_ERROR As Long = &H80093000
Private Const E_INVALIDARG As Long = &H80070057

Private m_strServer As String      ' The CA Server name

Private m_strCA As String          ' The CA Name

Private m_lCRLPointer As Long      ' Used to hold a CRL

Private m_bUseCRLToVerifyCerts As Boolean
```

Adding New Properties

Next, you need to add the property code for two new properties you're adding to the crypto class (Server and CertificateAuthority). Add these properties as in Listing 7.2.

LISTING 7.2　New Crypto Class Properties

```
Public Property Get Server() As String
    Server = m_strServer
End Property

Public Property Let Server(ByVal sNewValue As String)
    m_strServer = sNewValue
End Property

Public Property Get CertificateAuthority() As String
    CertificateAuthority = m_strCA
End Property

Public Property Let CertificateAuthority(ByVal sNewValue As String)
    m_strCA = sNewValue
End Property
```

Converting Bytes to Hex String

Now you can add a function to convert the certificate serial number from a byte string to a hex string. Remember that the bytes are in the reverse order that they need to be in the hex string. To add this functionality, add the function in Listing 7.3 to the crypto class.

LISTING 7.3   The `ConvertBytesToHexString` Function

```
Private Function ConvertBytesToHexString(sbOrg As String, _
        lbOrgLength As Long) As String
'****************************************************************
'* Written By: Davis Chapman
'* Date:       November 7, 1999
'*
'* Syntax:     ConvertBytesToHexString(sbOrg, lbOrgLength)
'*
'* Parameters: sbOrg As String
'*             lbOrgLength as Long
'*
'* Purpose: This will convert a byte string into a hex string.
'****************************************************************
    Dim strRtn As String
    Dim lPos As Long
    Dim strChr As String

    '--- Initialize the return string
    strRtn = ""
    '--- Loop through the bytes in reverse order
    For lPos = lbOrgLength To 1 Step -1
        '--- Get the current character's hex value
        strChr = Hex(Asc(Mid(sbOrg, lPos, 1)))
        '--- Do we need to pad it?
        If Len(strChr) < 2 Then
            '--- Pad the hex value so that it is 2 characters long
            If Len(strChr) = 1 Then
                strChr = "0" + strChr
            Else
                strChr = "00"
            End If
        End If
        '--- Append the hex value to the hex string
        strRtn = strRtn + strChr
    Next
    '--- Return the hex string
    ConvertBytesToHexString = strRtn
End Function
```

> **TIP**
>
> Because this function does not directly use any Crypto functionality, most programmers would not include it in the Crypto class. Instead, they would normally place it into a module. The placement of this function is really little more than a programming and object-oriented style issue. If I didn't make it clear at the beginning of this book, the Crypto class that you are creating in the examples is not intended to be an example of ideal object design (possibly not even good object design), but is intended to teach you how to interact with the CryptoAPI. By placing the code into a class, you can continue to use and extend it throughout all the example applications in all the chapters. I usually don't include all the CryptoAPI functionality in a single class, but instead organize it based on functional areas and how the classes will be used.

Checking Certificates Against the CA

Next, you need to add the functionality to verify the certificates against the Certificate Authority by using the CertAdmin object. You've basically seen all the key functionality in this process earlier in this chapter in the section "Verifying Certificates Against a CA." So, to add this functionality, add the function in Listing 7.4 to the crypto class.

LISTING 7.4   The CheckCertificateValidity Function

```
Public Function CheckCertificateValidity(lCertCtx As Long) As String
'****************************************************************
'* Written By: Davis Chapman
'* Date:       November 7, 1999
'*
'* Syntax:     CheckCertificateValidity(lCertCtx)
'*
'* Parameters:  lCertCtx As Long
'*
'* Purpose: This will extract the serial number from the
'*          certificate information type structure. It then
'*          uses the Certificate Administrator object to check
'*          the certificate status with the CA.
'****************************************************************
    Dim cAdm As CCertAdmin
    Dim ccTx As CERT_CONTEXT
    Dim crtInfo As CERT_INFO
    Dim strSn As String
    Dim strIssuer As String
    Dim lRtn As Long
    Dim lRsn As Long
```

continues

LISTING 7.4   Continued

```vb
Dim strMsg As String

On Error GoTo CheckCertificateValidityErr

'--- Initialize the return value
CheckCertificateValidity = ""
'--- Get the CERT_CONTEXT type structure
CopyMemory ccTx, lCertCtx, 20
'--- Get the CERT_INFO type structure
CopyMemory crtInfo, ccTx.pCertInfo, 112
'--- Size the serial number string to hold
'--- the certificate serial number
strSn = String(crtInfo.SerialNumber.cbData, vbNullChar)
'--- Copy the certificate serial number into the string
CopyMemory ByVal strSn, crtInfo.SerialNumber.pbData, _
            crtInfo.SerialNumber.cbData
'--- Convert the serial number into a hex string
strSn = ConvertBytesToHexString(strSn, crtInfo.SerialNumber.cbData)
'--- Create the Cert Admin object
Set cAdm = New CCertAdmin
'--- Check the validity of the certificate
lRtn = cAdm.IsValidCertificate(m_strServer + "\" + m_strCA, strSn)
'--- Determine what the status of the certificate is
Select Case lRtn
    Case CA_DISP_INCOMPLETE
        CheckCertificateValidity = _
                "The Certificate Check was Incomplete"
    Case CA_DISP_ERROR
        CheckCertificateValidity = _
                "The Certificate Check had an Error"
    Case CA_DISP_REVOKED
        strMsg = "Certificate has been Revoked"
        '--- The certificate has been revoked, get the reason
        lRsn = cAdm.GetRevocationReason
        Select Case lRsn
            Case CRL_REASON_UNSPECIFIED
                strMsg = strMsg + vbCrLf + " --> Unspecified reason"
            Case CRL_REASON_KEY_COMPROMISE
                strMsg = strMsg + vbCrLf + " --> Key was compromised"
            Case CRL_REASON_CA_COMPROMISE
                strMsg = strMsg + vbCrLf + _
                            " --> Certificate Authority was compromised"
            Case CRL_REASON_AFFILIATION_CHANGED
                strMsg = strMsg + vbCrLf + _
                            " --> Affiliation was changed"
            Case CRL_REASON_SUPERSEDED
```

Working with Certificate Revocation Lists

CHAPTER 7

241

7

WORKING WITH
CERTIFICATE
REVOCATION LISTS

```
                    strMsg = strMsg + vbCrLf + _
                            " --> Certificate was superseded"
                Case CRL_REASON_CESSATION_OF_OPERATION
                    strMsg = strMsg + vbCrLf + _
                            " --> Cessation of operation"
                Case CRL_REASON_CERTIFICATE_HOLD
                    strMsg = strMsg + vbCrLf + _
                            " --> Certificate placed on hold"
                Case CRL_REASON_REMOVE_FROM_CRL
                    strMsg = strMsg + vbCrLf + " --> Removed from CRL"
            End Select
            CheckCertificateValidity = strMsg
        Case CA_DISP_VALID
            CheckCertificateValidity = "Certificate is Valid"
        Case CA_DISP_INVALID
            CheckCertificateValidity = "Certificate is Invalid"
        Case CA_DISP_UNDER_SUBMISSION
            CheckCertificateValidity = "Certificate is Under Submission"
    End Select
    '--- Clean up
    Set cAdm = Nothing
    Exit Function

CheckCertificateValidityErr:
    '--- An error occurred, display it for the user
    MsgBox "Error: " + Str(Err.Number) + " - " + Err.Description
    Resume Next
End Function
```

In this listing, you first use the CopyMemory function to retrieve the CERT_CONTEXT type structure from the pointer that was passed in. Next, you use the pointer to the CERT_INFO to get the
actual CERT_INFO type structure. Finally, you retrieve the byte string containing the Certificate
serial number. You then call the ConvertBytesToHexString function to convert the serial number into a hex string.

At this point, you create an instance of the CertAdmin object. After you create it, you call the
IsValidCertificate method to verify the certificate. If the resulting certificate status was
"revoked," the GetRevocationReason method is called to find out why.

A string is returned from this function containing a message that specifies what the current status of the certificate is.

Creating a CRL from a File

Next, you can turn your attention to creating a CRL context from a CRL downloaded from the
Certificate Authority's Web site. Downloading a CRL through a Web browser, you'll most

likely save the CRL as a file. Therefore, you can assume that you'll be passed a filename for the CRL to be used as a parameter to the function.

After you've read the CRL into a string variable, you can use it to create a CRL context by using the `CertCreateCRLContext` function. When you have a CRL context, you can call the `ListCerts` function, passing the certificate store name that was passed in. You also need to set a Boolean flag to control whether the certificates are validated against the CRL or the CA. To add this functionality to the crypto class, add the function in Listing 7.5.

LISTING 7.5   The `CreateCRLAndCheckCerts` Function

```
Public Function CreateCRLAndCheckCerts(pszStoreName As String, _
                pszFileName As String) As String
'**************************************************************
'* Written By: Davis Chapman
'* Date:       November 7, 1999
'*
'* Syntax:     CreateCRLAndCheckCerts(pszStoreName As String,
'*                                    pszFileName As String)
'*
'* Parameters:  pszStoreName As String
'*              pszFileName As String
'*
'* Purpose: This will read in a CRL list from a file retrieved
'*          from a CA and create a CRL_CONTEXT type from it.
'*          It will then call the ListCerts function to list
'*          the certificates in the store, comparing them to
'*          the CRL to determine if they are valid.
'**************************************************************
    Dim strCRL As String
    Dim lFileLength As Long
    Dim lFileNbr As Long

    CreateCRLAndCheckCerts = ""
    '-- Get the length of the file to be decrypted
    lFileLength = FileLen(pszFileName)

    '-- Allocate the string to hold the entire file
    strCRL = String(lFileLength, vbNullChar)

    '-- Open the file in binary mode
    lFileNbr = FreeFile
    Open pszFileName For Binary Access Read As #lFileNbr

    '-- Read in the file
    Get #lFileNbr, , strCRL
```

```
    '-- Close the file
    Close #lFileNbr

    '--- Create the CRL from the file
    m_lCRLPointer = CertCreateCRLContext(X509_ASN_ENCODING Or _
            PKCS_7_ASN_ENCODING, strCRL, Len(strCRL))

    '--- Did we get a valid pointer?
    If m_lCRLPointer <> 0 Then
        '--- Specify that we'll be checking certs against the CRL
        m_bUseCRLToVerifyCerts = True
        '--- List the certs
        CreateCRLAndCheckCerts = ListCerts(pszStoreName)
        '--- Reset the flag
        m_bUseCRLToVerifyCerts = False
        '--- Release the CRL
        If Not CBool(CertFreeCRLContext(m_lCRLPointer)) Then
        End If
    End If
End Function
```

Checking Certificates Against a CRL

Now that you have a CRL context, you can validate certificates against it. You should get a pointer to the CRL_INFO type structure and load it into an array, as you saw earlier when looking at the CertVerifyCRLRevocation function. You also need to get a pointer to the CERT_INFO type structure from the pointer to the CERT_CONTEXT type structure.

When you have both of these pointers, you can call the CertVerifyCRLRevocation function to validate the certificate. You can format a string message to return, indicating whether the certificate is valid. To add this functionality to the crypto class, add the function in Listing 7.6.

LISTING 7.6 The CheckCertAgainstCRL Function

```
Private Function CheckCertAgainstCRL(lCertCtx As Long) As String
'*************************************************************
'* Written By: Davis Chapman
'* Date:       November 7, 1999
'*
'* Syntax:     CheckCertAgainstCRL(lCertCtx)
'*
'* Parameters:  lCertCtx As Long
'*
'* Purpose: This will compare the certificate context passed in
'*          to the CRL context currently held in memory to check
```

continues

LISTING 7.6   Continued

```
'*              whether the certificate is still valid.
'******************************************************************
    Dim ccTx As CERT_CONTEXT
    Dim cCrlTx As CRL_CONTEXT
    Dim strMsg As String
    Dim larrCrlInfos(1) As Long

    On Error GoTo CheckCertAgainstCRLErr

    '--- Initialize the return value
    CheckCertAgainstCRL = ""
    '--- Get the CERT_CONTEXT type structure
    CopyMemory ccTx, lCertCtx, 20
    '--- Get the CRL_CONTEXT type structure
    CopyMemory cCrlTx, m_lCRLPointer, 20
    '--- Put the pointer to the CRL_INFO type into an array
    larrCrlInfos(0) = cCrlTx.pCrlInfo
    '--- Check the validity of the certificate
    If CBool(CertVerifyCRLRevocation( _
            X509_ASN_ENCODING Or PKCS_7_ASN_ENCODING, _
            ccTx.pCertInfo, 1, larrCrlInfos(0))) Then
        strMsg = "Certificate is Valid"
    Else
        strMsg = "Certificate is NOT Valid!!!"
    End If
    '--- Return the results
    CheckCertAgainstCRL = strMsg
    Exit Function

CheckCertAgainstCRLErr:
    '--- An error occurred, display it for the user
    MsgBox "Error: " + Str(Err.Number) + " - " + Err.Description
    Resume Next
End Function
```

Adding a CRL to a Certificate Store

Next, you can add a function to take the CRL that you downloaded from the Certificate
Authority and import it into a certificate store. This function will read in the file containing the
CRL and use the `CertAddEncodedCRLToStore` function to import the CRL into the certificate
store opened using the `CertOpenSystemStore` function. To add this functionality, add the subroutine in Listing 7.7 to the crypto class.

LISTING 7.7   The GetCRLFromCA Subroutine

```
Public Sub GetCRLFromCA(pszStoreName As String, pszFileName As String)
'***************************************************************
'* Written By: Davis Chapman
'* Date:       November 7, 1999
'*
'* Syntax:     GetCRLFromCA(pszStoreName, pszFileName)
'*
'* Parameters:  pszStoreName As String
'*              pszFileName As String
'*
'* Purpose: This will read in a CRL list from a file retrieved
'*          from a CA and will load it into the certificate
'*          store.
'***************************************************************
    Dim hCertStore As Long
    Dim strCRL As String
    Dim strMsg As String
    Dim lCrlCtx As Long
    Dim lFileLength As Long
    Dim lFileNbr As Long

    '-- Get the length of the file to be decrypted
    lFileLength = FileLen(pszFileName)

    '-- Allocate the string to hold the entire file
    strCRL = String(lFileLength, vbNullChar)

    '-- Open the file in binary mode
    lFileNbr = FreeFile
    Open pszFileName For Binary Access Read As #lFileNbr

    '-- Read in the file
    Get #lFileNbr, , strCRL

    '-- Close the file
    Close #lFileNbr

    '--- Open a system certificate store.
    hCertStore = CertOpenSystemStore(0, pszStoreName)

    '--- Add the CRL to the certificate store
    If Not (CBool(CertAddEncodedCRLToStore(hCertStore, _
            X509_ASN_ENCODING Or PKCS_7_ASN_ENCODING, _
            strCRL, Len(strCRL), _
            CERT_STORE_ADD_REPLACE_EXISTING_INHERIT_PROPERTIES, 0))) Then
```

continues

7

WORKING WITH
CERTIFICATE
REVOCATION LISTS

LISTING 7.7 Continued

```
            '--- Determine why the CRL couldn't be added
            Select Case Err.LastDllError
                Case CRYPT_E_EXISTS
                    strMsg = "Certificate Revocation List already exists."
                Case CRYPT_E_OSS_ERROR
                    strMsg = "ASN.1 Decoding Error."
                Case E_INVALIDARG
                    strMsg = "Invalid argument."
                Case Else
                    strMsg = _
                        "Unable to import the Certificate Revocation List"
            End Select
            '--- Display the error message for the user
            MsgBox strMsg
        End If


        '--- Close the Certificate store
        CertCloseStore hCertStore, 0
    End Sub
```

Modifying the Certificate Listing

Two modifications need to be made to existing functionality in the crypto class to complete the
functionality that you need. The first is in the ListCerts function. Just after the subject name
is retrieved for a certificate, check the Boolean variable that is controlling which approach is
used to check the certificate validity, and call the appropriate function. To add this functionality, add the bolded code in Listing 7.8 to the ListCerts function in the crypto class (you originally created this function in the preceding chapter).

LISTING 7.8 The Modified ListCerts Function

```
Public Function ListCerts(pszStoreName As String) As String
'***************************************************************
'* Written By: Davis Chapman
'* Date:      October 12, 1999
'*
'* Syntax:    ListCerts(pszStoreName)
'*
'* Parameters: pszStoreName As String
'*
'* Purpose: This will loop through all of the certificates in
'*          the specified store, listing the available
'*          properties of each in turn. It builds this
'*          information as a large text string that is returned
```

```
'*          to the calling function to be displayed to the user.
'****************************************************************

    On Error GoTo ListCertsErr

    Dim hCertStore As Long
    Dim pszNameString As String * 256
    Dim pvData As String
    Dim dwData As Long
    Dim kcData As CERT_KEY_CONTEXT
    Dim kpiData As CRYPT_KEY_PROV_INFO
    Dim cbData As Long
    Dim dwPropId As Long
    Dim strMsg As String
    Dim lpCertContext As Long
    Dim szStoreName As String
    Dim szRtnMsg As String
    Dim iPos As Integer
    Dim iVerToUse As Integer


    szRtnMsg = ""
    dwPropId = 0

    '--- Open a system certificate store.
    hCertStore = CertOpenSystemStore(0, pszStoreName)

    '--- Did we open a store?
    If (hCertStore <> 0) Then
        szRtnMsg = "The " + pszStoreName + " store has been opened." + _
                vbCrLf
    Else
        m_sErrorMsg = "Error during CertOpenSystemStore - " & _
                CStr(Err.LastDllError) & Error$
        MsgBox m_sErrorMsg, vbOKOnly, "VB Crypto"
        Exit Function
    End If

    '--- Use CertEnumCertificatesInStore to get the certificates
    '--- from the open store.
    lpCertContext = CertEnumCertificatesInStore( _
        hCertStore, _
        0)

    '--- Loop until all certificates have been retrieved
    While (lpCertContext <> 0)
```

7

WORKING WITH
CERTIFICATE
REVOCATION LISTS

continues

LISTING 7.8   Continued

```
'--- A certificate was retrieved.
'--- Get the name from the certificate.
If (CertGetNameString( _
        lpCertContext, _
        CERT_NAME_SIMPLE_DISPLAY_TYPE, _
        0, _
        0, _
        pszNameString, _
        128)) Then

    '--- Find the end of the name
    iPos = InStr(1, pszNameString, vbNullChar, vbBinaryCompare)
    '--- Strip off the remaining NULL characters
    If iPos> 0 Then pszNameString = Left(pszNameString, _
            (iPos - 1))
    '--- Tell the user the name of the certificate
    szRtnMsg = szRtnMsg + vbCrLf + "Certificate for " + _
            Trim$(pszNameString) + vbCrLf
Else
    m_sErrorMsg = "Error during CertGetNameString - " & _
            CStr(Err.LastDllError) & Error$
    MsgBox m_sErrorMsg, vbOKOnly, "VB Crypto"
End If
'--- Check validity of certificate
If m_bUseCRLToVerifyCerts Then
    szRtnMsg = szRtnMsg + CheckCertAgainstCRL(lpCertContext) + _
                _vbCrLf
Else
    szRtnMsg = szRtnMsg + _
                CheckCertificateValidity(lpCertContext) + _
                vbCrLf
End If
'--- Loop to find all of the property identifiers for the
'--- specified certificate. The loop continues until
'--- CertEnumCertificateContextProperties returns zero.
.
.
.
End Function
```

The last change to the crypto class is the initialization of the Boolean value controlling which method is used to validate certificates. You need to initialize this variable as FALSE in the class initialization, as shown in the bolded code in Listing 7.9.

Listing 7.9 The Modified Class Initialization Subroutine

```
Private Sub Class_Initialize()
'****************************************************************
'* Written By: Davis Chapman
'* Date:        January 05, 2000
'*
'* Syntax:      Class_Initialize
'*
'* Parameters:  None
'*
'* Purpose: Calls the InitUser function to initialize the
'*          class. The initialization process loads the CSP
'*          and Public/Private key.
'****************************************************************
    If Not InitUser Then
        m_sErrorMsg = "Unable to initialize CryptoAPI."
        MsgBox m_sErrorMsg, vbOKOnly, "VB Crypto"
    End If

    m_bUseCRLToVerifyCerts = False
End Sub
```

Modifying the Form

Now you can turn your attention to the form portion of the application. You need to add a few new controls to the form to specify the server and Certificate Authority name, along with the filename where the CRL is saved. You also need to add some additional command buttons to trigger some of this additional functionality. Add these controls, modifying the form as shown in Figure 7.3. Set the properties of these new controls as specified in Table 7.7.

Table 7.7 Control Property Settings

Control	Property	Value
Label	Caption	Ser&ver Name:
TextBox	Name	txtServer
Label	Caption	Certi&ficate Authority:
TextBox	Name	txtCA
Combo Box (Existing)	Name	cboStore
	List	MY
		ROOT
		CA

continues

TABLE 7.7   Continued

Control	Property	Value
		SPC
		TRUST
Command Button (Existing)	Name	cmdList
	Caption	&List Certificates
CommonDialog	Name	cdFile
TextBox (Existing)	Name	txtCerts
	Multiline	True
Label	Caption	&CRL File:
TextBox	Name	txtFileName
Command Button	Name	cmdBrowse
	Caption	&Browse
Command Button	Name	cmdCreateCrlListCerts
	Caption	C&ompare Certs to CRL
Command Button	Name	cmdGetCRL
	Caption	&Import CRL List
Command Button (Existing)	Name	cmdExit
	Caption	E&xit

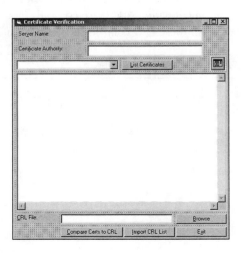

FIGURE 7.3

Designing the application form.

Working with Certificate Revocation Lists

CHAPTER 7

251

7

WORKING WITH
CERTIFICATE
REVOCATION LISTS

> **NOTE**
>
> All of the controls labeled as "Existing" should already be on the form from the pre-vious application you created. These controls should be kept without any changes.

Using the CA to Verify Certificates

Now that you've added the controls as specified, if you kept all the controls and code you cre-ated in the preceding chapter, you should be ready to check the validity of the certificates in your store. Before testing, it would be a good idea to revoke at least one of the certificates in your store so that you can see that the revoked certificate is recognized as being no longer valid. If you are testing against a copy of Microsoft's Certificate Server, and you have adminis-trative privileges, you might want to revoke one or more of your certificates, as shown in Figure 7.4. Select the certificate in the list of issued certificates, right-click, and select All Tasks, Revoke Certificates. You then can choose any reason you want from the list of available revocation reasons.

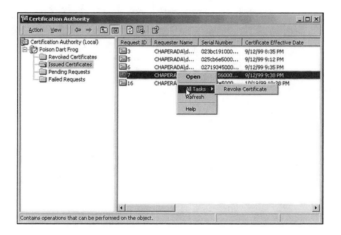

FIGURE 7.4
Revoking a certificate.

Before running your application, you'll want to make one last change to the existing applica-tion. Be sure to set the Server and Certificate Authority properties of the Crypto class to the values that the user has entered. To make this change, add the bolded lines of code to the Click event of the cmdList button, as in Listing 7.10.

LISTING 7.10 The cmdList Click Event

```
Private Sub cmdList_Click()
    Dim csCrypt As New clsCrypto

    '--- Retrieve and display the list of certificates
    csCrypt.Server = txtServer
    csCrypt.CertificateAuthority = txtCA
    txtCerts = csCrypt.ListCerts(cboStore)
End Sub
```

At this point, you should be ready to test the first method of validating certificates. Run your application, fill in the server and Certificate Authority names, and select the MY certificate store. Then click the List Certificates button to see a list of your certificates and their status, including the revoked one, as shown in Figure 7.5.

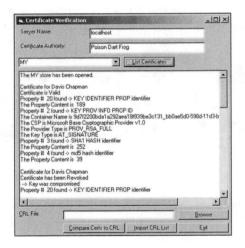

FIGURE 7.5
Listing the certificates with their validity status.

Using the CRL to Verify Certificates

Now that you have that portion of functionality working, it's time to add the pieces that enable you to verify certificates against a CRL. First, you can add an easy way of finding the CRL that has been downloaded. This is a simple matter of using the Common Dialog Control when the user clicks on the Browse button. You can filter the files, looking for the CRL file extension, as in Listing 7.11.

LISTING 7.11   The cmdBrowse Click Event

```
Private Sub cmdBrowse_Click()
    cdFile.Filter = "CRL File|*.crl|All Files|*.*"
    cdFile.ShowOpen
    txtFileName.Text = cdFile.FileName
End Sub
```

Next, when the user clicks on the Compare Certs to CRL button, you can call the CreateCRLAndCheckCerts function to use the CRL to validate the certificates. To add this functionality, add the code in Listing 7.12 to the Click event of the cmdCreateCrlListCerts button.

LISTING 7.12   The cmdCreateCrlListCerts Click Event

```
Private Sub cmdCreateCrlListCerts_Click()
    Dim csCrypt As New clsCrypto

    csCrypt.Server = txtServer
    csCrypt.CertificateAuthority = txtCA
    txtCerts = csCrypt.CreateCRLAndCheckCerts(cboStore, txtFileName)
End Sub
```

Before you try to validate your certificates against the CRL, you need to make sure that an updated CRL has been published by the Certificate Authority. To do so, select the Revoked Certificates folder in the Certificate Administration utility, right-click, and then select All Tasks, Publish, as shown in Figure 7.6.

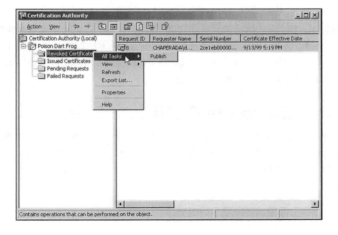

FIGURE 7.6
Publishing the Certificate Revocation List.

7

Now that you've made sure that an updated CRL has been published, you need to retrieve it. Using your Web browser, go to the Web site of the Certificate Authority, and follow the links to download the Certificate Revocation List, as shown in Figure 7.7. When prompted, save the CRL to your drive in the project directory.

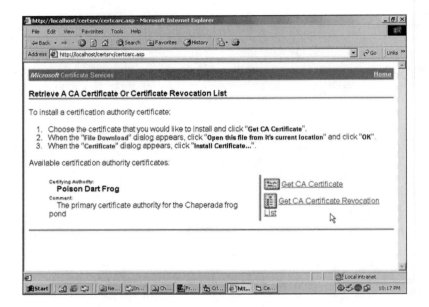

FIGURE 7.7

Retrieving the CRL from the Certificate Authority.

Now that you've retrieved the CRL from the Certificate Authority, you're ready to test your application's capability to verify certificates against the CRL. Run your application, specifying the MY certificate store in the combo box, and locate the CRL file you downloaded by using the Browse button. Next, click the Compare Certs to the CRL button to list the certificates, verifying them against the CRL, as shown in Figure 7.8.

Importing the CRL to the Certificate Store

You need to trigger one last piece of functionality to complete your application. When the user clicks on the Import CRL List button, you need to call the GetCRLFromCA method of the crypto class. To add this functionality, add the code in Listing 7.13 to the Click event of the cmdGetCRL button.

FIGURE 7.8
Listing the certificates with their status using the CRL.

LISTING 7.13   The cmdGetCRL Click Event

```
Private Sub cmdGetCRL_Click()
    Dim csCrypt As New clsCrypto

    csCrypt.Server = txtServer
    csCrypt.CertificateAuthority = txtCA
    csCrypt.GetCRLFromCA cboStore, txtFileName
    MsgBox "CRL Added to the Certificate Store."
End Sub
```

Summary

This chapter covers some significant ground. The whole area of using certificates to verify identity falls apart without some way of validating that a certificate has or hasn't been revoked. A certificate might be revoked for many reasons, not the least of which might be that the private key associated with the certificate has been compromised and is in the possession of someone other than the person you think it belongs to. As a result, this is a key area of functionality for building applications that communicate securely.

In the next chapter, you'll look at digital signatures, how to create them, and how to validate them. Digital signatures go hand-in-hand with digital certificates and are a key piece to verifying that messages and data you receive are from the people you think they are, and that they haven't been modified or corrupted.

Using Digital Signatures

IN THIS CHAPTER

- What Are Digital Signatures?
- Signing Messages and Verifying Signatures
- Enveloping Messages
- Building a Signing Utility

Now that you have an understanding of what digital certificates are and how to get, manage, and verify them, it's time to look at why you need them. In this chapter, you'll learn how digital certificates are used to sign messages so that the recipient can verify that the message came from you and that it hasn't been modified. By using these digital signatures, you can guarantee that the message received by someone is the same message you sent.

Along with signing messages, digital certificates are used as a means of exchanging public keys; you can use the message recipient's certificate to encrypt a message so that only the owner of that certificate can decrypt it. Combining the two uses of certificates, signing and encrypting, you can create a digital envelope, in which a signed message is then encrypted so that only the owner of the private key can decrypt it and verify the signature.

NOTE

This chapter requires that you have a system with a minimum of NT 4 with Service Pack 3 (or higher), or Windows 95 with Internet Explorer 3.02 (or higher). The material covered in this chapter is not available on the earliest versions of the Crypto API.

PREREQUISITES

Before reading this chapter, you need to make sure that you have a good understanding of the following:

- Digital certificates, digital signatures, and message enveloping, as covered in Chapter 1, "Understanding Encryption and Application Security"
- Selecting and opening Cryptographic Service Providers (CSP), as covered in Chapter 2, "Getting Started with the CryptoAPI"
- Hashing data, generating encryption keys, and encrypting and decrypting data, as covered in Chapter 3, "Symmetric and Password Encryption"
- Using public/private encryption keys, as covered in Chapter 4, "Public/Private Key Communications"
- Requesting and retrieving digital certificates, as covered in Chapter 5, "Requesting and Retrieving Certificates"
- Managing digital certificates in a certificate store, as covered in Chapter 6, "Working with Certificates"

What Are Digital Signatures?

A *digital signature* is a mechanism used to verify that a message, file, or other digital object has not been modified since it was signed. Second, it identifies the person (or persons) who signed the message, file, or other object.

You might be thinking, "Big deal!" You can make sure that a message or file hasn't been modified by making a hash of the message before sending it and then making a second hash after receiving it. You can then compare the two hashes to make sure that the message hasn't been modified.

To verify who created the first hash of the message, you could encrypt it using the sender's private key. This would mean that the recipient has to use the sender's public key to decrypt the hash before comparing the pre- and post-sending hashes. This process will verify who created the hash.

In a nutshell, this series of steps is what digital signatures do. A digital signature is created by first creating a hash of the message to be signed. The hash is then "signed" using the private key of the signer. This means that the hash is encrypted using an algorithm designed specifically for use in signing messages. This algorithm is designed not to keep the hash secret, but to prevent any possible modifications or other tampering with the hash. The whole process of creating a digital signature is illustrated in Figure 8.1.

8

> **NOTE**
>
> The primary aspect of digital signatures that has been left out of this description is the formatting of the signatures and signed messages. There are standard message formatting rules, which treat the entire signed message as a type structure, that you need to follow to be able to freely exchange signed messages with other people and applications. By using API functions that sign messages for you, the formatting is taken care of for you.

The signature is verified by the recipient creating his or her own hash of the original message. Then the new hash, the sender's public key (or rather the certificate that contains the sender's public key), and the signature are fed into a signature verification algorithm. This algorithm decrypts the signature using the sender's public key and then compares the hashes. If the hashes match, the signature is valid. This process is illustrated in Figure 8.2.

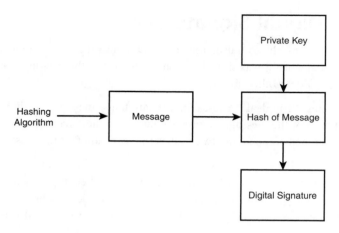

FIGURE 8.1
Creating a digital signature.

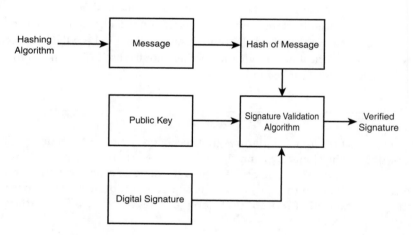

FIGURE 8.2
Verifying a digital signature.

Signatures can be packaged with the message or file that is being signed or can be kept separate. If a message or file needs to be signed by multiple people, it is often easier to keep the signatures separate from the message so that the later signers are not signing the signatures of the earlier signers. If this were the case, the signatures would have to be verified in a specific order and would be difficult to manage if you needed to be able to verify only a specific signature.

Signing Messages and Verifying Signatures

At this point, you already know how to perform all the necessary steps in creating a digital signature on your own. You know how to create a hash of an object and then how to encrypt that hash using an encryption key. What you don't know how to do is format the various pieces of information that make up a digital signature into a single object. Here, the process can get a little hairy.

The good news is that this process doesn't have to be as complicated as what you already know how to do. You can use a series of "simplified" functions that perform these tasks with a minimum of code. These functions not only create the digital signature with a single function call, but they also format the signature in the standardized object format used with digital signatures.

Encryption Algorithms and Pointers

One of the sticking points to using these "simplified" message functions is that you have to create some pointers for the type structures used by these functions. Does this mean that you'll have to finally dip into a little C code to supplement your Visual Basic code? Not yet. You can still find ways around this beast.

First, you need to be able to specify the encryption and signing algorithm to be used. It is specified through the CRYPT_ALGORITHM_IDENTIFIER type structure. In the preceding chapter, you defined this type as follows:

Syntax

```
Type CRYPT_ALGORITHM_IDENTIFIER
    pszObjId As Long      ' Pointer to String
    Parameters As CRYPT_INTEGER_BLOB
End Type
```

Now you need to be able to attach a string to the pszObjId member, which is a pointer to a string. This is a simple matter of redefining the pszObjId member as a string, as follows:

Syntax

```
Type CRYPT_ALGORITHM_IDENTIFIER
    pszObjId As String
    Parameters As CRYPT_INTEGER_BLOB
End Type
```

Visual Basic automatically handles this as a pointer to a string. You therefore can set the Object ID (OID) for the signing and encryption algorithms just as you would set any other string variable.

Next, you need to be able to create pointers to some nonstring variables. You can do so by using an undocumented function in Visual Basic called `VarPtr` (short for Variable Pointer). This simple function is a part of Visual Basic, starting with version 5. You pass it any variable, and it will return a pointer to that variable. The definition for this function is as follows:

Syntax

```
VarPtr(vVariable as Any) as Long
```

You also can use corresponding functions for creating pointers to strings and objects. These functions, `StrPtr` and `ObjPtr`, are also completely undocumented.

NOTE

Is it safe to use undocumented functions? The `VarPtr` function has actually been a part of Visual Basic for some time. It's just that, up through Visual Basic 4, you had to declare the function yourself, just like any other API function. With Visual Basic 5, it became a part of the base environment, eliminating the need for you to write a `declare` statement. With the addition of the two partner functions, for getting pointers to strings and objects, these clues all point toward these functions remaining a part of Visual Basic for some time.

Because these functions are undocumented, you will not be able to get help or support on any problems you encounter or bugs you find. This is the trade-off you make when you use them. Using pointers can be dangerous because you can crash your program very easily by using them incorrectly. However, sometimes you need them, and your choices are to use these undocumented functions or to create your own.

Signing a Message

When you need to sign a message, you can easily get this job done. You can wrap up the entire signing and packaging process by using the `CryptSignMessage` function. This function uses several lower-level functions, including `CryptCreateHash`, `CryptHashData`, and `CryptSignHash`. The syntax for this function is as follows:

Syntax

```
Public Declare Function CryptSignMessage Lib "Crypt32.dll" ( _
    pSignPara As CRYPT_SIGN_MESSAGE_PARA, _
    ByVal fDetachedSignature As Long, ByVal cToBeSigned As Long, _
    rgpbToBeSigned As String, rgcbToBeSigned As Long, _
    ByVal pbSignedBlob As String, pcbSignedBlob As Long) As Long
```

The first parameter (pSignPara) to this function is a new type structure, CRYPT_SIGN_
MESSAGE_PARA. You need to populate this type structure with numerous pieces of information
on how to perform the signing. The definition of this type structure is shown in the following
section.

The second parameter (fDetachedSignature) is a long Boolean value that specifies whether
the signature is to be detached from the message. If the signature is to be packaged with the
message, this parameter needs to be zero (0). If the signature is to be packaged separately from
the message, this parameter should be any nonzero value.

The third, fourth, and fifth parameters are used to pass the messages to be signed to the function. The third parameter (cToBeSigned) specifies the number of messages to be signed. The
fourth parameter (rgpbToBeSigned) is an array of strings, containing the messages to be signed.
The fifth parameter (rgcbToBeSigned) is an array of long values, specifying the length of each
of the messages in the fourth parameter. In using this function, you pass the first array element
of the message and message length arrays as the fourth and fifth parameters.

The sixth parameter (pbSignedBlob) contains the string variable into which the signature is
returned if it is to be detached, or the signed message if the signature is to be packaged with
the message. The seventh parameter (pcbSignedBlob) is a long variable specifying the length
of the string passed into the sixth parameter. If the string in the sixth parameter is not long
enough, this parameter will contain the length needed.

The Syntax for the CRYPT_SIGN_MESSAGE_PARA Type Structure

The definition of the CRYPT_SIGN_MESSAGE_PARA type structure, the first parameter of the
CryptSignMessage function, is as follows:

Syntax

```
Type CRYPT_SIGN_MESSAGE_PARA
    cbSize As Long
    dwMsgEncodingType As Long
    pSigningCert As Long        ' Pointer to signing certificate context
    HashAlgorithm As CRYPT_ALGORITHM_IDENTIFIER
    pvHashAuxInfo As Long
    cMsgCert As Long
    rgpMsgCert As Long          ' Pointer to array of certificate context
                                ' pointers
    cMsgCrl As Long
    rgpMsgCrl As Long           ' Pointer to array of CRL context pointers
    cAuthAttr As Long
    rgAuthAttr As Long          ' Pointer to CRYPT_ATTRIBUTE type
    cUnauthAttr As Long
    rgUnauthAttr As Long        ' Pointer to CRYPT_ATTRIBUTE type
```

8

USING DIGITAL
SIGNATURES

```
    dwFlags As Long
    dwInnerContentType As Long
End Type
```

The first member of this type, `cbSize`, is the size of this structure. Currently, this value should always be 68, but it could change if this type is ever redefined.

TIP

To calculate the size of a type structure, add up the number of bytes that each variable occupies. In this case, there are 14 long variables that use 4 bytes each (14 * 4 = 56), and one `CRYPT_ALGORITHM_IDENTIFIER` type structure. The `CRYPT_ALGORITHM_IDENTIFIER` is a pointer to a string (a long) and a `CRYPT_INTEGER_BLOB` type structure. The `CRYPT_INTEGER_BLOB` type structure consists of two more long variables. The grand total is 17 long variables (17 * 4 = 68).

The second member of this type structure, `dwMsgEncodingType`, is a flag that specifies how the signature should be encoded. The available values, which can be combined using `OR`, are listed in Table 8.1.

TABLE 8.1   Encoding Type Flag Values

Constant	Value	Description
X509_ASN_ENCODING	&H1	X.509 Encoding
PKCS_7_ASN_ENCODING	&H10000	PKCS #7 Message Formatting

The third member, `pSigningCert`, is the pointer to the certificate that should be used for signing the message. Although the certificate contains only the public key, and the message has to be signed using the associated private key, the `CryptSignMessage` function will retrieve the associated private key and use it to sign the message.

The fourth member, `HashAlgorithm`, is a `CRYPT_ALGORITHM_IDENTIFIER` type structure. You need to set the `pszObjId` member of this type structure to the OID of the signing algorithm to be used. Some of the available signing algorithm OIDs are listed in Table 8.2.

TABLE 8.2   Some Signing Algorithm OIDs

Algorithm	OID
MD2	1.2.840.113549.2.2
MD4	1.2.840.113549.2.4
MD5	1.2.840.113549.2.5

The fifth member, pvHashAuxInfo, is not currently used and should always be zero (0).

The sixth member, cMsgCert, specifies how many certificates are to be packaged with the message. If no certificates are to be packaged with the message, this value should be zero (0).

The seventh member, rgpMsgCert, is a pointer to an array of certificate context type structures. The certificate pointers in this array are the certificates that will be packaged with the message. You create this value by first declaring a variable as an array of long values. Next, you set the various array members to the certificate context pointers you need to include in the message. Finally, you use the VarPtr function to create a pointer to the first array position and set the rgpMsgCert value to this pointer. Your code should look something like the following:

```
Dim csmpSignParams As CRYPT_SIGN_MESSAGE_PARA
Dim lCertArray(1) As Long

'--- Number of certificates to be included with the
'--- signed message.
csmpSignParams.cMsgCert = 1
'--- Pointers to the certificate contexts of the certificates
'--- to be included in the signed message.
lCertArray(0) = m_lCertContextPointer
csmpSignParams.rgpMsgCert = VarPtr(lCertArray(0))
```

The eighth member, cMsgCrl, is the number of Certificate Revocation Lists (CRL) to be included in the message package. The ninth member, rgpMsgCrl, is an array of pointers to the CRL context type structures of the CRLs to be included. You can populate this array in the same way you populate the variables for the certificates to be included.

The next two members, cAuthAttr and rgAuthAttr, are for the authorized attributes for the signed message. The cAuthAttr member indicates the number of attributes, and the rgAuthAttr member is a pointer to an array of CRYPT_ATTRIBUTE type structures, specifying the attributes. The definition of the CRYPT_ATTRIBUTE type structure is shown in the following section.

The next two members, cUnauthAttr and rgUnauthAttr, are just like the previous two, except that they hold any unauthorized attributes.

The next member, dwFlags, is normally zero (0). This flag is sometimes used to control how the signed message is packaged.

The last member, dwInnerContentType, is also normally zero (0). This member is used to specify the encoding type of the message to be signed if that message is the encoded output from another function.

8

USING DIGITAL SIGNATURES

The Syntax for the CRYPT ATTRIBUTE Type Structure

The definition of the CRYPT_ATTRIBUTE type structure is as follows:

Syntax

```
Type CRYPT_ATTRIBUTE
    pszObjId As String
    cValue As Long
    rgValue As Long        ' Pointer to array of CRYPT_INTEGER_BLOB
End Type
```

For this type structure, the first member, pszObjId, is a string containing the OID of the attribute. The second member, cValue, is the number of values in the third member, rgValue. The third member, rgValue, is an array of pointers to CRYPT_INTEGER_BLOB type structures, which contain the attribute values.

Verifying a Message Signature

When you have a signed message, assuming that the signature is packaged with the message, you need to be able to verify the signature. Both the person doing the signing and the person who receives the message should verify the signature. You do so by using the CryptVerifyMessageSignature function. The syntax for this function is as follows:

Syntax

```
Public Declare Function CryptVerifyMessageSignature Lib "Crypt32.dll" ( _
    ➡pVerifyPara As CRYPT_VERIFY_MESSAGE_PARA, _
    ByVal dwSignerIndex As Long, ByVal pbSignedBlob As String, _
    ByVal cbSignedBlob As Long, ByVal pbDecoded As String, _
    pcbDecoded As Long, ppSignerCert As Long) As Long
```

> **NOTE**
>
> Why does the person signing the message need to verify the signature? The signature must be verified to make sure that it worked. If you are signing an important message, you don't want to be sending out the message with a bad signature on it. You want to be able to guarantee that the signature is valid, at least until the signed message leaves your possession.

The first parameter (pVerifyPara) to this function is a CRYPT_VERIFY_MESSAGE_PARA type structure. It performs the same purpose as the CRYPT_SIGN_MESSAGE_PARA type structure in the CryptSignMessage function. It is populated with various pieces of information that will be passed to the lower-level functions this function will call. The definition of the CRYPT_VERIFY_MESSAGE_PARA type structure is shown in the following section.

The second parameter (dwSignerIndex) is the index of the signature you want to verify. If a message has multiple signatures, you need to loop through all the signatures, starting with the first (0), incrementing each time to the next signature, until the function fails and a check of the Error object's LastDllError property returns CRYPT_E_NO_SIGNER (&H8009200E), indicating that all signatures have been validated.

The third parameter (pbSignedBlob) is a string buffer containing the signed message. The fourth parameter (cbSignedBlob) is the size of the message (including all the signatures and certificates packaged with it).

The fifth parameter (pbDecoded) is a string buffer into which will be placed the extracted message from the signed message package. The sixth parameter (pcbDecoded) is a long variable indicating the size of the string buffer in the previous parameter. You must allocate this string buffer prior to calling this function, either by using the String function to allocate it or by declaring the variable with a fixed length. As the extracted message is always smaller in size than the message package, allocating a string buffer the size of the message package guarantees that the buffer will be large enough to hold the extracted message. After the function returns, you'll need to strip off anything past the end of the actual message (using the size of the message returned in the sixth parameter).

The seventh parameter (ppSignerCert) is a pointer to a CERT_CONTEXT type structure into which will be placed the signer's certificate. If you don't need the signer's certificate, you can pass zero (0) for this value.

The Syntax for the CRYPT VERIFY MESSAGE PARA Type Structure

The definition of the CRYPT_VERIFY_MESSAGE_PARA type structure, the first parameter to the CryptVerifyMessageSignature function, is as follows:

Syntax

```
Type CRYPT_VERIFY_MESSAGE_PARA
    cbSize As Long
    dwMsgAndCertEncodingType As Long
    hCryptProv As Long
    pfnGetSignerCertificate As Long        ' Pointer to callback function
    pvGetArg As Long                       ' void Pointer
End Type
```

The first member of the CRYPT_VERIFY_MESSAGE_PARA type structure, cbSize, is the size of this type structure. For the current definition of this type, this value should always be 20.

8

USING DIGITAL
SIGNATURES

The second member of this type structure, dwMsgAndCertEncodingType, is the signature encoding type. The possible values for this member, which you can combine by using OR, are listed back in Table 8.1.

The third member, hCryptProv, is the handle of the CSP to be used to verify the signature. It should be the same CSP that was used to create the signature and used to create the keys in the certificate used to sign the message.

The fourth member, pfnGetSignerCertificate, is a pointer to a callback function that is used to retrieve the signing certificate. If this value is zero (0), the default function is used to locate and retrieve this certificate.

The fifth member, pvGetArg, is a pointer to an argument that you want to pass to the callback function in the pfnGetSignerCertificate member. If zero (0) is passed in the pfnGetSignerCertificate member, zero (0) should be passed in this member.

The Syntax for the Callback Function

If you want to create your own callback function to locate and retrieve the signer's certificate, you can use this function definition:

Syntax

```
Public Function PFN_CRYPT_GET_SIGNER_CERTIFICATE(pvGetArg As Long, _
             dwCertEncodingType As Long, pSignerId As Long, _
             hMsgCertStore As Long) As Long
```

The first parameter (pvGetArg) to this function is the pointer to an argument that you supplied to the CRYPT_VERIFY_MESSAGE_PARA type structure. This parameter can be used for any purpose specific to your implementation.

The second parameter (dwCertEncodingType) to this function is the encoding type flags. These flag values are listed in Table 8.1.

The third parameter (pSignerId) is a pointer to a CERT_INFO type structure that contains the signer's certificate issuer and serial number. You'll need this information to identify the certificate to be retrieved.

The fourth parameter (hMsgCertStore) is the handle of the certificate store that contains all the certificates and CRLs included in the signed message.

The return value that you have to return from this function is a pointer to the CERT_CONTEXT type structure of the signer's certificate. If you do not find a certificate and cannot create a certificate using the CertCreateCertificateContext function, you need to return zero (0).

> **NOTE**
>
> The CERT_CONTEXT that you return from this callback function must be freed by calling the CertFreeCertificateContext function.

Verifying a Detached Message Signature

If the signature is separate from the message, you need to use the CryptVerifyDetachedMessageSignature function to verify the signature. This function is defined as follows:

Syntax

```
Public Declare Function CryptVerifyDetachedMessageSignature Lib _
    "Crypt32.dll" (pVerifyPara As CRYPT_VERIFY_MESSAGE_PARA, _
    ByVal dwSignerIndex As Long, ByVal pbDetachedSignBlob As String, _
    ByVal cbDetachedSignBlob As Long, ByVal cToBeSigned As Long, _
    rgpbToBeSigned As String, rgcbToBeSigned As Long, _
    ppSignerCert As Long) As Long
```

The parameters for this function are basically a combination of the parameters for the CryptSignMessage and CryptVerifyMessageSignature functions. The first parameter (pVerifyPara) is a CRYPT_VERIFY_MESSAGE_PARA type structure, to be handled the same as with the CryptVerifyMessageSignature function.

The second parameter (dwSignerIndex) is the index of the signature to be verified. It works just as the same parameter did in the CryptVerifyMessageSignature function.

The third parameter (pbDetachedSignBlob) is a string buffer containing the message signatures. The fourth parameter (cbDetachedSignBlob) is the size of the string of signatures. These two parameters work just like the corresponding parameters for the signed message in the CryptVerifyMessageSignature function.

The fifth, sixth, and seventh parameters are straight from the CryptSignMessage function. The fifth parameter (cToBeSigned) is the number of messages to be verified. The sixth parameter (rgpbToBeSigned) is an array of strings containing the messages to be verified. The seventh parameter (rgcbToBeSigned) is an array of lengths for these messages. They need to be exactly the same as the corresponding values for the messages to be signed that are passed to the CryptSignMessage function.

The eighth parameter (ppSignerCert) is a pointer to a CRYPT_CONTEXT type structure. This type structure will be populated with the signer's certificate, just as in the CryptVerifyMessageSignature function.

Determining the Number of Signers

It is possible that a message can be signed multiple times, by multiple people. When you need to determine how many signatures have been placed on a message, you can use the `CryptGetMessageSignerCount` function. The definition of this function is as follows:

Syntax

```
Public Declare Function CryptGetMessageSignerCount Lib "Crypt32.dll" ( _
    ByVal dwMsgEncodingType As Long, ByVal pbSignedBlob As String, _
    ByVal cbSignedBlob As Long) As Long
```

The first parameter (`dwMsgEncodingType`) to this function is the encoding flag indicating how the signatures have been encoded and formatted. The possible values for this flag are given in Table 8.1.

The second parameter (`pbSignedBlob`) is a string buffer containing the signed message. The third parameter (`cbSignedBlob`) specifies the length of the signed message in the second parameter.

The return value from this function is a long value specifying the number of signatures in the signed message.

Enveloping Messages

One of the keys to signing and encrypting messages is the packaging of the signed and encrypted messages. You already know how to encrypt a message, but what you don't know is how to package the encrypted message with the certificate serial number so that the recipient can know which key pair to use to decrypt the message.

Along with formatting the encrypted message correctly, there is a practice of enclosing a signed message within an encrypted message. This practice is known as *enveloping*, in which only the intended recipient can decrypt the envelope and then read and verify the signed message.

Encrypting a Message

When you want to encrypt a message using the public key in the recipient's certificate, you can use the `CryptEncryptMessage` function. This function encrypts the message and packages the encrypted message with all the information needed by the recipient to determine what private key needs to be used to decrypt it. The definition of this function is as follows:

Syntax

```
Public Declare Function CryptEncryptMessage Lib "Crypt32.dll" ( _
    pEncryptPara As CRYPT_ENCRYPT_MESSAGE_PARA, _
```

```
ByVal cRecipientCert As Long, rgpRecipientCert As Long, _
ByVal pbToBeEncrypted As String, ByVal cbToBeEncrypted As Long, _
ByVal pbEncryptedBlob As String, pcbEncryptedBlob As Long) As Long
```

The first parameter (pEncryptPara) to this function is the CRYPT_ENCRYPT_MESSAGE_PARA type structure. As with the message signing functions, this type structure is populated with information that is passed to the lower-level functions that this function calls. This type structure is defined in the following section.

The second parameter (cRecipientCert) is a long value specifying the number of recipient certificates in the next parameter.

The third parameter (rgpRecipientCert) is an array of pointers to CERT_CONTEXT type structures. They are the recipients' certificates used to encrypt the message. You pass the first position in the array as the parameter.

The fourth parameter (pbToBeEncrypted) is the string buffer that contains the message to be encrypted. The fifth parameter (cbToBeEncrypted) specifies the length of this string buffer.

The sixth parameter (pbEncryptedBlob) is a string buffer into which the encrypted message will be placed. The seventh parameter (pcbEncryptedBlob) is a long variable that contains the length of the string buffer passed in the sixth parameter. If the string buffer isn't long enough, this variable will contain the required length of the string upon the function returning. If the function was successful, this variable will contain the actual length of the encrypted message. You will need to trim the encrypted string to the length specified in this variable, as the total buffer length required by this function is longer than the resulting encrypted message will be.

The Syntax for the CRYPT_ENCRYPT_MESSAGE_PARA Type Structure

The CRYPT_ENCRYPT_MESSAGE_PARA type structure, the first parameter of the CryptEncryptMessage function, is defined as follows:

Syntax

```
Type CRYPT_ENCRYPT_MESSAGE_PARA
    cbSize As Long
    dwMsgEncodingType As Long
    hCryptProv As Long
    ContentEncryptionAlgorithm As CRYPT_ALGORITHM_IDENTIFIER
    pvEncryptionAuxInfo As Long     ' void Pointer
    dwFlags As Long
    dwInnerContentType As Long
End Type
```

The first member of the CRYPT_ENCRYPT_MESSAGE_PARA type structure, cbSize, is the size of this type structure. Until this type structure is altered, this value will always be 32.

The second member, dwMsgEncodingType, is a flag that indicates the message encoding. The possible flag values for this member are listed in Table 8.1.

The third member, hCryptProv, is the handle to the CSP to be used for encrypting the message. If you set this member to zero (0), the default CSPs are used.

The fourth member, ContentEncryptionAlgorithm, is set to specify the encryption algorithm to be used. The pszObjId member of this element is set to the OID of the encryption algorithm to be used, and the Parameters member might need to be set to an initialization value. If the algorithm requires an initialization value, and none is provided, one is automatically generated by the CryptGenRandom function. Some of the possible encryption algorithms supported by the base CSP are listed in Table 8.3.

> **NOTE**
>
> It is important that the encryption algorithm specified be supported by the CSP being used to perform the encryption.

TABLE 8.3   Some Encryption Algorithm OIDs

Algorithm	OID
RC2	1.2.840.113549.3.2
RC4	1.2.840.113549.3.4
3DES	1.2.840.113549.3.7

The fifth member of this type structure, pvEncryptionAuxInfo, is a pointer to a CMSG_RC2_AUX_INFO type structure only if the RC2 algorithm is being used. Otherwise, this member should be zero (0). If you are using an RC2 encryption algorithm, you need to declare a variable of the CMSG_RC2_AUX_INFO type structure and get a pointer to it by using the VarPtr function. The CMSG_RC2_AUX_INFO type structure is defined in the following short section.

The sixth member, dwFlags, is normally set to zero (0). This flag is sometimes used to control how the signed message is packaged.

The seventh member, dwInnerContentType, is also normally set to zero (0). This member is used to specify the encoding type of the message to be encrypted if that message is the encoded output from another function.

The Syntax for the `CMSG_RC2_AUX_INFO` Type Structure

The `CMSG_RC2_AUX_INFO` type structure is defined as follows:

Syntax

```
Type CMSG_RC2_AUX_INFO
    cbSize As Long
    dwBitLen As Long
End Type
```

The first member of this type structure, `cbSize`, is the size of the type structure—in this case, 8. The second member, `dwBitLen`, is the length of the RC2 encryption key to be used. The currently supported values for this value are 40, 64, and 128.

Decrypting a Message

To decrypt a message that has been packaged using the `CryptEncryptMessage` function, you can use the `CryptDecryptMessage` function. This function decodes the encrypted message package, determining which key pair was used to encrypt the message, and retrieves the appropriate private key from the store. The declaration for this function is as follows:

Syntax

```
Public Declare Function CryptDecryptMessage Lib "Crypt32.dll" ( _
    pDecryptPara As CRYPT_DECRYPT_MESSAGE_PARA, _
    ByVal pbEncryptedBlob As String, ByVal cbEncryptedBlob As Long, _
    ByVal pbDecrypted As String, pcbDecrypted As Long, _
    ppXchgCert As Long) As Long
```

The first parameter (`pDecryptPara`) to this function is a `CRYPT_DECRYPT_MESSAGE_PARA` type structure. This type structure is populated with information that will be passed to the lower-level function that will perform the actual decryption. This type structure is defined in the following section.

The second parameter (`pbEncryptedBlob`) is the string buffer containing the encrypted message to be decrypted. The third parameter (`cbEncryptedBlob`) specifies the length of the encrypted message being passed in the second parameter.

The fourth parameter (`pbDecrypted`) is a string buffer into which will be placed the decrypted message. The fifth parameter (`pcbDecrypted`) is a long variable that specifies the length of the string buffer being passed in the fourth parameter. When this function returns, this parameter will contain the length of the actual message extracted from the encrypted message. If you don't want to make two calls—first to get the necessary size of this string and then to call with a sufficient string buffer—you can allocate the string to be the same size as the encrypted message because the resulting message will be shorter than this message package. When this function returns, you need to be sure to trim the returned message to the length specified in the fifth parameter.

The sixth parameter (ppXchgCert) is a pointer to a CERT_CONTEXT type structure into which will be placed the certificate used to encrypt the message. If you don't need this certificate, you can pass zero (0) for this parameter.

The Syntax for CRYPT_DECRYPT_MESSAGE_PARA Type Structure

The CRYPT_DECRYPT_MESSAGE_PARA type structure, the first parameter of the CryptDecryptMessage function, is defined as follows:

Syntax

```
Type CRYPT_DECRYPT_MESSAGE_PARA
    cbSize As Long
    dwMsgAndCertEncodingType As Long
    cCertStore As Long
    rghCertStore As Long            ' Pointer to Certificate Store handle
End Type
```

The first member of the CRYPT_DECRYPT_MESSAGE_PARA type structure, cbSize, specifies the size of this type structure. Until this type structure is redefined, it should always be 16.

The second member, dwMsgAndCertEncodingType, is a flag value that specifies the encoding used for the certificates and encryption. The possible values for this flag are listed in Table 8.1.

The third member, cCertStore, specifies the number of certificate store handles being passed in the fourth member. The fourth member, rghCertStore, is a pointer to an array of certificate store handles. They are handles to the certificate stores in which the encrypting certificate will be found. You populate this member by building an array of the handles to the open certificate stores and then use the VarPtr function to get a pointer to the first array position, as follows:

```
Dim cdmpDecryptParams As CRYPT_DECRYPT_MESSAGE_PARA
Dim lStoreArray(1) As Long

'--- The number of certificate store handles being passed
cdmpDecryptParams.cCertStore = 1
'--- Handles to the certificate stores to be searched for the decryption
'--- certificate and associated private key.
lStoreArray(0) = m_hCertStore
cdmpDecryptParams.rghCertStore = VarPtr(lStoreArray(0))
```

Signing and Encrypting a Message

If you don't want to make two function calls to first sign and then encrypt a message, you can use one. You can perform both of these steps by using the CryptSignAndEncryptMessage function. The definition of this function is as follows:

Syntax

```
Public Declare Function CryptSignAndEncryptMessage Lib "Crypt32.dll" ( _
    pSignPara As CRYPT_SIGN_MESSAGE_PARA, _
    pEncryptPara As CRYPT_ENCRYPT_MESSAGE_PARA, _
    ByVal cRecipientCert As Long, rgpRecipientCert As Long, _
    ByVal pbToBeSignedAndEncrypted As String, _
    ByVal cbToBeSignedAndEncrypted As Long, _
    ByVal pbSignedAndEncryptedBlob As String, _
    pcbSignedAndEncryptedBlob As Long) As Long
```

This function is very much a combination of the CryptSignMessage and CryptEncryptMessage functions. In fact, you can create the same resulting message by first calling CryptSignMessage and then feeding the output signed message into the CryptEncryptMessage function.

The first parameter (pSignPara) to this function is the CRYPT_SIGN_MESSAGE_PARA type structure. This type structure is populated just as it was for the CryptSignMessage function.

The second parameter (pEncryptPara) to this function is the CRYPT_ENCRYPT_MESSAGE_PARA type structure. This type structure is populated just as it was for the CryptEncryptMessage function.

The third parameter (cRecipientCert) specifies the number of recipient certificates in the fourth parameter. The fourth parameter (rgpRecipientCert) is an array of pointers to CERT_CONTEXT type structures for the recipient certificates. These two parameters are the same as the corresponding parameters in the CryptEncryptMessage function.

The fifth parameter (pbToBeSignedAndEncrypted) is the string buffer that contains the message to be signed and encrypted. The sixth parameter (cbToBeSignedAndEncrypted) specifies the size of the string.

The seventh parameter (pbSignedAndEncryptedBlob) is a string buffer into which will be placed the resulting signed and encrypted message. The eighth parameter (pcbSignedAndEncryptedBlob) is a long variable that specifies the length of the string buffer passed in the previous parameter. If the string isn't long enough, the eighth parameter will be returned with the needed length for the string buffer in the seventh parameter. If the string is long enough, the eighth parameter will be returned with the actual length of the resulting signed and encrypted message.

Decrypting and Verifying a Message

As you may have guessed, a corresponding function combines the `CryptDecryptMessage` and `CryptVerifyMessageSignature` functions into one. This function is `CryptDecryptAndVerify` ➥`MessageSignature`, which is defined as follows:

Syntax

```
Public Declare Function CryptDecryptAndVerifyMessageSignature _
    Lib "Crypt32.dll" (pDecryptPara As CRYPT_DECRYPT_MESSAGE_PARA, _
    pVerifyPara As CRYPT_VERIFY_MESSAGE_PARA, _
    ByVal dwSignerIndex As Long, ByVal pbEncryptedBlob As String, _
    ByVal cbEncryptedBlob As Long, ByVal pbDecrypted As String, _
    pcbDecrypted As Long, ppXchgCert As Long, _
    ppSignerCert As Long) As Long
```

The first parameter (`pDecryptPara`) to this function is the `CRYPT_DECRYPT_MESSAGE_PARA` type structure. This type structure is populated just the same as for the `CryptDecryptMessage` function.

The second parameter (`pVerifyPara`) is the `CRYPT_VERIFY_MESSAGE_PARA` type structure. This type structure is populated just as for the `CryptVerifyMessageSignature` function.

The third parameter (`dwSignerIndex`) is the index indicating which of the signatures on the message are to be verified. This function can be called multiple times to verify all the signatures on the message, just as with the `CryptVerifyMessageSignature` function.

The fourth parameter (`pbEncryptedBlob`) is string buffer that contains the signed and encrypted message to be decrypted and verified. The fifth parameter (`cbEncryptedBlob`) specifies the length of the encrypted and signed message.

The sixth parameter (`pbDecrypted`) is a string buffer into which will be placed the decrypted and verified message. The seventh parameter (`pcbDecrypted`) is a long variable that specifies the length of the string buffer in the sixth parameter. When this function returns, the variable in the seventh parameter will contain the actual length of the extracted message.

The eighth parameter (`ppXchgCert`) is a pointer to a `CERT_CONTEXT` type structure into which will be placed the certificate used to encrypt the message. If you don't want or need this certificate, you can pass zero (0) in this parameter.

The ninth parameter (`ppSignerCert`) is a pointer to a `CERT_CONTEXT` type structure into which will be placed the certificate used to sign the message. If you do not need or want this certificate, you can pass zero (0) for this parameter.

Decoding a Message

When you receive a message, and you're not sure what the packaging might be, you can use the CryptDecodeMessage function to try to unpackage the message one step at a time. Based on the possible packaging that you specify, this function tries to decode the message, determining what the topmost level of packaging might be. If you receive an encrypted, signed message, on the first pass, this function will decrypt the message and then on the second pass will verify the signature. If you receive an encrypted message that has been signed (the signature was applied to the entire encrypted message package), the CryptDecodeMessage function will try to verify the signature on the first pass and then decrypt the message on the second. The declaration for this function is as follows:

Syntax

```
Public Declare Function CryptDecodeMessage Lib "Crypt32.dll" ( _
    ByVal dwMsgTypeFlags As Long, _
    pDecryptPara As CRYPT_DECRYPT_MESSAGE_PARA, _
    pVerifyPara As CRYPT_VERIFY_MESSAGE_PARA, _
    ByVal dwSignerIndex As Long, ByVal pbEncodedBlob As String, _
    ByVal cbEncodedBlob As Long, ByVal dwPrevInnerContentType As Long, _
    pdwMsgType As Long, pdwInnerContentType As Long, _
    ByVal pbDecoded As String, pcbDecoded As Long, _
    ppXchgCert As Long, ppSignerCert As Long) As Long
```

The first parameter (dwMsgTypeFlags) to this function is a flag that specifies the message types that the message might be. These flag values should be combined using OR to indicate all the message types you think the message might be. The possible values for this flag are listed in Table 8.4.

TABLE 8.4 Message Type Flag Values

Constant	Value	Description
CMSG_DATA_FLAG	2	Raw data with no particular formatting
CMSG_SIGNED_FLAG	4	Signed message
CMSG_ENVELOPED_FLAG	8	Enveloped (encrypted) message
CMSG_SIGNED_AND_ENVELOPED_FLAG	16	Signed and encrypted message
CMSG_HASHED_FLAG	32	Hashed message
CMSG_ENCRYPTED_FLAG	64	Encrypted message

The second parameter (pDecryptPara) is a CRYPT_DECRYPT_MESSAGE_PARA type structure. This type structure should be populated just as for the CryptDecryptMessage function.

The third parameter (pVerifyPara) is a CRYPT_VERIFY_MESSAGE_PARA type structure. It should be populated just as for the CryptVerifyMessageSignature function.

The fourth parameter (dwSignerIndex) is the index of the signature to be verified. This parameter is used just like the corresponding parameter from the CryptVerifyMessageSignature function.

The fifth parameter (pbEncodedBlob) is the string buffer containing the message to be decoded. The sixth parameter (cbEncodedBlob) specifies the length of the encoded message in the fifth parameter.

The seventh parameter (dwPrevInnerContentType) indicates the previous inner content type. The first time this function is called, this value should be zero (0). On subsequent calls to this function, as you are decoding inner layers of the message, this parameter should be passed the value returned in the ninth parameter on the previous call to this function.

The eighth parameter (pdwMsgType) is a long variable in which the message type is returned. The possible return values in this variable are listed in Table 8.5.

TABLE 8.5   Message Type Values

Constant	Value	Description
CMSG_DATA	1	Raw data with no particular formatting
CMSG_SIGNED	2	Signed message
CMSG_ENVELOPED	3	Enveloped (encrypted) message
CMSG_SIGNED_AND_ENVELOPED	4	Signed and encrypted message
CMSG_HASHED	5	Hashed message
CMSG_ENCRYPTED	6	Encrypted message

The ninth parameter (pdwInnerContentType) is a variable in which the inner nesting type is returned. This value should be passed to this function on the next pass in the seventh parameter. The possible values for this variable are listed in Table 8.5. If there is no more nesting, the CMSG_DATA inner type is returned.

The tenth parameter (pbDecoded) is a string buffer into which will be placed the decoded message. If more decoding still needs to be done, this string will be passed as the encoded message in the subsequent call to this function.

The eleventh parameter (pcbDecoded) is a variable that specifies the size of the string buffer passed in the tenth parameter. When the function returns, the actual length of the message is returned in this variable.

The twelfth parameter (ppXchgCert) is a pointer to a CERT_CONTEXT type structure into which will be copied the certificate used to encrypt the message. It is the same as the corresponding parameter in the CryptDecryptMessage function. If you don't want or need this certificate, you can pass zero (0) in this parameter.

The thirteenth parameter (ppSignerCert) is a pointer to a CERT_CONTEXT type structure into which will be copied the certificate used to sign the message. It is the same as the corresponding parameter in the CryptVerifyMessageSignature function. If you don't want or need this certificate, you can pass zero (0) in this parameter.

> **NOTE**
>
> The CERT_CONTEXT that is returned from this function must be freed by calling the CertFreeCertificateContext function.

Building a Signing Utility

To see how these functions work in practice, you'll build a little utility that signs and verifies messages. It will also encrypt signed messages, along with decrypting them, all using the high-level functions you've looked at in this chapter.

To perform these tasks, this application will need to be able to retrieve either the Signature or the Key Exchange certificates from the certificate store and use them to sign and encrypt messages.

Creating the Project

To start this project, create a new, standard EXE project in Visual Basic. Copy the crypto class from the preceding chapter's sample application into the project directory, and include it in your new project. Edit the declaration section of the crypto class, adding the new constants, types, function, and variable declarations in Listing 8.1. Be sure to update the existing CRYPT_ALGORITHM_IDENTIFIER type structure definition as shown.

> **NOTE**
>
> At this point, this crypto class has been built and added to in just about every chapter, starting in Chapter 2. If you haven't kept up with all these chapters, you might want to go back and follow through the creation of this class through all the example applications before starting this project.

LISTING 8.1   New Constant, Type, and Declare Statements

```vb
Const CERT_FIND_ANY = 0
Const CERT_FIND_EXISTING = &HD0000
Const CERT_FIND_ISSUER_OF = &HC0000
Const CERT_FIND_ISSUER_STR = &H70004
Const CERT_FIND_KEY_SPEC = &H90000
Const CERT_FIND_PROPERTY = &H50000
Const CERT_FIND_SUBJECT_STR = &H70007


' Following are the definitions of various algorithm object identifiers
' RSA
Const szOID_RSA_MD5 = "1.2.840.113549.2.5"
Const szOID_RSA_RC4 = "1.2.840.113549.3.4"

'--- Change the following type definition that you already have in your
'--- Crypto class
Private Type CRYPT_ALGORITHM_IDENTIFIER
    pszObjId As String      ' Pointer to String
    Parameters As CRYPT_INTEGER_BLOB
End Type

Private Type CRYPT_SIGN_MESSAGE_PARA
    cbSize As Long
    dwMsgEncodingType As Long
    pSigningCert As Long        ' Pointer to signing certificate context
    HashAlgorithm As CRYPT_ALGORITHM_IDENTIFIER
    pvHashAuxInfo As Long
    cMsgCert As Long
    rgpMsgCert As Long              ' Pointer to array of certificate
                                    ' context pointers
    cMsgCrl As Long
    rgpMsgCrl As Long              ' Pointer to array of CRL context pointers
    cAuthAttr As Long
    rgAuthAttr As Long             ' Pointer to CRYPT_ATTRIBUTE type
    cUnauthAttr As Long
    rgUnauthAttr As Long           ' Pointer to CRYPT_ATTRIBUTE type
    dwFlags As Long
    dwInnerContentType As Long
End Type

Private Type CRYPT_VERIFY_MESSAGE_PARA
    cbSize As Long
    dwMsgAndCertEncodingType As Long
    hCryptProv As Long
    pfnGetSignerCertificate As Long         ' Pointer to callback function
    pvGetArg As Long                        ' void Pointer
End Type
```

```
Private Type CRYPT_ENCRYPT_MESSAGE_PARA
    cbSize As Long
    dwMsgEncodingType As Long
    hCryptProv As Long
    ContentEncryptionAlgorithm As CRYPT_ALGORITHM_IDENTIFIER
    pvEncryptionAuxInfo As Long      ' void Pointer
    dwFlags As Long
    dwInnerContentType As Long
End Type

Private Type CRYPT_DECRYPT_MESSAGE_PARA
    cbSize As Long
    dwMsgAndCertEncodingType As Long
    cCertStore As Long
    rghCertStore As Long            ' Pointer to Certificate Store handle
End Type

Private Declare Function CertFindCertificateInStore Lib "Crypt32.dll" ( _
    ByVal hCertStore As Long, ByVal dwCertEncodingType As Long, _
    ByVal dwFindFlags As Long, ByVal dwFindType As Long, _
    ByVal pvFindPara As String, ByVal pPrevCertContext As Long) As Long

Private Declare Function CryptSignMessage Lib "Crypt32.dll" ( _
    pSignPara As CRYPT_SIGN_MESSAGE_PARA, _
    ByVal fDetachedSignature As Long, ByVal cToBeSigned As Long, _
    rgpbToBeSigned As String, rgcbToBeSigned As Long, _
    ByVal pbSignedBlob As String, pcbSignedBlob As Long) As Long

Private Declare Function CryptVerifyMessageSignature Lib "Crypt32.dll" ( _
    pVerifyPara As CRYPT_VERIFY_MESSAGE_PARA, _
    ByVal dwSignerIndex As Long, ByVal pbSignedBlob As String, _
    ByVal cbSignedBlob As Long, ByVal pbDecoded As String, _
    pcbDecoded As Long, ppSignerCert As Long) As Long

Private Declare Function CryptSignAndEncryptMessage Lib "Crypt32.dll" ( _
    pSignPara As CRYPT_SIGN_MESSAGE_PARA, _
    pEncryptPara As CRYPT_ENCRYPT_MESSAGE_PARA, _
    ByVal cRecipientCert As Long, rgpRecipientCert As Long, _
    ByVal pbToBeSignedAndEncrypted As String, _
    ByVal cbToBeSignedAndEncrypted As Long, _
    ByVal pbSignedAndEncryptedBlob As String, _
    pcbSignedAndEncryptedBlob As Long) As Long

Private Declare Function CryptDecryptAndVerifyMessageSignature _
    Lib "Crypt32.dll" (pDecryptPara As CRYPT_DECRYPT_MESSAGE_PARA, _
    pVerifyPara As CRYPT_VERIFY_MESSAGE_PARA, _
    ByVal dwSignerIndex As Long, ByVal pbEncryptedBlob As String, _
```

8

continues

LISTING 8.1   Continued

```
      ByVal cbEncryptedBlob As Long, ByVal pbDecrypted As String, _
      pcbDecrypted As Long, ppXchgCert As Long, _
      ppSignerCert As Long) As Long

Private Declare Function CryptEncryptMessage Lib "Crypt32.dll" ( _
    pEncryptPara As CRYPT_ENCRYPT_MESSAGE_PARA, _
    ByVal cRecipientCert As Long, ByVal rgpRecipientCert As Long, _
    ByVal pbToBeEncrypted As String, ByVal cbToBeEncrypted As Long, _
    ByVal pbEncryptedBlob As String, pcbEncryptedBlob As Long) As Long

Private Declare Function CryptDecryptMessage Lib "Crypt32.dll" ( _
    pDecryptPara As CRYPT_DECRYPT_MESSAGE_PARA, _
    ByVal pbEncryptedBlob As String, ByVal cbEncryptedBlob As Long, _
    ByVal pbDecrypted As String, pcbDecrypted As Long, _
    ppXchgCert As Long) As Long

Private Const ERROR_MORE_DATA As Long = 234
Private Const CRYPT_E_NO_KEY_PROPERTY As Long = &H8009200B

Private m_lCertContextPointer As Long    ' Used to hold a pointer to a
                                         ' CERT_CONTEXT

Private m_hCertStore As Long      ' Used to hold a handle to the
                                  ' certificate store
```

Retrieving the Signing Certificate

The first addition to the crypto class will be a function to locate and retrieve the certificate to be used for signing messages. This function will open the certificate store specified and then loop while retrieving all certificates with the subject name specified until a signature certificate is found. To add this function to the crypto class, add the function in Listing 8.2.

LISTING 8.2   The *GetSignatureCertificate* Function

```
Public Function GetSignatureCertificate(pszStoreName As String, _
        pszCertName As String) As Boolean
'*******************************************************************
'* Written By: Davis Chapman
'* Date:       November 29, 1999
'*
'* Syntax:     GetSignatureCertificate(pszStoreName, pszCertName)
'*
'* Parameters: pszStoreName As String
'*             pszCertName As String
```

```
'*
'* Purpose: This function loops through the certificates in the
'*          specified certificate store, until the signature
'*          certificate for the specified user is found. This
'*          function returns a pointer to the first signature
'*          certificate found for the specified user, and doesn't
'*          perform any validation checking to determine if the
'*          certificate has either expired or been revoked.
'*****************************************************************
    Dim bContinue As Boolean
    Dim lCertCtxPtr As Long
    Dim hCertStore As Long

    On Error GoTo GetSignatureCertificateErr

    '--- Initialize the return value
    GetSignatureCertificate = False
    bContinue = True

    '--- Open a system certificate store.
    m_hCertStore = CertOpenSystemStore(0, pszStoreName)
    '--- If unable to open the specified store, exit
    If m_hCertStore = 0 Then Exit Function
    '--- Find the first certificate in the store for the
    '--- specified user.
    lCertCtxPtr = CertFindCertificateInStore(m_hCertStore, _
            X509_ASN_ENCODING Or PKCS_7_ASN_ENCODING, 0, _
            CERT_FIND_SUBJECT_STR, pszCertName, 0)
    '--- If no certificate found, exit
    If lCertCtxPtr = 0 Then Exit Function
    '--- Do we have a signature certificate? If so, then
    '--- set the flag to indicate that we don't need to
    '--- continue past this point.
    If GetKeyType(lCertCtxPtr) = AT_SIGNATURE Then bContinue = False
    '--- Loop until a signature certificate is found, or
    '--- there are no more certificates to be returned
    While bContinue
        '--- Get the next certificate for the specified user.
        lCertCtxPtr = CertFindCertificateInStore(m_hCertStore, _
            X509_ASN_ENCODING Or PKCS_7_ASN_ENCODING, 0, _
            CERT_FIND_SUBJECT_STR, pszCertName, lCertCtxPtr)
        '--- If no more certificates, end processing
        If lCertCtxPtr = 0 Then bContinue = False
        '--- If a signature certificate found, end processing
        If GetKeyType(lCertCtxPtr) = AT_SIGNATURE Then bContinue = False
    Wend
    '--- Set the certificate context pointer for the class signature
```

continues

LISTING 8.2   Continued

```
    '--- certificate variable.
    m_lCertContextPointer = lCertCtxPtr
    '--- Did we find a signature certificate, change the
    '--- return value to TRUE.
    If lCertCtxPtr <> 0 Then GetSignatureCertificate = True
    '--- Exit the function
    Exit Function

GetSignatureCertificateErr:
    '--- An error occurred, display it for the user
    MsgBox "Error: " + Str(Err.Number) + " - " + Err.Description
End Function
```

In this listing, you first open the certificate store using the `CertOpenSystemStore` function:

```
'--- Open a system certificate store.
m_hCertStore = CertOpenSystemStore(0, pszStoreName)
```

Next, you retrieve certificates from the store that match the username using the `CertFindCertificateInStore` function:

```
'--- Find the first certificate in the store for the
'--- specified user.
lCertCtxPtr = CertFindCertificateInStore(m_hCertStore, _
        X509_ASN_ENCODING Or PKCS_7_ASN_ENCODING, 0, _
        CERT_FIND_SUBJECT_STR, pszCertName, 0)
```

You are checking the certificate type using a function, `GetKeyType`, that doesn't exist yet:

```
'--- Do we have a signature certificate? If so, then
'--- set the flag to indicate that we don't need to
'--- continue past this point.
If GetKeyType(lCertCtxPtr) = AT_SIGNATURE Then bContinue = False
```

When you have a signature certificate, you copy it to a class-level variable for holding:

```
'--- Set the certificate context pointer for the class signature
'--- certificate variable.
m_lCertContextPointer = lCertCtxPtr
```

Determining the Certificate Type

In order for the function you just wrote to work, you need to be able to determine the key type of each certificate that you find in the certificate store. You do so by calling a new function, `GetKeyType`, that you still need to create. This function needs to extract the `CRYPT_KEY_PROV_INFO` property from the certificate context so that the key type can be extracted from this type structure. When you have the property, you can use an existing function, `GetKeySpecFromKPI` (which you created earlier), to get the key type. All the functionality in this function has been written before. All you need to do is repackage it in a new function. To do so, add the GetKeyType function to the crypto class, using the code in Listing 8.3.

LISTING 8.3   The GetKeyType Function

```
Private Function GetKeyType(lpCertCtx As Long) As Long
'*****************************************************************
'* Written By: Davis Chapman
'* Date:        November 29, 1999
'*
'* Syntax:      GetKeyType(lpCertCtx)
'*
'* Parameters:  lpCertCtx As Long
'*
'* Purpose: This function extracts the key type from the
'*          certificate context that is passed in.
'*****************************************************************
    Dim kpiData As CRYPT_KEY_PROV_INFO
    Dim dwData As Long
    Dim pvData As String
    Dim cbData As Long

    '--- Set the value size
    cbData = 28
    '--- Retrieve the property value
    If (CBool(CertGetCertificateContextKPIProperty( _
            lpCertCtx, _
            CERT_KEY_PROV_INFO_PROP_ID, _
            kpiData, _
            cbData))) Then
    End If

    '--- The call didn't succeed. Use the size to allocate memory
    '--- for the property.
    pvData = String(cbData, vbNullChar)

    '--- Allocation succeeded. Retrieve the property data.
    If (Not CBool(CertGetCertificateContextProperty( _
            lpCertCtx, _
            CERT_KEY_PROV_INFO_PROP_ID, _
            pvData, _
            cbData))) Then
        '--- Unable to retrieve the property value
        m_sErrorMsg = _
                ➥"Error during CertGetCertificateContextProperty - " _
```

continues

8

LISTING 8.3   Continued

```
                    & CStr(Err.LastDllError) & Error$
        MsgBox m_sErrorMsg, vbOKOnly, "VB Crypto"
    End If

    '--- Show the results.
    If cbData = 28 Then
        '--- We retrieved the type structure
        GetKeyType = kpiData.dwKeySpec
    Else
        '--- We received a byte array
        If GetKeySpecFromKPI(pvData) = "AT_SIGNATURE" Then
            GetKeyType = AT_SIGNATURE
        Else
            GetKeyType = AT_KEYEXCHANGE
        End If
    End If
End Function
```

Signing the Message

The next piece of functionality to add to your application is the capability to sign messages.
For this capability, you first need to populate a CRYPT_SIGN_MESSAGE_PARA type structure with
information on how to sign the message and then call the CryptSignMessage function to determine how large the string buffer needs to be to hold the signed message and then to actually
sign the message. To add this functionality, add the SignMessage function in Listing 8.4 to the
crypto class.

LISTING 8.4   The SignMessage Function

```
Public Function SignMessage() As Boolean
'*************************************************************
'* Written By: Davis Chapman
'* Date:       November 29, 1999
'*
'* Syntax:     SignMessage
'*
'* Parameters: None
'*
'* Purpose: This function uses the CryptSignMessage function
'*          to sign the message stored in the InBuffer property
'*          using the signature certificate held in the class
'*          variable, and to place the signed message in the
'*          OutBuffer property.
'*************************************************************
```

```
Dim csmpSignParams As CRYPT_SIGN_MESSAGE_PARA
Dim strSignedMsg As String
Dim lMsgSize As Long
Dim lRtnVal As Long
Dim lCertArray(1) As Long
Dim lMsgArray(1) As String
Dim lMsgLenArray(1) As Long

On Error GoTo SignMessageErr

'--- Initialize the return value
SignMessage = False
'--- Fill in the signature parameter type structure
'--- The type structure size
csmpSignParams.cbSize = 68
'--- The encoding type
csmpSignParams.dwMsgEncodingType = X509_ASN_ENCODING Or _
    PKCS_7_ASN_ENCODING
'--- The pointer to the certificate context of the certificate
'--- to be used for signing the message
csmpSignParams.pSigningCert = m_lCertContextPointer
'--- The hash algorithm to be used for signing
csmpSignParams.HashAlgorithm.pszObjId = szOID_RSA_MD5
'--- Any auxiliary information? No
csmpSignParams.pvHashAuxInfo = 0
'--- Number of certificates to be included with the
'--- signed message.
csmpSignParams.cMsgCert = 1
'--- Pointers to the certificate contexts of the certificates
'--- to be included in the signed message.
lCertArray(0) = m_lCertContextPointer
csmpSignParams.rgpMsgCert = VarPtr(lCertArray(0))
'--- Nothing else
csmpSignParams.cMsgCrl = 0
csmpSignParams.cAuthAttr = 0
csmpSignParams.cUnauthAttr = 0
csmpSignParams.dwFlags = 0
csmpSignParams.dwInnerContentType = 0
'--- Copy the message to the array of messages to be signed
lMsgArray(0) = m_sInBuffer
'-- And the length of the message
lMsgLenArray(0) = Len(m_sInBuffer)
'--- Initialize the signed message buffer
strSignedMsg = vbNullChar
'--- Call CryptSignMessage to get the required size of the
'--- signed message buffer.
lRtnVal = CryptSignMessage(csmpSignParams, 0, 1, lMsgArray(0), _
```

continues

8

USING DIGITAL
SIGNATURES

LISTING 8.4 Continued

```
                lMsgLenArray(0), strSignedMsg, lMsgSize)
    '--- Did we get a buffer size?
    If (lMsgSize> 0) Then
        '--- Size the buffer
        strSignedMsg = String(lMsgSize, vbNullChar)
        '--- Sign the message
        If Not CBool(CryptSignMessage(csmpSignParams, 0, 1, _
                ➥lMsgArray(0), lMsgLenArray(0), strSignedMsg, lMsgSize)) _
                Then
            '--- If something failed, then exit the function
            Exit Function
        End If
    Else
        '--- No message buffer size, something must have gone wrong.
        Exit Function
    End If
    '--- Copy the signed message to the output buffer.
    m_sOutBuffer = strSignedMsg
    '--- Update the return value.
    SignMessage = True
    '--- Exit the function
    Exit Function

SignMessageErr:
    '--- An error occurred, display it for the user
    MsgBox "Error: " + Str(Err.Number) + " - " + Err.Description
End Function
```

In this listing, you start by populating the CRYPT_SIGN_MESSAGE_PARA type structure. First, you set the size of the type structure:

```
'--- Fill in the signature parameter type structure
'--- The type structure size
csmpSignParams.cbSize = 68
```

Next, you specify the encoding format:

```
'--- The encoding type
csmpSignParams.dwMsgEncodingType = X509_ASN_ENCODING Or _
    PKCS_7_ASN_ENCODING
```

Then you set the pointer to the certificate context of the certificate to be used for signing the message:

```
'--- The pointer to the certificate context of the certificate
'--- to be used for signing the message
csmpSignParams.pSigningCert = m_lCertContextPointer
```

Next, you specify the signing algorithm to be used:

```
'--- The hash algorithm to be used for signing
csmpSignParams.HashAlgorithm.pszObjId = szOID_RSA_MD5
```

Finally, you specify the certificates to be included in the signed message package. This step involves copying the certificate context pointer into the array of pointers and then getting a pointer to the first position in the array:

```
'--- Number of certificates to be included with the
'--- signed message.
csmpSignParams.cMsgCert = 1
'--- Pointers to the certificate contexts of the certificates
'--- to be included in the signed message.
lCertArray(0) = m_lCertContextPointer
csmpSignParams.rgpMsgCert = VarPtr(lCertArray(0))
```

After you populate the type structure, you need to set the message arrays to the message in the `InBuffer` property:

```
'--- Copy the message to the array of messages to be signed
lMsgArray(0) = m_sInBuffer
'-- And the length of the message
lMsgLenArray(0) = Len(m_sInBuffer)
```

Finally, you pass all this information to the `CryptSignMessage` function, signing the message:

```
'--- Call CryptSignMessage to get the required size of the
'--- signed message buffer.
lRtnVal = CryptSignMessage(csmpSignParams, 0, 1, lMsgArray(0), _
          lMsgLenArray(0), strSignedMsg, lMsgSize)
```

After you sign the message successfully, you copy the signed message to the `OutBuffer` property:

```
'--- Copy the signed message to the output buffer.
m_sOutBuffer = strSignedMsg
```

This makes the signed message available to the calling application.

Verifying the Signature

The next piece of functionality is the verification of the signature. In this function, you'll need to populate a `CRYPT_VERIFY_MESSAGE_PARA` type structure and then pass the signed message to the `CryptVerifyMessageSignature` function. To add this functionality, add the `ValidateSignature` function in Listing 8.5 to the `crypto` class.

LISTING 8.5   The `ValidateSignature` Function

```vb
Public Function ValidateSignature() As Boolean
'*****************************************************************
'* Written By: Davis Chapman
'* Date:       November 29, 1999
'*
'* Syntax:     ValidateSignature
'*
'* Parameters:  None
'*
'* Purpose: This function uses the CryptValidateSignature
'*          function to validate the signature on the message.
'*          It also extracts the message from the encoded signed
'*          message.
'*****************************************************************
    Dim cvmpVerifyParams As CRYPT_VERIFY_MESSAGE_PARA
    Dim strDecodedMsg As String
    Dim lMsgLength As Long

    On Error GoTo ValidateSignatureErr

    '--- Initialize the return value
    ValidateSignature = False
    '--- Fill in the signature validation parameter type structure
    '--- The type structure size
    cvmpVerifyParams.cbSize = 20
    '--- The encoding type
    cvmpVerifyParams.dwMsgAndCertEncodingType = X509_ASN_ENCODING Or _
            PKCS_7_ASN_ENCODING
    '--- The CSP handle
    cvmpVerifyParams.hCryptProv = m_lHCryptProv
    '--- Get the length of the signed message
    lMsgLength = Len(m_sInBuffer)
    '--- Allocate the buffer to received the extracted message.
    strDecodedMsg = String(lMsgLength, vbNullChar)
    '--- Verify the message signature
    If CBool(CryptVerifyMessageSignature(cvmpVerifyParams, _
        ➥ 0, m_sInBuffer, _
          lMsgLength, strDecodedMsg, lMsgLength, 0)) Then
        '--- The signature was valid, set the return value
        ValidateSignature = True
        '--- Copy the extracted message to the output buffer
        m_sOutBuffer = Left(strDecodedMsg, lMsgLength)
    End If
    '--- Exit the function
    Exit Function
```

```
ValidateSignatureErr:
    '--- An error occurred, display it for the user
    MsgBox "Error: " + Str(Err.Number) + " - " + Err.Description
End Function
```

In this listing, you populate the `CRYPT_VERIFY_MESSAGE_PARA` type structure by first specifying the type structure's size:

```
'--- Fill in the signature validation parameter type structure
'--- The type structure size
cvmpVerifyParams.cbSize = 20
```

Next, you specify the encoding format of the signed message:

```
'--- The encoding type
cvmpVerifyParams.dwMsgAndCertEncodingType = X509_ASN_ENCODING Or _
        PKCS_7_ASN_ENCODING
```

Then you specify which CSP to use to verify the signature:

```
'--- The CSP handle
cvmpVerifyParams.hCryptProv = m_lHCryptProv
```

After you have all the information assembled, you verify the signature by calling the `CryptVerifyMessageSignature` function:

```
'--- Verify the message signature
If CBool(CryptVerifyMessageSignature(cvmpVerifyParams, 0, m_sInBuffer, _
        lMsgLength, strDecodedMsg, lMsgLength, 0)) Then
```

If the signature is valid, you copy the extracted message to the `OutBuffer` property so that the calling application can access it:

```
'--- Copy the extracted message to the output buffer
m_sOutBuffer = Left(strDecodedMsg, lMsgLength)
```

Retrieving the Exchange Certificate

Before you can start adding functionality to encrypt the message, you'll need to be able to retrieve the key exchange certificate of the message recipient. You could modify the `GetSignatureCertificate` function to add a flag to the parameters, specifying which certificate to retrieve, but you would also need to make changes to return the certificate context pointer instead of setting it to a class-level variable. You would also need to make it check whether the certificate store was already open. For the purposes of this application, you'll just create a new function that does only what you need it to do, instead of modifying the existing function. To add this functionality, add the `GetRecipientCertificate` function in Listing 8.6 to the `crypto` class.

LISTING 8.6   The `GetRecipientCertificate` Function

```
Public Function GetRecipientCertificate(pszCertName As String) As Long
'****************************************************************
'* Written By: Davis Chapman
'* Date:        November 29, 1999
'*
'* Syntax:      GetRecipientCertificate(pszCertName)
'*
'* Parameters:  pszCertName As String
'*
'* Purpose: This function retrieves the key exchange certificate
'*          for the user specified from the open certificate
'*          store.
'****************************************************************
    Dim bContinue As Boolean
    Dim lCertCtxPtr As Long
    Dim hCertStore As Long

    On Error GoTo GetRecipientCertificateErr
    '--- Initialize the return value
    GetRecipientCertificate = 0
    bContinue = True
    '--- If the certificate store is not already open, exit
    If m_hCertStore = 0 Then Exit Function
    '--- Find the first certificate in the store for the
    '--- specified user.
    lCertCtxPtr = CertFindCertificateInStore(m_hCertStore, _
            X509_ASN_ENCODING Or PKCS_7_ASN_ENCODING, 0, _
            CERT_FIND_SUBJECT_STR, pszCertName, 0)
    '--- If no certificate found, exit
    If lCertCtxPtr = 0 Then Exit Function
    '--- Do we have a key exchange certificate? If so, then
    '--- set the flag to indicate that we don't need to
    '--- continue past this point.
    If GetKeyType(lCertCtxPtr) = AT_KEYEXCHANGE Then bContinue = False
    '--- Loop until a key exchange certificate is found, or
    '--- there are no more certificates to be returned
    While bContinue
        '--- Get the next certificate for the specified user.
        lCertCtxPtr = CertFindCertificateInStore(m_hCertStore, _
            X509_ASN_ENCODING Or PKCS_7_ASN_ENCODING, 0, _
            CERT_FIND_SUBJECT_STR, pszCertName, lCertCtxPtr)
        '--- If no more certificates, end processing
        If lCertCtxPtr = 0 Then bContinue = False
        '--- If a key exchange certificate found, end processing
        If GetKeyType(lCertCtxPtr) = AT_KEYEXCHANGE Then _
```

```
                bContinue = False
        Wend
        '--- Did we find a key exchange certificate, change the
        '--- return value to the pointer to the certificate context.
        If lCertCtxPtr <> 0 Then GetRecipientCertificate = lCertCtxPtr
        '--- Exit the function
        Exit Function

GetRecipientCertificateErr:
        '--- An error occurred, display it for the user
        MsgBox "Error: " + Str(Err.Number) + " - " + Err.Description
End Function
```

In this listing, you assume that the certificate store is already open. If the certificate store is not open, there must be a problem, so you exit right away. This function works pretty much like the `GetSignatureCertificate` function, except that it returns the pointer to the certificate context for the first key exchange certificate it finds.

Encrypting the Message

Now, to add the function to sign and encrypt the message, you'll need to populate not only the `CRYPT_SIGN_MESSAGE_PARA` type structure, but also the `CRYPT_ENCRYPT_MESSAGE_PARA` type structure. After you populate both of these structures, you can call the `CryptSignAndEncryptMessage` function to sign and encrypt the message. To add this functionality to your crypto class, add the `SignAndEncryptMessage` function in Listing 8.7.

LISTING 8.7   The `SignAndEncryptMessage` Function

```
Public Function SignAndEncryptMessage(strName As String) As Boolean
'*************************************************************
'* Written By: Davis Chapman
'* Date:       November 29, 1999
'*
'* Syntax:     SignAndEncryptMessage(strName)
'*
'* Parameters:  strName As String
'*
'* Purpose: This function uses the CryptSignAndEncryptMessage
'*          function to perform both the signing and encrypting
'*          of the message in a single step.
'*************************************************************
    Dim csmpSignParams As CRYPT_SIGN_MESSAGE_PARA
    Dim cempEncryptParams As CRYPT_ENCRYPT_MESSAGE_PARA
    Dim strSignedMsg As String
    Dim lMsgSize As Long
```

continues

8

LISTING 8.7   Continued

```
Dim lRtnVal As Long
Dim lCertArray(1) As Long
Dim lRecpCertArray(1) As Long
Dim lMsgArray(1) As String
Dim lMsgLenArray(1) As Long

On Error GoTo SignAndEncryptMessageErr

'--- Initialize the return value
SignAndEncryptMessage = False
'--- Fill in the signature parameter type structure
'--- The type structure size
csmpSignParams.cbSize = 68
'--- The encoding type
csmpSignParams.dwMsgEncodingType = X509_ASN_ENCODING Or _
        PKCS_7_ASN_ENCODING
'--- The pointer to the certificate context of the certificate
'--- to be used for signing the message
csmpSignParams.pSigningCert = m_lCertContextPointer
'--- The hash algorithm to be used for signing
csmpSignParams.HashAlgorithm.pszObjId = szOID_RSA_MD5
'--- Any auxiliary information? No
csmpSignParams.pvHashAuxInfo = 0
'--- Number of certificates to be included with the
'--- signed message.
csmpSignParams.cMsgCert = 1
'--- Pointers to the certificate contexts of the certificates
'--- to be included in the signed message.
lCertArray(0) = m_lCertContextPointer
csmpSignParams.rgpMsgCert = VarPtr(lCertArray(0))
'--- Nothing else
csmpSignParams.cMsgCrl = 0
csmpSignParams.cAuthAttr = 0
csmpSignParams.cUnauthAttr = 0
csmpSignParams.dwFlags = 0
csmpSignParams.dwInnerContentType = 0
'--- Fill in the encryption parameter type structure
'--- The type structure size
cempEncryptParams.cbSize = 32
'--- The encoding type
cempEncryptParams.dwMsgEncodingType = X509_ASN_ENCODING Or _
        PKCS_7_ASN_ENCODING
'--- The handle of the CSP
cempEncryptParams.hCryptProv = m_lHCryptProv
'--- The encryption algorithm to use
cempEncryptParams.ContentEncryptionAlgorithm.pszObjId = szOID_RSA_RC4
```

```
'--- Get a pointer to the certificate context of the key
'--- exchange certificate of the recipient of the message.
lRecpCertArray(0) = GetRecipientCertificate(strName)
'--- Initialize the signed message buffer
strSignedMsg = vbNullChar
lMsgSize = 0
'--- Call CryptSignAndEncryptMessage to get the required size of the
'--- signed message buffer.
lRtnVal = CryptSignAndEncryptMessage(csmpSignParams, _
        ➥cempEncryptParams, 1, lRecpCertArray(0), m_sInBuffer, _
        Len(m_sInBuffer), strSignedMsg, lMsgSize)
'--- Did we get a buffer size?
If (lMsgSize> 0) Then
    '--- Size the buffer
    strSignedMsg = String(lMsgSize, vbNullChar)
    '--- Sign and encrypt the message
    If Not CBool(CryptSignAndEncryptMessage(csmpSignParams, _
            cempEncryptParams, 1, lRecpCertArray(0), m_sInBuffer, _
            Len(m_sInBuffer), strSignedMsg, lMsgSize)) Then
        '--- If something failed, then exit the function
        Exit Function
    End If
Else
    '--- No message buffer size, something must have gone wrong.
    Exit Function
End If
'--- Copy the signed and encrypted message to the output buffer
m_sOutBuffer = strSignedMsg
'--- Update the return value
SignAndEncryptMessage = True
'--- Release the recipient certificate
CertFreeCertificateContext lRecpCertArray(0)
'--- Exit the function
Exit Function

SignAndEncryptMessageErr:
    '--- An error occurred, display it for the user
    MsgBox "Error: " + Str(Err.Number) + " - " + Err.Description
End Function
```

In this listing, you populate the CRYPT_SIGN_MESSAGE_PARA type structure just as you did in the SignMessage function. Next, you populate the CRYPT_ENCRYPT_MESSAGE_PARA type structure, starting with the type structure size:

```
'--- Fill in the encryption parameter type structure
'--- The type structure size
cempEncryptParams.cbSize = 32
```

Then you specify the encoding type:

```
'--- The encoding type
cempEncryptParams.dwMsgEncodingType = X509_ASN_ENCODING Or _
        PKCS_7_ASN_ENCODING
```

Next, you specify the CSP to be used for performing the encryption.

```
'--- The handle of the CSP
cempEncryptParams.hCryptProv = m_lHCryptProv
```

Finally, you specify the encryption algorithm to use for encrypting the message:

```
'--- The encryption algorithm to use
cempEncryptParams.ContentEncryptionAlgorithm.pszObjId = szOID_RSA_RC4
```

After you populate all the information, specifying how to encrypt the message, you need to provide the certificate of the message recipient:

```
'--- Get a pointer to the certificate context of the key
'--- exchange certificate of the recipient of the message.
lRecpCertArray(0) = GetRecipientCertificate(strName)
```

Next, you perform the message signing and encryption:

```
'--- Call CryptSignAndEncryptMessage to get the required size of the
'--- signed message buffer.
lRtnVal = CryptSignAndEncryptMessage(csmpSignParams, cempEncryptParams, _
        1, lRecpCertArray(0), m_sInBuffer, Len(m_sInBuffer), _
        strSignedMsg, lMsgSize)
```

After you have a signed and encrypted message, you place it in the OutBuffer property for the calling application to be able to access it:

```
'--- Copy the signed and encrypted message to the output buffer
m_sOutBuffer = strSignedMsg
```

Then you release the recipient's certificate to clean up after yourself:

```
'--- Release the recipient certificate
CertFreeCertificateContext lRecpCertArray(0)
```

Decrypting the Message

Now you need to be able to decrypt the message and verify the signature. You can do so by using the CryptDecryptAndVerifyMessageSignature function. This function requires you to populate not only the CRYPT_VERIFY_MESSAGE_PARA type structure, but also the CRYPT_DECRYPT_MESSAGE_PARA type structure. To add this functionality, add the DecryptAndValidateMessage function in Listing 8.8 to the crypto class.

LISTING 8.8   The `DecryptAndValidateMessage` Function

```
Public Function DecryptAndValidateMessage() As Boolean
'***************************************************************
'* Written By: Davis Chapman
'* Date:       November 29, 1999
'*
'* Syntax:     DecryptAndValidateMessage
'*
'* Parameters: None
'*
'* Purpose: This function decrypts and verifies the signature
'*          on a message using the CryptDecryptAndVerifyMessage
'*          function. This performs both the decryption and
'*          signature verification in a single step.
'***************************************************************
    Dim cdmpDecryptParams As CRYPT_DECRYPT_MESSAGE_PARA
    Dim cvmpVerifyParams As CRYPT_VERIFY_MESSAGE_PARA
    Dim strDecodedMsg As String
    Dim lMsgLength As Long
    Dim lStoreArray(1) As Long

    On Error GoTo DecryptAndValidateMessageErr
    '--- Initialize the return value
    DecryptAndValidateMessage = False
    '--- Fill in the signature validation parameter type structure
    '--- The type structure size
    cvmpVerifyParams.cbSize = 20
    '--- The encoding type
    cvmpVerifyParams.dwMsgAndCertEncodingType = X509_ASN_ENCODING Or _
            PKCS_7_ASN_ENCODING
    '--- The handle of the CSP
    cvmpVerifyParams.hCryptProv = m_lHCryptProv
    '--- Fill in the decryption parameter type structure
    '--- The type structure size
    cdmpDecryptParams.cbSize = 16
    '--- The encoding type
    cdmpDecryptParams.dwMsgAndCertEncodingType = X509_ASN_ENCODING Or _
            PKCS_7_ASN_ENCODING
    '--- The number of certificate store handles being passed
    cdmpDecryptParams.cCertStore = 1
    '--- Handles to the certificate stores to be searched for the
➥'--- decryption certificate and associated private key.
    lStoreArray(0) = m_hCertStore
    cdmpDecryptParams.rghCertStore = VarPtr(lStoreArray(0))
    '--- Get the message length
    lMsgLength = Len(m_sInBuffer)
```

continues

8

USING DIGITAL
SIGNATURES

LISTING 8.8   Continued

```
'--- Allocate the buffer for the decrypted message
strDecodedMsg = String(lMsgLength, vbNullChar)
'--- Decrypt and verify the message
If CBool(CryptDecryptAndVerifyMessageSignature(cdmpDecryptParams, _
        cvmpVerifyParams, 0, m_sInBuffer, lMsgLength, _
        strDecodedMsg, lMsgLength, 0, 0)) Then
    '--- The signature was valid, set the return value
    DecryptAndValidateMessage = True
    '--- Copy the extracted message to the output buffer
    m_sOutBuffer = Left(strDecodedMsg, lMsgLength)
End If
'--- Exit the function
Exit Function


DecryptAndValidateMessageErr:
    '--- An error occurred, display it for the user
    MsgBox "Error: " + Str(Err.Number) + " - " + Err.Description
End Function
```

In this listing, you populate the `CRYPT_VERIFY_MESSAGE_PARA` type structure just as you did in the `ValidateSignature` function. Next, you populate the `CRYPT_DECRYPT_MESSAGE_PARA` type structure, starting with the type structure size:

```
'--- Fill in the decryption parameter type structure
'--- The type structure size
cdmpDecryptParams.cbSize = 16
```

Then you specify the encoding type:

```
'--- The encoding type
cdmpDecryptParams.dwMsgAndCertEncodingType = X509_ASN_ENCODING Or _
        PKCS_7_ASN_ENCODING
```

Finally, you specify the certificate stores to search for the private key to decrypt the message, supplying the certificate store handles in an array and then getting a pointer to the first position in the array:

```
'--- The number of certificate store handles being passed
cdmpDecryptParams.cCertStore = 1
'--- Handles to the certificate stores to be searched for the decryption
'--- certificate and associated private key.
lStoreArray(0) = m_hCertStore
cdmpDecryptParams.rghCertStore = VarPtr(lStoreArray(0))
```

At this point, you decrypt the message and validate the signature:

```
'--- Decrypt and verify the message
```

```
If CBool(CryptDecryptAndVerifyMessageSignature(cdmpDecryptParams, _
        cvmpVerifyParams, 0, m_sInBuffer, lMsgLength, _
        strDecodedMsg, lMsgLength, 0, 0)) Then
```

Then, after you extract a valid message, you copy it to the OutBuffer property so that the calling application can access it:

```
'--- Copy the extracted message to the output buffer
m_sOutBuffer = Left(strDecodedMsg, lMsgLength)
```

Releasing the Signature Certificate

The last piece of functionality you need to add to your crypto class is some cleanup functionality. When your application is finished, it needs to release the signature certificate and close the certificate store. To add this functionality, add the ReleaseSignatureCertificate function in Listing 8.9 to the crypto class.

LISTING 8.9   The ReleaseSignatureCertificate Subroutine

```
Public Sub ReleaseSignatureCertificate()
'**************************************************************
'* Written By: Davis Chapman
'* Date:       November 29, 1999
'*
'* Syntax:     ReleaseSignatureCertificate
'*
'* Parameters:  None
'*
'* Purpose: This subroutine releases certificate context of the
'*          signature certificate and closes the certificate
'*          store.
'**************************************************************
    '--- If we have a current certificate, then release it
    If m_lCertContextPointer <> 0 Then
        CertFreeCertificateContext m_lCertContextPointer
    End If
    '--- If we have a certificate store handle, then close it
    If m_hCertStore <> 0 Then
        '--- Close the Certificate store
        CertCloseStore m_hCertStore, 0
    End If
End Sub
```

Designing the Form

Now that you've added all the necessary functionality to the `crypto` class, it's time to turn your attention back to the application form. You'll need to have input controls to specify the username, the certificate store, and the message to work with. You'll also need controls to display the message in its signed/encrypted and verified/decrypted forms, along with buttons to trigger all this functionality. You can lay out your form as shown in Figure 8.3, configuring the controls as specified in Table 8.6.

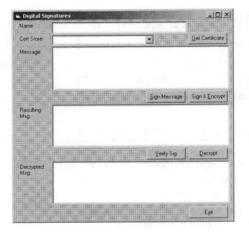

FIGURE 8.3.
Designing the application form.

TABLE 8.6   Control Property Settings

Control	Property	Value
Label	Caption	Name:
TextBox	Name	txtName
Label	Caption	Cert Store:
Combo Box	Name	cboStore
	List	MY
		ROOT
		CA
		SPC
		TRUST
Command Button	Name	cmdGetCert
	Caption	&Get Certificate

Control	Property	Value
Label	Caption	Message:
TextBox	Name	txtMsg
	Multiline	True
Command Button	Name	cmdSignMsg
	Caption	&Sign Message
	Enabled	False
Command Button	Name	cmdSignEncr
	Caption	Sign && &Encrypt
	Enabled	False
Label	Caption	Resulting Msg:
TextBox	Name	txtSignedMsg
	Multiline	True
Command Button	Name	cmdVerify
	Caption	&Verify Sig
	Enabled	False
Command Button	Name	cmdDecode
	Caption	&Decrypt
	Enabled	False
Label	Caption	Decrypted Msg:
TextBox	Name	txtDecryptMsg
	Multiline	True
Command Button	Name	cmdExit
	Caption	E&xit

Now that you have all the controls on the form, go to the code behind the form, and add declarations for a form-level instance of the crypto class and a variable to hold the signed or encrypted message, as in Listing 8.10.

LISTING 8.10 Form Variable Declarations

```
Option Explicit

Private csCrypt As clsCrypto
Private m_sSignedMsg As String
```

It's also a good time to add the code to clean up and close the application. To do so, add the code in Listing 8.11 to the Click event of the cmdExit command button.

LISTING 8.11   The cmdExit Click Event

```
Private Sub cmdExit_Click()
    '--- Do we have a crypto object?
    If Not (csCrypt Is Nothing) Then
        '--- Release the signature certificate
        csCrypt.ReleaseSignatureCertificate
        '--- Destroy the crypto object
        Set csCrypt = Nothing
    End If
    '--- Close the application
    Unload Me
End Sub
```

Getting the Signer Certificate

The first real functionality you need to be able to trigger is the creation of the instance of the crypto class and the retrieval of the certificate to be used for signing the messages. To add this functionality, add the code in Listing 8.12 to the Click event of the cmdGetCert button.

LISTING 8.12   The cmdGetCert Click Event

```
Private Sub cmdGetCert_Click()
    '--- Create the crypto object
    Set csCrypt = New clsCrypto
    '--- Get the signature certificate for the specified user
    If csCrypt.GetSignatureCertificate(cboStore, txtName) Then
        '--- Certificate found, enable the sign and encrypt buttons
        cmdSignMsg.Enabled = True
        cmdSignEncr.Enabled = True
    Else
        MsgBox "Unable to get certificate for " & txtName _
                & "Reason: &H" & Hex(Err.LastDllError)
    End If
End Sub
```

Performing the Signing

The next piece of functionality to add is the signing of the message the user has entered into the form. To do so, you'll need to copy the text message to the InBuffer of the Crypto object and then call the SignMessage method. When this function returns, you'll need to copy the signed message from the Crypto object's OutBuffer to the class variable that you created to hold this value, as well as display it for the user. To add this functionality, add the code in Listing 8.13 to the Click event of the cmdSignMsg button.

LISTING 8.13 The cmdSignMsg Click Event

```
Private Sub cmdSignMsg_Click()
    '--- Copy the message text to the input buffer
    csCrypt.InBuffer = txtMsg.Text
    '--- Sign the message
    If csCrypt.SignMessage Then
        '--- The message was signed, copy and hold onto
        '--- the signed message
        m_sSignedMsg = csCrypt.OutBuffer
        '--- Display the signed message blob to the user
        txtSignedMsg.Text = csCrypt.OutBuffer
        '--- Enable the verify button
        cmdVerify.Enabled = True
        cmdDecode.Enabled = False
    End If
End Sub
```

At this point, you can sign messages using your application. First, enter the username and the certificate store in which it will be found, and get the signing certificate. Next, enter a message to sign; then sign it, as shown in Figure 8.4.

FIGURE 8.4

Signing the message.

If you look at the signed message that is displayed, the message appears to be encrypted. This is not the case. The packaging of the message and signature place a lot of binary data in front of the actual message, and this binary data is all that is displayed in the text control. To see this for yourself, pause the application, and display the form-level variable that is holding the signed message, as shown in Figure 8.5. You'll see that, in the midst of a bunch of binary data, your message is clearly visible.

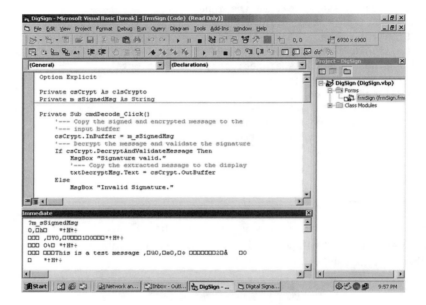

FIGURE 8.5

Examining the signed message.

Performing the Signature Verification

Next, you should perform the verification of the signature. To do so, you'll copy the saved and signed message to the InBuffer of the Crypto object (don't copy the version in the text box control, as it's been truncated) and then call the ValidateSignature method. Finally, you'll display for the user whether the signature is valid and display the extracted message on the form. To add this functionality, add the code in Listing 8.14 to the Click event of the cmdVerify button.

LISTING 8.14   The cmdVerify Click Event

```
Private Sub cmdVerify_Click()
    '--- Copy the signed message to the input buffer
    csCrypt.InBuffer = m_sSignedMsg
```

```
'--- Validate the signature
If csCrypt.ValidateSignature Then
    MsgBox "Signature valid."
    '--- Copy the extracted message to the display
    txtDecryptMsg.Text = csCrypt.OutBuffer
Else
    MsgBox "Invalid Signature."
End If
End Sub
```

At this point, you should be able to run your application, perform the steps you performed earlier, and then verify the signature, as shown in Figure 8.6.

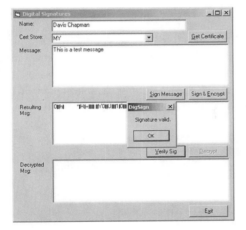

FIGURE 8.6
Verifying the message signature.

Performing the Encryption

Now that you can sign and verify the signature on messages, it's time to add the last few pieces so you can encrypt signed messages and decrypt and verify these messages. To do so, you'll need to take basically the same steps as you did to sign the message, except that you call the `SignAndEncryptMessage` method this time. To add this functionality, add the code in Listing 8.15 to the `Click` event of the `cmdSignEncr` button.

LISTING 8.15   The `cmdSignEncr` `Click` Event

```
Private Sub cmdSignEncr_Click()
    '--- Copy the message text to the input buffer
```

continues

LISTING 8.15   Continued

```
    csCrypt.InBuffer = txtMsg.Text
    '--- Sign and encrypt the message
    If csCrypt.SignAndEncryptMessage(txtName) Then
        '--- The message was encrypted, copy and hold onto
        '--- the encrypted message
        m_sSignedMsg = csCrypt.OutBuffer
        '--- Display the encrypted message to the user
        txtSignedMsg.Text = csCrypt.OutBuffer
        '--- Enable the decrypt button
        cmdDecode.Enabled = True
        cmdVerify.Enabled = False
    End If
End Sub
```

This time, when you run the application and encrypt the message instead of signing it, you won't immediately notice any difference. If you pause the application and examine the signed message form variable in the immediate window, as shown in Figure 8.7, you'll notice that the message is not visible in cleartext anywhere. You will see some cleartext from the certificates in the message, but that will be all the recognizable text you'll find.

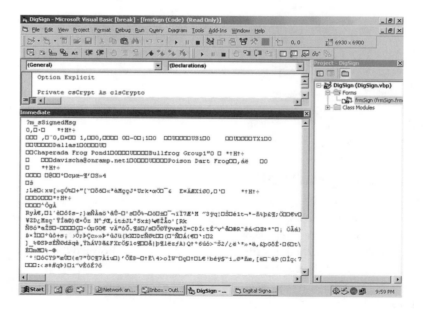

FIGURE 8.7

Examining the encrypted message.

Performing the Decryption

Finally, you need to be able to decrypt and verify the message. This process is basically the same as what you did to verify the signature, except that you call the DecryptAndValidateMessage method this time. To add this functionality, add the code in Listing 8.16 to the Click event of the cmdDecode button.

LISTING 8.16   The cmdDecode Click Event

```
Private Sub cmdDecode_Click()
    '--- Copy the signed and encrypted message to the
    '--- input buffer
    csCrypt.InBuffer = m_sSignedMsg
    '--- Decrypt the message and validate the signature
    If csCrypt.DecryptAndValidateMessage Then
        MsgBox "Signature valid."
        '--- Copy the extracted message to the display
        txtDecryptMsg.Text = csCrypt.OutBuffer
    Else
        MsgBox "Invalid Signature."
    End If
End Sub
```

At this point, you should be able to complete the process by actually decrypting the message and verifying the signature, displaying the decrypted message for the user, as shown in Figure 8.8.

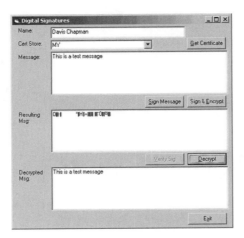

FIGURE 8.8

Decrypting and verifying the message.

8

**USING DIGITAL
SIGNATURES**

Summary

In this chapter, you learned about the "simplified" functions available in the Crypto API. You saw how you can use these functions to, in a single function call, perform what would have taken a significant amount of code given what you knew a few chapters ago. This functionality is all keyed on using certificates as a means to exchange public keys and is thus dependent on the information you learned in the previous few chapters, which dealt with how to get, manage, and validate certificates.

Now you know how, after you have your certificates and the key exchange certificates of the people you want to send messages to, you can send and receive messages in a secure manner. You also can verify that the message came from the other person and hasn't been modified in transit. These functions provide you with the key pieces of functionality to be able to build secure messaging applications.

In the next chapter, you'll look at how you can build an application that can communicate through the Secure Sockets Layer (SSL). You'll learn how this protocol works and how you can build applications that use it to communicate.

DCOM Through SSL

IN THIS CHAPTER

- **RDS and HTTP**
- **DCOM Tunneling Through TCP/IP**
- **Building a DCOM-HTTPS Application**

For C/C++ programmers, the normal way to activate Secure Sockets Layer (SSL) communications is through the Security Support Provider Interface (SSPI). Implementing the Security Support Provider Interface is a very difficult and complex way to use SSL communications. It would be preferable if there were a simpler way to perform secure communications between a client and a server.

Well, it just so happens that there is a much simpler way. In fact, you can accomplish this goal using two very similar methods. Both involve marshaling DCOM (Distributed COM, or Component Object Model) communications between client applications and server objects through the HTTP (or HTTPS for SSL communications) protocol. The older and more widely supported method of doing so is through Remote Data Services (RDS), which is a subset of the ActiveX Data Object (ADO) technology. The more recent method is tunneling DCOM communications through TCP/IP. Both accomplish the same goal using virtually identical processes and look almost identical to both the end user and the programmer.

> **NOTE**
>
> If you are working with Windows 2000, you can freely substitute COM+ for DCOM throughout this chapter. However, the technologies discussed here are readily available on Windows 95/98 and NT 4.0, not just Windows 2000.

RDS and HTTP

Remote Data Service (RDS) is a part of Microsoft's ActiveX Data Object technology. It is primarily designed for delivering recordsets from a Web site database to the Web browser, allowing the user to actively scroll through the recordset, make changes, and send the changes back to the server without making calls to the server between each row. Another aspect of RDS is that it is designed to move this recordset between the Web server and the browser via the HTTP protocol.

Another, not as well-advertised, feature of RDS is the capability to use it as a transport mechanism to marshal DCOM through the HTTP protocol. Using this capability, you can send and receive just about anything you need through the HTTP protocol to COM objects running on the Web server. And if you can send it through the HTTP protocol, then you can also send it through the Secure Sockets Layer (SSL) by using the HTTPS protocol (HTTP with SSL).

Standard DCOM Versus RDS DCOM

To understand what RDS enables you to do with DCOM, you need to know how DCOM performs its communications between objects. Standard DCOM uses a series of connections in communicating between computers. A Service Control Manager connection always uses port 135 on both TCP and UDP. This connection is used to get information about places to find COM objects on the server machine.

The actual COM objects running on any particular machine are dynamically allocated ports to use in the range 1024 to 65535, as shown in Figure 9.1. If you're using DCOM across a firewall, several ports in this range need to be open for use. Keeping these ports open makes for a large hole that is open in the firewall (and is not likely to make you many friends among the network security people responsible for the firewall).

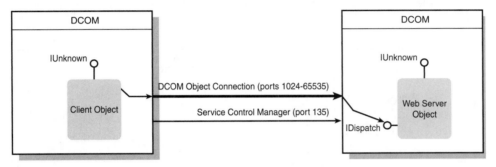

FIGURE 9.1
Standard DCOM uses numerous TCP/IP ports.

You can restrict the number of ports by adding a series of keys and values to the RPC settings in the NT Registry, documented in the Microsoft publications on DCOM with Firewalls (msdn.microsoft.com/library/backgrnd/html/msdn_dcomfirewall.htm). You also might need to specify which network protocol DCOM should be using, configurable through the DCOM configuration utility (DCOMCNFG.EXE), depending on how the firewall is set up. A limitation to this approach is that the firewall cannot be a proxy server. The IP address used by the server has to be the same as the one registered on the client computer.

What are the benefits of using DCOM in this configuration? The primary benefit is the integration with NT/MTS security. The (Microsoft) recommended approach for this configuration is to have a wrapper class on the client (Web server) that calls the desired COM object on the server. This way, the wrapper class can operate under NT/MTS security and pass that security information along to the server object.

Compare the number of ports used by DCOM to the single port used by RDS. RDS enables all DCOM communication to be marshaled through the HTTP protocol, as shown in Figure 9.2. This setup greatly simplifies the network configuration of DCOM. The result is that, although standard DCOM works great when all the communicating objects are located on machines physically close to each other on the same network, RDS is much more suitable for use over the Internet or other situations in which the objects are on computers that are far apart.

NOTE

The SOAP (Simple Object Access Protocol) technology is very similar to RDS in how it piggybacks on HTTP. SOAP is built on XML (eXtensible Markup Language) and is intended to be a platform- and language-neutral distributed object technology. While it is currently a very new technology, it will be a technology to watch over the next couple of years as another way of accomplishing this same goal.

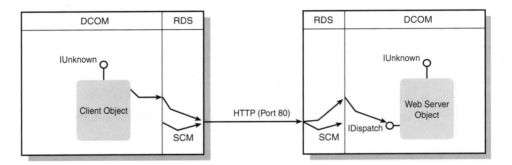

FIGURE 9.2
RDS marshals DCOM through a single TCP/IP port.

You must take into account some considerations when building an RDS solution. One of the biggest concerns is that you do not have integrated security between the COM objects on both systems. As a result, you need to take other measures to provide security if your application requires it.

CAUTION

One of the largest security problems with RDS is that any two calls to the server objects may be from different users. If your server objects use impersonation of the user to control access on the server, you could easily find your server objects executing as a different user than they should. The first call could be from one user, and the server would impersonate that user. The next call could be from someone else, while the server object was still impersonating the first user. I've heard rumors that this problem would be corrected in Windows 2000, but I haven't seen any verification.

RDS `DataSpace` Object

The RDS `DataSpace` object is the client proxy that performs the communications between the client application and the server objects. You use it to create object stubs in the client application and instance those same objects on the server. You do so by using the `CreateObject` method.

The RDS `DataSpace` object's `CreateObject` method is its only method. It is almost the same as the standard `CreateObject` method, except that you also have to specify the URL or server name of the server on which to create the object, as follows:

```
Dim ds As New RDS.DataSpace
Dim obj As Object

Set obj = ds.CreateObject("ExampleObject.ExampleClass", _
    "http://www.myserver.com")
```

RDS supports four protocols; they're listed in Table 9.1. Each of these protocols affects what you pass for the server name in the second parameter.

TABLE 9.1 Protocols Supported by RDS

Protocol	Server Parameter Format
HTTP	`"http://serverURL"`
HTTPS (HTTP with SSL)	`"https://serverURL"`
DCOM	`"machinename"`
In-Process (on the same computer as the client)	`""` (Empty string)

The `DataSpace` object also has a single property: the `InternetTimeout` property. The `InternetTimeout` property has an effect only if you're using either the HTTP or HTTPS protocols. It controls how long an RDS call to an object on the server will wait for a response. If the number of milliseconds to which this property is set passes and no response has arrived, the call fails and an exception is thrown in the client application.

RDSServer `DataFactory` Object

The `RDSServer DataFactory` object is a server-side object that you can use to create and retrieve recordsets and then send the updates back to the database. You create this object by using the `DataSpace CreateObject` method as follows:

```
Dim df As Object

Set df = ds.CreateObject("RDSServer.DataFactory", _
    "http://www.myserver.com")
```

To create a recordset from a query, you can call its `Query` method, passing the connection information and the SQL to run to create the recordset, as follows:

```
Dim rs As Object
Dim strSQL As String
Dim strConnect As String

strSQL = "Select Name, Address From User"
strConnect = "DSN=MyDB;UID=davis;PWD=mypassword"
Set rs = df.Query(strConnect, strSQL)
```

From here, you can treat the recordset as almost any ADO recordset object (almost all the same methods and properties are supported). After you make all the changes to the data that you're going to make, and you need to save the changes back to the database, you can pass the recordset to the `DataFactory` object's `SubmitChanges` method. This method is basically the same as the `Query`; you need to pass it both the connect string (to connect to the database) and the recordset object, as follows:

```
df.SubmitChanges strConnect, rs
```

When data changes are sent to the database, the changes are sent to the database as a batch transaction. This means that all the updates succeed or they all fail as a single transaction.

RDS `DataControl` Object

The RDS `DataControl` object is a combination of the `DataSpace` and `DataFactory` objects, as well as a recordset object. It is the last of the RDS objects, and it can be used only in Web pages. Because you cannot use this object in Visual Basic clients, I've mentioned this object here purely for reasons of completeness.

Interacting with Custom Server Controls

Before you can instantiate any objects on the Web server using either the HTTP or HTTPS protocols, you need to make an addition to the Registry on the server. Open the Registry using either the `regedit` or `regedt32` utilities and navigate to the HKEY_LOCAL_MACHINE\System\CurrentControlSet\Services\W3SVC\Parameters\ADCLaunch key. Under this key, you can find some keys that are named after COM objects, including one for `RDSServer.DataFactory`. You need to add a new key here for each server class that you want to be able to access through RDS using the HTTP or HTTPS protocols. For instance, if you want to use RDS to call the object `MyObject.MyClass` on the Web server, you add the Registry key HKEY_LOCAL_MACHINE\System\CurrentControlSet\Services\W3SVC\Parameters\ADCLaunch\MyObject.MyClass, as shown in Figure 9.3.

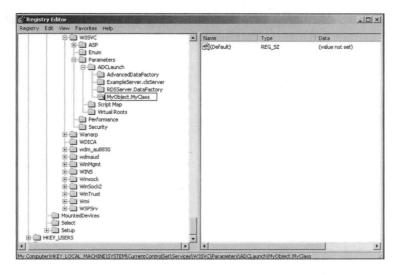

FIGURE 9.3
You need to add a Registry key before RDS can instantiate a server object.

After you instantiate the object on the server by using the `DataSpace` object's `CreateObject` method, you can call any method implemented by the object. You should not try to use any properties on the server object, as they are not supported by RDS (and even if they are, you cannot count on the properties maintaining their settings because any other client can reset them right after you set them). In fact, the best way to create server-side objects for calling through RDS is to design and create the objects just as you would for use with Microsoft's Transaction Server.

Enabling RDS Use

Before you can use RDS in an application, you must address a couple of requirements for the client and server machines. First, all machines, both client and server, need to have the latest version of MDAC (Microsoft Data Access Components) installed. The current version available for all platforms as I'm writing this chapter is MDAC 2.1 (the version shipping with Windows 2000 is MDAC 2.5), and the installation file is freely available from the Microsoft Web site.

If your client application is running either on Windows 95 or Windows 98, then you also need to install DCOM for the appropriate one of these operating systems. They also are freely available through the download center on the Microsoft Web site (`www.microsoft.com`).

Before you can use RDS in your Visual Basic applications, you need to add a reference to it in the project. For server-side objects, you need to add references to both the ActiveX Data

Objects Library and the Remote Data Services Server Library, as shown in Figure 9.4. For the client side, you need to add a reference to the Remote Data Services Library, as in Figure 9.5.

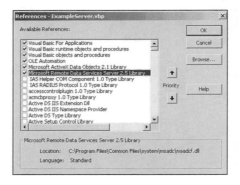

FIGURE 9.4
Adding references for RDS on a server-side object project.

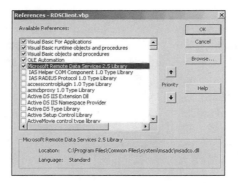

FIGURE 9.5
Adding references for RDS on a client-side project.

DCOM Tunneling Through TCP/IP

A different way of accomplishing the same result is by tunneling DCOM through TCP/IP. This method marshals an initial connection from the client to the server through the HTTP protocol, which then sets up a direct connection between the DCOM proxy on the server and the DCOM proxy on the client. From that point on, all DCOM communications between these two computers takes place through a single TCP/IP connection. This connection is often referred to as *SSL tunneling* and is part of Microsoft's COM Internet Services (CIS).

The attraction of this approach is that it requires nothing special from an application programming aspect. All you have to do is create a regular DCOM application with server-side objects and a client application. Tunneling DCOM through TCP/IP is purely a configuration matter.

> **CAUTION**
>
> DCOM tunneling requires special configuration consideration on firewalls that perform packet filtering. Most firewalls allow HTTP traffic through on port 80. Some firewalls actually examine the data that is passed through this port to make sure that it is HTTP traffic. This process is called *packet filtering*. When the initial connection is made, the rest of the communications between the client and the server do not use the HTTP protocol and thus are often rejected by packet-filtering firewalls. Therefore, if you need to tunnel DCOM through a packet-filtering firewall, you need to configure it to allow non-HTTP communications through on port 80.

Client Configuration

Your ability to tunnel DCOM through TCP/IP is dependent on various updates to the Windows operating systems (including the COM Internet Services). The minimum configurations are listed in Table 9.2.

TABLE 9.2   Minimum Configurations for DCOM Tunneling

Operating System	Minimum Software Upgrade
Windows 95	DCOM95 1.2
Windows 98	DCOM98 1.3
NT 4	Service Pack 4
Windows 2000	None

> **TIP**
>
> The CISCNFG utility required to configure COM Internet Services may require a separate download from Microsoft.

After you install the OS software upgrades, you need to configure DCOM to enable tunneling through TCP/IP. If you have Windows 95 or Windows 98, you do so from a DOS shell, using the CISCNFG utility, as follows:

CISCNFG tcp_http

The available arguments for the CISCNFG utility are listed in Table 9.3.

TABLE 9.3 CISCNFG Arguments

Argument	Description
tcp	Configures DCOM to use the standard communication model
http	Configures DCOM to use HTTP-TCP/IP tunneling only
tcp_http	Configures DCOM to try to use the standard DCOM communication model and then try to use HTTP-TCP/IP tunneling

If you use NT 4 or Windows 2000, you need to use the DCOMCNFG utility instead. You run this utility either from a DOS prompt or by choosing Start|Run. After you start the DCOMCNFG utility, select the Default Protocols tab, as shown in Figure 9.6. On this tab, click the Add button, and select Tunneling TCP/IP from the combo box, as shown in Figure 9.7. Click OK twice and then reboot your system. After your system has rebooted, all DCOM communications from your system to a DCOM server will try each of the communications protocols listed in the DCOMCNFG utility in the order listed.

FIGURE 9.6

The DCOMCNFG utility showing the configured communication protocols.

FIGURE 9.7

Adding the Tunneling TCP/IP protocol to the DCOM configuration.

At this point, your system is configured to use DCOM tunneling as a client. All that remains for you to do on the client is to install the client applications and configure the DCOM stubs as with any other standard DCOM application.

Server Configuration for DCOM

The server configuration for tunneling DCOM is a little more involved than the client. First, the server side can run only with Internet Information Server (IIS) 4.0 or higher. If you're running it on NT 4, you need to install Service Pack 4. A second requirement is that you cannot run the server side of tunneling DCOM on the same machine as Microsoft's Proxy Server.

NT 4 Server Configuration

To configure the server, you first need to create a new directory under the Inetpub directory. This new directory should be named RPC. For instance, if your Inetpub directory is in the root directory of your C drive, the new directory would be C:\Inetpub\rpc.

Next, you need to copy the rpcproxy.dll from the Windows system directory to the new Inetpub\rpc directory.

You need to perform the next few steps of the configuration in the Internet Service Manager. To run the Internet Service Manager, from the Start menu, select Programs|Windows NT 4 Option Pack|Microsoft Internet Information Server|Internet Server Manager. In the left pane, expand the tree views as follows:

- Console Root
- IIS
- *<your machine name>*
- Default Web Site

Now you need to create a virtual root for the Inetpub\rpc directory. To do so, select the Default Web Site node in the tree view, right-click, select New from the context menu that appears, and then select Virtual Directory from the cascading menu, as shown in Figure 9.8. Next, fill in the Virtual Directory Wizard using the information listed in Table 9.4.

TABLE 9.4   Virtual Directory Values

Wizard Screen	*Value to Provide*
Alias to be used to access virtual directory	RPC
Physical path	C:\Inetpub\rpc (the actual path for your Inetpub\rpc directory)
Permissions	Allow Execute Access (Unselect all others)

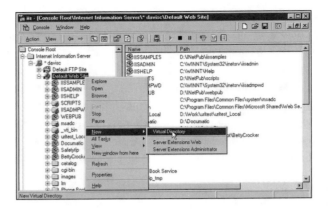

FIGURE 9.8
Adding a new virtual directory.

After you add the virtual directory, you need to change the connection timeout value for the default Web site. To do so, right-click over the Default Web Site node in the tree on the left side of the Internet Service Manager. From the context menu that appears, select Properties. Then select the Web Site tab in the Default Web Site Properties dialog, change the Connection Timeout value to 300 (5 minutes), and click OK to save this change and close the Default Web Site Properties dialog.

Finally, you need to install the RPCProxy ISAPI filter. To do so, move up one node on the tree on the left side of the Internet Service Manager, selecting the node with your computer name. Right-click and select Properties from the context menu that appears. On the Properties dialog, select the Internet Information Server tab, select WWW Service in the Master Properties combo box, and click the Edit button next to the combo box to open the WWW Service Master Properties dialog. On this dialog, select the ISAPI Filters tab, as shown in Figure 9.9, and click the Add button. In the Filter Properties dialog that appears, enter the information shown in Table 9.5. When you've finished, the dialog will look like the one shown in Figure 9.10.

TABLE 9.5   ISAPI Filter Properties

Property	Value to Provide
Filter Name	Rpcproxy
Executable	C:\Inetpub\rpc\rpcproxy.dll (the actual path for the rpcproxy.dll in your Inetpub\rpc directory)

After you save the RPCProxy filter information (by clicking OK three times to close the respective dialogs), you need to stop and restart the Internet Information Server for these changes to take effect. From here, you need to enable CIS on your server, which I'll get to shortly.

FIGURE 9.9
Adding a new ISAPI filter.

FIGURE 9.10
Specifying the new ISAPI filter's properties.

Windows 2000 Server Configuration

Configuring Windows 2000 to be a CIS server is a little easier than configuring NT 4. First, CIS is a part of the original shipping operating system, not an extension that was added after the OS originally shipped. This means that all the necessary CIS components are available as options from the Networking components on the installation CD-ROM, and you can use the Windows 2000 installation utilities to add and configure the service.

Adding the CIS services to a Windows 2000 server requires three simple steps. First, from the Control Panel, open the Add/Remove Programs utility. In the utility, click the Add/Remove Windows Components button.

When the Windows Components Wizard opens, select Networking Services and click the Details button. In the Networking Services dialog that appears, check the box beside COM Internet Services Proxy, as shown in Figure 9.11. Click OK a couple of times to add this service to your server (assuming that this networking option wasn't included in the initial installation of Windows 2000, in which case you'll find that the CIS Proxy option is already selected).

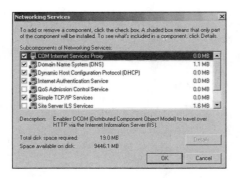

FIGURE 9.11
Adding COM Internet Services Proxy to your Windows 2000 Server.

Enabling CIS on the Server

After you have the RPCProxy installed on your server, you need to configure DCOM to use the tunneling TCP/IP protocol. This process requires two steps. The first step is adding the tunneling TCP/IP protocol using the DCOMCNFG utility, just as you added it to your NT 4 or Windows 2000 clients earlier in this chapter (refer to Figures 9.6 and 9.7). The second step, after you have rebooted your server, is to enable the COM Internet Services on your server. You do so by running the DCOMCNFG utility again and selecting the Default Properties tab. On this tab, check the Enable COM Internet Services on This Computer option, as shown in Figure 9.12.

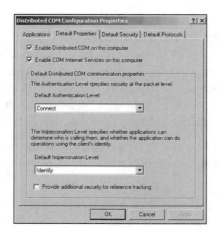

FIGURE 9.12
Enabling COM Internet Services on your server.

At this point, you are finished configuring the client and server computers for tunneling DCOM, so all you have to do is install the appropriate components on the server, their DCOM stubs on the client, and the client application on the client computers. The rest of the configuration responsibilities fall on the network administrator to configure any proxy servers or firewalls that these communications must pass through to allow non-HTTP traffic on port 80.

> **TIP**
>
> If you or your network administrator needs any additional information on how to configure any of the computers involved or on firewalls and proxy servers, you can refer to the white paper explaining how to do these tasks on Microsoft's Web site at msdn.Microsoft.com/library/backgrnd/html/CIS.htm.

Building a DCOM-HTTPS Application

Because tunneling DCOM through HTTP-TCP/IP requires nothing different in the design and construction from any other standard DCOM application, the sample application that you'll build now will use RDS as its means of marshaling DCOM through HTTP (or HTTPS if you're running SSL on your server). The sample application will be very simple, with three server-side methods that can be called. One method will create a custom recordset and return it, one will return a string, and the third will return a Boolean value. By creating this application, you'll see how different data types can be returned through RDS.

Creating the Server Object

To create the server object for this application, start a new Visual Basic project, specifying that you are creating an ActiveX DLL. For this example, name the project **ExampleServer**, and name the initial class **clsServer**. Open the project references dialog, and add the Microsoft ActiveX Data Object Library and the Microsoft Remote Data Services Server Library, as shown in Figure 9.4.

In this sample object, you'll be using the random number generator, so you need to initialize it upon the class initialization. To do so, add the code in Listing 9.1 to the class initialization event.

LISTING 9.1   Initializing the Class

```
Private Sub Class_Initialize()
    '--- Initialize the random number generator
    Randomize
End Sub
```

Returning a Recordset

For the method in which the server object will be returning a recordset, you'll build a recordset with three columns. The first column will contain a user-supplied name. The second column will contain a random number generated by the random number generator. The third column will contain the current date and time. The user will have the option of supplying one or two row names, and the server object will create one or two rows, depending on the names supplied. You'll therefore need to have two string parameters to this method, making the second parameter optional. To add this functionality to your server object, add the code in Listing 9.2 to the class in your server object project.

LISTING 9.2   The `GetRecordset` Function

```
Public Function GetRecordset(astrRow1String As String, _
                Optional astrRow2String As String = "") As Object
'*************************************************************
'* Written By: Davis Chapman
'* Date:       January 16, 2000
'*
'* Syntax:     GetRecordset(astrRow1String[, astrRow2String])
'*
'* Parameters:  astrRow1String As String
'*              astrRow2String As String
'*
'* Purpose: This will take one or two strings and create a
'*          recordset, using the strings passed in as row names,
'*          generates random values for the row value, and gets
'*          the current time for the row time. The recordset
'*          is then returned to the calling application.
'*************************************************************
    '--- Create a new recordset
    Dim objRtnRS As New ADODB.Recordset
On Error GoTo GetRecordset_Err

    '--- Build and initialize the return recordset
    objRtnRS.Fields.Append "RowName", adBSTR
    objRtnRS.Fields.Append "RowValue", adInteger
    objRtnRS.Fields.Append "RowTime", adDate
    '--- Open the recordset
    objRtnRS.Open
    '--- Add first row
    objRtnRS.AddNew
    '--- Populate the row values
    objRtnRS("RowName") = astrRow1String
    objRtnRS("RowValue") = ((50 * Rnd) + 1)
    objRtnRS("RowTime") = Now
    '--- Do we need to add a second row?
    If astrRow2String <> "" Then
```

```
        '--- Add second row
        objRtnRS.AddNew
        '--- Populate the row values
        objRtnRS("RowName") = astrRow2String
        objRtnRS("RowValue") = ((50 * Rnd) + 1)
        objRtnRS("RowTime") = Now
    End If
    '--- Set the return value to the recordset
    Set GetRecordset = objRtnRS
    '--- Exit the function
    Exit Function

GetRecordset_Err:
    '--- An error occurred, log the error
    App.LogEvent "GetRecordset Error = " & Err.Number & " = " & _
            Err.Description
    '--- Exit the function
    Exit Function
End Function
```

TIP

If you look at the exception handling in this code, you'll notice that you are calling the App object's LogEvent method. Because this object will be running on the server, you cannot and should not use the MsgBox function to alert the user of any exceptions that occur. The LogEvent method writes the error information to the server Application Event Log, which can be viewed through the Event Viewer utility.

The first thing you do in this function is to create a new, empty recordset, as follows:

```
'--- Create a new recordset
Dim objRtnRS As New ADODB.Recordset
```

After you create a new recordset, you add the columns to the recordset using the Append method, supplying the column name and data type:

```
'--- Build and initialize the return recordset
objRtnRS.Fields.Append "RowName", adBSTR
objRtnRS.Fields.Append "RowValue", adInteger
objRtnRS.Fields.Append "RowTime", adDate
```

After you define the recordset, you open it and add a new row like this:

```
'--- Open the recordset
objRtnRS.Open
'--- Add first row
objRtnRS.AddNew
```

After adding an empty row, you populate the columns in that row as follows:

```
'--- Populate the row values
objRtnRS("RowName") = astrRow1String
objRtnRS("RowValue") = ((50 * Rnd) + 1)
objRtnRS("RowTime") = Now
```

If the user supplies two row names, you next add a second row and populate its columns. After you populate the recordset, you set the return value to the recordset that you created:

```
'--- Set the return value to the recordset
Set GetRecordset = objRtnRS
```

Returning a String

The next method you need to add to the server object is the method that will return a string. In this method, you'll allow the user to specify a number, and you'll return a string specifying what the number is. You'll give the user the option of not supplying any number, in which case you'll tell the user that no number was returned. This flexibility requires that the only parameter to this function be optional. To add this functionality to your server object, add the function in Listing 9.3.

LISTING 9.3   The GetString Function

```
Public Function GetString(Optional aiValue As Integer = 0) As String
'*************************************************************
'* Written By: Davis Chapman
'* Date:       January 16, 2000
'*
'* Syntax:     GetString([aiValue])
'*
'* Parameters: aiValue As Integer
'*
'* Purpose: This will build a string that specifies what the
'*          numeric value that was passed in is. The string
'*          that was built is returned.
'*************************************************************
    Dim strRtnValue As String
On Error GoTo GetString_Err

    '--- Initialize the return value
    GetString = ""

    '--- Was a non-zero value passed in?
    If aiValue <> 0 Then
        '--- Yes, build a return string specifying the value
        strRtnValue = "The value passed is " + CStr(aiValue) + "."
```

```
    Else
        '--- No, build a return string stating that no value was passed
        strRtnValue = "There was no value passed, or the value was 0."
    End If
    '--- Return the string
    GetString = strRtnValue
    '--- Exit the function
    Exit Function

GetString_Err:
    '--- An error occurred, log the error
    App.LogEvent "GetString Error = " & Err.Number & " = " & _
            Err.Description
    '--- Exit the function
    Exit Function
End Function
```

Returning a Boolean

The last method that you need to add to the server object is the method that will return a
Boolean value. In this method, you'll compare two strings that are passed in and return a
Boolean value specifying whether the two strings match. To add this method to your server
object, add the function in Listing 9.4.

LISTING 9.4   The GetBoolean Function

```
Public Function GetBoolean(astrFirstValue As String, _
                            astrSecondValue As String) As Boolean
'*************************************************************
'* Written By: Davis Chapman
'* Date:       January 16, 2000
'*
'* Syntax:     GetBoolean(astrFirstValue, astrSecondValue)
'*
'* Parameters:   astrFirstValue As String
'*               astrSecondValue As String
'*
'* Purpose: This will compare the two strings passed in, compare
'*          them, and return a boolean specifying whether or
'*          not they match.
'*************************************************************
On Error GoTo GetBoolean_Err

    '--- Initialize the return value to FALSE
    GetBoolean = False
```

continues

LISTING 9.4   Continued

```
    '--- If the two strings match, change the return value to TRUE
    If (astrFirstValue = astrSecondValue) Then GetBoolean = True
    '--- Exit the function
    Exit Function

GetBoolean_Err:
    '--- An error occurred, log the error
    App.LogEvent "GetBoolean Error = " & Err.Number & " = " & _
            Err.Description
    '--- Exit the function
    Exit Function
End Function
```

Configuring the Server

Now you are ready to compile your application into a DLL. After you do so, you need to add it to the Registry so that it can be called. Add the Registry key HKEY_LOCAL_MACHINE\System\CurrentControlSet\Services\W3SVC\Parameters\ADCLaunch\ExampleServer.clsServer, as shown in Figure 9.13.

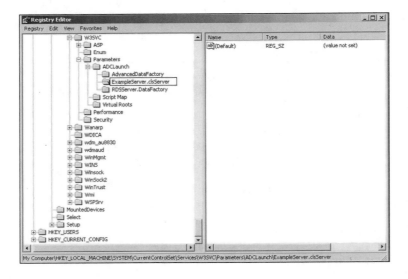

FIGURE 9.13

Adding the Registry key for your server object.

> **NOTE**
>
> This last set of instructions makes the assumption that you will be using your development machine as the server. If you're going to place the DLL you created on a different server, you need to create an installation program using the Package & Deployment Wizard so that all the Visual Basic runtime and supporting controls and DLLs are installed on the server. If all the necessary components are already installed on the server, you just need to copy the DLL you created to the server and register it using `regsvr32`.

Creating the Client Application

Now it's time to turn your attention to the client application. To create it, you need to create a new Visual Basic project for a standard EXE. After you create the project, add a reference for the Microsoft Remote Data Services Library, as shown in Figure 9.14.

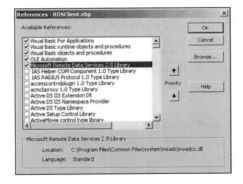

FIGURE 9.14
Adding references for RDS to the client project.

Designing the Form

The first step that you need to take from here is to design the layout of the application form. The user needs to be able to specify the server (and protocol) where the server object is running, the row names for the recordset, and a number (you'll reuse the row names for comparing two strings). You also need command buttons for the user to connect to the server, to call each of the server methods, and then to close the connection and exit the application. To provide this functionality to the user, lay out the application form as shown in Figure 9.15, configuring the controls as listed in Table 9.6.

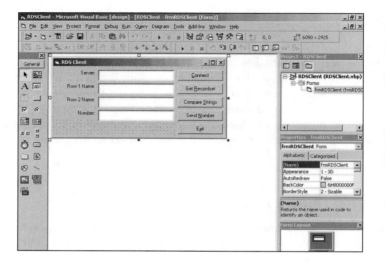

FIGURE 9.15
Designing the application form.

TABLE 9.6   Control Property Settings

Control	Property	Value
Label	Caption	Server:
TextBox	Name	txtServer
Command Button	Name	cmdConnect
	Caption	&Connect
Label	Caption	Row 1 Name:
TextBox	Name	txtRow1Name
Command Button	Name	cmdGetRecordset
	Caption	Get &Recordset
Label	Caption	Row 2 Name:
TextBox	Name	txtRow2Name
Command Button	Name	cmdCompareStrings
	Caption	Compare &Strings
Label	Caption	Number:
TextBox	Name	txtNumber
Command Button	Name	cmdSendNumber
	Caption	Send &Number
Command Button	Name	cmdClose
	Caption	E&xit

The next step is to declare the variables that you're going to use in your form. It's a good idea to provide a default server name, along with the object name that you'll be connecting to on the server. You also should declare a form-level instance of the RDS.DataSpace, along with the object that will be the instance of the server object. By doing so, you can connect to the server and instantiate the object once, instead of within each event that interacts with the server object. To add these variables to your form, add the variable declarations in Listing 9.5.

LISTING 9.5   Declaring the Form Variables

```
Option Explicit

'--- Define the default servers, objects, domains, etc.
Const m_def_Server = "http://localhost"
Const m_def_Obj = "ExampleServer.clsServer"

'--- Declare the RDS dataspace object
Private m_ds As New RDS.DataSpace
'--- Declare the COM object to be created on the server
Private m_rs As Object
```

Initializing and Closing the Form

After you add all the necessary variables to the form, you can initialize the form by populating the server text box with the default server and protocol string. To do so, add the code in Listing 9.6 to the form load event.

LISTING 9.6   Initializing the Form

```
Private Sub Form_Load()
    '--- Initialize the server name
    txtServer = m_def_Server
End Sub
```

The next step to take in preparing to call the methods on the server is to connect to the server and create an instance of the server object. You do so by using the RDS.DataSpace object's CreateObject method, passing the object name you defined in the variable declarations and the server (and protocol) specified by the user. To add this functionality, add the code in Listing 9.7 to the Click event of the cmdConnect button.

LISTING 9.7   Connecting to the Server

```
Private Sub cmdConnect_Click()
On Error GoTo cmdConnect_Click_Err

    '--- Create the object on the server
    Set m_rs = m_ds.CreateObject(m_def_Obj, txtServer)
```

continues

9

DCOM
THROUGH SSL

LISTING 9.7   Continued

```
    '--- Exit the sub
    Exit Sub

cmdConnect_Click_Err:
    '--- Report the error that occurred
    MsgBox "Error : " + CStr(Err.Number) + " - " + Err.Description
End Sub
```

The last piece of form functionality that you need to define is the cleanup and closing of the application. You should check to see whether an instance of the server object has been created and, if so, destroy it before you unload the form. To add this functionality, add the code in Listing 9.8 to the Click event of the cmdClose button.

LISTING 9.8   Closing the Form

```
Private Sub cmdClose_Click()
    '--- Have we created a COM object on the server?
    If Not (m_rs Is Nothing) Then
        '--- Yes, destroy it.
        Set m_rs = Nothing
    End If
    '--- Close the application
    Unload Me
End Sub
```

Retrieving the Recordset

Now that you have the preliminary work out of the way, you can start calling the methods of the server object. The first method that you'll call is the GetRecordset method, which creates and returns a recordset. For this procedure, you need to make sure that the user has entered at least one row name and then call the method passing one or two strings, depending on how many the user entered. When the recordset is returned, cycle through the rows, displaying the row values for the user. To add this functionality, add the code in Listing 9.9 to the Click event of the cmdGetRecordset button.

LISTING 9.9   Retrieving the Recordset

```
Private Sub cmdGetRecordset_Click()
    Dim ieUserObj As Object
    Dim strMsg As String
On Error GoTo cmdGetRecordset_Click_Err

    '--- Do we have at least one row name?
    If (txtRow1Name = "") Then
```

```
                '--- No, tell the user to fill in a value
            MsgBox "You need to supply at least 1 row name."
                '--- Exit the sub
            Exit Sub
        End If
        '--- Do we have two row names?
        If (txtRow2Name = "") Then
            '--- No, only pass the first row name
            Set ieUserObj = m_rs.GetRecordset(txtRow1Name.Text)
        Else
            '--- Yes, pass both row names
            Set ieUserObj = m_rs.GetRecordset(txtRow1Name.Text, _
                ➥txtRow2Name.Text)
        End If
        '--- Did we get something back?
        If Not (ieUserObj Is Nothing) Then
            '--- Yes we did
            With ieUserObj
                '--- Are there any rows in the recordset?
                If .recordcount> 0 Then
                    '--- Yes, move to the first row
                    .movefirst
                    '--- Loop until the end of the recordset
                    While Not .EOF
                        '--- Build a message listing the row values
                        strMsg = "Row Values:" + vbCrLf + _
                            "RowName = " + .fields("RowName") + vbCrLf + _
                            "RowValue = " + CStr(.fields("RowValue")) + _
                            ➥vbCrLf + _
                            "RowTime = " + CStr(.fields("RowTime"))
                        '--- Display the values to the user
                        MsgBox strMsg
                        '--- Move to the next row
                        .movenext
                    Wend
                End If
            End With
            '--- Destroy the recordset
            Set ieUserObj = Nothing
        End If
        '--- Exit the sub
        Exit Sub

cmdGetRecordset_Click_Err:
        '--- Report the error that occurred
        MsgBox "Error : " + CStr(Err.Number) + " - " + Err.Description
End Sub
```

9

**DCOM
THROUGH SSL**

CAUTION

When you're passing the values in the text boxes to the server object, you have to be explicit on which property of the control you are passing, as follows:

```
Set ieUserObj = m_rs.GetRecordset(txtRow1Name.Text)
```

You cannot pass just the control, depending on the default property to pass the value in the control, because the client application does not know what parameters the server object's methods take, including the data types that the methods' parameters require. As a result, the entire control is passed, not just the default property. Passing the entire control results in an interface error, raising an exception in the client application.

NOTE

Because you have to declare the object on the server, and the objects return from the server as the Object data type, Visual Basic doesn't know what properties or methods are available for the objects. Therefore, none of the Auto-Complete functionality in the Visual Basic IDE works for these objects. As a result, you have to be careful to make sure that you are spelling all the method and property names correctly. If you mistype any of the method or property names, the application throws a runtime exception when you try to run it.

At this point, you should be able to run your application, connect to the server object, and enter one or two row names to pass to the server object, as shown in Figure 9.16. Upon receiving the recordset, you should be presented with the values in each row of the recordset, as shown in Figure 9.17.

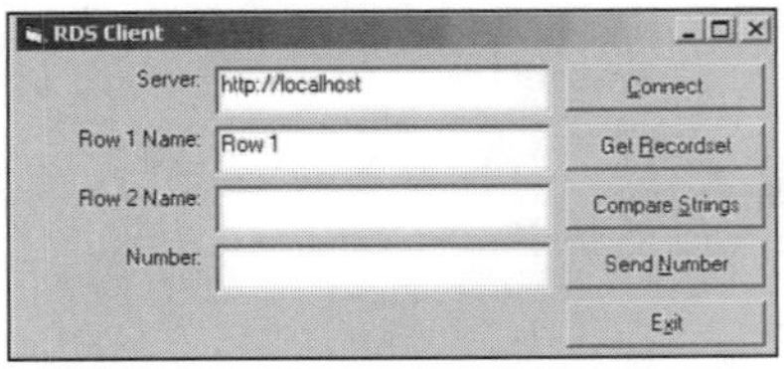

FIGURE 9.16

Running the application.

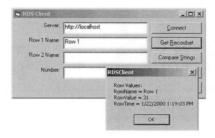

FIGURE 9.17
Displaying the contents of a recordset row.

Retrieving the String Value

The next piece of functionality that you'll add to the client application is the call to the
`GetString` method of the server object. For this functionality, you need to make sure that the
user either didn't enter a value into the txtNumber text box or that the user did enter a number.
Depending on the user's actions, you'll either convert the value entered to a number and pass it
to the server object, or you'll call the `GetString` method without any parameters. When the
call to the server method returns, you'll display the returned string for the user. To add this
functionality to the application, add the code in Listing 9.10 to the `Click` event of the
cmdSendNumber button.

LISTING 9.10   Retrieving the String Value

```
Private Sub cmdSendNumber_Click()
    Dim strRtn As String
On Error GoTo cmdSendNumber_Click_Err

    '--- Do we have a numeric value?
    If Not IsNumeric(txtNumber) And (txtNumber <> "") Then Exit Sub
    '--- Do we have a value?
    If (txtNumber <> "") Then
        '--- Yes, convert it to a number and pass it to the server
        strRtn = m_rs.GetString(CInt(txtNumber))
    Else
        '--- No, pass nothing to the server
        strRtn = m_rs.GetString
    End If
    '--- Display the returned message
    MsgBox strRtn
    '--- Exit the sub
    Exit Sub
```

continues

LISTING 9.10   Continued

```
cmdSendNumber_Click_Err:
    '--- Report the error that occurred
    MsgBox "Error : " + CStr(Err.Number) + " - " + Err.Description
End Sub
```

If you run the application, you can pass the number value to the server object and receive back a string value, as shown in Figure 9.18.

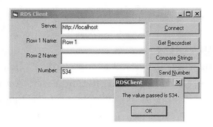

FIGURE 9.18
Displaying the string returned from the server object.

Retrieving the Boolean Value

The final piece of functionality will be to pass both of the row names to the GetBoolean method of the server object. For this method, you need to make sure that the user has provided two row names. After you pass both row names to the server object, you can display for the user a message indicating whether the server returned a TRUE or FALSE value. To add this functionality to the application, add the code in Listing 9.11 to the Click event of the cmdCompareStrings button.

LISTING 9.11   Retrieving the Boolean Value

```
Private Sub cmdCompareStrings_Click()
    Dim bRtnValue As Boolean
On Error GoTo cmdCompareStrings_Click_Err

    '--- Do we have values to send to the server?
    If (txtRow1Name = "") Or (txtRow2Name = "") Then
        '--- No, tell the user to fill in the values
        MsgBox "You need to provide two row names to compare."
        '--- Exit the sub
        Exit Sub
    End If
```

```
    '--- Compare the two string values
    bRtnValue = m_rs.GetBoolean(txtRow1Name.Text, txtRow2Name.Text)
    '--- Do they match?
    If bRtnValue Then
        '--- Yes, tell the user
        MsgBox "The two row names match."
    Else
        '--- No, tell the user
        MsgBox "The two row names do not match."
    End If
    '--- Exit the sub
    Exit Sub

cmdCompareStrings_Click_Err:
    '--- Report the error that occurred
    MsgBox "Error : " + CStr(Err.Number) + " - " + Err.Description
End Sub
```

Now you can run the application and pass both row names to the server object, displaying the result to the user, which tells the user that the row names do not match.

Summary

In this chapter, you learned about a simple and practical way of building applications that communicate through SSL using DCOM. By building server components that sit on the server with IIS, if you have SSL enabled on IIS, you can pass secure information to and from the client. You learned how easily you can do so by using RDS: when you have the appropriate software installed on the client, you don't have to do any further configuration. You also learned how to configure DCOM to tunnel through HTTP and TCP/IP, without any special programming effort, although this method does involve all the client DCOM configuration effort for every server object that you need to call from the client.

At this point, you should have a relatively good understanding of how you can incorporate encryption with your Visual Basic applications. In the next few chapters, you'll learn how to interact with the security in NT 4 and Windows 2000. You'll learn how to impersonate a user to control access based on the OS-configured security and how to validate a user login against the OS domain. You'll also see how you can interact with the Active Directory Security Interface (ADSI), along with Lightweight Directory Access Protocol (LDAP) servers. Finally, you'll look at the new security model being introduced with COM+ and learn how it is similar and different from the security model used in Microsoft's Transaction Server.

9

DCOM THROUGH SSL

Understanding Windows 2000 Security and Security Descriptors

IN THIS CHAPTER

- Windows 2000 Security Overview
- Fundamental Security Data Structures
- Trustee-Based Access Control
- Impersonating a Client

This chapter discusses distributed security in Windows 2000. Security has been a key part of Windows NT programming since the operating system was introduced to developers in 1992. Although the original security manipulation functions were very low-level and difficult to use, security programming became much easier with the release of Windows NT 4.0, which included high-level functions for access control. Windows 2000 extends these functions to offer support for security when interacting with non-Windows operating systems.

This chapter includes a number of sample functions you can use to simplify your security programming. It also includes an example that illustrates how a server can use impersonation to properly handle the access of securable objects on behalf of a client.

NOTE

The topic discussed in this chapter is only applicable to NT 4.0 and Windows 2000. The information discussed in this chapter is not available on Windows 95 or Windows 98.

Windows 2000 Security Overview

Windows 2000 security has two aspects: authorization and authentication. *Authentication* is the process used by the operating system to ensure that you are who you say you are. *Authorization* is the process used by the operating system to allow access to objects or tasks based on the security credentials of a user.

Although authentication and authorization are two sides of the same coin (and work closely together), they are not two names for the same topic. Authentication is involved only with guaranteeing the identity of a user and does not concern itself with access control. Similarly, authorization is concerned only with granting or denying access to an authenticated user.

Prior to Windows 2000, Windows NT used the Windows NT LAN Manager (NTLM) protocol as its sole network authentication protocol. Windows 2000 has expanded its horizons somewhat and uses the industry-standard Kerberos version 5 protocol as its default authentication protocol. Kerberos has many advantages over NTLM, such as the capability to authenticate both client and server. Authentication via NTLM is still available when interacting with NT 4.0 and earlier machines. Windows 2000 also supports the Crypto API, Secure Sockets Layer (SSL), and public key encryption as additional authentication tools.

Before a user is allowed access to any resources, the Windows 2000 logon process must authenticate the user. Access tokens that describe the user's security information are associated with the user and can be used to identify the user on the computer and network. This will be discussed in more detail later in this and the next chapter.

After a user has been authenticated, Windows 2000 allows or denies access to securable objects, based on comparisons between the access rights granted to the user and the access control lists attached to the securable objects. Windows 2000 performs these checks automatically; you usually do not need to test access permissions programmatically in your code.

Server applications that perform work on behalf of clients use an operating system feature known as *impersonation*. Impersonation enables the server thread to assume the security identity of the client in order to access securable objects. Later in the chapter, you'll see an example of a server object that uses impersonation to provide the proper security access to clients.

Fundamental Security Data Structures

Several type structures are used constantly in Windows 2000 security programming. Many of the type structures are often referred to by abbreviated names—which doesn't simplify your life if you're a newcomer to security programming. Here are a few of the most commonly used security structures:

- **SID**. Short for *security identifier*. This is a type structure that uniquely identifies a user or group.
- **ACE**. Short for *access control entry*. This is a type structure that defines how a SID can interact with securable objects. An ACE may allow or deny access to a particular SID. It may also define security-auditing parameters for a SID.
- **ACL**. Short for *access control list*. This is an array of zero or more ACEs. An ACL may contain both access-allowed and access-denied ACEs.
- **DACL**. Short for *discretionary access control list*. This is an ACL that's used to allow or deny access to a securable object.
- **SACL**. Short for *system access control list*. This is an ACL that's used to audit access to a securable object.
- **SECURITY_DESCRIPTOR**. A type structure that contains security information for an object. This information includes the DACL and SACL associated with the object, as well information about its owner and group membership.

These type structures interact with each other as shown in Figure 10.1.

Understanding Process and Thread Security Tokens

When a thread or process is created, it's provided with an *access token*. The access token describes the security attributes associated with the process or thread. The access token is normally obtained from the owner of the process. Later in the chapter, you'll see how the access token can be adjusted programmatically.

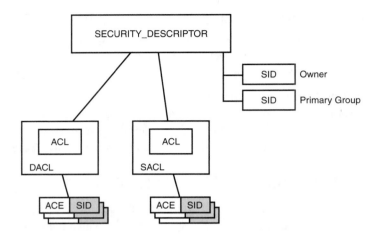

FIGURE 10.1

The relationships between basic low-level security structures.

An access token carries information that can be used to determine the privileges and rights for a process or thread. In Windows 2000, privileges and rights refer to the capabilities of a user to perform certain actions, but they are different concepts. The following is an explanation of each:

- A *privilege* is the capability to perform a system-level action, such as the capability to modify the system time, and is granted by a system administrator.

- A *right* is the capability to access a securable object and is allowed or denied by the DACL associated with the object.

In short, you may have the *right* to access a particular object, such as a registry key, but not have the *privilege* to modify it. Your access *rights* determine what objects you can access, and your *privileges* determine what you can do with those objects.

Access tokens carry a great deal of information about the user. The following is a list of the most commonly used information:

- The SID for the user's account
- The SID for the user's primary group
- SIDs for groups that the user belongs to
- A logon SID that identifies the logon session
- A list of privileges held by the user and the user's groups
- A DACL, known as the *default DACL*, that's assigned to objects created without a security descriptor

Every process has a primary access token. In addition, each thread has an impersonation token that's used when a server impersonates a client in order to assume the security context of the calling process. During impersonation, Windows 2000 uses the impersonation token when authorizing access to resources.

Manipulating Process and Thread Access Tokens

Several Windows 2000 functions are used to interact with access tokens. Here are four commonly used functions:

- **OpenProcessToken**. Returns an access token handle.
- **OpenThreadToken**. Returns an impersonation token handle that identifies a client.
- **GetTokenInformation**. Returns security information stored in the access token.
- **SetTokenInformation**. Modifies security information stored in the access token.

Modifying Token Privileges

Various Win32 and Windows 2000 functions require that the caller have certain privileges enabled. If the access token of the calling process does not possess the required set of privileges, the function call will be rejected by the operating system.

Two functions are used to modify the privileges of an access token:

- **LookupPrivilegeValue**. Returns a locally unique identifier (LUID) that's used to identify a specific privilege.
- **AdjustTokenPrivileges**. Enables or disables privileges in an access token.

For example, some security functions require that the calling process have the SE_SECURITY_NAME privilege. A user in an administrator group may enable this privilege, but it's not normally enabled by default; the calling process must adjust its access token. Listing 10.1 contains an example of a function that enables or disables the SE_SECURITY_NAME privilege for the calling process.

LISTING 10.1   A Function That Adjusts the SE_SECURITY_NAME Privilege on a Process Token

```
Option Explicit

Private Const SE_SECURITY_NAME = "SeSecurityPrivilege"
Private Const SE_PRIVILEGE_ENABLED = &H2
Private Const STANDARD_RIGHTS_REQUIRED = &HF0000

'
' Token Specific Access Rights.
'
```

continues

10

LISTING 10.1   Continued

```vb
Private Const TOKEN_ASSIGN_PRIMARY = &H1
Private Const TOKEN_DUPLICATE = &H2
Private Const TOKEN_IMPERSONATE = &H4
Private Const TOKEN_QUERY = &H8
Private Const TOKEN_QUERY_SOURCE = &H10
Private Const TOKEN_ADJUST_PRIVILEGES = &H20
Private Const TOKEN_ADJUST_GROUPS = &H40
Private Const TOKEN_ADJUST_DEFAULT = &H80
Private Const TOKEN_ADJUST_SESSIONID = &H100

Private Const TOKEN_ALL_ACCESS = (STANDARD_RIGHTS_REQUIRED Or _
    TOKEN_ASSIGN_PRIMARY Or TOKEN_DUPLICATE Or TOKEN_IMPERSONATE Or _
    TOKEN_QUERY Or TOKEN_QUERY_SOURCE Or TOKEN_ADJUST_PRIVILEGES Or _
    TOKEN_ADJUST_GROUPS Or TOKEN_ADJUST_SESSIONID Or TOKEN_ADJUST_DEFAULT)

Private Type LUID
    lowpart As Long
    highpart As Long
End Type

Private Type LUID_AND_ATTRIBUTES
    lLuid As LUID
    Attributes As Long
End Type

Private Type TOKEN_PRIVILEGES
    PrivilegeCount As Long
    Privileges(1) As LUID_AND_ATTRIBUTES
End Type

Private Declare Function GetCurrentProcess Lib "kernel32" () As Long

Private Declare Function OpenProcessToken Lib "advapi32.dll" ( _
    ByVal ProcessHandle As Long, ByVal DesiredAccess As Long, _
    TokenHandle As Long) As Long

Private Declare Function LookupPrivilegeValue Lib "advapi32.dll" _
    Alias "LookupPrivilegeValueA" (ByVal lpSystemName As String, _
    ByVal lpName As String, lpLuid As LUID) As Long

Private Declare Function AdjustTokenPrivileges Lib "advapi32.dll" ( _
    ByVal TokenHandle As Long, ByVal DisableAllPrivileges As Long, _
    NewState As TOKEN_PRIVILEGES, ByVal BufferLength As Long, _
    PreviousState As TOKEN_PRIVILEGES, ReturnLength As Long) As Long
```

```
'--- Declare a second version for passing a NULL pointer in place
'--- of the PreviousState TOKEN_PRIVILEGES type
Private Declare Function AdjustTokenPrivileges2 Lib "advapi32.dll" _
    Alias "AdjustTokenPrivileges" (ByVal TokenHandle As Long, _
    ByVal DisableAllPrivileges As Long, NewState As TOKEN_PRIVILEGES, _
    ByVal BufferLength As Long, PreviousState As Long, _
    ReturnLength As Long) As Long

Public Function EnableSecurityNamePrivilege(bEnable As Boolean) As Boolean
'***************************************************************
'* Written By: Mickey Williams/Davis Chapman
'* Date:       January 29, 2000
'*
'* Syntax:     EnableSecurityNamePrivilege(bEnable)
'*
'* Parameters: bEnable As Boolean
'*
'* Purpose: Enables or disables the SE_SECURITY_NAME privilege for the
'*          current process. This privilege must be explicitly enabled
'*          to access some security information. Returns FALSE
'*          if the privilege was adjusted, or TRUE otherwise.
'***************************************************************

    EnableSecurityNamePrivilege = False

    Dim hProcess As Long
    Dim hToken As Long
    Dim tpNew As TOKEN_PRIVILEGES
    Dim bLookup As Boolean
    Dim strSysName As String
    Dim bAdjusted As Boolean

    '--- Get the handle of the current process
    hProcess = GetCurrentProcess

    '--- Open a token for the process
    If (Not CBool(OpenProcessToken(hProcess, TOKEN_ALL_ACCESS, hToken))) Then
        Exit Function
    End If

    '--- Lookup the security name privilege value for the current process
    strSysName = vbNullChar
    bLookup = CBool(LookupPrivilegeValue(strSysName, _
        SE_SECURITY_NAME, tpNew.Privileges(0).lLuid))
    '--- If unable to lookup the value, exit
```

continues

LISTING 10.1   Continued

```
If (Not bLookup) Then Exit Function

'--- Is the security name privilege to be enabled or disabled?
If (bEnable) Then
    '--- Enable
    tpNew.Privileges(0).Attributes = SE_PRIVILEGE_ENABLED
Else
    '--- Disable
    tpNew.Privileges(0).Attributes = 0
End If

'--- Set the privilege count
tpNew.PrivilegeCount = 1

'--- Adjust the process privilege
bAdjusted = CBool(AdjustTokenPrivileges2(hToken, 0, tpNew, 0, 0, 0))
'--- If unable to adjust the privilege, exit
If (Not bAdjusted) Then Exit Function

'--- Set the return value to true
EnableSecurityNamePrivilege = True

End Function
```

In Listing 10.1, the `EnableSecurityNamePrivilege` function begins by obtaining a pseudohandle for the current process by calling `GetCurrentProcess`. Next, calling `OpenProcessToken` retrieves a handle to the process access token.

The `LookupPrivilegeValue` function is then called to determine the `LUID` used to identify the `SE_SECURITY_NAME` privilege. This `LUID` is passed to the `AdjustTokenPrivileges` function to enable or disable the `SE_SECURITY_NAME` privilege for the process's access token.

Understanding the Security Identifier

The security identifier structure, or `SID`, is used to uniquely identify a user or group in a Windows 2000 domain. In general, you should not manipulate a `SID` directly; however, it is instructive to take a look at a `SID` to get some understanding about how it's put together.

A security identifier contains the following items:

- The revision level of the `SID`.
- The 48-bit identifier for the Windows 2000 domain that issued the `SID`.
- A list of subauthority or relative identifiers (`RID`s) that uniquely identify the `SID`. This list is guaranteed to be unique within a Windows 2000 domain.

A SID always uniquely identifies a user or group. In the event that two users or groups have identical rights, the list of RIDs is guaranteed to be unique.

Converting SIDs to Strings

The SID is stored as a binary value that shouldn't be examined directly. You can, however, convert the SID into a format that's easily displayed with the ConvertSidToStringSid function:

Syntax

```
Public Declare Function ConvertSidToStringSid Lib "advapi32.dll" _
    Alias "ConvertSidToStringSidA" (ByVal Sid As Long, _
    StringSid As Long) As Long
```

The ConvertSidToStringSid function has two parameters:

- A pointer to the SID to be converted.
- A pointer to a string buffer that will be allocated and filled with the string representation of the SID. This buffer must be freed using the LocalFree function. The string pointer can be converted to a Visual Basic string by using the CopyMemory function.

Syntax

```
Public Declare Function LocalFree Lib "kernel32" ( _
    ByVal hMem As Long) As Long
```

The string representation of a SID follows a specific format, known as *SRIS*. Each SID string is composed of four or more elements:

- *S.* The letter S
- *R.* A number that represents the revision level
- *I.* An identifier for the authority that issued the SID
- *S.* One or more subauthority values or relative identifiers

As an example of a SID, here's the current value of the mickeyw security identifier in the code-vtech.com domain:

S-1-5-21-854245398-515967899-1417001333-1105

The ConvertStringSidToSid function is used to convert a SID from a string format into its native binary format:

Syntax

```
Public Declare Function ConvertStringSidToSid Lib "advapi32.dll" _
    Alias "ConvertStringSidToSidA" (ByVal StringSid As String, _
    Sid As Long) As Long
```

The `ConvertStringSidToSid` function has two parameters:

- The `SID`, in string form, to be converted.
- A pointer to a `SID` that will be allocated and filled with the binary form of the `SID`. This buffer must be freed using the `LocalFree` function.

A *well-known* `SID` is a security identifier that specifies a commonly used, generic user or group. Well-known `SID`s include the Everyone group, the Local Administrators group, and the Local System group.

Retrieving a `SID` for a User or Group

The `LookupAccountName` function is used to retrieve a `SID` for a particular user or group:

Syntax

```
Private Declare Function LookupAccountName Lib "advapi32.dll" _
    Alias "LookupAccountNameA" (ByVal lpSystemName As String, _
    ByVal lpAccountName As String, Sid As Long, _
    cbSid As Long, ByVal ReferencedDomainName As String, _
    cbReferencedDomainName As Long, peUse As SID_NAME_USE) As Long
```

The `LookupAccountName` function has seven parameters:

- The name of the system where the lookup will take place (or `vbNullString` to specify the local system).
- The account name you're searching for.
- A pointer to a `SID` that will receive the account's security identifier.
- A pointer to a `Long` that contains the length, in bytes, of the `SID` buffer. If the buffer is too small, the function will fail with a return code of `ERROR_INSUFFICIENT_BUFFER` (122), and this parameter will be filled with the minimum required size for the `SID` buffer.
- A string buffer that will be filled with the account's domain name.
- A pointer to a `Long` that contains the length, in bytes, of the previous parameter. If the buffer is too small, the function will fail with a return code of `ERROR_INSUFFICIENT_BUFFER`, and this parameter will be filled with the minimum required size for the domain name.
- A `SID_NAME_USE` variable that will be filled with a value from the `SID_NAME_USE` enumeration that defines the type of account. The `SID_NAME_USE` enumeration is defined as follows:

Syntax

```
Enum SID_NAME_USE
    SidTypeUser = 1
    SidTypeGroup = 2
    SidTypeDomain = 3
    SidTypeAlias = 4
    SidTypeWellKnownGroup = 5
    SidTypeDeletedAccount = 6
    SidTypeInvalid = 7
    SidTypeUnknown = 8
    SidTypeComputer = 9
End Enum
```

Typically, you'll call LookupAccountName twice—the first time with the SID buffer size set to zero to determine the size of the account's SID, and the second time with a properly sized SID buffer to retrieve the SID. Listing 10.2 contains a wrapper function around the LookupAccountName function that retrieves the SID for a specified account and then converts the SID into string form.

LISTING 10.2   A Function That Retrieves SIDs in String Form

```
Option Explicit

Private Const ERROR_INSUFFICIENT_BUFFER = 122

Private Const LMEM_FIXED = &H0
Private Const LMEM_ZEROINIT = &H40
Private Const LPTR = (LMEM_FIXED Or LMEM_ZEROINIT)

Enum SID_NAME_USE
    SidTypeUser = 1
    SidTypeGroup = 2
    SidTypeDomain = 3
    SidTypeAlias = 4
    SidTypeWellKnownGroup = 5
    SidTypeDeletedAccount = 6
    SidTypeInvalid = 7
    SidTypeUnknown = 8
    SidTypeComputer = 9
End Enum

Private Declare Function LookupAccountName Lib "advapi32.dll" _
    Alias "LookupAccountNameA" (ByVal lpSystemName As String, _
    ByVal lpAccountName As String, ByVal Sid As Long, _
```

continues

10

UNDERSTANDING
WINDOWS 2000
SECURITY

LISTING 10.2   Continued

```vb
    cbSid As Long, ByVal ReferencedDomainName As String, _
    cbReferencedDomainName As Long, peUse As SID_NAME_USE) As Long

Private Declare Function LocalAlloc Lib "kernel32" ( _
    ByVal wFlags As Long, ByVal wBytes As Long) As Long

Private Declare Function LocalFree Lib "kernel32" ( _
    ByVal hMem As Long) As Long

Private Declare Function ConvertSidToStringSid Lib "advapi32.dll" _
    Alias "ConvertSidToStringSidA" (ByVal Sid As Long, _
    StringSid As Long) As Long

Private Declare Sub CopyMemory Lib "kernel32" Alias "RtlMoveMemory" ( _
    Destination As Any, ByVal Source As Long, _
    ByVal Length As Long)

Public Sub AccountNameToSidString(lpszSystem As String, _
        lpszAccountName As String, pszSidBuffer As String, _
        cbSidBuffer As Long)
'**************************************************************
'* Written By: Mickey Williams/Davis Chapman
'* Date:       January 29, 2000
'*
'* Syntax:     AccountNameToSidString(lpszSystem, lpszAccountName,
'*                        pszSidBuffer, cbSidBuffer)
'*
'* Parameters: lpszSystem As String
'*             lpszAccountName As String
'*             pszSidBuffer As String
'*             cbSidBuffer As Long
'*
'* Purpose: Gets the SID for the specified account name, then
'*          converts it into a string and returns it.
'**************************************************************
    Dim pSid As Long   'PSID
    Dim cbSid As Long
    Dim lpszRefDomain As String * 256
    Dim cbRefDomain As Long
    Dim sne As SID_NAME_USE
    Dim bRet As Boolean
    Dim dwErr As Long
    Dim pszSidString As Long 'LPTSTR

    '--- Initialize the variables
    pSid = 0
```

```vb
cbSid = 0
cbRefDomain = 256

'--- Lookup the account name
bRet = CBool(LookupAccountName(lpszSystem, lpszAccountName, _
        pSid, cbSid, lpszRefDomain, cbRefDomain, sne))
'--- First call is expected to fail
If (bRet <> False) Then
    MsgBox "LookupAccountName returned invalid val"
    Exit Sub
End If
'--- Check the error
dwErr = Err.LastDllError
'--- If ERROR_INSUFFICIENT_BUFFER then allocate the buffer
If (dwErr = ERROR_INSUFFICIENT_BUFFER) Then
    pSid = LocalAlloc(LPTR, cbSid)
    If (pSid = 0) Then
        MsgBox "LocalAlloc for SID failed"
        Exit Sub
    End If
    '--- Lookup the account name again
    bRet = CBool(LookupAccountName(lpszSystem, lpszAccountName, _
            pSid, cbSid, lpszRefDomain, cbRefDomain, sne))
    '--- If we failed this time, then we really failed
    If (bRet = False) Then
        MsgBox "LookupAccountName #2 failed"
        '--- Free the buffer
        LocalFree pSid
        Exit Sub
    End If
Else
    MsgBox "GetLastError returned invalid val"
    Exit Sub
End If

'--- Initialize the SID string
pszSidString = 0

'--- Convert the SID to a string
bRet = CBool(ConvertSidToStringSid(pSid, pszSidString))
'--- Allocate the string to copy the SID string into
pszSidBuffer = String(cbSidBuffer + 1, vbNullChar)
'--- Copy the SID string
CopyMemory ByVal pszSidBuffer, pszSidString, cbSidBuffer
'--- Free the allocated buffers
LocalFree pszSidString
LocalFree pSid
End Sub
```

In Listing 10.2, the `AccountNameToSidString` function begins by calling `LookupAccountName` with a `SID` buffer that has a length of zero. The function is expected to fail with an error code of `ERROR_INSUFFICIENT_BUFFER`. The `SID` buffer is allocated using the minimum buffer length returned in the `cbSid` parameter, and the `LookupAccountName` function is called again to retrieve the account's `SID`.

After the `SID` is obtained, it's converted into a string using the `ConvertSidToStringSid` function and then copied into the caller's string buffer.

A simple wrapper for the `LookupAccountName` function is provided in Listing 10.3. The `AccountNameToSid` function dynamically allocates a `SID` for a user passed as a parameter to the function. The declarations for this function are the same as for Listing 10.2, so they are not repeated in this listing.

LISTING 10.3   A Function That Creates a `SID` Based on a Username

```
Public Function AccountNameToSid(lpszAccountName As String) As Long
'****************************************************************
'* Written By: Mickey Williams/Davis Chapman
'* Date:       January 29, 2000
'*
'* Syntax:     AccountNameToSid(lpszAccountName)
'*
'* Parameters: lpszAccountName As String
'*
'* Purpose: Gets and returns the SID for the specified account
'*          name.
'****************************************************************
    Dim pSid As Long
    Dim cbSid As Long
    Dim lpszRefDomain As String * 256
    Dim cbRefDomain As Long
    Dim sne As SID_NAME_USE
    Dim bRet As Boolean
    Dim dwErr As Long

    '--- Initialize the variables
    pSid = 0
    cbSid = 0
    cbRefDomain = 256

    '--- Lookup the account name
    bRet = CBool(LookupAccountName(vbNullString, _
                          lpszAccountName, _
                          pSid, _
```

```
                                    cbSid, _
                                    lpszRefDomain, _
                                    cbRefDomain, _
                                    sne))
    '--- First call is expected to fail
    If (bRet <> False) Then
        AccountNameToSid = 0
        Exit Function
    End If
    '--- Check the error
    dwErr = Err.LastDllError
    '--- If ERROR_INSUFFICIENT_BUFFER then allocate the buffer
    If (dwErr = ERROR_INSUFFICIENT_BUFFER) Then
        pSid = LocalAlloc(LPTR, cbSid)
        If (pSid = 0) Then
            AccountNameToSid = 0
            Exit Function
        End If
        '--- Lookup the account name again
        bRet = CBool(LookupAccountName(vbNullString, _
                                lpszAccountName, _
                                pSid, _
                                cbSid, _
                                lpszRefDomain, _
                                cbRefDomain, _
                                sne))
        '--- If we failed this time, then we really failed
        If (bRet = False) Then
            '--- Free the buffer
            LocalFree pSid
            AccountNameToSid = 0
            Exit Function
        End If
    Else
        AccountNameToSid = 0
        Exit Function
    End If
    '--- Return the pointer to the SID
    AccountNameToSid = pSid
End Function
```

In Listing 10.3, the AccountNameToSid function works in much the same way as the AccountNameToSidString function presented in Listing 10.2. The only difference is that instead of converting the SID into string form, the AccountNameToSid function passes the dynamically allocated SID back to the caller.

Understanding ACE, DACL, and SACL Structures

The ACE, DACL, and SACL structures form the heart of Windows 2000 security. The next few sections discuss how these structures are used.

The ACE Structure

An ACE, or access control entry structure, is used to specify a type of action to be taken for a particular user or group with respect to security. Each ACE contains a SID that identifies a security trustee and a set of masks that contain the rights for the trustee.

Here are the six types of ACE structures:

- **ACCESS_ALLOWED_ACE**. An ACE that specifies a user or group that's allowed access to a securable object.

- **ACCESS_DENIED_ACE**. An ACE that specifies a user or group that's denied access to a securable object.

- **SYSTEM_AUDIT_ACE**. An ACE that specifies a user or group that causes a security audit event to be generated when the user or group attempts to access a securable object.

- **ACCESS_ALLOWED_OBJECT_ACE**. An ACE used in Active Directory that's similar to the ACCESS_ALLOWED_ACE structure. It adds information that controls the inheritance of the ACE by child objects.

- **ACCESS_DENIED_OBJECT_ACE**. An ACE used in Active Directory that's similar to the ACCESS_DENIED_ACE structure. It adds information that controls inheritance of the ACE by child objects.

- **SYSTEM_AUDIT_OBJECT_ACE**. An ACE used in Active Directory that's similar to the ACCESS_ALLOWED_ACE structure. It adds information that controls inheritance of the ACE by child objects.

All ACE structures have a similar format. Figure 10.2 shows the memory layout for an ACCESS_ALLOWED_ACE structure.

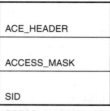

FIGURE 10.2

The layout of an ACCESS_ALLOWED_ACE.

The DACL and SACL Structures

Every securable object may have two ACLs, or access control lists, associated with it:

- A DACL, or discretionary access list, which specifies the users and groups permitted access to the object
- A SACL, or system access control list, which specifies the conditions that cause a security audit event to be generated for the object

Both DACLs and SACLs are arrays of ACE structures, beginning with an ACL structure used as a header for the list. A SACL contains only system audit ACE structures, and a DACL contains only access-allowed or access-denied ACE structures. ACEs in a DACL must be arranged in proper order: ACEs that deny access must come before ACEs that allow access.

Determining the Size Required for an ACL

Occasionally, you may need to copy or add an entry to an ACL. Because an ACL is a variable-length structure, you'll need to determine the size of the ACL and allocate a new buffer that's large enough to store the (possibly larger) new ACL.

The size of an ACL is determined by adding the size of the ACL structure to the size of all ACLs contained in the list. The simplest way to determine the size is to call the GetAclInformation function, as shown in the Listing 10.4:

LISTING 10.4 A Function That Determines the Size of an ACL Type Structure

```
Option Explicit

Enum ACL_INFORMATION_CLASS
    AclRevisionInformation = 1
    AclSizeInformation = 2
End Enum

Private Type ACL_SIZE_INFORMATION
        AceCount As Long
        AclBytesInUse As Long
        AclBytesFree As Long
End Type

Private Type ACL
        AclRevision As Byte
        Sbz1 As Byte
        AclSize As Integer
        AceCount As Integer
        Sbz2 As Integer
End Type
```

10

continues

LISTING 10.4   Continued

```
Private Declare Function GetAclInformation Lib "advapi32.dll" ( _
    pAcl As ACL, pAclInformation As Any, _
    ByVal nAclInformationLength As Long, _
    ByVal dwAclInformationClass As ACL_INFORMATION_CLASS) As Long

'--- Declare a second version for passing a NULL pointer in place
'--- of the pAcl ACL type
Private Declare Function GetAclInformation2 Lib "advapi32.dll" _
    Alias "GetAclInformation" (ByVal pAcl As Long, _
    pAclInformation As Any, ByVal nAclInformationLength As Long, _
    ByVal dwAclInformationClass As ACL_INFORMATION_CLASS) As Long
Public Function GetAclSize(pAcl As Long, pdw As Long) As Boolean
'**************************************************************
'* Written By: Mickey Williams/Davis Chapman
'* Date:       January 29, 2000
'*
'* Syntax:     GetAclSize(pAcl, pdw)
'*
'* Parameters: pAcl As Long
'*             pdw As Long
'*
'* Purpose: Gets the current size of an ACL.
'**************************************************************
    Dim info As ACL_SIZE_INFORMATION
    Dim bInfo As Boolean

    '--- Get the size information on the ACL
    bInfo = CBool(GetAclInformation2(pAcl, _
                                     info, _
                                     12, _
                                     AclSizeInformation))
    '--- Did we get the info?
    If (bInfo) Then
        '--- Get the size of the ACL
        pdw = info.AclBytesInUse
    End If
    '--- Return whether we succeeded or failed
    GetAclSize = bInfo
End Function
```

The GetAclInformation function has four parameters:

- A pointer to an ACL

- Either an ACL_SIZE_INFORMATION type structure, if you're retrieving the size of an ACL, or an ACL_REVISION_INFORMATION type structure, to retrieve revision information about the ACL

- The size of the type structure in the previous parameter
- Either AclSizeInformation, to retrieve size information from the ACL, or AclRevisionInformation, to retrieve revision information

Adding an Access-Allowed ACE to a DACL

An access-allowed ACE is added to a DACL using the AddAccessAllowedAceEx function in Listing 10.5.

LISTING 10.5 A Function That Adds an Access-Allowed ACE to a DACL

```
Option Explicit

Private Const GENERIC_ALL = &H10000000
Private Const ACL_REVISION = 2

Private Declare Function AddAccessAllowedAceEx Lib "advapi32.dll" ( _
    pAcl As ACL, ByVal dwAceRevision As Long, _
    ByVal AceFlags As Long, ByVal AccessMask As Long, _
    ByVal pSid As Long) As Long

'--- Declare a second version for passing a NULL pointer in place
'--- of the pAcl ACL type
Private Declare Function AddAccessAllowedAceEx2 Lib "advapi32.dll" _
    Alias "AddAccessAllowedAceEx" (ByVal pAcl As Long, _
    ByVal dwAceRevision As Long, ByVal AceFlags As Long, _
    ByVal AccessMask As Long, ByVal pSid As Long) As Long

Public Function AllowUserAccessThroughAcl(pAcl As Long, _
                lpszUser As String) As Boolean
'*****************************************************************
'* Written By: Mickey Williams/Davis Chapman
'* Date:       January 29, 2000
'*
'* Syntax:     AllowUserAccessThroughAcl(pAcl, lpszUser)
'*
'* Parameters: pAcl As Long
'*             lpszUser As String
'*
'* Purpose: Modifies an ACL to allow the specified user access
'*          to whatever it is that the ACL controls.
'*****************************************************************
    Dim pSid As Long
    Dim bAdded As Boolean
```

continues

LISTING 10.5 Continued

```
'--- Get a pointer to the SID for this user
pSid = AccountNameToSid(lpszUser)
'--- Did we get a SID pointer?
If (Not pSid) Then
    '--- No, return a failure
    AllowUserAccessThroughAcl = False
    Exit Function
End If

'--- Add the SID to the access list for the ACL
bAdded = CBool(AddAccessAllowedAceEx2(pAcl, _
                                      ACL_REVISION, _
                                      0, _
                                      GENERIC_ALL, _
                                      pSid))
'--- Free the SID
LocalFree pSid
'--- Return whether the SID was added to the ACL
AllowUserAccessThroughAcl = bAdded
End Function
```

TIP

API functions, type structures, and other declarations that have been made in previous listings in this chapter are not being repeated. If an API function or type is being used and is not included in the current listing, check the previous listings for its declaration.

As shown in this code fragment, you don't need to create the ACCESS_ALLOWED_ACE yourself; you simply pass a SID to the AddAccessAllowedAceEx function. AddAccessAllowedAceEx has five parameters:

- A pointer to the ACL.
- The revision level of the ACL. This parameter is ACL_REVISION_DS (4) when working with ACLs in Active Directory. Otherwise, this parameter is ACL_REVISION (2).
- Zero or more flags that specify the inheritance characteristics of the new ACE. Possible values for this parameter are discussed later.
- One or more flags that specify the access rights affected by this ACL. Possible values for this parameter are discussed later.
- A pointer to the SID that will be added to the ACL as an access-allowed ACE.

For DACLs that are applied to containers (such as Registry keys, directories, and printers), child objects may inherit ACEs. The following inheritance flags control the type of inheritance allowed:

> **NOTE**
>
> In a security context, inheritance means that a child object, like a subdirectory or a file in a directory, inherits the same rights and privileges that the parent has. So if you have a directory that has a specific security configuration, and the subdirectories under it inherit the security settings, the subdirectories will have the same specific security configuration as the parent directory. With ACE inheritance, this means that the child will inherit an ACE that duplicates the ACE that was inherited.

- **CONTAINER_INHERIT_ACE (&H2)**. Enables the ACE to be inherited by child objects that are container objects, such as directories, printers, and Registry keys.
- **INHERIT_ONLY_ACE (&H8)**. Specifies that the ACE does not apply to this object. However, child objects can inherit it.
- **INHERITED_ACE (&H10)**. Specifies an inherited ACE for use in operations on child objects.
- **NO_PROPAGATE_INHERIT_ACE (&H4)**. Inhibits the OBJECT_INHERIT_ACE and CONTAINER_INHERIT_ACE flags from being copied to an inherited ACE.
- **OBJECT_INHERIT_ACE (&H1)**. Enables the ACE to be inherited by noncontainer child objects, such as files, Registry values, and printer shares.

The access rights controlled by the ACL are a combination of one or more of the following flags:

- **DELETE (&H10000)**. The ACE affects the right to delete the object.
- **READ_CONTROL (&H20000)**. The ACE affects the right to read non-SACL security descriptor information.
- **SYNCHRONIZE (&H100000)**. The ACE affects the right to use the object for process and thread synchronization.
- **WRITE_DAC (&H40000)**. The ACE affects the right to modify the object's DACL.
- **WRITE_OWNER (&H80000)**. The ACE affects the right to change the owner in the object's security descriptor.

To simplify things, here are a number of constants that combine one or more of the preceding flags:

- **STANDARD_RIGHTS_ALL (&H1F0000).** Combines all rights from the previous list.
- **STANDARD_RIGHTS_EXECUTE.** Same as READ_CONTROL.
- **STANDARD_RIGHTS_READ.** Same as READ_CONTROL.
- **STANDARD_RIGHTS_REQUIRED (&HF0000).** Combines all flags except SYNCHRONIZE.
- **STANDARD_RIGHTS_WRITE.** Same as READ_CONTROL.

A set of generic rights also can be applied to securable objects in Windows 2000. You can use the following generic rights with an ACE in place of the preceding flags:

- **GENERIC_ALL (&H10000000).** Includes read, write, and execute access
- **GENERIC_EXECUTE (&H20000000).** Execute access
- **GENERIC_READ (&H80000000).** Read access
- **GENERIC_WRITE (&H40000000).** Write access

The AddAccessDeniedAceEx function works the same as AddAccessAllowedAceEx, except that it adds an access-denied ACE to the end of the DACL. Both functions may result in a DACL that contains ACE structures in the wrong order. When using low-level security functions such as AddAccessAllowedAceEx and AddAccessDeniedAceEx, you need to make sure that all access-denied entries are located before any access-allowed entries. If necessary, you must manually reorder the list. The syntax for the AddAccessDeniedAceEx function is shown next:

Syntax

```
Public Declare Function AddAccessDeniedAceEx Lib "advapi32.dll" ( _
    ByVal pAcl As Long, ByVal dwAceRevision As Long, _
    ByVal AceFlags As Long, ByVal AccessMask As Long, _
    ByVal pSid As Long) As Long
```

The AddAccessAllowedAceEx function does not allocate new storage for an ACL—it simply adds the new ACE to the end of an existing ACL. You must calculate the required size of your new ACL and allocate a new ACL if necessary. In cases where you're adding an ACE to an existing ACL, it's easier to use a newer TRUSTEE-based access control function, such as SetEntriesInAccessList. These functions are discussed later in this chapter.

Security Descriptors

The SECURITY_DESCRIPTOR type structure is used to store security information for a securable object. The security descriptor for an object includes the following items:

- An optional DACL that specifies access rights for the object
- An optional SACL that specifies what type of access results in security audit events
- An owner SID that identifies the owner of the object
- A group SID that identifies group membership of the object

The two basic types of security descriptors follow:

- A security descriptor in *absolute format* contains pointers to the SID and ACL information. SID and ACL information is usually not located in the same contiguous chunk of memory as the SECURITY_DESCRIPTOR structure.
- A security descriptor in *self-relative format* contains the SID and ACL information in the same contiguous chunk of memory as the SECURITY_DESCRIPTOR structure. Instead of pointers, the structure contains offsets to the SID and ACL information. This type of security descriptor is useful in COM because it can easily be transmitted to another machine on the network.

Figure 10.3 illustrates the difference between absolute and self-relative security descriptors.

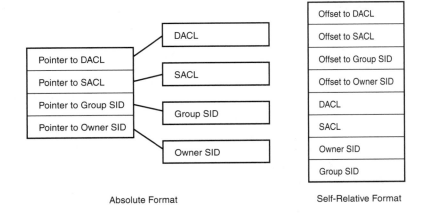

Absolute Format   Self-Relative Format

FIGURE 10.3

The layout of self-relative format and absolute format security descriptors.

The process of creating a security descriptor begins by initializing it. Listing 10.6 contains a wrapper function that illustrates how to allocate and initialize an empty security descriptor.

LISTING 10.6   Creating an Empty Security Descriptor

```
Option Explicit

Private Const SECURITY_DESCRIPTOR_MIN_LENGTH = 20
Private Const SECURITY_DESCRIPTOR_REVISION = 1

Private Type SECURITY_DESCRIPTOR
        Revision As Byte
        Sbz1 As Byte
        Control As Long
        Owner As Long
        Group As Long
        Sacl As ACL
        Dacl As ACL
End Type

Private Declare Function InitializeSecurityDescriptor Lib "advapi32.dll" ( _
    pSecurityDescriptor As SECURITY_DESCRIPTOR, _
    ByVal dwRevision As Long) As Long

'--- Declare a second version for passing a NULL pointer in place
'--- of the pSecurityDescriptor SECURITY_DESCRIPTOR type
Private Declare Function InitializeSecurityDescriptor2 Lib "advapi32.dll" _
    Alias "InitializeSecurityDescriptor" ( _
    ByVal pSecurityDescriptor As Long, _
    ByVal dwRevision As Long) As Long



Public Function CreateEmptySecurityDescriptor() As Long
'****************************************************************
'* Written By: Mickey Williams/Davis Chapman
'* Date:       January 29, 2000
'*
'* Syntax:     CreateEmptySecurityDescriptor
'*
'* Parameters: None
'*
'* Purpose: Creates and returns a pointer to an empty security
'*          descriptor.
'****************************************************************
    Dim psd As Long
    Dim bInit As Boolean

    '--- Initialize the pointer to the security descriptor buffer
```

```
    psd = 0

    '--- Allocate the security descriptor buffer
    psd = LocalAlloc(LPTR, SECURITY_DESCRIPTOR_MIN_LENGTH)
    '--- Did we allocate the buffer?
    If (psd <> 0) Then
        '--- Yes, initialize the security descriptor
        bInit = CBool(InitializeSecurityDescriptor2(psd, _
                                 SECURITY_DESCRIPTOR_REVISION))
        '--- Did we initialize it?
        If (Not bInit) Then
            '--- No, free the buffer and reset the pointer
            LocalFree psd
            psd = 0
        End If
    End If
    '--- Return the pointer
    CreateEmptySecurityDescriptor = psd
End Function
```

In Listing 10.6, the `CreateEmptySecurityDescriptor` function begins by allocating a buffer with a length of `SECURITY_DESCRIPTOR_MIN_LENGTH`. This is the size of a security descriptor that does not include `SID` or `DACL` information in the same memory block as the `SECURITY_DESCRIPTOR` structure. Next, the security descriptor is initialized into an empty state with the `InitializeSecurityDescriptor` function. Note that the security descriptor returned from the function in Listing 10.6 is allocated using `LocalAlloc`. Any function that calls this function must free the returned security descriptor using `LocalFree`.

The `SetSecurityDescriptorDacl` function is used to add a `DACL` to a security descriptor. The syntax for this function is seen as follows:

Syntax

```
Public Declare Function SetSecurityDescriptorDacl Lib "advapi32.dll" ( _
    pSecurityDescriptor As SECURITY_DESCRIPTOR, ByVal bDaclPresent As Long, _
    ByVal pDacl As Long, ByVal bDaclDefaulted As Long) As Long
```

The `SetSecurityDescriptorDacl` function has four parameters:

- A security descriptor
- A flag that indicates whether a `DACL` is included in the security descriptor
- A pointer to the `ACL` to be used as the security descriptor's `DACL`
- A flag that's set to `True` (`<> 0`) if the `DACL` is a default `DACL`

To create a security descriptor that contains a DACL, you need to allocate and initialize the security descriptor and ACL, and then use SetSecurityDescriptorDacl to add the ACL to the security descriptor. Listing 10.7 is an example of a function that creates a security descriptor that grants access to a specific user.

LISTING 10.7   Creating a Security Descriptor That Allows Access to a Specific User

```
Private Declare Function IsValidSid Lib "advapi32.dll" ( _
    ByVal pSid As Long) As Long

Private Declare Function GetLengthSid Lib "advapi32.dll" ( _
    ByVal pSid As Long) As Long

Private Declare Function SetSecurityDescriptorDacl Lib "advapi32.dll" ( _
    ByVal pSecurityDescriptor As Long, ByVal bDaclPresent As Long, _
    ByVal pDacl As Long, ByVal bDaclDefaulted As Long) As Long

Private Declare Function InitializeAcl Lib "advapi32.dll" ( _
    ByVal pAcl As Long, ByVal nAclLength As Long, _
    ByVal dwAclRevision As Long) As Long

Public Function CreateAllowedSDForUser(lpszUser As String) As Long
'****************************************************************
'* Written By: Mickey Williams/Davis Chapman
'* Date:       January 29, 2000
'*
'* Syntax:     CreateAllowedSDForUser(lpszUser)
'*
'* Parameters: lpszUser As String
'*
'* Purpose: Creates an access allowed security descriptor for
'*          the specified user. The pointer to the security
'*          descriptor that is created is returned.
'****************************************************************
    Dim psd As Long
    Dim pSid As Long
    Dim cbSid As Long
    Dim pAcl As Long
    Dim cbAcl As Long
    Dim bAdded As Boolean
    Dim bInitialized As Boolean

    '--- Initialize the pointer
    psd = 0
```

```
'--- Create the empty security descriptor
psd = CreateEmptySecurityDescriptor
'--- If unable to create the security descriptor, return a NULL pointer
If (psd = 0) Then
    CreateAllowedSDForUser = 0
    Exit Function
End If


'--- Convert the account name to a SID
pSid = AccountNameToSid(lpszUser)
'--- Did we get a SID?
If ((pSid = 0) Or Not CBool(IsValidSid(pSid))) Then
    '--- No, free the SID and security descriptors
    LocalFree pSid
    LocalFree psd
    '--- Return a NULL pointer
    CreateAllowedSDForUser = 0
    Exit Function
End If


'--- Get the length of the SID
cbSid = GetLengthSid(pSid)
'--- Calculate the required size for the ACL
pAcl = 0
cbAcl = 8 + 14 + cbSid
'--- Allocate the ACL
pAcl = LocalAlloc(LPTR, cbAcl)

'--- Initialize the Acl
bInitialized = InitializeAcl(pAcl, cbAcl, ACL_REVISION)

'--- Add the SID to the ACL
bAdded = CBool(AddAccessAllowedAceEx2(pAcl, _
                                      ACL_REVISION, _
                                      0, _
                                      GENERIC_ALL, _
                                      pSid))
'--- Free the SID
LocalFree pSid
'--- Set the ACL for the security descriptor
bAdded = CBool(SetSecurityDescriptorDacl(psd, -1, pAcl, 0))

'--- Return the pointer for the security descriptor
CreateAllowedSDForUser = psd
End Function
```

In Listing 10.7, the CreateAllowedSDForUser function begins by calling the CreateEmpty SecurityDescriptor function presented earlier in Listing 10.6. Next, a SID for the specified user is created using the AccountNameToSid function. The SID is then added to a new ACL, and the ACL is added to the security descriptor before the security descriptor is returned to the caller.

Retrieving a Security Descriptor

Retrieving an existing security descriptor is much easier than creating a new security descriptor. To retrieve a security descriptor, use the GetNamedSecurityInfo function:

Syntax

```
Enum SE_OBJECT_TYPE
    SE_UNKNOWN_OBJECT_TYPE = 0
    SE_FILE_OBJECT = 1
    SE_SERVICE = 2
    SE_PRINTER = 3
    SE_REGISTRY_KEY = 4
    SE_LMSHARE = 5
    SE_KERNEL_OBJECT = 6
    SE_WINDOW_OBJECT = 7
    SE_DS_OBJECT = 8
    SE_DS_OBJECT_ALL = 9
    SE_PROVIDER_DEFINED_OBJECT = 10
    SE_WMIGUID_OBJECT = 11
End Enum

Public Declare Function GetNamedSecurityInfo Lib "advapi32.dll" _
    Alias "GetNamedSecurityInfoA" (ByVal pObjectName As String, _
    ByVal ObjectType As SE_OBJECT_TYPE, ByVal SecurityInfo As Long, _
    ppsidOwner As Long, ppsidGroup As Long, ppDacl As Long, _
    ppSacl As Long, ppSecurityDescriptor As Long) As Long
```

The GetNamedSecurityInfo function has eight parameters:

- A string that identifies the securable object. For a file, this parameter is the path to the file. Each type of securable object has a different name format. For details about specific types, consult the online documentation.

- An identifier for the object type. Possible values for this parameter are listed later.

- One or more flags that specify the type of information to be returned by the function. Possible values for this parameter are listed later.

- A pointer to a SID that will be set to the address of the owner SID contained in the security descriptor. This parameter can be NULL (0) if the OWNER_SECURITY_INFORMATION flag is not included in the third parameter.

- A pointer to a SID that will be set to the address of the group SID contained in the security descriptor. This parameter can be NULL (0) if the GROUP_SECURITY_INFORMATION flag is not included in the third parameter.

- A pointer to an ACL that will be set to the address of the DACL contained in the security descriptor. This parameter can be NULL (0) if the DACL_SECURITY_INFORMATION flag is not included in the third parameter.

- A pointer to an ACL that will be set to the address of the SACL contained in the security descriptor. This parameter can be NULL (0) if the SACL_SECURITY_INFORMATION flag is not included in the third parameter.

- A pointer to a SECURITY_DESCRIPTOR structure that will be set when the function returns. This structure is dynamically allocated and must be freed using LocalFree when the structure is no longer needed.

The object type identifier SE_OBJECT_TYPE is an enumerated type that is used to indicate the type of object named in the first parameter. Possible values for this parameter are the following:

- **SE_FILE_OBJECT**. The object is a file or directory.
- **SE_SERVICE**. The object is a Windows 2000 service.
- **SE_PRINTER**. The object is a printer.
- **SE_REGISTRY_KEY**. The object is a Registry key.
- **SE_LMSHARE**. The object is a network share.
- **SE_KERNEL_OBJECT**. The object is a Windows 2000 kernel object, such as a pipe, mutex, waitable timer, or similar object.
- **SE_WINDOW_OBJECT**. The object is a window station or desktop object.
- **SE_DS_OBJECT**. The object is an Active Directory object. The object can also be a property or property set of an Active Directory object.
- **SE_DS_OBJECT_ALL**. The object is an Active Directory object that includes all its property sets and properties.
- **SE_PROVIDER_DEFINED_OBJECT**. The object is a user-defined object.

The following security information flags are combined to specify the types of information returned by the function:

- **OWNER_SECURITY_INFORMATION (&H1)**. A pointer to the owner SID will be returned.
- **GROUP_SECURITY_INFORMATION (&H2)**. A pointer to the group SID will be returned.
- **DACL_SECURITY_INFORMATION (&H4)**. A pointer to the DACL will be returned.
- **SACL_SECURITY_INFORMATION (&H8)**. A pointer to the SACL will be returned.

10

An example of a function that returns a security descriptor for a given filename is provided in Listing 10.8. The `GetFileSecurityDescriptor` function returns a pointer to a `SECURITY_DESCRIPTOR` type structure that must be freed using `LocalFree`.

LISTING 10.8   A Function That Retrieves a Security Descriptor for a File

```
Option Explicit

Private Const OWNER_SECURITY_INFORMATION = &H1
Private Const GROUP_SECURITY_INFORMATION = &H2
Private Const DACL_SECURITY_INFORMATION = &H4
Private Const SACL_SECURITY_INFORMATION = &H8

Enum SE_OBJECT_TYPE
    SE_UNKNOWN_OBJECT_TYPE = 0
    SE_FILE_OBJECT = 1
    SE_SERVICE = 2
    SE_PRINTER = 3
    SE_REGISTRY_KEY = 4
    SE_LMSHARE = 5
    SE_KERNEL_OBJECT = 6
    SE_WINDOW_OBJECT = 7
    SE_DS_OBJECT = 8
    SE_DS_OBJECT_ALL = 9
    SE_PROVIDER_DEFINED_OBJECT = 10
    SE_WMIGUID_OBJECT = 11
End Enum

Private Declare Function GetNamedSecurityInfo Lib "advapi32.dll" _
    Alias "GetNamedSecurityInfoA" (ByVal pObjectName As String, _
    ByVal ObjectType As SE_OBJECT_TYPE, ByVal SecurityInfo As Long, _
    ppsidOwner As Long, ppsidGroup As Long, ppDacl As Long, _
    ppSacl As Long, ppSecurityDescriptor As Long) As Long

Public Function GetFileSecurityDescriptor(pszPath As String) As Long
'***************************************************************
'* Written By: Mickey Williams/Davis Chapman
'* Date:        January 29, 2000
'*
'* Syntax:     GetFileSecurityDescriptor(pszPath)
'*
'* Parameters: pszPath As String
'*
'* Purpose: Returns a pointer to the security descriptor for
'*          the specified file.
'***************************************************************
```

```
Dim psidOwner As Long    'PSID
Dim psidGroup As Long    'PSID
Dim pAcl As Long         'PACL
Dim pSacl As Long        'PACL
Dim psd As Long          'PSECURITY_DESCRIPTOR
Dim lRtn As Long

'--- Initialize the pointers
psidOwner = 0
psidGroup = 0
pAcl = 0
pSacl = 0
psd = 0

'--- Get the security information for the file
lRtn = GetNamedSecurityInfo(pszPath, _
                SE_FILE_OBJECT, _
                (OWNER_SECURITY_INFORMATION Or _
                GROUP_SECURITY_INFORMATION Or _
                DACL_SECURITY_INFORMATION), _
                psidOwner, _
                psidGroup, _
                pAcl, _
                pSacl, _
                psd)
'--- Return the pointer for the security descriptor
'--- This pointer will need to be released
'--- using the LocalFree function
GetFileSecurityDescriptor = psd
End Function
```

Using the SECURITY_ATTRIBUTES Structure

The SECURITY_ATTRIBUTES structure is used by most Win32 functions that create or access securable objects. For example, CreateFile, CreateNamedPipe, and CreateMutex (to name three) all accept a pointer to a SECURITY_ATTRIBUTES structure as a parameter.

It's a common practice to pass NULL (0) in place of a pointer to a valid SECURITY_ATTRIBUTES structure. When a securable object is created using a NULL security attributes structure, the default security attributes from the creator's access token are used.

Syntax

The `SECURITY_ATTRIBUTES` structure is very straightforward:

```
Public Type SECURITY_ATTRIBUTES
    nLength As Long
    lpSecurityDescriptor As Long      'LPVOID
    bInheritHandle As Long     'BOOL
End Type
```

The following are the three member variables in the `SECURITY_ATTRIBUTES` structure:

- **nLength**. The size of the `SECURITY_ATTRIBUTES` type structure (12)
- **lpSecurityDescriptor**. A pointer to a `SECURITY_DESCRIPTOR` structure
- **bInheritHandle**. A flag that's set to `True` (`<> 0`) to allow the handle to the created object to be inherited

As you can see, the `SECURITY_ATTRIBUTES` structure is basically just a wrapper around a `SECURITY_DESCRIPTOR` pointer.

Trustee-Based Access Control

Trustee-based access control was originally introduced in Windows NT 4.0, where it was commonly known as Windows NT 4.0 Access Control. Windows 2000 has extended the trustee-based access control functions to include support for Active Directory objects as well as support for alternate security providers. In Windows 2000, you can also interact with securable objects on non-Windows systems.

Trustee-Based Access Control

Trustee-based access control is an access control system in which users, groups, or other objects are granted a series of rights and privileges to various objects within the domain. There are various elements that are considered to be trustees, such as user accounts, groups, trusted domains, computers, and so on.

The structures used in trustee-based access control are nested several layers deep, as shown in Figure 10.4.

Four elements (type structures and arrays) are used in Windows 2000 access control:

- **TRUSTEE**. A type structure that represents a trustee or security principal. A trustee may be a user, a group, or a login session.

- **EXPLICIT_ACCESS**. A type structure that contains access control information about a single TRUSTEE, including a mask of the rights that are controlled by the TRUSTEE as well as whether those rights are allowed or denied. This structure includes a TRUSTEE as one of its member variables.

- An array that represents the actual access control list. This is an array of zero or more EXPLICIT_ACCESS type structures.

- An array that contains access control lists for an object. A new feature in Windows 2000 is the capability to set attributes for properties located on some objects. This array contains pointers to arrays of EXPLICIT_ACCESS type structures, with one structure for each managed property.

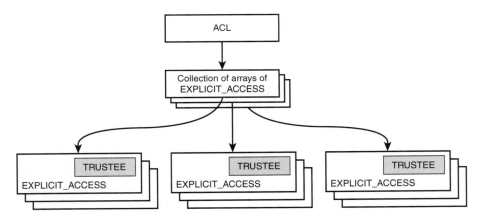

Using the TRUSTEE Structure

The TRUSTEE type structure is used to identify a security principal, and it can easily be initialized using either the security principal's name or a SID that refers to the principal.

The TRUSTEE structure is defined as follows:

Syntax

```
Enum TRUSTEE_TYPE
    TRUSTEE_IS_UNKNOWN = 0
    TRUSTEE_IS_USER = 1
    TRUSTEE_IS_GROUP = 2
    TRUSTEE_IS_DOMAIN = 3
    TRUSTEE_IS_ALIAS = 4
    TRUSTEE_IS_WELL_KNOWN_GROUP = 5
    TRUSTEE_IS_DELETED = 6
    TRUSTEE_IS_INVALID = 7
End Enum
```

```
Enum TRUSTEE_FORM
    TRUSTEE_IS_SID = 0
    TRUSTEE_IS_NAME = 1
    TRUSTEE_BAD_FORM = 2
End Enum

Enum MULTIPLE_TRUSTEE_OPERATION
    NO_MULTIPLE_TRUSTEE = 0
    TRUSTEE_IS_IMPERSONATE = 1
End Enum

Public Type TRUSTEE
    pMultipleTrustee As Long     'Pointer to other TRUSTEE
    tMultipleTrusteeOperation As MULTIPLE_TRUSTEE_OPERATION
    tTrusteeForm As TRUSTEE_FORM
    tTrusteeType As TRUSTEE_TYPE
    ptstrName As String
End Type
```

The following are the members of the TRUSTEE structure:

- **pMultipleTrustee**. Reserved for future use. Must be set to NULL (0).

- **MultipleTrusteeOperation**. The only valid value for this member is NO_MULTIPLE_TRUSTEE.

- **TrusteeForm**. Indicates whether the TRUSTEE structure contains a SID or the name of a security principal. If the structure contains a SID, the value of this member is TRUSTEE_IS_SID; if the structure contains a principal name, the value of this member is TRUSTEE_IS_NAME. A value of TRUSTEE_BAD_FORM indicates neither member is valid.

- **TrusteeType**. Indicates the type of trustee identified by the structure. Values for this member are discussed later.

- **ptstrName**. A pointer to a SID or security principal name. If TrusteeForm is TRUSTEE_IS_SID, this member is a pointer to the trustee's SID. If TrusteeForm is TRUSTEE_IS_NAME, this member is a string containing the trustee's name.

The following values can be used for the TrusteeType member variable:

- **TRUSTEE_IS_UNKNOWN**. The trustee has an unknown trustee type.

- **TRUSTEE_IS_USER**. The trustee is a user account.

- **TRUSTEE_IS_GROUP**. The trustee is a group account.

- **TRUSTEE_IS_DOMAIN**. The trustee is a domain.

- **TRUSTEE_IS_ALIAS**. The trustee is an alias account.

- **TRUSTEE_IS_WELL_KNOWN_GROUP**. The trustee is a well-known group, such as Everyone.

- **TRUSTEE_IS_DELETED**. The trustee refers to a deleted account.
- **TRUSTEE_IS_INVALID**. The trustee is an invalid trustee type.

Although you're free to manipulate the TRUSTEE structure directly, Windows 2000 includes two functions that make it easy to initialize a TRUSTEE structure:

- **BuildTrusteeWithName**. Initializes a TRUSTEE structure from a trustee's name
- **BuildTrusteeWithSid**. Initializes a TRUSTEE structure from a trustee's SID

The BuildTrusteeWithName subroutine properly initializes a TRUSTEE structure from a trustee's name:

Syntax

```
Public Declare Sub BuildTrusteeWithName Lib "advapi32.dll" _
    Alias "BuildTrusteeWithNameA" (pTrustee As Any, _
    ByVal pName As String)
```

The BuildTrusteeWithName subroutine has two parameters:

- The TRUSTEE structure to be initialized
- A string that contains the trustee name

The BuildTrusteeWithName subroutine doesn't allocate any data for the TRUSTEE type structure, particularly the ptstrName member variable. The string passed to the function must remain valid for the lifetime of the TRUSTEE type structure; otherwise, you'll have unpredictable results. Functions such as the one in Listing 10.9 must be avoided.

LISTING 10.9   Improper Use of the BuildTrusteeWithName Function

```
Private Declare Sub BuildTrusteeWithName Lib "advapi32.dll" _
    Alias "BuildTrusteeWithNameA" (pTrustee As Any, _
    ByVal pName As String)

'--- Declare a second version for passing a NULL pointer in place
'--- of the pTrustee Any type
Private Declare Sub BuildTrusteeWithName2 Lib "advapi32.dll" _
    Alias "BuildTrusteeWithNameA" (ByVal pTrustee As Long, _
    ByVal pName As String)

Public Sub BuildBadTrusteeStruct(pTrustee As Long)
'********************************************************************
'* Written By: Mickey Williams/Davis Chapman
'* Date:       January 29, 2000
'*
```

continues

LISTING 10.9   Continued

```
'* Syntax:      BuildBadTrusteeStruct(pTrustee)
'*
'* Parameters: pTrustee As Long
'*
'* Purpose: Create a TRUSTEE type structure in the wrong way.
'*****************************************************************
    Dim lTempString As String

    '--- Create a nonexistent username string
    lTempString = "chaperada\harvey"
    '--- Get a pointer to the TRUSTEE type structure
    BuildTrusteeWithName2 pTrustee, lTempString
End Sub
```

Inside BuildBadTrusteeStruct, the variable with local scope (lTempString), is used to initialize the TRUSTEE structure. The lTempString variable is allocated on the thread's stack; when the function returns to the caller, the variable will be discarded. Any attempt to use the TRUSTEE structure will result in difficult-to-trace faults.

The proper way to use BuildTrusteeWithName is to allocate a buffer that exists for the lifetime of the TRUSTEE structure.

The BuildTrusteeWithSid function is similar to the BuildTrusteeWithName function, except that it uses a trustee's SID to initialize the structure:

```
Private Declare Sub BuildTrusteeWithSid Lib "advapi32.dll" _
    Alias "BuildTrusteeWithSidA" (pTrustee As Any, _
    ByVal pSid As Long)
```

The BuildTrusteeWithSid function has two parameters:

- The TRUSTEE structure to be initialized
- A pointer to the trustee's SID

The SID passed as a parameter to BuildTrusteeWithSid must be valid for the lifetime of the TRUSTEE structure. As is the case with the BuildTrusteeWithName function discussed earlier, the BuildTrusteeWithSid function does not allocate data for the TRUSTEE member variables.

Windows 2000 also provides functions that can be used to extract information from a TRUSTEE structure, thus saving you the trouble of picking the structure apart explicitly. Each of these functions accepts a TRUSTEE pointer as a parameter and returns the value of a TRUSTEE member variable:

- GetTrusteeForm
- GetTrusteeSid
- GetTrusteeType

The EXPLICIT_ACCESS Structure

The EXPLICIT_ACCESS type structure contains access control information for a specific trustee. The EXPLICIT_ACCESS structure is similar to the ACE structure discussed earlier in the chapter, except that it has the capability to work with provider-independent security functions.

The EXPLICIT_ACCESS type structure is defined as follows:

Syntax

```
Enum ACCESS_MODE
    NOT_USED_ACCESS = 0
    GRANT_ACCESS = 1
    SET_ACCESS = 2
    DENY_ACCESS = 3
    REVOKE_ACCESS = 4
    SET_AUDIT_SUCCESS = 5
    SET_AUDIT_FAILURE = 6
End Enum

Public Type EXPLICIT_ACCESS
    grfAccessPermissions As Long
    grfAccessMode As ACCESS_MODE
    grfInheritance As Long
    eaTrustee As TRUSTEE
End Type
```

The following are the members of the EXPLICIT_ACCESS type structure:

- **grfAccessPermissions**. Contains one or more flags that specify the access rights controlled by the access entry. You must use the standard or generic flags, such as STANDARD_RIGHTS_WRITE (&H20000). Commonly used flags are discussed later.

- **grfAccessMode**. Contains flags that specify how access control is to be applied to the trustee. Values for this member are discussed next.

- **grfInheritance**. One or more flags that specify the inheritance characteristics of the access entry. This value is set to NO_INHERITANCE unless the secured object is stored in Active Directory.

- **eaTrustee**. A TRUSTEE type structure that identifies the trustee represented by this structure.

The value of grfAccessMode must be one of the following values:

- **GRANT_ACCESS**. Rights are granted to the trustee.
- **DENY_ACCESS**. Rights are denied to the trustee.

- **SET_ACCESS**. The specified rights are set for the trustee. This will remove existing access modes from the trustee.
- **REVOKE_ACCESS**. All existing rights are removed.
- **SET_AUDIT_FAILURE**. Audit messages are generated for failed attempts to use the rights.
- **SET_AUDIT_SUCCESS**. Audit messages are generated for successful attempts to use the rights.

The value of the grfAccessPermissions member variable must be taken from the provider-independent flags defined next. A complete list of values is provided in the Platform SDK online Help. The following are some common flags used with the Windows 2000 file system:

- **GENERIC_EXECUTE (&H20000000)**. Controls the right to execute a binary file
- **GENERIC_READ (&H80000000)**. Controls the right to read a file
- **GENERIC_WRITE (&H40000000)**. Controls the right to write to a file
- **GENERIC_ALL (&H10000000)**. Controls the right to read, write, and execute a file

Listing 10.10 contains a function that loads an EXPLICIT_ACCESS type structure so that any user or group name passed as a parameter has file-access rights.

LISTING 10.10   An Example of Filling in an EXPLICIT_ACCESS Type Structure

```
Option Explicit

Private Const GENERIC_ALL = &H10000000
Private Const GENERIC_READ = &H80000000
Private Const GENERIC_WRITE = &H40000000
Private Const OPEN_EXISTING = 3
Private Const FILE_ATTRIBUTE_NORMAL = &H80
Private Const DELETE = &H10000
Private Const READ_CONTROL = &H20000
Private Const WRITE_DAC = &H40000
Private Const WRITE_OWNER = &H80000
Private Const SYNCHRONIZE = &H100000
Private Const STANDARD_RIGHTS_REQUIRED = &HF0000
Private Const STANDARD_RIGHTS_READ = READ_CONTROL
Private Const STANDARD_RIGHTS_WRITE = READ_CONTROL
Private Const STANDARD_RIGHTS_EXECUTE = READ_CONTROL
Private Const STANDARD_RIGHTS_ALL = &H1F0000
Private Const SPECIFIC_RIGHTS_ALL = &HFFFF
Private Const NO_INHERITANCE = &H0
Private Const SUB_OBJECTS_ONLY_INHERIT = &H1
Private Const SUB_CONTAINERS_ONLY_INHERIT = &H2
Private Const SUB_CONTAINERS_AND_OBJECTS_INHERIT = &H3
```

```
Private Const INHERIT_NO_PROPAGATE = &H4
Private Const INHERIT_ONLY = &H8
Private Const FILE_READ_DATA = &H1                   ' file & pipe
Private Const FILE_LIST_DIRECTORY = &H1              ' directory
Private Const FILE_WRITE_DATA = &H2                  ' file & pipe
Private Const FILE_ADD_FILE = &H2                    ' directory
Private Const FILE_APPEND_DATA = &H4                 ' file
Private Const FILE_ADD_SUBDIRECTORY = &H4            ' directory
Private Const FILE_CREATE_PIPE_INSTANCE = &H4        ' named pipe
Private Const FILE_READ_EA = &H8                     ' file & directory
Private Const FILE_WRITE_EA = &H10                   ' file & directory
Private Const FILE_EXECUTE = &H20                    ' file
Private Const FILE_TRAVERSE = &H20                   ' directory
Private Const FILE_DELETE_CHILD = &H40               ' directory
Private Const FILE_READ_ATTRIBUTES = &H80            ' all
Private Const FILE_WRITE_ATTRIBUTES = &H100          ' all
Private Const FILE_ALL_ACCESS = (STANDARD_RIGHTS_REQUIRED Or _
                            SYNCHRONIZE Or &H1FF)
Private Const FILE_GENERIC_READ = (STANDARD_RIGHTS_READ Or _
                FILE_READ_DATA Or FILE_READ_ATTRIBUTES Or _
                FILE_READ_EA Or SYNCHRONIZE)
Private Const FILE_GENERIC_WRITE = (STANDARD_RIGHTS_WRITE Or _
                FILE_WRITE_DATA Or FILE_WRITE_ATTRIBUTES Or _
                FILE_WRITE_EA Or FILE_APPEND_DATA Or SYNCHRONIZE)
Private Const FILE_GENERIC_EXECUTE = (STANDARD_RIGHTS_EXECUTE Or _
                FILE_READ_ATTRIBUTES Or FILE_EXECUTE Or SYNCHRONIZE)


Enum ACCESS_MODE
    NOT_USED_ACCESS = 0
    GRANT_ACCESS = 1
    SET_ACCESS = 2
    DENY_ACCESS = 3
    REVOKE_ACCESS = 4
    SET_AUDIT_SUCCESS = 5
    SET_AUDIT_FAILURE = 6
End Enum


Enum TRUSTEE_TYPE
    TRUSTEE_IS_UNKNOWN = 0
    TRUSTEE_IS_USER = 1
    TRUSTEE_IS_GROUP = 2
    TRUSTEE_IS_DOMAIN = 3
    TRUSTEE_IS_ALIAS = 4
    TRUSTEE_IS_WELL_KNOWN_GROUP = 5
    TRUSTEE_IS_DELETED = 6
    TRUSTEE_IS_INVALID = 7
End Enum
```

10

UNDERSTANDING
WINDOWS 2000
SECURITY

continues

LISTING 10.10   Continued

```
Enum TRUSTEE_FORM
    TRUSTEE_IS_SID = 0
    TRUSTEE_IS_NAME = 1
    TRUSTEE_BAD_FORM = 2
End Enum

Enum MULTIPLE_TRUSTEE_OPERATION
    NO_MULTIPLE_TRUSTEE = 0
    TRUSTEE_IS_IMPERSONATE = 1
End Enum

Private Type TRUSTEE
    pMultipleTrustee As Long        'PTRUSTEE
    tMultipleTrusteeOperation As MULTIPLE_TRUSTEE_OPERATION
    tTrusteeForm As TRUSTEE_FORM
    tTrusteeType As TRUSTEE_TYPE
    ptstrName As String
End Type

Private Type EXPLICIT_ACCESS
    grfAccessPermissions As Long
    grfAccessMode As ACCESS_MODE
    grfInheritance As Long
    eaTrustee As TRUSTEE
End Type

Private Declare Sub ZeroMemory Lib "kernel32" Alias "RtlZeroMemory" ( _
    dest As Any, ByVal numBytes As Long)

Public Sub FillAccessEntry(pae As Long, pszName As String)
'*************************************************************
'* Written By: Mickey Williams/Davis Chapman
'* Date:       January 29, 2000
'*
'* Syntax:     FillAccessEntry(pae, pszName)
'*
'* Parameters: pae As Long
'*             pszName As String
'*
'* Purpose: Initialize an EXPLICIT_ACCESS type structure with
'*          generic access values.
'*************************************************************
    Dim aaePae As EXPLICIT_ACCESS
```

```
'--- Clear the memory for the structure
ZeroMemory aaePae, 32
'--- Create the TRUSTEE type structure
BuildTrusteeWithName aaePae. eaTrustee, pszName

'--- Specify the security values
aaePae.grfInheritance = NO_INHERITANCE
aaePae.grfAccessMode = GRANT_ACCESS
aaePae.grfAccessPermissions = (FILE_WRITE_DATA Or FILE_READ_DATA Or _
            FILE_EXECUTE Or FILE_APPEND_DATA Or _
            FILE_READ_ATTRIBUTES Or FILE_WRITE_ATTRIBUTES Or _
            FILE_READ_EA Or FILE_WRITE_EA)
'--- Copy the type structure back to the pointer
CopyMemory ByVal pae, VarPtr(aaePae), 32
End Sub
```

Using `SetEntriesInAcl` to Create and Modify Access Control Lists

Earlier in the chapter, the `AddAccessAllowedAceEx` function was used to add an `ACE` to the end of an `ACL`. This function, like many of the low-level Windows security functions, requires you to manage the order and size of the access control list. When using trustee-based security, you can often eliminate the need to manage the low-level details of the access control list.

For example, the `SetEntriesInAcl` function is used to add, modify, or remove the entries in an access control list:

Syntax

```
Public Declare Function SetEntriesInAcl Lib "advapi32.dll" _
    Alias "SetEntriesInAclA" (ByVal cCountOfExplicitEntries As Long, _
    pListOfExplicitEntries As EXPLICIT_ACCESS, OldAcl As ACL, _
    NewAcl As Long) As Long
```

The `SetEntriesInAcl` function returns zero when it's successful and the Win32 error code when it fails. `SetEntriesInAcl` has four parameters:

- The number of `EXPLICIT_ACCESS` elements in the array passed as the next parameter.

- An array of `EXPLICIT_ACCESS` type structures that each define the access control for a single trustee.

- A pointer to the current `ACL` structure that contains the access control list, if any. This parameter is optional if you're creating a new access control list. It's required if you're removing an entry from the list or if you're merging new entries into an existing list.

- A pointer to an ACL type structure that will receive the new access control list. The ACL type structure and access control list will be dynamically allocated and must be freed using the LocalFree function.

An example of using the SetEntriesInAcl trustee-based access control function is provided in Listing 10.11. The function in Listing 10.11 creates an ACL that denies access to the author.

LISTING 10.11   Creating an ACL

```
Private Declare Function SetEntriesInAcl Lib "advapi32.dll" _
    Alias "SetEntriesInAclA" (ByVal cCountOfExplicitEntries As Long, _
    pListOfExplicitEntries As EXPLICIT_ACCESS, OldAcl As ACL, _
    NewAcl As Long) As Long

'--- Declare a second version for passing a NULL pointer in place
'--- of the OldAcl ACL type
Private Declare Function SetEntriesInAcl2 Lib "advapi32.dll" _
    Alias "SetEntriesInAclA" (ByVal cCountOfExplicitEntries As Long, _
    pListOfExplicitEntries As EXPLICIT_ACCESS, ByVal OldAcl As Long, _
    NewAcl As Long) As Long

Public Function CreateAntiAuthorSecurityDescriptor() As Long
'*******************************************************************
'* Written By: Mickey Williams/Davis Chapman
'* Date:       January 29, 2000
'*
'* Syntax:     CreateAntiAuthorSecurityDescriptor
'*
'* Parameters: None
'*
'* Purpose: Create a security descriptor that restricts the author from
'*          accessing an object. The caller must use LocalFree to release
'*          the memory used by the security descriptor.
'*******************************************************************

    Dim ae As EXPLICIT_ACCESS
    Dim pal As Long      'PACL
    Dim dwErr As Long

    '--- Initialize the pointer
    pal = 0
    dwErr = 0

On Error GoTo CreateAntiAuthorSecurityDescriptor_Err
    '--- Clear the memory for the structure
    ZeroMemory ae, 32
```

```
    '--- Create the TRUSTEE type structure
    BuildTrusteeWithName ae.eaTrustee, "chaperada\davis"

    '--- Specify the security values
    ae.grfInheritance = NO_INHERITANCE
    ae.grfAccessPermissions = STANDARD_RIGHTS_ALL
    ae.grfAccessMode = DENY_ACCESS
    '--- Create an ACL with these permissions
    dwErr = SetEntriesInAcl2(1, ae, 0, pal)
CreateAntiAuthorSecurityDescriptor_Err:
    '--- Did we have an error?
    If (dwErr <> 0) Then
        MsgBox "Security Error"
    End If
    '--- Return the pointer to the ACL
    CreateAntiAuthorSecurityDescriptor = pal
End Function
```

In Listing 10.11, the function starts by calling the `BuildTrusteeWithName` function to initialize a `TRUSTEE` type structure. Next, an `EXPLICIT_ACCESS` structure is created. Then it's converted into an ACL with the `SetEntriesInAcl` function.

Impersonating a Client

As discussed at the beginning of this chapter, to access secured objects, servers typically impersonate a client. During the impersonation process, the server's impersonation token assumes the security characteristics of the client. This simplifies the security model because Windows 2000 simply uses the thread's impersonation token to perform access checks.

To begin impersonation, the server calls one of the following impersonation functions:

- **ImpersonateNamedPipeClient**. Used when the client and server are connected via a named pipe
- **ImpersonateLoggedOnUser**. Used when the client is the currently logged on user

After a server has finished accessing resources on behalf of the client, it stops impersonating the client by calling the `RevertToSelf` function.

Syntax

```
Public Declare Function ImpersonateNamedPipeClient Lib "advapi32.dll" ( _
    ByVal hNamedPipe As Long) As Long
```

10

UNDERSTANDING
WINDOWS 2000
SECURITY

```
Public Declare Function ImpersonateLoggedOnUser Lib "advapi32.dll" ( _
    ByVal hToken As Long) As Long

Public Declare Function RevertToSelf Lib "advapi32.dll" () As Long
```

As an example of how a server process uses impersonation to use the client's security context, the example in the next chapter takes you through the process of logging a user on and then impersonating that user. It uses the TestFileForAccess function in Listing 10.12. In the TestFileForAccess function, the server impersonates the logged-on user and attempts to open a filename passed as a parameter.

LISTING 10.12   A Function That Impersonates a Client Before Attempting File Access

```
Private Declare Function ImpersonateLoggedOnUser Lib "advapi32.dll" ( _
    ByVal hToken As Long) As Long

Private Declare Function RevertToSelf Lib "advapi32.dll" () As Long

Public Function TestFileForAccess(hUser As Long, _
        szFileName As String) As Boolean
'***************************************************************
'* Written By: Mickey Williams/Davis Chapman
'* Date:       January 29, 2000
'*
'* Syntax:     TestFileForAccess(hUser, szFileName)
'*
'* Parameters: hUser As Long
'*             szFileName As String
'*
'* Purpose: Impersonate the logged in user and try to open the
'*          specified file to see if the user has access to the
'*          file.
'***************************************************************
    Dim hFile As Long
    Dim bAllowed As Boolean

    On Error GoTo TestFileForAccess_Err
    '--- Initialize the return value
    bAllowed = False

    '--- impersonate the client
    ImpersonateLoggedOnUser hUser

    '--- Open file for reading and writing
    hFile = FreeFile
```

```
    Open szFileName For Random Access Read Write As hFile
    '--- Able to open the file, change the return value
    bAllowed = True
    '--- Close the file
    Close hFile

TestFileForAccess_Err:
    '--- Revert to primary access token
    RevertToSelf
    TestFileForAccess = bAllowed
End Function
```

In Listing 10.12, the `TestFileForAccess` function begins by impersonating the client that is logged in. Next, the function attempts to open the file using the filename passed as a parameter. The file is accessed using the client's access token rather than the server's. Before returning, the function calls `RevertToSelf` to start using the server's access token rather than the impersonation token.

Summary

This chapter discussed Windows 2000 security, including both the traditional low-level security structures and functions and the newer trustee-based access control functions offered by Windows 2000. This chapter also included an example of how a server can use impersonation to properly handle access requests from a client.

The next chapter looks at the other side of this coin—the authentication of a user. Through the combination of these two topics, you can provide a server object that logs a user in and then uses that user's access token to limit that user's access on the server.

Using NT Login Authentication

IN THIS CHAPTER

- Validating a Domain Login
- Granting Account Permissions
- Building a Login Validation Utility

In the previous chapter, you took a look at how Windows 2000 manages access to objects and services. This is only half of the security picture. The other half is user authentication. There are two methods of user authentication: the Windows NT LAN Manager (NTLM) protocol and the Kerberos protocol. In this chapter, you look at the NTLM authentication protocol, and then you'll look at the Kerberos protocol, as part of the Active Directory Security Interface (ADSI), in the next chapter.

> **NOTE**
>
> The topic discussed in this chapter is only applicable for NT 4 and Windows 2000, and really requires that these systems be configured to use NTFS-formatted drives. This functionality is not available on Windows 95 or Windows 98.

> **PREREQUISITES**
>
> Before reading this chapter, you need to make sure you have a good understanding of the following:
>
> - NT security and security descriptors, Chapter 10, "Understanding Windows 2000 Security and Security Descriptors"

Validating a Domain Login

The NTLM and Kerberos protocols solve the same problem in different scenarios. The NTLM protocol uses the standard username and password for authentication over a local area network (LAN). The Kerberos protocol is part of the Security Support Provider Interface (SSPI), which is used for performing authentication and authorization over a distributed network using certificates.

The basic function that NTLM authentication performs is validating a username and password and providing a logon session handle. This handle can then be used to impersonate the user that is logging in, and thus allow the operating system to perform its access control functions.

Modifying Access Permissions

Before you are able to validate a user login, you have to modify your access permissions to make sure that you have the proper access to perform this task. This is basically the same task you saw in the previous chapter in Listing 10.1, except you need to enable a different permission. In Listing 10.1, you enabled (or disabled) the SE_SECURITY_NAME (able to manage audit-ing and security) privilege. The privilege you need to enable is the SE_TCB_NAME (able to act as part of the operating system) privilege. This is accomplished by modifying the function in Listing 10.1, making it more flexible, as shown in Listing 11.1.

LISTING 11.1   A Generic Function for Enabling and Disabling Access Privileges

```
Option Explicit

Private Const ANYSIZE_ARRAY = 1

'--- Error Codes
Const ERROR_SUCCESS = 0&
Const ERROR_NO_TOKEN = 1008&
Const ERROR_NOT_ALL_ASSIGNED = 1300&
Const ERROR_LOGON_FAILURE = 1326&

'--- Enable privilege constant
Const SE_PRIVILEGE_ENABLED = &H2

'--- Security Privilege types and structures
Private Type luid
    LowPart As Long
    HighPart As Long
End Type

Private Type LUID_AND_ATTRIBUTES
        pLuid As luid
        Attributes As Long
End Type

Private Type TOKEN_PRIVILEGES
    PrivilegeCount As Long
    Privileges(ANYSIZE_ARRAY) As LUID_AND_ATTRIBUTES
End Type

'--- Security and privilege API declarations
Private Declare Function LookupPrivilegeValue Lib "advapi32.dll" _
    Alias "LookupPrivilegeValueA" (ByVal lpSystemName As String, _
    ByVal lpName As String, lpLuid As luid) As Long

Private Declare Function AdjustTokenPrivileges Lib "advapi32.dll" ( _
    ByVal TokenHandle As Long, ByVal DisableAllPrivileges As Long, _
    NewState As TOKEN_PRIVILEGES, ByVal BufferLength As Long, _
    PreviousState As Long, ReturnLength As Long) As Long
```

continues

LISTING 11.1   Continued

```
Private Function SetPrivilege(hToken As Long, strPrivilege As String, _
                bEnablePriv As Boolean) As Boolean
'**************************************************************
'* Written By: Davis Chapman
'* Date:       April 7, 1999
'*
'* Syntax:     SetPrivilege(hToken, strPrivilege, bEnablePriv)
'*
'* Parameters: hToken As Long - The token of the current process/thread
'*             strPrivilege As String - The privilege to be modified
'*             bEnablePriv As Boolean - Enable or disable the privilege
'*
'* Purpose: This method is called to modify the privileges of
'*          the current process/thread so that restricted API
'*          functions can be called.
'**************************************************************
On Error GoTo SetPrivilege_Err
    Dim tp As TOKEN_PRIVILEGES
    Dim lLuid As luid
    Dim dwErr As Long
    Dim lRtnVal As Long

    '--- Initialize the return value
    SetPrivilege = False
    '--- Lookup the LUID of the requested privilege
    lRtnVal = LookupPrivilegeValue(vbNullString, strPrivilege, lLuid)
    '--- Were we successful?
    If lRtnVal = 0 Then
        '--- No, get the error ID and log the error
        dwErr = Err.LastDllError
        App.LogEvent "Login validation error = " & dwErr, _
                vbLogEventTypeError
        Exit Function
    End If
    '--- Initialize the token privileges structure with the LUID
    tp.PrivilegeCount = 1
    tp.Privileges(0).pLuid.LowPart = lLuid.LowPart
    tp.Privileges(0).pLuid.HighPart = lLuid.HighPart
    '--- Specify whether to enable or disable the specified privilege
    If bEnablePriv Then
        tp.Privileges(0).Attributes = SE_PRIVILEGE_ENABLED
    Else
        tp.Privileges(0).Attributes = 0
    End If
```

```
'--- Enable or disable the privilege
AdjustTokenPrivileges hToken, 0, tp, 16, 0, 0
'--- Get the error code to determine if we were successful
dwErr = Err.LastDllError
'--- Did we have an error occur?
If (dwErr <> ERROR_SUCCESS) And _
        (dwErr <> ERROR_NOT_ALL_ASSIGNED) Then
    '--- Yes, log the error and exit
    App.LogEvent "Login validation error = " & dwErr, _
            vbLogEventTypeError
    Exit Function
Else
    '--- Possibly not, check to see if there
    '--- might have been a problem
    If (dwErr = ERROR_NOT_ALL_ASSIGNED) Then
        '--- Log the error but continue on
        App.LogEvent "Login validation error = " & dwErr, _
                vbLogEventTypeError
    End If
End If
'--- Return TRUE
SetPrivilege = True
'--- Exit the function
Exit Function

SetPrivilege_Err:
    '--- An error occurred, log the error
    App.LogEvent "Login validation error = " & Err.Number & " - " & _
            Err.Description
    '--- Exit the function
    Exit Function
End Function
```

This function is basically the same as the one in Listing 10.1, with a couple of subtle differences. First, the access privilege is being passed in as a function parameter instead of being hard coded in the function. Second, the process token is not retrieved in the function, but instead is also passed in as a parameter. This allows this function to perform only the task of enabling or disabling the access privilege and enables it to perform this task for any of the available access permissions.

Checking a Login Against a Domain

After you have granted your process the needed permissions, the next step is logging in the user. To do this, you need to have the username and password in an unencrypted form. When you have the username and password, you can log the user in using the LogonUser function. The declaration for this function is as follows:

```
Private Declare Function LogonUser Lib "advapi32" Alias "LogonUserA" ( _
    ByVal lpszUsername As String, ByVal lpszDomain As String, _
    ByVal lpszPassword As String, ByVal dwLogonType As Long, _
    ByVal dwLogonProvider As Long, phToken As Long) As Long
```

The first parameter (lpszUsername) to this function is the username. This is the username for the account for which the user is logging in to the system.

The second parameter (lpszDomain) is the network domain into which the user is logging in. For NT 4 and earlier versions of NT, if this parameter is ".", the local account database is used (the accounts set up on the machine on which this process is running). For Windows 2000, this value must be the NULL string (vbNullString) to use the local account database. Otherwise, you must provide a domain name to use.

The third parameter (lpszPassword) for this function is the password for the account specified with the username. This must be in clear, unencrypted form.

The fourth parameter (dwLogonType) specifies the type of logon operation to perform. The available values for this parameter are listed in Table 11.1.

TABLE 11.1   Logon Types

Constant	Value	Description
LOGON32_ LOGON_BATCH	4	Intended for use with unattended, noninteractive applications. This is also used with high-activity processes that need to validate a large number of user logins at one time. Using this logon type prevents the LogonUser function from caching the user credentials. It is also intended for use with applications in which the server process is performing actions on the behalf of a remote user.
LOGON32_LOGON_ INTERACTIVE	2	This logon type is intended for use with users who are interactively using the machine on which the logon process is taking place. This logon process does cache the account credentials, so it is not appropriate for use with a noninteractive type of process such as a mail or Web server.
LOGON32_LOGON_ NETWORK	3	This logon type is intended for use with high-performance servers. It does not cache user credentials. The logon token returned from this logon type can be used only to impersonate the user. You have to duplicate the token to get a token that can be used to create other processes as the user.

Constant	Value	Description
LOGON32_LOGON_NETWORK_CLEARTEXT WINDOWS 2000-98	8	This logon type maintains the username and password, allowing it to interact with other servers while impersonating the user.
LOGON32_LOGON_NEW_CREDENTIALS WINDOWS 2000-98	9	This logon type allows the user to use one logon identity for all local access, but requires a new set of logon credentials for making connections to other servers.
LOGON32_LOGON_SERVICE	5	This logon type is for use with processes that need to run as services on NT. To use this logon type, the account must have the privilege to run as a service.
LOGON32_LOGON_UNLOCK	7	For use with GINA (Graphical Identification and Authentication) DLLs, this logon type issues a unique audit record to show when the workstation was unlocked.

GINA

GINA (Graphical Identification and Authentication) DLLs provide the interface for accepting user credentials during the WinLogon process. Third-party GINA DLLs are most often used to allow user account credentials to be entered via Smart Cards, retinal scans, or other means of authenticating the user other than the default username/password method.

The fifth parameter (dwLogonProvider) specifies the logon provider to be used. The available values for use in this parameter are listed in Table 11.2.

TABLE 11.2   Logon Providers

Provider	Value	Description
LOGON32_PROVIDER_DEFAULT	0	This is the standard logon provider for the system and is the recommended provider to use.
LOGON32_PROVIDER_WINNT50 WINDOWS 2000-98	3	This is the logon provider for Windows 2
LOGON32_PROVIDER_WINNT40	2	This is the logon provider for NT 4.0.
LOGON32_PROVIDER_WINNT35	1	This is the logon provider for NT 3.5.

The last parameter (phToken) is a long variable into which will be placed the handle to a logon token that can be used to impersonate the user or to create separate processes as the user.

A typical use of this function is to logon the user and return the logon token handle, as shown in Listing 11.2.

LISTING 11.2   Logging a User into the System

```
Option Explicit

'--- Error Codes
Const ERROR_SUCCESS = 0&
Const ERROR_NO_TOKEN = 1008&
Const ERROR_NOT_ALL_ASSIGNED = 1300&
Const ERROR_LOGON_FAILURE = 1326&
'--- Security Privileges to be adjusted
Const SE_TCB_NAME = "SeTcbPrivilege"
'--- Security check types and providers
Const LOGON32_LOGON_BATCH = 4
Const LOGON32_LOGON_INTERACTIVE = 2
Const LOGON32_LOGON_SERVICE = 5
Const LOGON32_LOGON_NETWORK = 3
Const LOGON32_PROVIDER_DEFAULT = 0
Const LOGON32_PROVIDER_WINNT35 = 1
Const LOGON32_PROVIDER_WINNT40 = 2
Const LOGON32_PROVIDER_WINNT50 = 3
'--- Permission constants
Const DELETE = &H10000
Const READ_CONTROL = &H20000
Const WRITE_DAC = &H40000
Const WRITE_OWNER = &H80000
Const SYNCHRONIZE = &H100000
Const STANDARD_RIGHTS_REQUIRED = &HF0000
Const STANDARD_RIGHTS_READ = READ_CONTROL
Const STANDARD_RIGHTS_WRITE = READ_CONTROL
Const STANDARD_RIGHTS_EXECUTE = READ_CONTROL
Const STANDARD_RIGHTS_ALL = &H1F0000
'--- Token permission constants
Const TOKEN_ASSIGN_PRIMARY = &H1
Const TOKEN_DUPLICATE = &H2
Const TOKEN_IMPERSONATE = &H4
Const TOKEN_QUERY = &H8
Const TOKEN_QUERY_SOURCE = &H10
Const TOKEN_ADJUST_PRIVILEGES = &H20
Const TOKEN_ADJUST_GROUPS = &H40
Const TOKEN_ADJUST_DEFAULT = &H80
Const TOKEN_ADJUST_SESSIONID = &H100
```

```
Const TOKEN_ALL_ACCESS = (STANDARD_RIGHTS_REQUIRED Or _
        TOKEN_ASSIGN_PRIMARY Or TOKEN_DUPLICATE Or _
        TOKEN_IMPERSONATE Or TOKEN_QUERY Or TOKEN_QUERY_SOURCE Or _
        TOKEN_ADJUST_PRIVILEGES Or TOKEN_ADJUST_GROUPS Or _
        TOKEN_ADJUST_SESSIONID Or TOKEN_ADJUST_DEFAULT)

Const TOKEN_READ = (STANDARD_RIGHTS_READ Or TOKEN_QUERY)

Const TOKEN_WRITE = (STANDARD_RIGHTS_WRITE Or TOKEN_ADJUST_PRIVILEGES _
        Or TOKEN_ADJUST_GROUPS Or TOKEN_ADJUST_DEFAULT)

Const TOKEN_EXECUTE = (STANDARD_RIGHTS_EXECUTE)

Const TOKEN_MY_ACCESS = (TOKEN_READ Or TOKEN_WRITE)

'--- Security and privilege API declarations
Private Declare Function LogonUser Lib "advapi32" Alias "LogonUserA" ( _
    ByVal lpszUsername As String, ByVal lpszDomain As String, _
    ByVal lpszPassword As String, ByVal dwLogonType As Long, _
    ByVal dwLogonProvider As Long, phToken As Long) As Long

Private Declare Function CloseHandle Lib "kernel32" ( _
    ByVal hObject As Long) As Long

Private Declare Function OpenThreadToken Lib "advapi32.dll" ( _
    ByVal ThreadHandle As Long, ByVal DesiredAccess As Long, _
    ByVal OpenAsSelf As Long, TokenHandle As Long) As Long

Private Declare Function OpenProcessToken Lib "advapi32.dll" ( _
    ByVal ProcessHandle As Long, ByVal DesiredAccess As Long, _
    TokenHandle As Long) As Long

Private Declare Function GetCurrentProcess Lib "kernel32" () As Long

Private Declare Function GetCurrentThread Lib "kernel32" () As Long


Public Function LoginUser(sUserName As String, sDomain As String, _
                sPassword As String) As Long
'**************************************************************
'* Written By: Davis Chapman
'* Date:       April 7, 1999
'*
'* Syntax:     LoginUser(sUserName, sDomain, sPassword)
'*
'* Parameters: sUserName As String - The logon name to be validated
'*             sDomain As String - The domain to validate the logon name
```

continues

LISTING 11.2   Continued

```
'*              sPassword As String - The password for the logon name
'*
'* Purpose: This method validates the user name/password
'*          combination in the NT domain specified. It creates
'*          a recordset to return the Boolean value in,
'*          initializing the return value to FALSE. Next, it
'*          opens a context token to be used in setting the
'*          privileges so that the logon can be validated (as
'*          well as setting the privileges back). Finally, it
'*          calls the LogonUser API call to validate the logon.
'***************************************************************
    Dim lToken As Long
    Dim lHandle As Long
    Dim lRtnVal As Long
    Dim lType As Long
    Dim lProv As Long
    Dim dwErr As Long
On Error GoTo CheckLogin_Err

    '--- Set the default return value to the initialized recordset
    LoginUser = 0
    '--- Set the logon type and provider to be used
    lType = LOGON32_LOGON_INTERACTIVE
    lProv = LOGON32_PROVIDER_DEFAULT
    '--- Get a thread or process token that can be used for
    '--- setting the privileges so that the logon can be validated
    lRtnVal = OpenThreadToken(GetCurrentThread, TOKEN_MY_ACCESS, _
            0, lHandle)
    '--- Were we successful?
    If (lRtnVal = 0) Then
        '--- No, check the error
        dwErr = Err.LastDllError
        '--- Did we not get a token?
        If (dwErr = ERROR_NO_TOKEN) Then
            '--- Try to get a process token
            lRtnVal = OpenProcessToken(GetCurrentProcess, _
                    TOKEN_MY_ACCESS, lHandle)
            '--- Were we successful?
            If (lRtnVal = 0) Then
                '--- No, check the error
                dwErr = Err.LastDllError
                '--- Log the error and exit the function
                App.LogEvent "Login validation error = " & dwErr, _
                        vbLogEventTypeError
                Exit Function
            End If
        End If
```

```
        Else
            '--- Log the error and exit the function
            App.LogEvent "Login validation error = " & dwErr, _
                    vbLogEventTypeError
            Exit Function
        End If
    End If
End If
'--- Set the necessary privilege
If (Not SetPrivilege(lHandle, SE_TCB_NAME, True)) Then Exit Function
'--- Validate the user logon
lRtnVal = LogonUser(sUserName, sDomain, sPassword, lType, _
        lProv, lToken)
'--- Were we successful?
If lRtnVal <> 0 Then
    '--- Non-zero, the call worked. Check the error status to see
    '--- if there were problems
    dwErr = Err.LastDllError
    Select Case dwErr
        '--- Invalid logon combination
        Case ERROR_LOGON_FAILURE
            '--- Do nothing
            'App.LogEvent "Login validation error = "_
                        & "ERROR_LOGON_FAILURE", vbLogEventTypeError
        '--- No error, valid logon
        Case 0
            '--- Reset the return value to return the logon token
            LoginUser = lToken
        '--- Some other error occurred
        Case Else
            '--- Log the error
            App.LogEvent "Login validation error = " & dwErr, _
                        vbLogEventTypeError
    End Select
Else
    '--- Zero, the call failed. Check the error status to see
    '--- what problems were
    lRtnVal = Err.LastDllError
    '--- Invalid logon combination?
    If lRtnVal <> ERROR_LOGON_FAILURE Then
        '--- No, log the error
        App.LogEvent "Login validation error = " & dwErr, _
                    vbLogEventTypeError
    Else
        '--- Yes, do nothing
        'App.LogEvent "Login validation error = " _
                    & "ERROR_LOGON_FAILURE", vbLogEventTypeError
```

continues

LISTING 11.2   Continued

```
        End If
    End If
    '--- Reset the necessary privilege
    If (Not SetPrivilege(lHandle, SE_TCB_NAME, False)) Then Exit Function
    '--- Close the thread or process handle
    '--- that is used to set the privilege
    lRtnVal = CloseHandle(lHandle)
    '--- Exit the function
    Exit Function

CheckLogin_Err:
    '--- An error occurred, log the error
    App.LogEvent "Logon validation error = " & Err.Number & " = " & _
                Err.Description
    '--- Exit the function
    Exit Function
End Function
```

NOTE

To perform the tasks in Listings 11.1 and 11.2, you'll need to have the "Act as part of the operating system" privilege enabled. This privilege is not granted by default to any user accounts, including the Administrator account, on either NT 4 or Windows 2000. Directions on how to grant this privilege will be provided later in this chapter.

In this function, the first thing that you did was to specify the logon type and provider.

```
'--- Set the logon type and provider to be used
lType = LOGON32_LOGON_INTERACTIVE
lProv = LOGON32_PROVIDER_DEFAULT
```

Next, you need to get a token for the thread or the process. You first tried to get the token for the current thread using a combination of the GetCurrentThread and OpenThreadToken functions.

```
'--- Get a thread or process token that can be used for
'--- setting the privileges so that the logon can be validated
lRtnVal = OpenThreadToken(GetCurrentThread, TOKEN_MY_ACCESS, 0, lHandle)
```

If that didn't work, you then tried to get a token for the current process using a combination of the GetCurrentProcess and OpenProcessToken functions.

```
'--- Try to get a process token
lRtnVal = OpenProcessToken(GetCurrentProcess, TOKEN_MY_ACCESS, lHandle)
```

The `GetCurrentThread` and `GetCurrentProcess` functions both return pseudo handles for the current thread and process respectively. These pseudo handles are not very usable as is, but instead have to be passed to other API functions to become something useful. Neither of these functions requires any parameters, and the function declarations are in the declarations portion of Listing 11.2.

The `OpenThreadToken` and `OpenProcessToken` functions are almost alike. For both functions, the first parameter is the handle, or pseudo handle, to the thread or process, respectively. The second parameter to both of these functions is an access mask specifying the type of access desired. The available access masks are listed in the declaration section of Listing 11.2. The final parameter for both of these functions is a long variable into which the token for either the thread or the process will be placed. The `OpenThreadToken` function has an additional parameter (the third), which specifies whether the security check should be made against the thread or the process in which the thread is running. A value of 0 means that the security will be checked against the thread, and a value of -1 will check the security against the process.

NOTE

Although a thread will normally have the same security context as the process in which it is running, if a thread is impersonating another account, it may have a different security context.

After you had a token for either the thread or the process, you enabled the `SE_TCB_NAME` privilege by calling the generic function in Listing 11.1.

```
'--- Set the necessary privilege
If (Not SetPrivilege(lHandle, SE_TCB_NAME, True)) Then Exit Function
```

Finally, you tried to log the user on to the system using the `LogonUser` function.

```
'--- Validate the user logon
lRtnVal = LogonUser(sUserName, sDomain, sPassword, lType, lProv, lToken)
```

After you had the user logged on, you did some cleaning after yourself by unsetting the SE_TCB_NAME privilege and then closing the thread or the process token using the `CloseHandle` function.

```
'--- Reset the necessary privilege
If (Not SetPrivilege(lHandle, SE_TCB_NAME, False)) Then Exit Function
'--- Close the thread or process handle that is used to set the privilege
lRtnVal = CloseHandle(lHandle)
```

When you are finished with a user login session, you can log the user out by using the `CloseHandle` function to close the logon token, as shown in Listing 11.3.

LISTING 11.3   Logging a User Out

```
Public Sub CloseLogin(lToken As Long)
    Dim lRtnVal As Long

    '--- Close the token created
    lRtnVal = CloseHandle(lToken)
End Sub
```

Granting Account Permissions

Before you can run the preceding code modules, you need to compile them into either a DLL or a server module that will be running independently from the user interface. This DLL or executable will need to be running on the server under a controlled user account that can be granted permission to execute as part of the operating system. The account needs to have permission configured to operate as part of the operating system before the code module can grant the privilege to itself.

Granting Permissions on NT 4.0

Granting a user account permission to act as part of the operating system is a fairly simple task. First, you need to be logged in either to the administrator account or to another account that is a member of the administrators group. Next, run the User Manager (Start|Programs|Administrative Tools|User Manager), as shown in Figure 11.1.

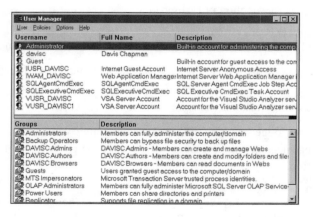

FIGURE 11.1

Running the User Manager utility.

In the User Manager, you might want to consider adding a special account specifically for running modules like this that need to run as part of the operating system. After you have an account picked out, select Policies|User Rights from the menu, which opens the User Rights Policy dialog. Click the Show Advanced User Rights check box near the bottom left of the dialog, and then select Act as part of the operating system in the combo box, as shown in Figure 11.2.

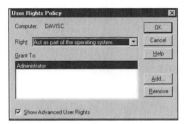

FIGURE 11.2
Selecting the user rights to configure.

Click the Add button to add an account to have this right. This opens the Add Users and Groups dialog, which presents you with a list of active groups and accounts in the domain. Click the Show Users button to be able to select individual accounts and not just groups. Click the Add button to add the selected account to the list at the bottom of the dialog, as shown in Figure 11.3. Click the OK button to add the selected accounts to the User Rights Policy dialog, and then click OK on the User Rights Policy to add the selected accounts to have permission to act as part of the operating system.

FIGURE 11.3
Selecting the accounts for which to add a privilege.

If you are currently logged on to the account for which you are granting new privileges, you will need to log out and back in before the privileges will be granted.

Granting Permissions on Windows 2000

Granting the appropriate permissions on Windows 2000 is a little more involved than on NT 4.0, primarily because the privilege needs to be set in more places. First, you need to use the Active Directory Users and Computers utility to set up and configure the user account under which the login module needs to run, as shown in Figure 11.4.

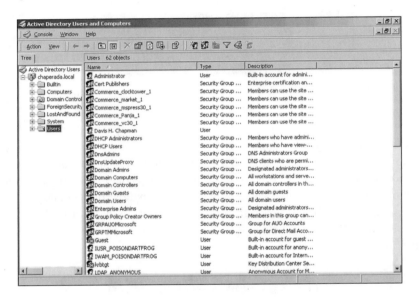

FIGURE 11.4
Running the Active Directory Users and Computers utility.

After the account is set up and configured, two or three policy maintenance utilities need to be used to add the privilege, depending on the configuration of the server on which the login module will be run. The Local Security Policy utility maintains and modifies privileges on the computer on which it is run; the Domain Controller Security Policy utility maintains privileges on the Domain controller; and the Domain Security Policy utility maintains privileges across the domain. Any settings in the Domain policy override settings in the local policy, and if you are configuring the Domain Controller, the Domain Controller policy settings override the local settings.

To configure the policy, choose the appropriate security policy utility, expand the security settings tree, and select User Rights Assignment, as shown in Figure 11.5.

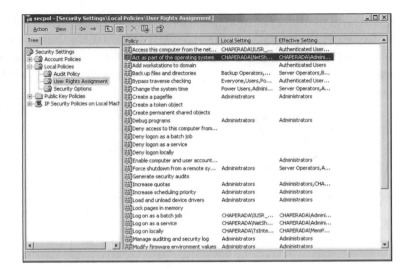

FIGURE 11.5

Selecting the user rights assignment to configure.

Double-click on the right to act as part of the operating system (or right-click it and select Security from the context menu) to display the Security Policy Setting dialog, as shown in Figure 11.6. In here, you can enable or disable the policy setting as needed, by toggling the check box next to the accounts shown.

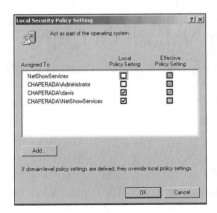

FIGURE 11.6

Configuring the security policy.

To add a new account to the displayed list of accounts, click the Add button. This opens the Select Users or Groups dialog, as shown in Figure 11.7. In here, you can select the desired accounts, add them to the list of accounts in the bottom half of the dialog, and then add the selected accounts to the Security Policy Setting dialog, enabling you to enable or disable the specified privilege for those accounts.

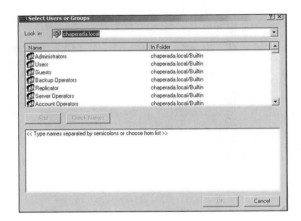

FIGURE 11.7
Selecting the accounts to add to the Security Policy.

If you are currently logged on to the account for which you are granting new privileges, you will need to log out and back in before the privileges will be granted.

Building a Login Validation Utility

To see some of what has been covered in this and the previous chapter, you'll build a two (or three) piece application. This application consists of one or two DLLs containing some of the code provided in this and the previous chapter. This code is Listings 11.1, 11.2, 11.3, and 10.12. The other part of the application is a user front end that enables you to enter a username and password to validate and a file to check for access.

Creating the DLLs

Package the code listings into a couple of DLLs. For the first DLL, create a project named **SecurLoginBO** and place the code listings from this chapter, 11.1, 11.2, and 11.3, into a class named clsLoginDomain. For the second DLL, create a project named **Authorize** and place the code listing 10.12 from the previous chapter into a class named clsAuthorize. Compile both of these projects into DLLs.

Creating the User Interface

Start a new project to create a standard EXE. Include in this project references to the two DLLs that you just created. Next, add the Microsoft Common Dialog Component to the project, as shown in Figure 11.8.

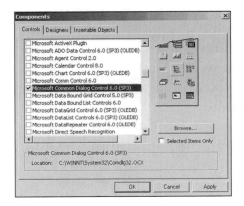

FIGURE 11.8
Adding the Common Dialog Control to the project.

Next, lay out the application dialog as shown in Figure 11.9, configuring the controls as listed in Table 11.3.

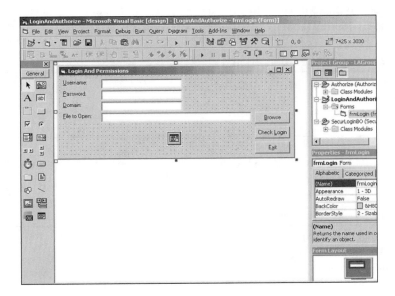

FIGURE 11.9
Application Screen Layout.

TABLE 11.3   Control Property Settings

Control	Property	Value
Label	Caption	&Username:
TextBox	Name	txtUsername
Label	Caption	&Password:
TextBox	Name	txtPassword
	PasswordChar	*
Label	Caption	&Domain:
TextBox	Name	txtDomain
Label	Caption	&File to Open:
TextBox	Name	txtFilename
Command Button	Name	cmdBrowse
	Caption	&Browse
CommonDialog	Name	cdDialogs
Command Button	Name	cmdLogin
	Caption	Check &Login
Command Button	Name	cmdExit
	Caption	E&xit

Next, attach code to the Exit button to close the application by adding the code in Listing 11.4 to the Click event for this button.

LISTING 11.4   Closing the Application

```
Private Sub cmdExit_Click()
    '--- Close the application
    Unload Me
End Sub
```

And then allow the user the ability to browse to select the file to try and open by adding the code in Listing 11.5 to the Click event of the Browse button.

LISTING 11.5   Allowing Browsing for the File to Open

```
Private Sub cmdBrowse_Click()
    '--- Get the file name to open
    cdDialogs.ShowOpen
    txtFilename = cdDialogs.FileName
End Sub
```

Checking the User Logon

The remaining functionality for the application is to perform the user logon and to test the specified file for access privileges. To do this, you need to create new instances of both the DLLs that you created, call the LoginUser method in the first DLL, and if successfully logged in, pass the filename and the login token to the TestFileForAccess method in the second DLL. After you have tested the access of the user, you need to call the CloseLogin method in the first DLL to end the user session that you created. To add this functionality, attach the code in Listing 11.6 to the Check Login button.

LISTING **11.6**   Validating the User Logon and Testing for Access

```
Private Sub cmdLogin_Click()
    '--- Create instances of the security objects
    Dim objLogin As New SecurLoginBO.clsLoginDomain
    Dim objAuth As New Authorize.clsAuthorize
    Dim hToken As Long

    '--- Try and log in the user
    hToken = objLogin.LoginUser(txtUsername, txtDomain, txtPassword)
    '--- Were we able to log the user in?
    If (hToken <> 0) Then
        '--- Test the specified file for access
        If objAuth.TestFileForAccess(hToken, txtFilename) Then
            MsgBox "Login has access"
        Else
            MsgBox "Login does not have access"
        End If
        '--- Log the user out
        objLogin.CloseLogin hToken
    Else
        MsgBox "Invalid Login"
    End If
End Sub
```

At this point you should be able to run this application, if you are logged in as an account that has permission to act as part of the operating system, and test user accounts that you have configured on your system, as shown in Figure 11.10. What you might want to do is configure a directory so that a specific account does not have access to that directory, and then try creating files in that directory using several accounts. This should provide a good feel for how you can leverage impersonation using a logon token as a way to restrict user access to resources on a server in a distributed application.

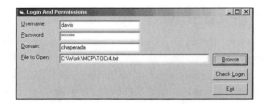

FIGURE 11.10
Testing user login accounts for access.

Summary

In this chapter you got a look at how you can take a username and password and log that user into a domain so that you can use impersonation of that user to restrict access to resources on the server and network. This can be a powerful means of implementing integrated security into a networked application, leveraging the security profiles that the network administrator is already configuring and maintaining.

In the next chapter, you'll begin to learn how to access and interact with Active Directory servers using the Active Directory Security Interface (ADSI). This will include connecting to the Active Directory server using the Kerberos authentication protocol, as well as accessing NT 4 domains and computers. If you want to learn how to access Active Directory servers—as well as several other types of directory servers—using the ADSI interface, read on.

Working with Active Directory Security (ADSI) and an LDAP Server

IN THIS CHAPTER

One of the newest technologies being introduced with Windows 2000 is the Active Directory. This is a directory service that enables objects and services to be published in a distributed directory. Active Directory makes it easy for applications to locate and use network services such as printers, databases, and email and fax servers. If you have an application that many people within an organization need to have access to, you can publish the application in the organization's Active Directory, and any user who needs to locate your application can easily find it.

Active Directory also provides you with access to the security of each of the objects published within. Assuming that you have sufficient rights to examine the permissions on various objects, you can examine what permissions each group has for every one of the objects in the directory.

Active Directory and Security

The Active Directory Security Interface (ADSI) goes well beyond the Active Directory in Windows 2000. Using ADSI, you can access not only Active Directory, but also Novell's NDS directory service, any X.500 directory service, Microsoft's Exchange directory, NT 4 directory, and several others. The Active Directory directory service is accessed through the Lightweight Directory Access Protocol (LDAP), the protocol that is also used to access Exchange and X.500 directories. In this chapter, you'll be working with the NT 4 directory service (WinNT), and the Active Directory service (LDAP), but you can also just as easily work with Novell NetWare 3.x (NWCOMPAT), or Novell NetWare Directory Service (NDS) using the same objects and methods.

Opening an ADSI Session

Binding to an ADSI object interface opens all ADSI sessions. All ADSI object interfaces can be bound to an object by using the GetObject function. This function is declared as

Syntax

```
GetObject("URL [, class]") As Object
```

The URL parameter to the GetObject function consists of two parts. The first part specifies the provider to user. The provider can be one of the default providers listed in Table 12.1 or any additional providers that are installed on the client machine.

TABLE 12.1 ADSI Providers That Are Provided with the ADSI Interface

Provider	Description
WinNT:	This provider allows you to communicate with an NT 4 Domain Controller (either primary or backup).
LDAP:	This provider enables you to communicate with any LDAP servers, including Exchange 5.x and Windows 2000 Active Directory.

Provider	Description
NDS:	This provider allows you to communicate with any Novell Directory Services server.
NWCOMPAT:	This provider enables you to communicate with any Novell 3.x NetWare server.

The second part of the URL parameter is the path to the object. If you are trying to bind to a domain controller, this is the name of the domain. If you are trying to bind to a specific user on the domain, you specify the domain, the domain controller, and the username, as follows:

```
Dim obj As Object

Set obj = GetObject("WinNT://TheDomain/DomainController/Bill")
```

The second parameter (class) specifies the object class for the object that you are trying to bind to. This specifies the type of object interface that you are wanting to bind to and will thus determine what properties and methods you have available to you after you retrieve the object interface. Some of the possible interface classes that are available are listed in Table 12.2.

TABLE 12.2   Some Possible Interface Classes

Class	Description
user	A user account on the computer or in the domain
group	A group on the computer or in the domain
domain	A domain in the namespace
computer	A computer in the domain
organization	An organization in the domain
organizationalUnit	An organizational unit or department within the organization
fileShare	A file share on a computer
printQueue	A printer or print queue in the domain

The way that you might bind to a specific class interface using the GetObject function would work like this: If you were wanting to bind to a user account Davis on the domain controller Frog in the domain Pond, your call to GetObject would look something like this:

```
Dim obj As Object
Set obj = GetObject("WinNT://Pond/Frog/Davis,user")
```

> **NOTE**
>
> Be sure to take note that, even though these are technically two different parameters, they are passed as part of the same string.

> **CAUTION**
>
> Any spaces in the string being passed to the GetObject function will result in an automation error. You need to be sure that you don't include any spaces between the parameters within the string.

> **TIP**
>
> If you have trouble connecting to your domain by just using the domain name in the `GetObject` parameter string, as in the following:
>
> ```
> Set obj = GetObject("WinNT://Pond/Frog/Davis,user")
> ```
>
> you might need to use the fully qualified Internet name for the machine, as follows:
>
> ```
> Set obj = GetObject("WinNT://frog.pond.com/Davis,user")
> ```

LDAP Active Directory Path

LDAP Active Directory paths always start with the specification of the LDAP provider, as follows:

```
LDAP:
```

If you are just initializing the LDAP provider and will be binding to specific objects using a secure connection, the preceding LDAP specification may be all that is in the initial call to the `GetObject` function. If you are needing to bind to a specific object within the Active Directory service, you'll need to add some additional elements to the specification.

The rest of the LDAP path resembles a combination of a URL and the X.500 Distinguished Name Fields that you learned about in Chapter 5, "Requesting and Receiving Certificates." The reason for this is that they are the same Distinguished Name Fields, as listed in Table 12.3.

TABLE 12.3 X.500 Distinguished Name Fields

Code	Description
DC	Domain Component—Identifies a part of an object's network domain.
CN	Common Name—The user's name, or if this is a request for a certificate for a server, the fully qualified hostname/URL.
O	Organization—The name of the organization or company for which the certificate is being requested. This should be the legal name for the company or organization.
OU	Organizational Unit—This is used to differentiate divisions within an organization or company. This can also be used to specify a DBA (Doing Business As) name for the certificate.
L	Locality—The city in which the organization or person resides.
S	State—The state in which the organization or person resides.
C	Country—The country in which the organization or person resides. The X.500 naming scheme limits this to a two-character country code. The code for the United States is "US" and the code for Canada is "CA."
E	Email Address—The email address for the person requesting the certificate (this is an optional element).

If you look closely, you'll notice that this table begins with an element that wasn't in this table in Chapter 5. The Domain Component (DC) element was added for specifying pieces of a domain. For instance, if your Active Directory domain is mydomain.com, you would bind to the domain using the following LDAP binding string:

```
LDAP://DC=mydomain,DC=com
```

If you want to bind to the user davis in the organizational unit authors, you might use the LDAP path as

```
LDAP://CN=davis,OU=authors,DC=mydomain,DC=com
```

You might also define the LDAP path as follows:

```
LDAP://DC=mydomain,DC=com/OU=authors/CN=davis
```

Basically, you are defining the path through the Active Directory tree to the object that you are looking for. In Chapter 13, "Active Directory Security and Searching," you'll build a utility that will build the entire Active Directory tree for the specified domain. Examine the Active Directory path properties for the various objects in the tree, analyzing them to understand how the path is constructed.

WinNT Active Directory Path

The NT 4 Active Directory path is more like a standard URL than the LDAP path. It starts by specifying the provider as WinNT, and then gives the path through the directory tree starting with the domain, as follows:

```
WinNT://MyDomain/davis
```

You can also include the class on the end of the path for a NT 4 path, separated by a comma, as follows:

```
WinNT://MyDomain/davis,user
```

WinNT paths may include a specific computer in the domain for the paths to printers and other objects associated with a computer, as follows:

```
WinNT://MyDomain/MyComputer/MyPrinter,printQueue
```

NDS Active Directory Path

The NDS Active Directory path is virtually the same as the LDAP paths, only with the NDS provider specified, as follows:

```
NDS://DC=mydomain,DC=com/OU=authors/CN=davis
```

NWCOMPAT Active Directory Path

The Novell 3.x Active Directory path is virtually the same as the LDAP paths, only with the NWCOMPAT provider specified, as follows:

```
NWCOMPAT://DC=mydomain,DC=com/OU=authors/CN=davis
```

The IADs Object Interface

The IADs object interface is the base interface that all ADSI objects support. All the methods and properties available in the IADs object interface are available in all the ADSI objects. The available properties in this interface are listed in Table 12.4.

TABLE 12.4   *IADs* Properties

Property	Description
Name	The name of this object
Class	The interface class of this object
GUID	The Globally Unique ID (GUID) of this object
AdsPath	The Active Directory path for this object that uniquely identifies this object within the directory
Parent	The Active Directory path for the parent of this object
Schema	The Active Directory path for the schema object that describes this object (you'll learn about schema objects later in this chapter).

Getting Any Property Value

Any property of an object can be retrieved using the Get method. This method can be used on the IADs object interface even if the property being retrieved is not one available through the IADs interface. The syntax for the Get method is as follows:

Syntax

```
object.Get(strName As String) As Variant
```

The one parameter (strName) to this method is the name of the property that you want to retrieve. For instance, you could retrieve the name of an IADs object in either of two ways. You could use the property to get the name, as follows:

```
Dim obj As IADs
Dim strName As String

Set obj = GetObject("WinNT://TheDomain/DomainController/Bill")
strName = obj.Name
```

You could also use the Get method to retrieve the same property, as follows:

```
Dim obj As IADs
Dim strName As Variant

Set obj = GetObject("WinNT://TheDomain/DomainController/Bill")
strName = obj.Get("cn")
```

> **TIP**
>
> If you are using the Get method to retrieve properties of an object, you'll need to use the internal name for the property. The internal names of properties are often different from the exposed property name for those properties that are externally visible. For instance, externally exposed Name property may have an internal name of objectName, cn (Common Name), Name, or any other internal name the object designer decided to use.

Setting a Property Value

Assuming that you have the proper authorization, you can set the value of various properties of an object using the Put method. The syntax for the Put method is as follows:

Syntax

```
object.Put(strName As String, varValue As Variant)
```

The first parameter (strName) to this method is the name of the property that you are wanting to update. The second parameter (varValue) is the value that you are setting for the property. The value has to be in the form of a Variant value.

Updating the Active Directory

If you have changed the values of any of the properties of an ADSI object, you need to flush those changes to the Active Directory server. You do this with the SetInfo method. This method doesn't take any parameters and should be called only after all the properties that are being updated have been set. An example of how you might use this method is as follows:

```
Dim obj As IADs

obj.Put(property1, value1)
obj.Put(property2, value2)
obj.Put(property3, value3)
obj.SetInfo
```

Refreshing the Property Values

If there is any chance that some of the property values of an object have been changed, you can refresh the properties from the Active Directory server using the GetInfo method. If you have updated some properties and don't want to save these changes to the Active Directory server, you can also use the GetInfo method to reset the object properties to their initial settings. Like the SetInfo method, the GetInfo method doesn't take any parameters.

The IADsContainer Object Interface

The IADsContainer object interface is available for all objects that contain other objects within the Active Directory tree. The objects contained within IADsContainer objects can be enumerated using a For Each loop. The available properties in the IADsContainer object interface are listed in Table 12.5.

TABLE 12.5   *IADsContainer* Properties

Property	Description
Count	The number of objects contained within this object.
Filter	A variant array of object classes that will be available for enumeration. Setting this property enables you to limit the enumeration to objects of a specific class.
Hints	A variant array of names of properties for each enumerated object.

Getting a Specific Object

If you know the object that you want to get from the collection, you can use the GetObject method. The syntax for this method is as follows:

Syntax

```
object.GetObject(strClass As String, strRelativeName As String) As Object
```

The first parameter (strClass) is the class of the object that you are wanting to retrieve. The second parameter (strRelativeName) is the relative path from the container object for the object that you want to retrieve. This method returns an Active Directory object interface for the object requested.

For instance, if you have an IADsContainer object that contains users, and you want to retrieve a user named Bob, you could retrieve it using the following code:

```
Dim objUser As Object

Set objUser = objContainer.GetObject("user", "CN=Bob")
```

Creating an Object

If you need to create a new object as a member of the collection, you'll use the Create method. This syntax for this method is

Syntax

```
object.Create(strClass As String, strRelativeName As String) As Object
```

This method takes the same parameters as the GetObject method examined earlier. It returns the object that has been created.

Deleting an Object

If you need to delete an object from a collection, you can use the Delete method. The syntax for this method is the following:

Syntax

```
object.Delete(strClass As String, strRelativeName As String)
```

The parameters for this method are the same as for the Create and GetObject methods.

Copying an Object

If you need to copy an object from anywhere in the Active Directory namespace into the current collection, you can use the `CopyHere` method. The syntax for this method is as follows:

Syntax

```
object.CopyHere(strPath As String, strNewName As String) As Object
```

The first parameter (`strPath`) to this method is the Active Directory path to the current object that is being copied. The second parameter (`strNewName`) is the name for the new copy of the object to be added to the current collection.

This method returns the new object that has been added to the current collection. An example of how this method might be used is as follows:

```
Dim objUser As Object

Set objUser = objContainer.CopyHere( _
    "LDAP://CN=JohnSmith,OU=myDepartment,O=myCompany,DC=mDomain,DC=com", _
    "CN=BobSmith")
```

Moving an Object

If you need to move or rename an object, you can use the `MoveHere` method. The syntax for this method is as follows:

Syntax

```
object.MoveHere(strPath As String, strNewName As String) As Object
```

The parameters and return value for this method are the same as for the `CopyHere` method. If you just need to move an object into the current collection without renaming the object, you can pass the NULL string (`vbNullString`) as the second parameter (`strNewName`).

The `IADsNamespaces` Object Interface

The highest level object in the Active Directory tree is the `IADsNamespaces` object. The `IADsNamespaces` object is a collection of providers that are currently installed in the Active Directory namespace. The `IADsNamespaces` object has a single property beyond those provided by the `IADs` and `IADsContainer` interfaces. This property is listed in Table 12.6.

TABLE 12.6   *IADsNamespaces* Properties

Property	Description
DefaultContainer	The Active Directory path to the base container for the current user.

You can bind to the IADsNamespaces object interface by calling the GetObject function, specifying the ADs provider, as follows:

```
Dim obj As IADsNamespaces

Set obj = GetObject("ADs:")
```

After you have opened an instance of the IADsNamespaces object, you can use it to enumerate all the namespaces available to you. This can be done using a For Each loop, listing the Name property of each object contained in the IADsNamespaces object, as shown in Listing 12.1.

LISTING 12.1   Enumerating the Namespaces

```
Private Sub GetNamespaces()
'*************************************************************
'* Written By: Davis Chapman
'* Date:        February 12, 2000
'*
'* Syntax:      GetNamespaces
'*
'* Parameters: None
'*
'* Purpose: This subroutine builds a list of all the names
'*          in the ADS namespace.
'*************************************************************
    Dim objNameSpaces As Object
    Dim nsSpaces As Object
    Dim strMsg As String

    On Error Resume Next
    '--- Get the root object for the name spaces
    Set objNameSpaces = GetObject("ADs:")
    '--- Initialize the display string
    strMsg = ""
    '--- Loop through all the names in the namespaces
    For Each nsSpaces In objNameSpaces
        '--- Add the name to the list
        strMsg = strMsg + nsSpaces.Name + vbCrLf
    Next
    '--- Display the information for the user
    MsgBox strMsg
End Sub
```

ADSI Security and Authentication

If you need to have a secure connection to the Active Directory service that you are connected to, you can use the IADsOpenDSObject interface. This object has a single method,

OpenDSObject, that is used to authenticate the user and then maintain the security context for the session. The syntax for this method is as follows:

Syntax

```
object.OpenDSObject(strPath As String, strUserName As String, _
         strPassword As String, lAuthFlags As Long) As Object
```

The first parameter (strPath) is the Active Directory path to the object to be opened. The second parameter (strUserName) is the user account name to use. The third parameter (strPassword) is the password for the account specified in the second parameter. The fourth parameter (lAuthFlags) specifies how the connection is made, how the user is authenticated, and how the session is maintained. The possible values to be used for this parameter are listed in Table 12.7.

TABLE 12.7   *OpenDSObject* Authentication Flags

Flag	Value	Description
ADS_SECURE_ AUTHENTICATION	&H1	Causes ADSI to perform secure authentication. The authentication method used depends on the provider being used. The WinNT provider uses the NT Lan Manager (NTLM) authentication. The Active Directory provider uses Kerberos, if possible, or NTLM if not. If the NULL string (vbNullString) is passed in place of the username and password (second and third parameters), the current security context is used.
ADS_USE_ENCRYPTION	&H2	Causes ADSI to use encryption on all data transfers across the network.
ADS_USE_SSL	&H2	Causes the data to be encrypted using SSL, if available. Certificate Services must be installed for Active Directory to use SSL.
ADS_READONLY_SERVER	&H4	With a WinNT provider, this flag causes ADSI to bind to either a primary domain controller or a backup domain controller. With an Active Directory provider, this flag allows a read-only server to be used.
ADS_PROMPT_CREDENTIALS	&H8	This flag causes the Security Support Provider Interface (SSPI) to prompt the user for authentication credentials, assuming that the selected SSPI provides a user interface for this.

Flag	Value	Description
ADS_NO_AUTHENTICATION	&H10	This flag requests that an anonymous connection be made, providing the user with limited access to the Active Directory.
ADS_FAST_BIND	&H20	This flag will not provide all the properties and methods for objects, but will provide only the base properties and methods that are available to all ADSI objects.
ADS_USE_SIGNING	&H40	This flag causes all data sent between the Active Directory server and the client to be signed so that the data is verified to not change in the transfer. This flag can be used only with the ADS_SECURE_AUTHENTICATION flag.
ADS_USE_SEALING	&H80	This flag causes all the data transferred to be encrypted using Kerberos. This flag can be used only with the ADS_SECURE_AUTHENTICATION flag.

The IADsOpenDSObject object is retrieved using the GetObject function, passing in just the namespace to be used. An example of how this might be used shown in the following:

```
Dim openDS As IADsOpenDSObject
Dim obj As IADs

'--- Open the LDAP interface
Set openDS = GetObject("LDAP:")
'--- Open the security context using secure authentication
Set obj = openDS.OpenDSObject( _
    "LDAP://CN=JohnSmith,OU=myDepartment,O=myCompany,DC=myDomain,DC=com", _
    "davis", "password", ADS_SECURE_AUTHENTICATION)
```

NOTE

The specific syntax used in the example above depends on how your Active Directory is organized. The syntax above will retrieve a user or contact from an organizational unit. This will only work if you have an organizational unit set up and configured in your Active Directory. If you are on an Active Directory that only has users and groups, then you might try a syntax like the following:

```
"LDAP://CN=John Smith,CN=Users,DC=myDomain,DC=com"
```

Active Directory Object Schemas

You may have noticed a property of the IADs object interface called Schema. This property is the Active Directory path to an object that contains a description of the class of each and every object in the Active Directory tree. The schema can be examined to determine what each of the properties in any class are and what their data types are.

The IADsClass Object Interface

If you use the GetObject function to retrieve the schema of an Active Directory class, the object you'll receive will implement the IADsClass object interface. This object interface has the properties in Table 12.8.

TABLE 12.8   *IADsClass* Properties

Property	Description
PrimaryInterface	The GUID for the primary interface for this class.
CLSID	The CLSID of the COM object implementing this object class.
OID	The provider-specific Object Identifier (OID) for this object class.
Abstract	A Boolean value specifying whether this class is abstract. An abstract class cannot be instantiated, but can only be inherited by other classes.
Auxiliary	A Boolean value that indicates whether this class is an auxiliary class to another class. If this class is an auxiliary class, it cannot be directly instantiated, but provides additional properties for another class.
MandatoryProperties	An array of properties that must have values for this class to be stored in the Active Directory.
OptionalProperties	An array of properties that are optional and that don't have to have values.
NamingProperties	An array of properties that are used for naming this class, such as OU, CN, and O.
DerivedFrom	An array of Active Directory paths for the classes that this class was derived from.
AuxDerivedFrom	An array of Active Directory paths for the auxiliary classes that this class was derived from.
PossibleSuperiors	An array of Active Directory paths for the classes that may contain this class.
Containment	An array of container types that may contain this class.
Container	A Boolean value indicating whether this class is a container.

Property	Description
HelpFileName	The name of a help file that contains information about objects of this class.
HelpFileContext	The help context ID for locating the specific information about this class within the help file.

An example of how you might use the schema of an object to get various properties of the object is shown in the following:

```
Dim objSchema As IADsClass
Dim strMsg As String
Dim lTotalNbr As Long
Dim lCurNbr As Long

On Error Resume Next
'--- Get the object's schema
Set objSchema = GetObject(obj.Schema)
'--- Get the number of mandatory properties
lTotalNbr = UBound(objSchema.MandatoryProperties)
'--- Initialize the return string
strMsg = "Mandatory Properties" + vbCrLf
'--- Loop through the mandatory properties
For lCurNbr = 0 To lTotalNbr
    '--- Add the property to the return string
    strMsg = strMsg & vbTab & objSchema.MandatoryProperties(lCurNbr) _
        & ": " & obj.Get(objSchema.MandatoryProperties(lCurNbr)) & vbCrLf
Next
```

The IADsProperty Object Interface

When you need information about a specific property of a class, you can bind to the IADsProperty object interface for that property. This object interface provides the properties in Table 12.9.

TABLE 12.9 *IADsProperty* Properties

Property	Description
OID	The directory-specific Object Identifier (OID)
Syntax	The Active Directory path for the syntax object for this property
MaxRange	A long value indicating the maximum value that this property can hold
MinRange	A long value indicating the minimum value that this property can hold
MultiValued	A Boolean value indicating whether this property supports single or multiple values.

Binding to the `IADsProperty` object interface for a specific object property requires several steps:

1. Get an object's `schema` class (`IADsClass`).
2. Verify that the desired property is in the class mandatory or optional properties.
3. Bind to the `container` class (`IADsContainer`) of the `schema` class.
4. Use the `GetObject` method to retrieve the property class (`IADsProperty`).

An example of this could look like the following:

```
Dim objSchema As IADsClass
Dim objParent As IADsContainer
Dim objProperty As IADsProperty

On Error Resume Next
'--- Get the object's schema
Set objSchema = GetObject(obj.Schema)
'--- Get the schema's container
Set objParent = GetObject(objSchema.Parent)
'--- Get the property
Set objProperty = objParent.GetObject("Property", "Owner")
```

The `IADsSyntax` Object Interface

The final piece of the schema objects is the `IADsSyntax` object interface. The path to this object is one of the properties of the `IADsProperty` object interface. This object interface provides you with a single piece of information—the data type of the property. This one property is the `OleAutoDataType` property and can be one of the possible values listed in Table 12.10.

TABLE 12.10   `OleAutoDataType` Data Type Values

Data Type	Value
Boolean	11
String	8 (vbVString)
Currency	6 (vbVCurrency)
Date	7 (vbVDate)
Empty	0 (vbVEmpty)
Error (Invalid)	10
Integer	2 (vbVInteger)
Long	3 (vbVLong)
Single	4 (vbVSingle)
Double	5 (vbVDouble)
Byte	17

To get the `IADsSyntax` object interface for a property, you need to append the `Syntax` property of the `IADsProperty` object interface to the Active Directory path for the `schema` object's parent `container` object. An example of this would look something like the following:

```
Dim objSchema As IADsClass
Dim objParent As IADsContainer
Dim objProperty As IADsProperty
Dim objSyntax As IADsSyntax

On Error Resume Next
'--- Get the object's schema
Set objSchema = GetObject(obj.Schema)
'--- Get the schema's container
Set objParent = GetObject(objSchema.Parent)
'--- Get the property
Set objProperty = objParent.GetObject("Property", "Owner")
'--- Get the property syntax
Set objSyntax = GetObject(objParent.AdsPath + "/" + objProperty.Syntax)
```

Network Groups and Users

Some of the object types that you might want to work with in Active Directory are users and groups. This will enable you to determine who is in a particular group and what groups a user belongs to. After you start examining the security of particular objects, this information is likely to come in handy.

The `IADsCollection` Object Interface

The `IADsCollection` object is similar to the `IADsContainer` class that you learned about in the previous chapter. A distinct difference exists between the two. Whereas the `IADsContainer` class could hold a mixture of classes, the `IADsCollection` can hold only a collection of objects of the same class. Like the `IADsContainer` class, the `IADsCollection` class can be enumerated using a For Each loop to retrieve all the objects in the collection.

Getting a Specific Object from the Collection

If you want to retrieve a specific object from a collection, you can use the `GetObject` method. The syntax for this method is as follows:

Syntax

```
object.GetObject(strName As String) As Object
```

The only parameter (`strName`) to this method is the name of the object to be retrieved from the collection. The object name is the same name as the one provided when the object was added to the collection. This method returns the object from the collection.

Adding an Object to the Collection

When you need to add an object to a collection, you can use the Add method. The syntax for this method is as follows:

Syntax

```
object.Add(strName As String, obj As Any) As Object
```

The first parameter (strName) is the name of the object being added to the collection. The second parameter (obj) is the object being added to the collection.

Removing an Object from the Collection

If you need to remove an object from a collection, you can use the Remove method. The syntax for this method is as follows:

Syntax

```
object.Remove(strName As String)
```

The only parameter (strName) to this method is the name of the object to be retrieved from the collection. The object name is the same name as was provided when the object was added to the collection.

The IADsDomain Object Interface

The IADsDomain object interface allows you to interact directly with the domain. When using the WinNT provider, an IADsDomain object is a container that contains Computers, Groups, and Users. In addition to the IADs and IADsContainer interfaces, the IADsDomain interface has the properties shown in Table 12.11.

TABLE 12.11   *IADsDomain* Properties

Property	Description
IsWorkgroup	A Boolean flag indicating whether the domain is a workstation that belongs to a workgroup.
MinPasswordLength	A long value indicating the minimum length allowed for a user password.
MinPasswordAge	A long value indicating the minimum number of seconds that have to pass before a user is allowed to change a password.
MaxPasswordAge	A long value indicating the maximum number of seconds that is allowed before a user is forced to change a password.
MaxBadPasswordsAllowed	A long value specifying the maximum number of failed login attempts allowed before the account is locked out.

Working with Active Directory Security (ADSI) and an LDAP Server

CHAPTER 12

425

12

WORKING WITH
ADSI AND AN
LDAP SERVER

Property	Description
PasswordHistoryLength	A long value specifying how many past passwords are kept in the history list. A user is not allowed to reuse any password in the history list.
PasswordAttributes	A flag value that indicates any restrictions on passwords. The possible values for this property are listed in Table 12.12.
AutoUnlockInterval	A long value indicating the amount of time that must pass before a locked-out account is automatically reenabled.
LockoutObservationInterval	A long value indicating the interval of time that the number of failed login attempts is monitored to determine whether an account needs to be locked out. If the number of failed login attempts exceeds the number in the MaxBadPasswordsAllowed property within the time specified in this property, the account is automatically locked out.

TABLE 12.12 Password Restriction Flags

Flag	Value	Description
PASSWORD_ATTR_NONE	&H0	No restrictions on passwords.
PASSWORD_ATTR_MIXED_CASE	&H1	Password must use mixed-case letters.
PASSWORD_ATTR_COMPLEX	&H2	Password must contain at least one punctuation mark or nonprintable character.

NOTE

The IADsDomain object interface is available only with the WinNT provider. It is not available with the other ADSI providers.

The IADsGroup Object Interface

The IADsGroup object interface represents a user group in the directory. It has only one property, Description, which is a description of the group.

> **TIP**
>
> Remember when I state that a particular interface has only a single property, the interface also has all the properties from the IADs object interface. Keeping this in mind, you see that the IADsGroup object interface doesn't have only the Description property, but it also has the Name, Class, AdsPath, Parent, and Schema properties from the IADs interface.

Getting the Group Members

If you need to get a collection of the members in the group, you can use the Members method. The syntax for this method is as follows:

Syntax

```
object.Members As IADsMembers
```

This method returns the IADsMembers object interface, which is a collection object that contains all the users that are members of this group. You'll look at the IADsMembers object interface shortly.

Checking for Membership

If you just want to check to see whether a particular user is a member of a group, you can use the IsMember method. The syntax for this method is as follows:

Syntax

```
object.IsMember(strName As String) As Boolean
```

The one parameter (strName) to this method is the Active Directory path for an IADsUser object. The IADsUser object represents a user account in the domain; you'll look at this object interface shortly. This method returns a Boolean value, specifying whether the user is a member of the group.

Adding Members

If you need to add members to a group, you can use the Add method. The syntax for this method is as follows:

Syntax

```
object.Add(strName As String)
```

The one parameter (strName) to this method is the Active Directory path for the IADsUser object to be added to this group.

Removing Members

If you need to remove a member from a group, you can use the Remove method. The syntax for this method is as follows:

Syntax

```
object.Remove(strName As String)
```

The one parameter (strName) to this method is the Active Directory path for the IADsUser object to be removed from this group.

The IADsMembers Object Interface

The IADsMembers object interface is a collection object that contains group member objects, primarily users and other groups. This object interface has two properties, listed in Table 12.13. Like all other collection objects, this object can be enumerated to get all the member objects.

TABLE 12.13   IADsMembers Properties

Property	Description
Count	The number of members in the collection.
Filter	A variant array of object classes that will be available for enumeration. Setting this property enables you to limit the enumeration to objects of a specific class.

The IADsUser Object Interface

The IADsUser object interface enables you to directly interact with a user account. The properties of this object interface are listed in Table 12.14.

TABLE 12.14   IADsUser Properties

Property	Description
AccountDisabled	A Boolean value indicating whether the account is disabled
AccountExpirationDate	The date and time after which the account will be disabled and the user will not be able to log in
BadLoginAddress	The network address of the workstation that is considered to be a possible intruder (available only if Intruder detection has been activated)

continues

TABLE 12.14   Continued

Property	Description
BadLoginCount	The number of failed login attempts since the last reset
Department	The organizational unit in which the user belongs
Description	A description of the user
Division	The division within the organization in which the user works
EmailAddress	The email address for the user
EmployeeID	The employer identification number for the user
FaxNumber	A variant array of fax numbers for the user
FirstName	The first name of the user
FullName	The full name of the user
GraceLoginsAllowed	The number of times the user is allowed to login without changing the password after the password has expired
GraceLoginsRemaining	The number of grace logins remaining before the user is forced to change the password
HomeDirectory	The user's home directory
HomePage	The URL for the user's home page
IsAccountLocked	A Boolean value indicating whether the user account is locked
Languages	A variant array of language names for the user
LastFailedLogin	The date and time of the last failed login attempt by this user
LastLogin	The date and time of the last successful login by the user
LastLogoff	The date and time of the last time the user logged off the network
LastName	The last name of the user
LoginHours	A table of Boolean values for each time slot during the week, indicating which time slots the user is allowed to log in
LoginScript	The path for the user's login script
LoginWorkstations	A variant array of network addresses or workstation names where the user is allowed to login
Manager	The manager of the user
MaxLogins	The maximum number of simultaneous logins that the user is allowed
MaxStorage	The maximum amount of disk space that the user is allowed to use

Property	Description
NamePrefix	The name prefix for the user
NameSuffix	The name suffix for the user
OfficeLocations	A variant array of office locations for the user
OtherName	An additional name for the user
PasswordExpirationDate	The date and time when the user's password expires
PasswordLastChanged	The date and time when the user's password was last changed
PasswordMinimumLength	The minimum password length allowed for the user
PasswordRequired	A Boolean flag indicating whether a password is required for the user
Picture	The picture of the user
PostalAddresses	A variant array of strings that hold the address of the user
PostalCodes	A variant array of strings holding the postal codes that go with the postal addresses
Profile	The path to the user profile
RequireUniquePassword	A Boolean flag indicating whether the user is allowed to reuse a password in the user's password history list
SeeAlso	An array of Active Directory paths to other objects related to the user
TelephoneHome	An array of home telephone numbers for the user
TelephoneMobile	An array of mobile telephone numbers for the user
TelephoneNumber	An array of work-related telephone numbers for the user
TelephonePager	An array of pager numbers for the user
Title	The user's title

Getting the Groups in Which the User is a Member

If you need to get a collection of the groups in which this user is a member, you can use the Groups method. The syntax for this method is as follows:

Syntax

```
object.Groups As IADsMembers
```

This method returns the IADsMembers object interface, which is a collection object that contains all the groups in which the user is a member.

Setting the User Password

If you need to set the password for a particular user, you can use the SetPassword method. The syntax of this method is as follows:

Syntax

```
object.SetPassword(strNewPassword As String)
```

The only parameter to this method (strNewPassword) is the new password for the user account.

Changing the User Password

If you need to change the password for a particular user, you can use the ChangePassword method. The syntax for this method is as follows:

Syntax

```
object.ChangePassword(strOldPassword As String, strNewPassword As String)
```

The first parameter (strOldPassword) to this method is the current password for this user account. The second parameter (strNewPassword) is the new password for the user account.

The IADsComputer Object Interface

The IADsComputer object interface provides you with direct access to information about a computer in the domain. This object interface provides the properties shown in Table 12.15.

TABLE 12.15   *IADsComputer* Properties

Property	Description
ComputerID	The globally unique identifier assigned to each computer
Department	The department within the organization to which this computer belongs
Description	The description of this computer
Division	The division of the organization to which this computer belongs
Location	The physical location of this computer
MemorySize	The size, in megabytes (MB), of the RAM in this computer
Model	The make/model of this computer
NetAddresses	A variant array of network addresses assigned to this computer
OperatingSystem	The operating system running on this computer

Property	Description
OperatingSystemVersion	The version of the operating system running on this computer
Owner	The name of the user who normally uses this computer and has a license to run the software loaded on it
PrimaryUser	The name of the contact person who needs to be contacted in case a problem occurs with this computer
Processor	The type of processor in this computer
ProcessorCount	The number of processors in this computer
Role	The role of this computer (for example, workstation, server, domain controller)
Site	The globally unique identifier for the site in which this computer is installed
StorageCapacity	The disk space, in megabytes, on this computer

The `IADsFileShare` Object Interface

The `IADsFileShare` object provides information about file shares on an NT 4 or Novell NetWare network. The configuration of this file share is available through the properties shown in Table 12.16.

TABLE 12.16 `IADsFileShare` Properties

Property	Description
CurrentUserCount	The number of users currently connected to this file share
Description	The description of this file share
HostComputer	The Active Directory path to the computer that is hosting this file share
MaxUserCount	The maximum number of users that may be connected to this file share at one time
Path	The file system path to this file share

NOTE

Several more defined classes are available that you can work with without having to use the class `schema` to learn what properties are available. You can find the definitions for these classes in the Microsoft Developer Network library, either on CD or on the Web (www.msdn.microsoft.com). Look under Platform SDK|Networking and Directory Services|Active Directory, ADSI, and Directory Services|Active Directory Service Interfaces (ADSI)|ADSI Reference|ADSI Interfaces to locate information about other miscellaneous interfaces you can use in your applications.

Examining Groups and Users

To see how this portion of the ADSI interface works and how it can be used, you'll build a utility that allows you to see all the users and groups in a particular domain. You'll be able to enter the name of any domain to which you have access and select whether you want to see the groups, the groups with the users in them, the users, or the users and which groups they are in.

Designing the User Interface

To start this application, create a new standard executable Visual Basic project. Open the project references and add a reference for the Active DS Type Library, as shown in Figure 12.1.

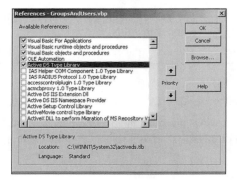

FIGURE 12.1

Adding a reference for the Active Directory objects.

Next, add controls to the project form as shown in Figure 12.2. Configure the controls as specified in Table 12.17.

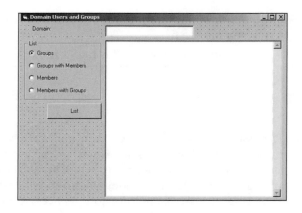

FIGURE 12.2

The application screen layout.

TABLE 12.17   Control Property Settings

Control	Property	Value
Label	Caption	Domain:
TextBox	Name	txtDomain
Frame	Caption	List
RadioButton	Name	optGroups
	Caption	Groups
RadioButton	Name	optGroupsUsers
	Caption	Groups with Members
RadioButton	Name	optMembers
	Caption	Members
RadioButton	Name	optMemGroups
	Caption	Members with Groups
Command Button	Name	cmdList
	Caption	List
TextBox	Name	txtResults
	MultiLine	True

Listing the Groups

The first method that you'll add to your application is the one to create a list of all the groups in the domain. This method binds itself to the domain using the WinNT provider. Next it adds a filter for groups, and then it enumerates the groups in the domain. To add this functionality, add the method in Listing 12.2 to your project.

LISTING 12.2   The ListGroups Method

```
Private Sub ListGroups()
'*************************************************************
'* Written By: Davis Chapman
'* Date:       February 12, 2000
'*
'* Syntax:     ListGroups
'*
'* Parameters: None
'*
'* Purpose: This subroutine builds a list of the groups in the
'*          specified domain. The list of groups is displayed
'*          in the txtResults text box.
```

continues

LISTING 12.2   Continued

```
'*****************************************************************
    Dim myDomain As Object
    Dim objGroup As IADsGroup
    Dim strMsg As String
    Dim strDomain As String

    '--- Build the domain string
    strDomain = "WinNT://" + txtDomain
    '--- Get the domain object
    Set myDomain = GetObject(strDomain)
    '--- Filter for groups
    myDomain.Filter = Array("group")
    '--- Initialize the display string
    strMsg = ""
    '--- Loop through the groups in the domain
    For Each objGroup In myDomain
        '--- Add the current group to the display string
        strMsg = strMsg + objGroup.Name + vbCrLf
    Next
    '--- Display the list of groups
    txtResults = strMsg
End Sub
```

Listing the Group Members

The next method that you'll add to your project will duplicate what you just did and extend it by adding a sublist of all the users in each group. In this method, for each group object in the domain, you'll get the IADsMembers object from the Members property, and then enumerate it for all the users in the group. To add this method to your project, add the method in Listing 12.3.

LISTING 12.3   The ListGroupUsers Method

```
Private Sub ListGroupUsers()
'*****************************************************************
'* Written By: Davis Chapman
'* Date:       February 12, 2000
'*
'* Syntax:     ListGroupUsers
'*
'* Parameters: None
'*
'* Purpose: This subroutine builds a list of the groups in the
'*          specified domain and the users in each group. The
'*          list of groups is displayed in the txtResults text
'*          box.
'*****************************************************************
```

```
        Dim myDomain As Object
        Dim objGroup As IADsGroup
        Dim objUser As IADsUser
        Dim objUsers As IADsMembers
        Dim strMsg As String
        Dim strDomain As String

        On Error Resume Next
        '--- Build the domain string
        strDomain = "WinNT://" + txtDomain
        '--- Get the domain object
        Set myDomain = GetObject(strDomain)
        '--- Filter for groups
        myDomain.Filter = Array("group")
        '--- Initialize the display string
        strMsg = ""
        '--- Loop through the groups in the domain
        For Each objGroup In myDomain
            '--- Add the current user to the display string
            strMsg = strMsg + objGroup.Name + vbCrLf
            '--- Get the collection of users in the group
            Set objUsers = objGroup.Members
            '--- Loop through the users in the group
            For Each objUser In objUsers
                '--- Add the current user to the display string
                strMsg = strMsg + vbTab + objUser.Name + vbCrLf
            Next
        Next
        '--- Display the list of users
        txtResults = strMsg
End Sub
```

NOTE

For an interesting twist on this method, change the object type of the objUser variable from IADsUser to Object. Next, change the line where you are adding each member to the list from the following:

```
    strMsg = strMsg + vbTab + objUser.Name + vbCrLf
```

to the following:

```
    strMsg = strMsg + vbTab + objUser.Name + " - " + _
        objUser.Class + vbCrLf
```

After you are able to run this application, you might be able to find a few groups that are members of other groups.

Listing the Users

The next method that you'll add to your application lists all the users in the domain. This method is almost the same as the first method that you added to this application, except that you'll be filtering for users instead of groups. To add this functionality to your application, add the method in Listing 12.4.

LISTING 12.4   The `ListUsers` Method

```
Private Sub ListUsers()
'***************************************************************
'* Written By: Davis Chapman
'* Date:        February 12, 2000
'*
'* Syntax:      ListUsers
'*
'* Parameters: None
'*
'* Purpose: This subroutine builds a list of the users in the
'*          specified domain. The list of users is displayed
'*          in the txtResults text box.
'***************************************************************
    Dim myDomain As Object
    Dim objUser As IADsUser
    Dim strMsg As String
    Dim strDomain As String

    '--- Build the domain string
    strDomain = "WinNT://" + txtDomain
    '--- Get the domain object
    Set myDomain = GetObject(strDomain)
    '--- Filter for users
    myDomain.Filter = Array("user")
    '--- Initialize the display string
    strMsg = ""
    '--- Loop through the users in the domain
    For Each objUser In myDomain
        '--- Add the current user to the display string
        strMsg = strMsg + objUser.Name + vbCrLf
    Next
    '--- Display the list of users
    txtResults = strMsg
End Sub
```

Listing the User Memberships

The next piece of functionality that you'll add is to specify to which groups a user is a member. This is basically the same as what you did to list the members of each group, binding to the `IADsMembers` object by getting the `Groups` property of each user, and then enumerating all the groups. To add this functionality to your application, add the method in Listing 12.5.

LISTING 12.5   The `ListUserGroups` Method

```
Private Sub ListUserGroups()
'*****************************************************************
'* Written By: Davis Chapman
'* Date:       February 12, 2000
'*
'* Syntax:     ListUserGroups
'*
'* Parameters: None
'*
'* Purpose: This subroutine builds a list of the users in the
'*          specified domain and the groups in which the users
'*          are members. The list of users is displayed
'*          in the txtResults text box.
'*****************************************************************
    Dim myDomain As Object
    Dim objUser As IADsUser
    Dim objGroups As IADsMembers
    Dim objGroup As IADsGroup
    Dim strMsg As String
    Dim strDomain As String

    '--- Build the domain string
    strDomain = "WinNT://" + txtDomain
    '--- Get the domain object
    Set myDomain = GetObject(strDomain)
    '--- Filter for users
    myDomain.Filter = Array("user")
    '--- Initialize the display string
    strMsg = ""
    '--- Loop through the users in the domain
    For Each objUser In myDomain
        '--- Add the current user to the display string
        strMsg = strMsg + objUser.Name + vbCrLf
        '--- Get the collection of groups the user is in
        Set objGroups = objUser.Groups
        '--- Loop through the groups the user is a member of
```

continues

LISTING 12.5   Continued

```
        For Each objGroup In objGroups
            '--- Add the current group to the display string
            strMsg = strMsg + vbTab + objGroup.Name + vbCrLf
        Next
    Next
    '--- Display the list of users
    txtResults = strMsg
End Sub
```

Calling the List Methods

Finally, you'll add the functionality to call each of the methods that you've added to your application. You'll trigger this functionality with the Click event of the cmdList button that you placed on the form. This method makes sure that the user has specified a domain to check and then uses a select case to determine which method to call based on which option button is selected. To add this functionality to your application, add the method in Listing 12.6 to the Click event of the cmdList button.

LISTING 12.6   The cmdList Click event

```
Private Sub cmdList_Click()
'****************************************************************
'* Written By: Davis Chapman
'* Date:       February 12, 2000
'*
'* Syntax:     cmdList_Click
'*
'* Parameters: None
'*
'* Purpose: This subroutine determines which option the user
'*          selected and calls the appropriate subroutine.
'****************************************************************
    '--- Make sure a domain has been specified
    If txtDomain = "" Then
        '--- No domain, tell the user
        MsgBox "You must specify a domain to list the user or group in."
        Exit Sub
    End If
    '--- Which list does the user want?
    Select Case True
        '--- A list of groups
        Case optGroups
```

```
        ListGroups
        '--- A list of groups with the users in the groups
        Case optGroupsUsers
            ListGroupUsers
        '--- A list of users
        Case optMembers
            ListUsers
        '--- A list of users with the groups they are in
        Case optMemGroups
            ListUserGroups
    End Select
End Sub
```

At this point, you can run your application and look at all the users and groups in your domain, as shown in Figure 12.3.

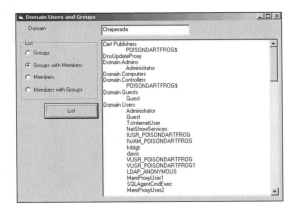

FIGURE 12.3
The domain groups with their members.

Summary

In this chapter you learned how to open an Active Directory Security Interface (ADSI) session and how to bind to a domain or other objects with one of several directory services. You also learned about several of the core object classes available within the ADSI interface. You used these object classes to build a utility application that allowed you to display all the users and groups in a particular domain.

In the next chapter, you'll be building on what you learned in this chapter, learning about more of the ADSI object classes and how to extract the security configuration of each. You'll also learn how to use ADO to search a directory for a specific object for which you don't know the path. There's quite a lot still to come, so turn the page and let's get going.

Active Directory Security and Searching

IN THIS CHAPTER

In the previous chapter, you learned the basics about working with the Active Directory Security Interface. You learned how to initialize an ADSI session and how to enumerate objects contained in collection objects. You also learned how to create a secure connection to an Active Directory server and what options to pass to maintain a secure session. You learned how to read the schema of an object to learn what properties are available, what their data types are, and how to interpret this on an unknown class type.

In this chapter, you'll dig a little deeper into some of the classes available in Active Directory. You'll learn about some of the other Active Directory classes that will extend your knowledge of the available classes. You'll also learn about the security objects within Active Directory and how you can query them to determine which groups have what permissions on a particular object. Finally, you'll learn how to use Active Data Objects (ADO) to query an Active Directory server to locate objects for which you don't know the Active Directory path.

PREREQUISITES

Before reading this chapter, you need to have a good understanding of the following:

- The basics of the Active Directory Security Interface (ADSI), Chapter 12, "Working with Active Directory Security (ADSI) and an LDAP Server"

Active Directory Object Security

Every object in the Active Directory tree has a security configuration specifying who has access to that object and what type of access that person has. This information is provided using three security class interfaces:

- IADsSecurityDescriptor
- IADsAccessControlList
- IADsAccessControlEntry

The three of these objects work together to describe the security configuration of an object. The first object, IADsSecurityDescriptor, describes various general information about the object, such as who the user and group are that own the object. The second object, IADsAccessControlList, is basically a collection of the third object, IADsAccessControlEntry, which describes the types of access that a particular group has for the object.

The `IADsSecurityDescriptor` Object Interface

The `IADsSecurityDescriptor` object interface provides basic top-level information about the ownership of a particular object. This object interface is retrieved by using the `IADs` object interface's `Get` method to retrieve the `ntSecurityDescriptor` property, as follows:

```
Dim objSecur As SecurityDescriptor

'--- Get the Security Descriptor for the object passed in
Set objSecur = obj.Get("ntSecurityDescriptor")
```

The `IADsSecurityDescriptor` exposes the properties in Table 13.1 to describe the ownership of the object.

TABLE 13.1 `IADsSecurityDescriptor` Properties

Property	Description
Revision	The revision level of the security descriptor. All Access Control Entries in the Access Control List should have the same revision level.
Owner	The owner of the object.
OwnerDefaulted	A Boolean value indicating whether the owner was derived from a default mechanism.
Group	The group to which the object belongs.
GroupDefaulted	A Boolean value indicating whether the group was derived from a default mechanism.
DiscretionaryAcl	This property is the access control list that specifies which users and groups have what access rights to the object.
DaclDefaulted	A Boolean value indicating whether the access control list was derived from a default mechanism.
SystemAcl	This property is an access control list that is used to generate audit records for the object.
SaclDefaulted	A Boolean value indicating whether the system access control list was derived from a default mechanism.

The `IADsAccessControlList` Object Interface

The `IADsAccessControlList` object interface is retrieved from the `DiscretionaryAcl` property of the `IADsSecurityDescriptor` object. This object is a collection of Access Control Entries (ACE) that describes each group that has access to the object and what kind of access that group has. The properties exposed by this object are listed in Table 13.2.

TABLE 13.2   `IADsAccessControlList` Properties

Property	Description
`AclRevision`	The revision level of the Access Control List (ACL). All Access Control Entries in the ACL should be at the same revision level.
`AceCount`	The number of ACEs in the ACL.

This object can be enumerated to retrieve all the Access Control Entries contained within it.

Adding an ACE

If you need to add an ACE to an ACL, you can use the `AddAce` method. The syntax for this method is as follows:

Syntax

```
object.AddAce(aceNewAce As IADsAccessControlEntry)
```

The one parameter (`aceNewAce`) to this method is the ACE that you need to add to the ACL.

Removing an ACE

If you need to remove an ACE from an ACL, you can use the `RemoveAce` method. The syntax for this method is as follows:

Syntax

```
object.RemoveAce(aceAce As IADsAccessControlEntry)
```

The one parameter (`aceAce`) to this method is the ACE that you need to remove from the ACL.

Copying an ACL

If you need to make a copy of an ACL, you can use the `CopyAccessList` method. The syntax for this method is as follows:

Syntax

```
object.CopyAccessList as IADsAccessControlList
```

The return value from this method is the copy Access Control List.

The `IADsAccessControlEntry` Object Interface

The final security object is the `IADsAccessControlEntry`. This is the object that specifies what kind of access a specific group has to the object. This object is retrieved by enumerating the Access Control List using a `For Each` loop. The properties exposed by this object are listed in Table 13.3.

TABLE 13.3 IADsAccessControlEntry Properties

Property	Description
AccessMask	This is a mask of access rights that have been combined using OR. The possible values for this value are listed in Table 13.4.
AceType	This is a long value that specifies what type of ACE this is— whether it is granting or revoking the rights specified in the AccessMask property. The possible values for this property are listed in Table 13.5.
AceFlags	This is a long value that specifies whether this ACE can be inherited from the owner of the ACL. The possible values for this property are listed in Table 13.6.
Flags	This is a flag that indicates whether either of the following two properties have values. If the value is 0, neither of the following two properties have values. The possible values for this property are listed in Table 13.7.
ObjectType	This property contains a string that specifies the object type. This may be a GUID of an object type.
InheritedObjectType	This property contains a string that specifies the inherited object type. This may be a GUID of an object type.
Trustee	This property contains a string specifying the user or group that has the access permissions described in this ACE.

13

ACTIVE DIRECTORY
SECURITY AND
SEARCHING

TABLE 13.4 AccessMask Rights

Right	Value	Description
ADS_RIGHT_DELETE	&H10000	The user has permission to delete the object.
ADS_RIGHT_READ_CONTROL	&H20000	The user has permission to read information from the security descriptor of the object. This does not include the right to read information from the SACL (the audit list).
ADS_RIGHT_WRITE_DAC	&H40000	The user has permission to modify the discretionary access control list.
ADS_RIGHT_WRITE_OWNER	&H80000	The user has permission to take ownership of the object.

continues

TABLE 13.4 Continued

Right	Value	Description
ADS_RIGHT_SYNCHRONIZE	&H100000	The user has permission to use the object for synchronization.
ADS_RIGHT_ACCESS_SYSTEM_ SECURITY	&H1000000	The user has permission to access the SACL in the object security descriptor.
ADS_RIGHT_GENERIC_READ	&H80000000	The user has permission to read from the security descriptor, examine the object, and to read all the object's properties.
ADS_RIGHT_GENERIC_WRITE	&H40000000	The user has permission to write to all the object's properties and to the DACL. The user has the ability to add and remove the object from the directory.
ADS_RIGHT_GENERIC_EXECUTE	&H20000000	The user has permission to list all the children of the object.
ADS_RIGHT_GENERIC_ALL	&H10000000	The user has permission to create or delete children and subtrees, read and write properties, and to add or delete the object from the directory.
ADS_RIGHT_DS_CREATE_CHILD	&H1	The user has permission to create children of the object.
ADS_RIGHT_DS_DELETE_CHILD	&H2	The user has permission to delete children of the object.
ADS_RIGHT_ACTRL_DS_LIST	&H4	The user has permission to list children of the object.
ADS_RIGHT_DS_SELF	&H8	The user has permission to modify the group membership of the object.
ADS_RIGHT_DS_READ_PROP	&H10	The user has permission to read the properties of the object.
ADS_RIGHT_DS_WRITE_PROP	&H20	The user has permission to write properties of the object.
ADS_RIGHT_DS_DELETE_TREE	&H40	The user has permission to delete all children of the object, regardless of the permissions of the children.
ADS_RIGHT_DS_LIST_OBJECT	&H80	The user has permission to list the object. If the user does not have this right, the object is hidden from the user.
ADS_RIGHT_DS_CONTROL_ACCESS	&H100	The user has permission to perform operations that are controlled by extended rights of the object.

TABLE 13.5 AceType Access Types

Type	Value	Description
ADS_ACETYPE_ACCESS_ALLOWED	0	The ACE allows the access rights specified in the AccessMask property.
ADS_ACETYPE_ACCESS_DENIED	&H1	The ACE denies the access rights specified in the AccessMask property.
ADS_ACETYPE_SYSTEM_AUDIT	&H2	The ACE specifies standard audit rights on the rights specified in the AccessMask property.
ADS_ACETYPE_ACCESS_ALLOWED_OBJECT	&H5	The ACE allows the access rights specified in the AccessMask property, and either the ObjectType property, the InheritedObjectType property, or both contain a GUID.
ADS_ACETYPE_ACCESS_DENIED_OBJECT	&H6	The ACE denies the access rights specified in the AccessMask property, and either the ObjectType property, the InheritedObjectType property, or both contain a GUID.
ADS_ACETYPE_SYSTEM_AUDIT_OBJECT	&H7	The ACE specifies standard audit rights on the rights specified in the AccessMask property, and the ObjectType or InheritedObjectType or both contain a GUID.

TABLE 13.6 AceFlags Inheritance Types

Type	Value	Description
ADS_ACEFLAG_INHERIT_ACE	&H2	Children will inherit ACE.
ADS_ACEFLAG_NO_PROPAGATE_INHERIT_ACE	&H4	ACE will not be inherited by children's children.
ADS_ACEFLAG_INHERIT_ONLY_ACE	&H8	ACE applies only to children.
ADS_ACEFLAG_INHERITED_ACE	&H10	ACE was inherited.
ADS_ACEFLAG_VALID_INHERIT_FLAGS	&H1F	Inherit flags are valid.
ADS_ACEFLAG_SUCCESSFUL_ACCESS	&H40	Generates audit messages for successful access.
ADS_ACEFLAG_FAILED_ACCESS	&H80	Generates audit messages for failed access.

13

ACTIVE DIRECTORY SECURITY AND SEARCHING

TABLE 13.7   Flags Object Types

Type	Value	Description
ADS_FLAG_OBJECT_TYPE_PRESENT	&H1	The ObjectType property has a value.
ADS_FLAG_INHERITED_OBJECT_TYPE_PRESENT	&H2	The InheritedObject Type property has a value.

Searching Active Directory

When you need to find an object within an Active Directory tree, and you don't want to traverse through the entire tree until you find the object, you can use ADO to perform SQL-like queries to find the object. This requires a strange combination of SQL syntax, and the LDAP paths, to define the search criteria and search scope, but the result is a standard ADO recordset.

LDAP Scope Syntax

First, when you are using ADO to search an Active Directory tree, you use the LDAP path in the place of the database table to define the scope of where you are searching from. This is much like specifying a specific directory from which you want to perform a search for a file. The directory you specify is the starting point, and the search is performed on that directory and on all the subdirectories under it. The search doesn't look at any directories above where you specified.

Specifying the LDAP path works in much the same way. You specify an LDAP path for the starting point in the Active Directory tree, and the search is performed from that point down. For instance, the following path:

```
LDAP://DC=microsoft,DC=com
```

performs the search on the entire Microsoft.com directory tree. However, the following path:

```
LDAP://OU=Sales,DC=Dallas,DC=Microsoft,DC=com
```

limits the search to the sales organizational unit in the Dallas.Microsoft.com domain.

Building the SQL Syntax

When you build the SQL query to perform the search, the LDAP path is used in place of the table name in the query. The fields that you want to return are just those that you need to identify and retrieve the desired object from the Active Directory. This means that you'll probably want to return the Active Directory Path (AdsPath) and the common name (cn) of the object. This will provide you with the information that you need.

For the Where clause of the SQL query, you'll start working with some object properties that you are unfamiliar with to this point. The first of these properties are the objectClass and objectCategory properties. These are basically the same as the object class property that you are familiar with, only with a couple of twists. First, the objectClass property has multiple values, listing not only the primary class of the object, but also the other classes from which the object is derived. The objectCategory property has a single value and is the primary category for the object. As a result of the differences between these two properties, searching on the objectClass property will be slow and inefficient, whereas searching on the objectCategory property will be much faster and more efficient.

Next, when you are searching off of object properties, you'll probably want to examine the properties listed in the object schema to get the property names to be used. The object properties used in the SQL queries are not necessarily given the same names as the same properties are exposed with in their ADSI object interfaces. For instance, with the user object, the user's last name property is exposed as LastName, whereas the actual class property is sn (for surname). For example, to search the Chaperada.com domain for the users with the last name of Chapman, you'd build a query like the following:

```
SELECT AdsPath, cn
FROM 'LDAP://DC=chaperada,DC=com'
WHERE objectCategory='user'
AND sn='Chapman'
```

Performing SQL Queries

To actually perform the SQL queries against an Active Directory, you need to perform a few steps. First, you need to make sure that you have included a reference to the ADO type library (msadoXX.dll) in your project. The current ADO type library shipping with Windows 2000 is "Microsoft ActiveX Data Objects Library 2.5." Next, you need to create a Connection object and set the provider to ADsDSOObject. Third, you need to create a Command object and set its active connection to the Connection object. Then you need to set the CommandText property to the SQL query. Finally, you need to call the Execute method on the Command object to create the recordset. This might look something like the following:

```
Dim Con As New Connection
Dim Cmd As New Command
Dim Rs As Recordset

'--- Set the provider to Active Directory Search Object
Con.Provider = "AdsDSOObject"
'--- Open the connection
Con.Open "LDAP:"
'--- Set the active connection
Set Cmd.ActiveConnection = Con
'--- Set the SQL query to execute
```

13

```
Cmd.CommandText = "SELECT AdsPath, cn " + _
    "FROM 'LDAP://DC=chaperada,DC=com' " + _
    "WHERE objectCategory='user' AND sn='Chapman'"
'--- Run the query
Set Rs = Cmd.Execute
'--- While not past the last row in the recordset...
While Not Rs.EOF
'--- So on and so forth
```

> **NOTE**
>
> Active Directory queries using ADO cannot be updated at this time. If you need to update some of the properties of the objects that you retrieve in the ADO query, you'll need to use the standard LDAP retrieval methods to retrieve the actual object to be updated.

Examining Active Directory Objects

To finish this chapter, you'll build a second ADSI application, this time using the LDAP provider. This utility starts at the top of an Active Directory tree and fills in a tree-view control with all the objects in the tree. Next, as the user selects each individual object in the tree, the utility retrieves information about the object, including its security, and displays it for the user.

Starting the Project

To start this application, start a new standard EXE project in Visual Basic and include a reference to the Active DS Type library, as you did in Figure 12.1. Next, add the Microsoft Common Controls to the project, as shown in Figure 13.1, so that you'll be able to use the Tree View control.

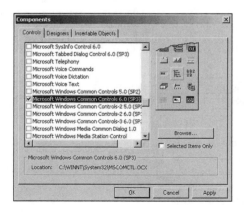

FIGURE 13.1

Adding the Windows Common Controls to the project.

Next, add controls to the project form as shown in Figure 13.2. Configure the controls as specified in Table 13.8.

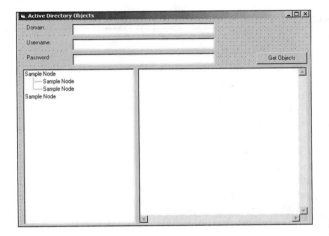

FIGURE 13.2

The application screen layout.

TABLE 13.8 Control Property Settings

Control	Property	Value
Label	Caption	Domain:
TextBox	Name	txtDomain
Label	Caption	Username:
TextBox	Name	txtUsername
Label	Caption	Password:
TextBox	Name	txtPassword
	PasswordChar	*
Command Button	Name	cmdGetObjs
	Caption	Get Objects
TreeView	Name	tvNodes
TextBox	Name	txtDetails
	MultiLine	True

Now it's time to turn your attention to the code for this application. Before any real code can be written, you need to define all the constants that you've seen in this and the previous chapter so that you can use them in the code. To do this, add the declarations in Listing 13.1 to the declaration section of the code behind the form.

LISTING 13.1   Constant Declarations

```
Option Explicit

'--- ADS_RIGHTS_ENUM
Const ADS_RIGHT_DELETE = &H10000
Const ADS_RIGHT_READ_CONTROL = &H20000
Const ADS_RIGHT_WRITE_DAC = &H40000
Const ADS_RIGHT_WRITE_OWNER = &H80000
Const ADS_RIGHT_SYNCHRONIZE = &H100000
Const ADS_RIGHT_ACCESS_SYSTEM_SECURITY = &H1000000
Const ADS_RIGHT_GENERIC_READ = &H80000000
Const ADS_RIGHT_GENERIC_WRITE = &H40000000
Const ADS_RIGHT_GENERIC_EXECUTE = &H20000000
Const ADS_RIGHT_GENERIC_ALL = &H10000000
Const ADS_RIGHT_DS_CREATE_CHILD = &H1
Const ADS_RIGHT_DS_DELETE_CHILD = &H2
Const ADS_RIGHT_ACTRL_DS_LIST = &H4
Const ADS_RIGHT_DS_SELF = &H8
Const ADS_RIGHT_DS_READ_PROP = &H10
Const ADS_RIGHT_DS_WRITE_PROP = &H20
Const ADS_RIGHT_DS_DELETE_TREE = &H40
Const ADS_RIGHT_DS_LIST_OBJECT = &H80
Const ADS_RIGHT_DS_CONTROL_ACCESS = &H100

'--- ADS_ACETYPE_ENUM
Const ADS_ACETYPE_ACCESS_ALLOWED = 0
Const ADS_ACETYPE_ACCESS_DENIED = &H1
Const ADS_ACETYPE_SYSTEM_AUDIT = &H2
Const ADS_ACETYPE_ACCESS_ALLOWED_OBJECT = &H5
Const ADS_ACETYPE_ACCESS_DENIED_OBJECT = &H6
Const ADS_ACETYPE_SYSTEM_AUDIT_OBJECT = &H7

'--- ADS_ACEFLAG_ENUM
Const ADS_ACEFLAG_INHERIT_ACE = &H2
Const ADS_ACEFLAG_NO_PROPAGATE_INHERIT_ACE = &H4
Const ADS_ACEFLAG_INHERIT_ONLY_ACE = &H8
Const ADS_ACEFLAG_INHERITED_ACE = &H10
Const ADS_ACEFLAG_VALID_INHERIT_FLAGS = &H1F
Const ADS_ACEFLAG_SUCCESSFUL_ACCESS = &H40
Const ADS_ACEFLAG_FAILED_ACCESS = &H80

'--- ADS_FLAGTYPE_ENUM
```

```
Const ADS_FLAG_OBJECT_TYPE_PRESENT = &H1
Const ADS_FLAG_INHERITED_OBJECT_TYPE_PRESENT = &H2


'--- ADS_AUTHENTICATION_ENUM
Const ADS_SECURE_AUTHENTICATION = &H1
Const ADS_USE_ENCRYPTION = &H2
Const ADS_USE_SSL = &H2
Const ADS_READONLY_SERVER = &H4
Const ADS_PROMPT_CREDENTIALS = &H8
Const ADS_NO_AUTHENTICATION = &H10
Const ADS_FAST_BIND = &H20
Const ADS_USE_SIGNING = &H40
Const ADS_USE_SEALING = &H80
```

Traversing the Active Directory Tree

Now you'll start creating the code that will traverse the Active Directory tree and fill in the Tree View control. You'll need to use the username and password that the user entered to make a secure connection to the server, using the IADsOpenDSObject. You'll also need to convert the domain as the user typed it into the syntax that the LDAP provider will expect. Finally, after you've connected and retrieved the base object, add it to the Tree View and then call an as yet undefined method to populate the Tree View with the rest of the objects. To add this code to your application, add the method in Listing 13.2 to the form in your application.

13

ACTIVE DIRECTORY
SECURITY AND
SEARCHING

LISTING 13.2   The GetUnits Method

```
Private Sub GetUnits()
'*******************************************************
'* Written By: Davis Chapman
'* Date:       February 12, 2000
'*
'* Syntax:     GetUnits
'*
'* Parameters: None
'*
'* Purpose: This subroutine opens a security context to the
'*          root of the domain specified by the user. It uses
'*          this as the starting point for the tree view of
'*          the domain.
'*******************************************************
    Dim openDS As IADsOpenDSObject
    Dim obj As IADs
    Dim strName As String
```

continues

LISTING 13.2 Continued

```
Dim ndNewNode As Node
Dim strDomain As String
Dim lDotPos As Long
Dim lLastDotPos As Long
Dim strOrgDomain As String
Dim lStringLen As Long

'--- Build the object LDAP name for the domain
If (InStr(1, txtDomain, ".", vbTextCompare)> 0) Then
    strOrgDomain = txtDomain
     '---Cache the length of the dot domain string
    lStringLen = Len(strOrgDomain)

    '---Loop through the string, extracting each sub-domain
    '---and finally the top domain
    Do
        '--- Get the position of the next . in the string
        lDotPos = InStr(lLastDotPos + 1, strOrgDomain, ".")
        '--- If there are no more dots, set the dot position to the
        '--- string length plus 1
        If lDotPos = 0 Then lDotPos = lStringLen + 1
        '--- If there is already text in the LDAP string, we know
        '--- we need a comma separator
        If Len(strDomain)> 0 Then strDomain = strDomain & ","
        '--- Append the domain element to the LDAP domain path
        strDomain = strDomain & "DC=" & Mid$(strOrgDomain, _
                lLastDotPos + 1, lDotPos - lLastDotPos - 1)
        '---Remember our position in the string
        lLastDotPos = lDotPos
    Loop While lDotPos < lStringLen
    strDomain = "LDAP://" & strDomain
Else
    strDomain = "LDAP://" + txtDomain
End If
'--- Open the LDAP interface
Set openDS = GetObject("LDAP:")
'--- Open the security context using secure authentication
Set obj = openDS.OpenDSObject(strDomain, _
                txtUsername, txtPassword, ADS_SECURE_AUTHENTICATION)
'--- Strip the unneeded portion from the domain name
strName = obj.Name
If (InStr(1, strName, "=", vbTextCompare)> 0) Then
    strName = Mid(strName, (InStr(1, strName, "=", _
            vbTextCompare) + 1))
```

```
      End If
      '--- Clear the tree from any previous objects
      tvNodes.Nodes.Clear
      '--- Add the domain name as the root node in the tree view
      Set ndNewNode = tvNodes.Nodes.Add(, , obj.ADsPath, strName)
      '--- Add all the children nodes to the tree view
      ListChildren obj
      '--- Clean up
      Set openDS = Nothing
End Sub
```

Now that you've got a connection to the Active Directory server, you can create a recursive method to traverse through the Active Directory tree, adding all the objects that you can find to the Tree View control. You'll want to try and enumerate each object, adding the objects found to the Tree View and then calling this method again with each of the child objects as the root object to get the next level of objects. To add this functionality, add the `ListChildren` method in Listing 13.3 to the project.

LISTING 13.3   The `ListChildren` Method

```
Private Sub ListChildren(obj As IADs)
'***************************************************************
'* Written By: Davis Chapman
'* Date:       February 12, 2000
'*
'* Syntax:     ListChildren(obj)
'*
'* Parameters: obj As IADs
'*
'* Purpose: This subroutine recursively adds all the children
'*          nodes to the tree view.
'***************************************************************
    Dim objCont As IADsContainer
    Dim objChild As IADs
    Dim strName As String
    Dim strParent As String
    Dim ndNewNode As Node

    '--- Hold onto the name of the parent node
    strParent = obj.ADsPath
    '--- Get the IADsContainer interface for the object passed in
    Set objCont = obj
    '--- If an error occurred, then there are no children
    If Err = 0 Then
```

continues

LISTING 13.3   Continued

```
        '--- Loop through all the children of the current node
        For Each objChild In objCont
            '--- Get the child's name and strip off the prefix
            strName = objChild.Name
            If (InStr(1, strName, "=", vbTextCompare)> 0) Then
                strName = Mid(strName, (InStr(1, strName, "=", _
                    vbTextCompare) + 1))
            End If
            '--- Add the child as a new node to the tree view
            Set ndNewNode = tvNodes.Nodes.Add(strParent, tvwChild, _
                objChild.ADsPath, strName)
            '--- Add all the children nodes to the tree view
            ListChildren objChild
        Next
    End If
End Sub
```

> **TIP**
>
> You've probably noticed that you are using the Active Directory path as the key for each node in the Tree View control. This will be useful when retrieving the object information to display for the user. By retrieving the Active Directory path from the key, it can be used to directly retrieve the selected object, as you'll see later.

Now that you have the functionality to go through and populate the Tree View with all the objects in the Active Directory tree, you'll need to be able to trigger this process. You'll do this from the Click event of the cmdGetObjs button, as in Listing 13.4.

LISTING 13.4   The cmdGetObjs Click Event

```
Private Sub cmdGetObjs_Click()
'************************************************************
'* Written By: Davis Chapman
'* Date:        February 12, 2000
'*
'* Syntax:      cmdGetObjs_Click
'*
'* Parameters: None
'*
'* Purpose: This subroutine loads the tree view control with
'*          the ADS objects in the domain specified by the user.
```

```
'****************************************************************
    '--- Load the tree view control
    GetUnits
End Sub
```

Examining Users and Groups

The next set of functionality that you need to add to your application is the capability to examine each object and display information about that object for the user. You'll start with a couple
of known object classes—users and groups. For the user, list the class type, the user's name,
and various organizational information about the user. After you've listed all the readily available properties on the user object, call a currently nonexistent function, GetSecurity, to get
the object's security configuration. To add this functionality to your project, add the
GetUserDetails method in Listing 13.5 to your form.

LISTING 13.5   The GetUserDetails Method

```
Private Sub GetUserDetails(obj As IADs)
'****************************************************************
'* Written By: Davis Chapman
'* Date:        February 12, 2000
'*
'* Syntax:       GetUserDetails(obj)
'*
'* Parameters: obj As IADs
'*
'* Purpose: This method extracts and formats all the details
'*          about the user object that is passed in.
'****************************************************************
    Dim objUser As IADsUser
    Dim strMsg As String
    Dim strName As String

    On Error Resume Next
    '--- Get the IADsUser interface for the object
    Set objUser = obj
    '--- Extract the object name from the name string
    strName = objUser.Name
    If (InStr(1, strName, "=", vbTextCompare)> 0) Then
        strName = Mid(strName, (InStr(1, strName, "=", _
                vbTextCompare) + 1))
    End If
```

continues

LISTING 13.5   Continued

```
'--- Specify the object type
strMsg = "Object Type: " + objUser.Class + vbCrLf
'--- Specify the user's name
strMsg = strMsg + "Name: " + strName + vbCrLf
'--- Specify the user's full name
strMsg = strMsg + "Full Name: " + objUser.FullName + vbCrLf
'--- Specify the user's description
strMsg = strMsg + "Description: " + objUser.Description + vbCrLf
'--- Specify the user's department
strMsg = strMsg + "Department: " + objUser.Department + vbCrLf
'--- Specify the user's division
strMsg = strMsg + "Division: " + objUser.Division + vbCrLf
'--- Specify the user's email address
strMsg = strMsg + "EMail Address: " + objUser.EmailAddress + vbCrLf
'--- Specify the user's home directory
strMsg = strMsg + "Home Directory: " + objUser.HomeDirectory + vbCrLf
'--- Specify the user's manager
strMsg = strMsg + "Manager: " + objUser.Manager + vbCrLf
'--- Specify the user's password expiration date
strMsg = strMsg + "Password Expires: " + _
        CStr(objUser.PasswordExpirationDate) + vbCrLf
'--- Specify the user's account expiration date
strMsg = strMsg + "Account Expires: " + _
        CStr(objUser.AccountExpirationDate) + vbCrLf
'--- Specify the object's security descriptor
strMsg = strMsg + GetSecurity(objUser)
'--- Display the user details
txtDetails = strMsg
End Sub
```

> **NOTE**
>
> It is important to use the "On Error Resume Next" method of error handling when accessing object properties with the ADSI interface. If a particular property, like FullName, doesn't have a value, then that property is not included in the object cache and an error occurs when you try to access it.

Next, you'll do a similar thing with group objects as you did with users. You'll give the object class, name, and description. Next, you'll list all the members of the group. Finally, you'll call the GetSecurity function to get the object's security configuration information. To add this functionality to your application, add the GetGroupDetails method in Listing 13.6 to your application.

LISTING 13.6   The GetGroupDetails Method

```
Private Sub GetGroupDetails(obj As IADs)
'***************************************************************
'* Written By: Davis Chapman
'* Date:        February 12, 2000
'*
'* Syntax:      GetGroupDetails(obj)
'*
'* Parameters: obj As IADs
'*
'* Purpose: This method extracts and formats all the details
'*          about the group object that is passed in.
'***************************************************************
    Dim objGroup As IADsGroup
    Dim strMsg As String
    Dim strName As String
    Dim objMem As IADsMembers
    Dim objM As Object

    '--- Get the IADsGroup interface for the object
    Set objGroup = obj
    '--- Extract the object name from the name string
    strName = objGroup.Name
    If (InStr(1, strName, "=", vbTextCompare)> 0) Then
        strName = Mid(strName, (InStr(1, strName, "=", _
            vbTextCompare) + 1))
    End If
    '--- Specify the object type
    strMsg = "Object Type: " + objGroup.Class + vbCrLf
    '--- Specify the object's name
    strMsg = strMsg + "Name: " + strName + vbCrLf
    '--- Specify the object's description
    strMsg = strMsg + "Description: " + objGroup.Description + vbCrLf
    '--- Get the IADsMembers interface for the object
    Set objMem = objGroup.Members
    '--- Get the number of members in the group
    If objMem.Count> 0 Then
        '--- If there are members, list them
        strMsg = strMsg + "Members:" + vbCrLf
        '--- Loop through all the members in the group
        For Each objM In objMem
            '--- Extract the member name from the name string
            strName = objM.Name
            If (InStr(1, strName, "=", vbTextCompare)> 0) Then
                strName = Mid(strName, (InStr(1, strName, "=", _
```

13

ACTIVE DIRECTORY
SECURITY AND
SEARCHING

continues

LISTING 13.6   Continued

```
                          vbTextCompare) + 1))
            End If
            '--- Specify the member's name
            strMsg = strMsg + vbTab + strName + vbCrLf
        Next
    End If
    '--- Specify the object's security descriptor
    strMsg = strMsg + GetSecurity(objGroup)
    '--- Display the user details
    txtDetails = strMsg
End Sub
```

Examining Collections

Next, you'll display the properties of any containers that you find in the Active Directory tree. You'll basically do the same with this object as you did with the group objects. You'll display the basic information about the object and then list the members contained within the object, using the `GetContainerMembers` function (which has not been created yet), and then list the security configuration of this object using the `GetSecurity` function (which also has still not been created). To add this functionality, add the `GetContainerDetails` method in Listing 13.7 to your application.

LISTING 13.7   The `GetContainerDetails` Method

```
Private Sub GetContainerDetails(obj As IADs)
'***************************************************************
'* Written By: Davis Chapman
'* Date:       February 12, 2000
'*
'* Syntax:     GetContainerDetails(obj)
'*
'* Parameters: obj As IADs
'*
'* Purpose: This method extracts and formats all the details
'*          about the container object that is passed in.
'***************************************************************
    Dim objGroup As IADsContainer
    Dim strMsg As String
    Dim strName As String
    Dim objMem As Object

    '--- Get the IADsContainer interface for the object
    Set objGroup = obj
    strMsg = ""
```

```
    '--- Extract the object name from the name string
    strName = obj.Name
    If (InStr(1, strName, "=", vbTextCompare)> 0) Then
        strName = Mid(strName, (InStr(1, strName, "=", _
            vbTextCompare) + 1))
    End If
    '--- Specify the object type
    strMsg = "Object Type: " + obj.Class + vbCrLf
    '--- Specify the object's name
    strMsg = strMsg + "Name: " + strName + vbCrLf
    '--- Specify the container's hints
    strMsg = strMsg + "Hints: " + objGroup.Hints + vbCrLf
    '--- Get the container's members
    strMsg = strMsg + GetContainerMembers(obj)
    '--- Specify the object's security descriptor
    strMsg = strMsg + GetSecurity(obj)
    '--- Display the user details
    txtDetails = strMsg
End Sub
```

For the GetContainerMembers function, you'll loop through all the members in the container, listing the name of each object found. To add this functionality, add the method in Listing 13.8 to your application.

LISTING 13.8   The GetContainerMembers Function

```
Private Function GetContainerMembers(obj As IADs) As String
'**************************************************************
'* Written By: Davis Chapman
'* Date:        February 12, 2000
'*
'* Syntax:      GetContainerMembers(obj)
'*
'* Parameters: obj As IADs
'*
'* Purpose: This method extracts and formats the names of the
'*          objects in the container object that is passed in.
'**************************************************************
    Dim objGroup As IADsContainer
    Dim strMsg As String
    Dim strName As String
    Dim objMem As Object

    '--- Get the IADsContainer interface for the object
    Set objGroup = obj
```

continues

13

ACTIVE DIRECTORY
SECURITY AND
SEARCHING

LISTING 13.8   Continued

```
    '--- Initialize the return string
    strMsg = ""
    '--- There are members
    strMsg = "Members:" + vbCrLf
    '--- Loop through each member in the container
    For Each objMem In objGroup
        '--- Extract the object name from the name string
        strName = objMem.Name
        If (InStr(1, strName, "=", vbTextCompare)> 0) Then
            strName = Mid(strName, (InStr(1, strName, "=", _
                vbTextCompare) + 1))
        End If
        '--- Specify the object's name
        strMsg = strMsg + vbTab + strName + vbCrLf
    Next
    '--- Return the list of members
    GetContainerMembers = strMsg
End Function
```

Examining Miscellaneous Objects

The last object type that you'll add functionality to display information about is a general object type. This is a default object type for any object in the tree that doesn't fall into any of the previous object types (users, groups, and containers). For this, you'll list the object type and name, and then call another method to extract information from the object schema for properties to display. To add this functionality, add the method in Listing 13.9 to your application.

LISTING 13.9   The GetObjDetails Method

```
Private Sub GetObjDetails(obj As IADs)
'**************************************************************
'* Written By: Davis Chapman
'* Date:       February 12, 2000
'*
'* Syntax:     GetObjDetails(obj)
'*
'* Parameters: obj As IADs
'*
'* Purpose: This method extracts and formats all the details
'*          about the object that is passed in.
'**************************************************************
    Dim strMsg As String
```

```
    Dim strName As String

    '--- Extract the object name from the name string
    strName = obj.Name
    If (InStr(1, strName, "=", vbTextCompare)> 0) Then
        strName = Mid(strName, (InStr(1, strName, "=", _
                vbTextCompare) + 1))
    End If
    '--- Specify the object type
    strMsg = "Object Type: " + obj.Class + vbCrLf
    '--- Specify the object's name
    strMsg = strMsg + "Name: " + strName + vbCrLf
    '--- Get the schema properties
    strMsg = strMsg + GetSchemaAttribs(obj)
    '--- Specify the object's security descriptor
    strMsg = strMsg + GetSecurity(obj)
    '--- Display the user details
    txtDetails = strMsg
End Sub
```

For extracting properties from the schema to display, you'll want to get the object schema, and then loop through the mandatory and then the optional properties, getting the property value from the object using the Get method. To add this functionality to your application, add the GetSchemaAttribs function in Listing 13.10 to your application.

LISTING 13.10   The GetSchemaAttribs Function

```
Private Function GetSchemaAttribs(obj As IADs) As String
'****************************************************************
'* Written By: Davis Chapman
'* Date:       February 12, 2000
'*
'* Syntax:     GetSchemaAttribs(obj)
'*
'* Parameters: obj As IADs
'*
'* Purpose: This function gets the object's schema and loops
'*          through the lists of mandatory and optional
'*          properties to add to the displayed list.
'****************************************************************
    Dim objSchema As IADsClass
    Dim objMem As Object
    Dim strMsg As String
    Dim lTotalNbr As Long
```

13

ACTIVE DIRECTORY
SECURITY AND
SEARCHING

continues

LISTING 13.10   Continued

```
      Dim lCurNbr As Long

      On Error Resume Next
      '--- Get the object's schema
      Set objSchema = GetObject(obj.Schema)
      '--- Get the number of mandatory properties
      lTotalNbr = UBound(objSchema.MandatoryProperties)
      '--- Initialize the return string
      strMsg = "Mandatory Properties" + vbCrLf
      '--- Loop through the mandatory properties
      For lCurNbr = 0 To lTotalNbr
          '--- Add the property to the return string
          strMsg = strMsg & vbTab & _
              objSchema.MandatoryProperties(lCurNbr) & ": " & _
              obj.Get(objSchema.MandatoryProperties(lCurNbr)) & vbCrLf
      Next
      '--- Get the number of optional properties
      lTotalNbr = UBound(objSchema.OptionalProperties)
      '--- Add the section header to the return string
      strMsg = strMsg + "Optional Properties" + vbCrLf
      '--- Loop through the optional properties
      For lCurNbr = 0 To lTotalNbr
          '--- Add the property to the return string
          strMsg = strMsg & vbTab & _
              objSchema.OptionalProperties(lCurNbr) & ": " & _
              obj.Get(objSchema.OptionalProperties(lCurNbr)) & vbCrLf
      Next
      '--- Return the schema properties
      GetSchemaAttribs = strMsg
End Function
```

Examining Object Security

Now it's time to turn your attention to the GetSecurity function that you've been using, but haven't written yet. This function needs to retrieve the object's security descriptor. Next, it needs to display the object's owner and group information. Finally, it has to go through the Access Control List, displaying the information from each of the Access Control Entries about groups and what permissions they each have to the object. To add this functionality, add the GetSecurity function in Listing 13.11 to your project.

LISTING 13.11   The GetSecurity Function

```
Private Function GetSecurity(obj As IADs) As String
'****************************************************************
'* Written By: Davis Chapman
'* Date:       February 12, 2000
'*
'* Syntax:     GetSecurity(obj)
'*
'* Parameters: obj As IADs
'*
'* Purpose: This function builds a string that describes the
'*          security descriptor of the object passed in. It
'*          specifies the owner and group of the object and
'*          includes all the entries in the object's Access
'*          Control List.
'****************************************************************
    Dim objSecur As SecurityDescriptor
    Dim objDacl As AccessControlList
    Dim objDace As AccessControlEntry
    Dim strRtn As String
    Dim lAccMask As Long

    '--- Get the Security Descriptor for the object passed in
    Set objSecur = obj.Get("ntSecurityDescriptor")
    '--- Initialize the return string
    strRtn = vbCrLf + "Security:" + vbCrLf
    '--- Add the owner to the return string
    strRtn = strRtn + vbTab + "Owner: " + objSecur.Owner + vbCrLf
    '--- Add the group to the return string
    strRtn = strRtn + vbTab + "Group: " + objSecur.Group + vbCrLf
    '--- Get the Access Control List from the Security Descriptor
    Set objDacl = objSecur.DiscretionaryAcl
    '--- Get the number of Access Control Entries
    '--- in the Access Control List
    strRtn = strRtn + vbTab + "ACE Count: " + CStr(objDacl.AceCount) + _
            vbCrLf
    '--- Loop through the Access Control Entries
    For Each objDace In objDacl
        '--- Add the ACE Trustee to the return string
        strRtn = strRtn + vbTab + "Trustee: " + objDace.Trustee + vbCrLf
        '--- Add the access rights to the return string
        strRtn = strRtn + vbTab + vbTab + "Access Rights: " + vbCrLf
        strRtn = strRtn + GetAccessRights(objDace.AccessMask)
```

13

ACTIVE DIRECTORY
SECURITY AND
SEARCHING

continues

LISTING 13.11   Continued

```
                '--- Add the Ace Flags to the return string
                If (objDace.AceFlags> 0) Then
                    strRtn = strRtn + vbTab + vbTab + "Ace Flags: " + vbCrLf
                    strRtn = strRtn + GetAccessFlags(objDace.AceFlags)
                End If
                '--- Add the Ace Type to the return string
                strRtn = strRtn + vbTab + vbTab + "Ace Type: " + _
                    GetAccessType(objDace.AceType)
                '--- If there is an object type included,
                '--- add it to the return string
                If ((objDace.Flags And ADS_FLAG_OBJECT_TYPE_PRESENT)> 0) Then _
                    strRtn = strRtn + vbTab + vbTab + "Object Type: " + _
                        objDace.ObjectType + vbCrLf
                '--- If there is an inherited object type included, add it
                '--- to the return string
                If ((objDace.Flags And ADS_FLAG_INHERITED_OBJECT_TYPE_PRESENT) _
                        > 0) Then strRtn = strRtn + vbTab + vbTab + _
                        "Inherited Object Type: " _
                        + objDace.InheritedObjectType + vbCrLf
        Next
        '--- Return the security descriptor string
        GetSecurity = strRtn
End Function
```

In the previous function, you called three functions that don't exist, GetAccessRights, GetAccessType, and GetAccessFlags. These functions decode the access rights, masks, types, and other properties of the Access Control Entries. The first of these, GetAccessRights, uses the AND operator to see which of the access rights the group has to the object. This function puts these rights into understandable messages. To add this function to your application, add the function in Listing 13.12 to the application.

LISTING 13.12   The GetAccessRights Function

```
Private Function GetAccessRights(lAccMask As Long) As String
'************************************************************
'* Written By: Davis Chapman
'* Date:        February 12, 2000
'*
'* Syntax:      GetAccessRights(lAccMask)
'*
'* Parameters: lAccMask As Long
'*
'* Purpose: This function builds a list of the access rights
```

```
'*          that are included in an Access Control Entry.
'*****************************************************************
    Dim strRtn As String

    '--- Initialize the return string
    strRtn = ""
    '--- Is the ADS_RIGHT_DELETE right included?
    If ((lAccMask And ADS_RIGHT_DELETE)> 0) Then _
        strRtn = strRtn + vbTab + vbTab + vbTab + "Delete" + vbCrLf
    '--- Is the ADS_RIGHT_READ_CONTROL right included?
    If ((lAccMask And ADS_RIGHT_READ_CONTROL)> 0) Then _
        strRtn = strRtn + vbTab + vbTab + vbTab + _
            "Read Security Descriptor" + vbCrLf
    '--- Is the ADS_RIGHT_WRITE_DAC right included?
    If ((lAccMask And ADS_RIGHT_WRITE_DAC)> 0) Then _
        strRtn = strRtn + vbTab + vbTab + vbTab + "Modify ACL" + vbCrLf
    '--- Is the ADS_RIGHT_WRITE_OWNER right included?
    If ((lAccMask And ADS_RIGHT_WRITE_OWNER)> 0) Then _
        strRtn = strRtn + vbTab + vbTab + vbTab + "Assume Ownership" + _
                vbCrLf
    '--- Is the ADS_RIGHT_SYNCHRONIZE right included?
    If ((lAccMask And ADS_RIGHT_SYNCHRONIZE)> 0) Then _
        strRtn = strRtn + vbTab + vbTab + vbTab + _
            "Use for Synchronization" + vbCrLf
    '--- Is the ADS_RIGHT_ACCESS_SYSTEM_SECURITY right included?
    If ((lAccMask And ADS_RIGHT_ACCESS_SYSTEM_SECURITY)> 0) Then _
        strRtn = strRtn + vbTab + vbTab + vbTab + _
            "Can Get or Set System ACL" + vbCrLf
    '--- Is the ADS_RIGHT_GENERIC_READ right included?
    If ((lAccMask And ADS_RIGHT_GENERIC_READ)> 0) Then _
        strRtn = strRtn + vbTab + vbTab + vbTab + "Read" + vbCrLf
    '--- Is the ADS_RIGHT_GENERIC_WRITE right included?
    If ((lAccMask And ADS_RIGHT_GENERIC_WRITE)> 0) Then _
        strRtn = strRtn + vbTab + vbTab + vbTab + "Write" + vbCrLf
    '--- Is the ADS_RIGHT_GENERIC_EXECUTE right included?
    If ((lAccMask And ADS_RIGHT_GENERIC_EXECUTE)> 0) Then _
        strRtn = strRtn + vbTab + vbTab + vbTab + "List Children" + _
            vbCrLf
    '--- Is the ADS_RIGHT_GENERIC_ALL right included?
    If ((lAccMask And ADS_RIGHT_GENERIC_ALL)> 0) Then _
        strRtn = strRtn + vbTab + vbTab + vbTab + "All" + vbCrLf
    '--- Is the ADS_RIGHT_DS_CREATE_CHILD right included?
    If ((lAccMask And ADS_RIGHT_DS_CREATE_CHILD)> 0) Then _
        strRtn = strRtn + vbTab + vbTab + vbTab + "Create Children" + _
            vbCrLf
```

13

ACTIVE DIRECTORY
SECURITY AND
SEARCHING

continues

LISTING 13.12   Continued

```
        '--- Is the ADS_RIGHT_DS_DELETE_CHILD right included?
        If ((lAccMask And ADS_RIGHT_DS_DELETE_CHILD)> 0) Then _
            strRtn = strRtn + vbTab + vbTab + vbTab + "Delete Children" + _
                vbCrLf
        '--- Is the ADS_RIGHT_ACTRL_DS_LIST right included?
        If ((lAccMask And ADS_RIGHT_ACTRL_DS_LIST)> 0) Then _
            strRtn = strRtn + vbTab + vbTab + vbTab + "List Children" + _
                vbCrLf
        '--- Is the ADS_RIGHT_DS_SELF right included?
        If ((lAccMask And ADS_RIGHT_DS_SELF)> 0) Then _
            strRtn = strRtn + vbTab + vbTab + vbTab + _
                "Modify Group Membership" + vbCrLf
        '--- Is the ADS_RIGHT_DS_READ_PROP right included?
        If ((lAccMask And ADS_RIGHT_DS_READ_PROP)> 0) Then _
            strRtn = strRtn + vbTab + vbTab + vbTab + "Read Properties" + _
                vbCrLf
        '--- Is the ADS_RIGHT_DS_WRITE_PROP right included?
        If ((lAccMask And ADS_RIGHT_DS_WRITE_PROP)> 0) Then _
            strRtn = strRtn + vbTab + vbTab + vbTab + "Write Properties" + _
                vbCrLf
        '--- Is the ADS_RIGHT_DS_DELETE_TREE right included?
        If ((lAccMask And ADS_RIGHT_DS_DELETE_TREE)> 0) Then _
            strRtn = strRtn + vbTab + vbTab + vbTab + _
                "Delete All Children" + vbCrLf
        '--- Is the ADS_RIGHT_DS_LIST_OBJECT right included?
        If ((lAccMask And ADS_RIGHT_DS_LIST_OBJECT)> 0) Then _
            strRtn = strRtn + vbTab + vbTab + vbTab + "List Object" + vbCrLf
        '--- Is the ADS_RIGHT_DS_CONTROL_ACCESS right included?
        If ((lAccMask And ADS_RIGHT_DS_CONTROL_ACCESS)> 0) Then _
            strRtn = strRtn + vbTab + vbTab + vbTab + _
                "Extended Access Rights" + vbCrLf
    '--- Return the rights list
    GetAccessRights = strRtn
End Function
```

The next of these functions, GetAccessType, determines whether the ACE is granting the rights or revoking them. This function is able to use a standard Select Case structure to determine which type of ACE this is and to return an understandable message. To add this function, add the code in Listing 13.13 to your application.

LISTING 13.13   The GetAccessType Function

```
Private Function GetAccessType(lAceType As Long) As String
'**************************************************************
```

```
'* Written By: Davis Chapman
'* Date:       February 12, 2000
'*
'* Syntax:     GetAccessType(lAceType)
'*
'* Parameters: lAceType As Long
'*
'* Purpose: This function builds a list of the access type
'*          of an Access Control Entry.
'*************************************************************
    Dim strRtn As String

    '--- Initialize the return string
    strRtn = ""
    '--- Determine which type of ACE this is
    Select Case lAceType
        Case ADS_ACETYPE_ACCESS_ALLOWED
            strRtn = "Access Allowed" + vbCrLf
        Case ADS_ACETYPE_ACCESS_DENIED
            strRtn = "Access Denied" + vbCrLf
        Case ADS_ACETYPE_SYSTEM_AUDIT
            strRtn = "Standard Access" + vbCrLf
        Case ADS_ACETYPE_ACCESS_ALLOWED_OBJECT
            strRtn = "Access Allowed" + vbCrLf
        Case ADS_ACETYPE_ACCESS_DENIED_OBJECT
            strRtn = "Access Denied" + vbCrLf
        Case ADS_ACETYPE_SYSTEM_AUDIT_OBJECT
            strRtn = "Standard Access" + vbCrLf
    End Select
    '--- Return the access type
    GetAccessType = strRtn
End Function
```

The third function, GetAccessFlags, uses the AND operator to determine how this object can and will be inherited. For each aspect of the inheritance, the function provides a readable message. To add this, add the GetAccessFlags function in Listing 13.14 to your application.

LISTING 13.14   The GetAccessFlags Function

```
Private Function GetAccessFlags(lAccFlag As Long) As String
'*************************************************************
'* Written By: Davis Chapman
'* Date:       February 12, 2000
'*
'* Syntax:     GetAccessFlags(lAccFlag)
```

continues

13

ACTIVE DIRECTORY
SECURITY AND
SEARCHING

LISTING 13.14   Continued

```
'*
'* Parameters: lAccFlag As Long
'*
'* Purpose: This function builds a list of the access flags
'*          that are included in an Access Control Entry.
'****************************************************************
    Dim strRtn As String

    '--- Initialize the return string
    strRtn = ""
    '--- Is the ADS_ACEFLAG_INHERIT_ACE flag included?
    If ((lAccFlag And ADS_ACEFLAG_INHERIT_ACE)> 0) Then _
        strRtn = strRtn + vbTab + vbTab + vbTab + _
            "Children will inherit ACE" + vbCrLf
    '--- Is the ADS_ACEFLAG_NO_PROPAGATE_INHERIT_ACE flag included?
    If ((lAccFlag And ADS_ACEFLAG_NO_PROPAGATE_INHERIT_ACE)> 0) Then _
        strRtn = strRtn + vbTab + vbTab + vbTab + _
            "ACE will not be inherited by children's children" + vbCrLf
    '--- Is the ADS_ACEFLAG_INHERIT_ONLY_ACE flag included?
    If ((lAccFlag And ADS_ACEFLAG_INHERIT_ONLY_ACE)> 0) Then _
        strRtn = strRtn + vbTab + vbTab + vbTab + _
            "ACE applies only to children" + vbCrLf
    '--- Is the ADS_ACEFLAG_INHERITED_ACE flag included?
    If ((lAccFlag And ADS_ACEFLAG_INHERITED_ACE)> 0) Then _
        strRtn = strRtn + vbTab + vbTab + vbTab + _
            "ACE was inherited" + vbCrLf
    '--- Is the ADS_ACEFLAG_VALID_INHERIT_FLAGS flag included?
    If ((lAccFlag And ADS_ACEFLAG_VALID_INHERIT_FLAGS)> 0) Then _
        strRtn = strRtn + vbTab + vbTab + vbTab + _
            "Inherit flags are valid" + vbCrLf
    '--- Is the ADS_ACEFLAG_SUCCESSFUL_ACCESS flag included?
    If ((lAccFlag And ADS_ACEFLAG_SUCCESSFUL_ACCESS)> 0) Then _
        strRtn = strRtn + vbTab + vbTab + vbTab + _
            "Generates audit messages for successful access" + vbCrLf
    '--- Is the ADS_ACEFLAG_FAILED_ACCESS flag included?
    If ((lAccFlag And ADS_ACEFLAG_FAILED_ACCESS)> 0) Then _
        strRtn = strRtn + vbTab + vbTab + vbTab + _
            "Generates audit messages for failed access" + vbCrLf
    '--- Return the flags list
    GetAccessFlags = strRtn
End Function
```

Looking Up Object Details

Now that you've got the functionality included to display all the details of any object in the Active Directory tree, you need to retrieve the object, determine which class type the object is, and pass it along to the appropriate method. This method needs to use the `IADsOpenDSObject` class interface to make a secure connection to the LDAP server, to retrieve the specified object, and then to call the appropriate method using a `Select Case` statement. To add this functionality, add the `GetDetails` method in Listing 13.15 to your project.

Listing 13.15   The `GetDetails` Method

```
Private Sub GetDetails(strPath As String)
'*************************************************************
'* Written By: Davis Chapman
'* Date:       February 12, 2000
'*
'* Syntax:     GetDetails(strPath)
'*
'* Parameters: strPath As String
'*
'* Purpose: This subroutine retrieves the specified object
'*          using the LDAP interface, determines the class of
'*          the object, and then calls the appropriate method to
'*          display the details of the object.
'*************************************************************
    Dim openDS As IADsOpenDSObject
    Dim obj As IADs

    '--- Open the LDAP interface
    Set openDS = GetObject("LDAP:")
    '--- Open the security context using secure authentication
    Set obj = openDS.OpenDSObject(strPath, _
                  txtUsername, txtPassword, ADS_SECURE_AUTHENTICATION)
    '--- Determine the class of the object and call the appropriate
    '--- method to display the details of the object
    Select Case obj.Class
        '--- The object is a user
        Case "user"
            GetUserDetails obj
        '--- The object is a group
        Case "group"
            GetGroupDetails obj
        '--- The object is a container
        Case "container"
```

continues

13

ACTIVE DIRECTORY
SECURITY AND
SEARCHING

LISTING 13.15   Continued

```
            GetContainerDetails obj
        '--- The object is a miscellaneous object
        Case Else
            GetObjDetails obj
    End Select
End Sub
```

Finally, you need to trigger all this object retrieval and display functionality when the user selects one of the objects in the Tree View. To do this, you'll get the selected node's key, which is the Active Directory path for that object, and pass this path to the GetDetails method. The rest will take care of itself. To add this last bit of functionality, add the code in Listing 13.16 to the Click event for the Tree View control.

LISTING 13.16   The tvNodes Click Event

```
Private Sub tvNodes_Click()
'***********************************************************
'* Written By: Davis Chapman
'* Date:       February 12, 2000
'*
'* Syntax:     tvNodes_Click
'*
'* Parameters: None
'*
'* Purpose: This subroutine gets the details of the selected
'*          node in the tree view control.
'***********************************************************
    Dim ndItem As Node
    Dim strADS As String

    '--- Get the selected node
    Set ndItem = tvNodes.SelectedItem
    '--- Get the key of the selected node
    strADS = ndItem.Key
    '--- Get the details of the selected node
    GetDetails strADS
End Sub
```

Now you should be able to run your application, load the Tree View with all the objects in the Active Directory (assuming you have sufficient access rights), and then examine the details of each object in the directory, as shown in Figure 13.3.

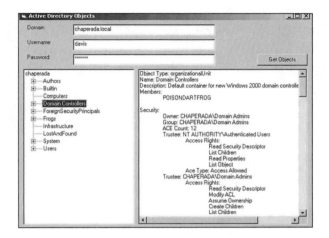

FIGURE 13.3
The Domain Controllers with their members and security.

Summary

In this chapter you learned how to extract the security configuration of each object, building on what you learned in the preceding chapter. You also learned how to use ADO to search a directory for a specific object that you don't know the path of. Finally, you got to see a good portion of this in action by building an application that traversed the entire Active Directory tree, allowing you to examine every object in the tree.

In the next chapter, you'll learn about COM+ and how its security model works. You'll learn how it is the same—and how it's different—from the security model used in previous versions of Microsoft's Transaction Server.

13

ACTIVE DIRECTORY
SECURITY AND
SEARCHING

Developing with COM+ Security

IN THIS CHAPTER

- What Is COM+?
- COM+ and Security
- Building Security-Aware COM+ Components

In this chapter, you will look at COM+ and see how you can incorporate it into your applications and modules. You will also learn about the COM+ security model and how to build security-aware COM+ modules. In the first portion of this chapter, you will review COM+ terminology and component creation and usage. Then in the last part of this chapter, you will find out how straightforward it is to add security to this component.

PREREQUISITES

Before reading this chapter, you need to make sure you have a good understanding of the following:

- The distinction between class and object
- Creating and using classes in Visual Basic
- NT users and groups, Chapter 12, "Working with Active Directory Security (ADSI) and an LDAP Server"
- Impersonation and delegation, Chapter 10, "Understanding Windows 2000 Security and Security Descriptors"

What Is COM+?

Microsoft is positioning COM+ as one of the main reasons to upgrade from NT to Windows 2000 because of the role COM+ plays in letting you build bigger and better applications. In this section, you will learn what COM+ is. A sample project demonstrates how to use COM+ to create and use a component. Later in this chapter, you will see how you can control who can access this COM+ component with COM+ security.

COM+'s Ancestry: COM/DCOM

COM is a Microsoft acronym for Component Object Model. COM is a programming model for packaging software running on the Windows family of operating systems. The term *programming model* is used merely to indicate that COM consists of two distinct parts.

NOTE

While COM began as a Windows technology, its use has spread beyond the Windows platform. Over the past few years, COM has been ported to the Macintosh and various UNIX platforms. Thanks to this wider availability, COM is now a cross-platform object model that can be used to build enterprise-wide distributed applications.

The first part of COM is a specification used mainly by development-tool vendors to write COM-capable compilers. You, in turn, can use these tools to create COM components (component is another term for software package). With COM, software is, by definition, packaged in a binary, language-independent format. (The specification mainly consists of a description of this format.) As a result, you can create COM components in a variety of development tools, including Visual Basic, Visual C++, Delphi, and many others. And herein lies the beauty of COM: you could use all these COM components in a variety of development tools, regardless of the language each component was written in. You can, for example, create a component in Visual Basic and use it in a Visual C++ program. Of course, because this is a Visual Basic book, our coverage will focus on VB, both for creating and using components.

> **NOTE**
>
> In the preceding text, the term *software package* is used in a generic way, as a more intuitive replacement for component. However, you see next that *package* is used for a group of components put under control of Microsoft Transaction Server.

The second part of COM is the system-level infrastructure that is needed for these software packages. Microsoft provides this infrastructure, shipping in the form of DLLs, with the Windows family of operating systems (this includes Windows 95, Windows 98, Windows NT, and Windows 2000). With COM, a component and the application using it reside on a single computer. DCOM (the D stands for distributed) is simply "COM over the network." DCOM allows your application to call a component located on another PC on the network (typically a server).

COM+ is the next version of COM/DCOM shipping with Windows 2000. COM+ is a programming model used to write scalable distributed applications on Windows 2000. This programming model is made possible by Windows 2000's component services, the COM+ system-level infrastructure. Thus, whatever you read about COM also applies to COM+. However, COM+ adds some new features (such as method-level security) that are not available under plain COM.

In Visual Basic, you can create several types of COM packages. The primary ones are ActiveX DLLs, ActiveX EXEs, and ActiveX Controls. Typically, you select the type in the New tab of the New Project dialog when you start a new application.

> **TIP**
>
> In the vast majority of cases, you want to create ActiveX DLLs. Check your Visual Basic documentation to find out what the differences are between an ActiveX DLL, an ActiveX EXE, and an ActiveX Control.

When you create a COM component in VB, the public methods (methods is used as a collective for Subs and Functions) and properties of the classes contained in this ActiveX DLL or ActiveX EXE are made available to other applications by the COM infrastructure. In the next section, you see how straightforward it is to create a COM component using Visual Basic.

Creating a COM Component in VB

During the course of this chapter, you'll learn about COM+ and its security model by building a simple banking application. This application will consist of a COM+ component that you will build throughout the chapter. To start building this COM+ component, begin a new VB project, selecting ActiveX DLL as the project type. Change the default name of the class from Class1 to **BankAccount** and add the following code, shown in Listing 14.1, to the class.

LISTING 14.1   BankAccount Implements a Very Rudimentary Bank Account

```
Option Explicit

Private m_cBalance As Currency

Public Function Deposit(Amount As Currency) As Boolean
'***********************************************************************
'* Written By: Pierre G. Boutquin
'* Date:        January 31, 2000
'*
'* Syntax:      Deposit(Amount)
'*
'* Parameters:  Amount As Currency
'*
'* Purpose: This function will increase the account balance by the
'*          amount passed as a parameter. This amount must
'*          be positive. Returns True on Success, False otherwise.
'***********************************************************************
    '--- Check the amount to make sure it's positive
    Deposit = (Amount>= 0)
    '--- If a good amount, add it to the balance
    If Deposit Then m_cBalance = m_cBalance + Amount
End Function

Public Function Withdraw(Amount As Currency) As Boolean
'***********************************************************************
'* Written By: Pierre G. Boutquin
'* Date:        January 31, 2000
'*
'* Syntax:      Deposit(Amount)
'*
'* Parameters:  Amount As Currency
'*
```

```
'* Purpose: This function will decrease the account balance by the
'*          amount passed as a parameter. This amount must
'*          be positive and there must be sufficient funds in
'*          the account to cover the amount.  Returns True on
'*          Success, False otherwise.
'***********************************************************************
    '--- Check the withdraw amount to make sure it's available
    WithDraw = (Amount>= 0) And (m_cBalance>= Amount)
    '--- If a valid amount, adjust the balance
    If WithDraw Then m_cBalance = m_cBalance - Amount
End Function

Public Property Get Balance() As Currency
'***********************************************************************
'* Written By: Pierre G. Boutquin
'* Date:       January 31, 2000
'*
'* Syntax:     Balance()
'*
'* Parameters:  Amount As Currency
'*
'* Purpose: This property will return the account balance.
'***********************************************************************
    Balance = m_cBalance
End Property
```

Select Project|Project1 Properties from the menu and change the project name to **SimpleBank**. It is important to choose a descriptive name for the ActiveX component because you use this name to indicate that you will use this component in other projects. (You will build such a project in the next section.) Save this project and create the ActiveX DLL by selecting File|Make ActiveX DLL. You may save the DLL in the same directory as the project.

That is all there is to creating COM components in Visual Basic—you just create an ActiveX DLL (or EXE). Visual Basic and COM take care of the behind-the-scenes magic so that the public methods and properties of the classes created within that project are made available to other programs. In the next section, you create a small test program for our COM component. Again, you will see that Visual Basic makes this task a walk in the park.

Using a COM Component in VB

Start a new VB project, selecting Standard EXE as the project type. Change the default name of the form from Form1 to **frmTestBankAccount**. Select Project|References. This gives you a dialog box with a list of all the COM components on your development PC. Scroll down until you find SimpleBank (or whatever name you used for the previous project) and check it off to indicate that this project will use the SimpleBank component, as seen in Figure 14.1. After you have done this, you may use all the classes created in the SimpleBank component in the same way as if they were part of this project.

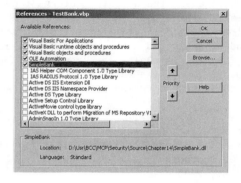

The References dialog lets you select which components your project will use.

Ok, now let's implement our test harness. Lay out the form as seen in Figure 14.02, and configure the controls as specified in Table 14.1.

FIGURE 14.2
The form in our test harness contains two labels, three buttons, and a text box.

TABLE 14.1 Control Property Settings

Control	Property	Value
Label	Name	lblDesc
	Caption	Balance
Label	Name	lblBalance
	Caption	$$$$$$$$
TextBox	Name	txtAmount
	Text	100
Command Button	Name	cmdDeposit
	Caption	Deposit

Control	Property	Value
Command Button	Name	cmdWithdraw
	Caption	Withdraw
Command Button	Name	cmdExit
	Caption	Exit

Add the following code to the form. As you can see in this simple project, after you have set a reference to a component, you can use the classes contained in this component the same way as if the classes were implemented in the current project. The only indication that a class is implemented in a component is that the class name is prefixed by the component name.

```
Private m_oBankAccount As SimpleBank.BankAccount
```

This is a good habit, but you can actually omit the component name and completely hide the fact that a component was used.

```
Private m_oBankAccount As BankAccount
```

Adding the component name avoids problems when several components have the same class name (you could for example have a RealWorldBank component that also has a BankAccount class). Of course, a name conflict arises only when both components are used within the same project.

Listing 14.2 shows how to implement the test harness. The code is fairly straightforward and includes some basic input validation. Because this is a test harness, validation is not necessarily implemented in the most effective way and may not catch all input errors.

LISTING 14.2 frmTestBankAccount Implements a Test Harness for Our Rudimentary Bank Account

14

DEVELOPING WITH
COM+ SECURITY

```
Option Explicit

Private m_oBankAccount As SimpleBank.BankAccount

Private Sub Form_Load()
    '--- Create the Bank Account object
    Set m_oBankAccount = New SimpleBank.BankAccount
    '--- Update the User Interface
    UpdateUI
End Sub

Private Sub Form_Terminate()
    '--- Clean up
    Set m_oBankAccount = Nothing
```

continues

LISTING 14.2   Continued

```
End Sub

Private Sub cmdExit_Click()
    '--- Close the application
    Unload Me
End Sub

Private Sub cmdDeposit_Click()
Dim cAmount As Currency

    '--- Check to make sure that a number was entered by the user
    If IsNumeric(txtAmount.Text) Then
        '--- Convert the user input into currency
        cAmount = CCur(txtAmount.Text)
        '--- Call the Deposit method
        If m_oBankAccount.Deposit(cAmount) Then
            '--- Update the display
            UpdateUI
        Else
            '--- Error, tell the user
            ErrMsgBox "Deposit failed!"
        End If
    Else
        '--- The user didn't enter a number, tell them
        ErrMsgBox "Please enter a number!"
        '--- Put the focus on the amount text box
        txtAmount.SetFocus
        '--- Select all of the text in the box
        txtAmount.SelStart = 0
        txtAmount.SelLength = Len(txtAmount.Text)
    End If
End Sub

Private Sub cmdWithdraw_Click()
Dim cAmount As Currency

    '--- Check to make sure that a number was entered by the user
    If IsNumeric(txtAmount.Text) Then
        '--- Convert the user input into currency
        cAmount = CCur(txtAmount.Text)
        '--- Call the Withdraw method
        If m_oBankAccount.Withdraw(cAmount) Then
            '--- Update the display
            UpdateUI
        Else
            '--- Error, tell the user
            ErrMsgBox "Withdraw failed!"
```

```
      End If
   Else
      '--- The user didn't enter a number, tell them
      ErrMsgBox "Please enter a number!"
      '--- Put the focus on the amount text box
      txtAmount.SetFocus
      '--- Select all of the text in the box
      txtAmount.SelStart = 0
      txtAmount.SelLength = Len(txtAmount.Text)
   End If
End Sub

Private Sub UpdateUI()
   '--- Update the balance display
   lblBalance.Caption = CStr(m_oBankAccount.Balance)
   '--- Refresh the screen
   Me.Refresh
End Sub

Private Sub ErrMsgBox(sMessage As String)
   '--- Display the error message for the user
   MsgBox sMessage, vbExclamation, "Error!"
End Sub
```

When you run this project, nothing indicates that the project is divided into two parts. The COM infrastructure operates behind the scenes as the glue between the standard EXE and the ActiveX DLL. Figure 14.3 shows the test harness in action.

FIGURE 14.3
Nothing indicates that the test harness uses a component.

COM/DCOM in Perspective

The $64,000 question, of course, is why you want to use this cool-looking COM/DCOM technology in the real world. The answer is that DCOM allows you to create more powerful server applications. Using DCOM, you can place a COM component on the server and have the applications on the client access it almost as if it were local (that is, sitting on the client). This new type of application, made possible by technology such as DCOM, is called a distributed application because its functionality is distributed over several computers. Distributed applications offer major benefits at the cost of some drawbacks. The major benefit is the centralized access to functionality. Many applications can use a component placed on the server. This eases upgrading this functionality because you need to update only one component on one server for all the clients to gain access to the upgraded functionality. The trade-off is that you need to become familiar with a new way of designing applications.

TIP

Realizing the learning curve involved with COM/DCOM and distributed application design, Microsoft has created tons of technical articles and samples to help programmers understand this new way of building applications; look under the heading Distributed interNet Application Architecture (DNA). Many books are also available to help you master this paradigm shift.

Other trade-offs include the more complex installation of client software (you need to ensure that the client knows where to find the server-side components) and the performance hit due to the network traffic turnaround time. The performance hit of a server-side component in comparison to a client-side component is the major reason why applications using server-side components need to be designed differently. Calls to server-side components need to be minimized as much as possible. When using client-side components (or a standalone program, not using programs), there is no harm in writing code such as the following:

```
Dim oPerson As CPerson
Set oPerson = New CPerson
oPerson.FirstName = " Jean-Paul"
oPerson.LastName = " Sartre"
oPerson.Occupation = " Philosophizer"
```

However, when the CPerson class is implemented in a server-side component, this code causes a network trip to set each property. The following code reduces the number of network trips and is much more efficient:

```
Dim oPerson As CPerson
Set oPerson = New CPerson
oPerson.Init " Jean-Paul", " Sartre", " Philosophizer"
```

TIP

When designing and building components for running on a shared server, it's a good idea not to use properties, but to pass everything needed as parameters to the methods of the classes in the component. Properties on a component may be reset by another user between calls, thus leading to unpredictable results.

Introducing Microsoft Transaction Server

The biggest challenge building distributed applications is to build highly scalable applications that can handle a very large number of simultaneous users, like a Web application. Having a large number of simultaneous users complicates matters because as server resources become scarce, you have to deal with complex issues such concurrency, contention, and congestion. Luckily, Microsoft decided that, as the leading operating system vendor, it needed to help application programmers solve these complex issues so that they can more easily build powerful applications running on the Windows servers. The result was Microsoft Transaction Server (MTS). MTS is a runtime environment for server-side COM components that provides a set of services to help you build scalable distributed applications. In Windows 2000, MTS is completely integrated in COM+ and provides all its services in the background. These services include

- Transaction management
- Resource pooling
- Security

Transactions are a way to execute a set of code as one batch that either completely succeeds or completely fails. The classic example is a bank transfer, where you want to debit one account and credit another; either both succeed or both fail.

Resource pooling is a crucial technique that allows more components to coexist on the same server. Suppose you host the previously created SimpleBank component on a server; each client requires its own copy of this component to be put in memory. Because a COM component is fairly expensive in terms of memory footprint, this limits the number of concurrent users that your application can handle. Now it turns out that these components typically are idle the majority of the time. Only when the user presses the Withdraw or Deposit buttons does the component need to do something. This need led to the creation of object pools and just-in-time activation within MTS. Therefore, to increase the scalability of your banking application, you can host the SimpleBank component within MTS. MTS creates a pool of BankAccount objects. When a client application requests a BankAccount object, it tricks the application into believing it receives a BankAccount object, but in reality, it gives the application a fake BankAccount object. These fake BankAccount objects consume much less memory than the real objects (enabling more concurrent users). When the client asks a fake object to do work, MTS grabs a real object from its pool and replaces the fake with a real object. When the real object is finished, MTS replaces the real object with another fake and returns the real object to the pool. This process, which is invisible to the client application, is what is meant by just-in-time activation.

Another area where MTS pools resources is database connections. Like COM objects, database connections are resource hogs. To give each client or server component a dedicated database connection limits the number of concurrent users your users can handle. MTS solves this in a fashion similar to object creation—by keeping a pool of database connections.

> **TIP**
>
> To be able to take advantage of database connection pooling requires certain techniques and approaches in the design of MTS components. If you want to be able to take advantage of this capability, you might want to pick up a good book on MTS or COM+. Check out Sams *Pure COM+* or *COM+ Unleashed* to enhance your understanding of these topics.

MTS also offers a scalable security model, which is discussed in the next section.

Let us see what is involved in hosting our SimpleBank component in MTS running on Windows 2000 Server. (MTS is also available for Windows NT. Hosting a component in MTS running on NT Server is similar and is done within the Transaction Server Explorer.) Bring up the component service administration tool, called the COM+ Explorer, by selecting Programs|Administrative Tools|Component Services from the Start menu. Under Console Root, open COM+ Applications by expanding Component Services|Computers|My Computer. You should see something similar to Figure 14.4.

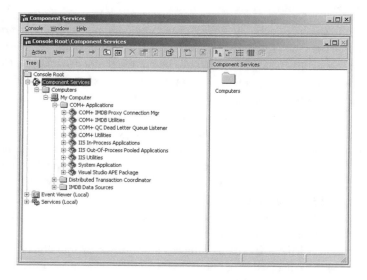

FIGURE 14.4
In Windows 2000, you use the COM+ Explorer to host components under MTS.

Bring up the COM+ Application Wizard by right-clicking COM+ Applications and selecting New|Application.

Click Next to move on to the next Window and click Create an Empty Application. An application, previously called a package, can hold more than one component. On the next window, name the application **SimpleBank Application** and select Server Application.

Click Next to bring up the next window. Leave the account under which the application will run as the current logged on user.

Click Next. This brings up the final screen14. Click Finish to create the empty application. The newly created application can now be viewed in the COM+ Explorer, as seen in Figure 14.5.

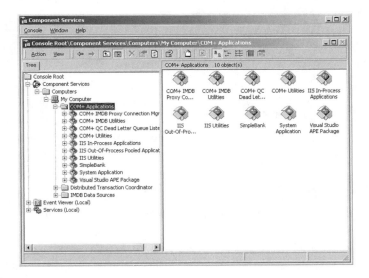

FIGURE 14.5
The newly created application shows up in the COM+ Explorer.

Now you can drag and drop the SimpleBank DLL into the COM+ runtime environment. Click the Components folder of the SimpleBank application. Open Explorer and drag the Simple-Bank DLL into this folder. (Alternatively, you can right-click the component and bring up the Component Install Wizard by selecting New|Component.) As you can see in Figure 14.6, the component then shows up in the component folder.

Keep the COM+ Explorer open and run the test harness application. You will see the ball representing the BankAccount class spinning to indicate activity. You may close COM+ Explorer when you are tired of looking at the spinning balls.

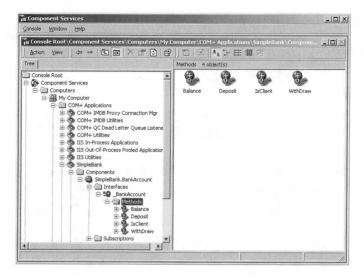

FIGURE 14.6
The freshly installed component shows up in the COM+ Explorer.

COM+ and Security

You now know how to create and use COM+ components. COM+ components support what is called attribute-based programming. This new paradigm allows you to create a component and then decide what COM+ services that component will use. You can make these choices after you have built the component. For example, you can decide whether a component supports or requires transactions. You can also decide whether a component requires security. In addition to this attribute-based programming, you can programmatically control who can access your component.

Introducing MTS/COM+ Security

Many applications, both Client/Server and Web-based, work with sensitive information. If the application is a Web store-front, then the sensitive information may be in the form of credit card numbers. If the application is a Client/Server application, then the sensitive information may be salary and personnel information. Any application that works with sensitive information requires security. The larger the application, the more scaleable the security mechanism needs to be.

It turns out that providing scalable security is yet another challenging task. You do not want to use the built-in security mechanism of the database because this will result in a database connection for each user requiring security clearance. This defeats the purpose of database connection pooling. Luckily, COM+ also solves this problem for you by providing a scalable security mechanism. COM+ provides two ways to implement security for COM+ components: declarative security and programmatic security. These ways are not mutually exclusive and may be used together. Declarative security puts the control into the hands of the Administrator. Programmatic security lets the programmer decide on the access privileges.

Declarative Security in COM+

Declarative security is implemented through the use of what COM+ calls *roles*. You assign users or group accounts to a role. Declarative security is added to a component after it has been developed, typically by an administrator during deployment. Programmers benefit because while they are coding, they do not need to worry who will have what permissions. When they are done coding and it is time to deploy the applications, the network administrator can set permissions to the components (or to the methods of the components).

A role is similar to Windows NT user groups and is simply a name that is used to identify a group of related users for the set of components in a COM+ application. Each role defines which users are allowed to call which methods of each component. After roles have been created and populated with users, an administrator grants access to the components and their methods by using role membership.

Let's see how this works by adding roles to our SimpleBank application. Bring up the COM+ Explorer (Start|Programs|Administrative Tools|Component Services). Under Console Root, open COM+ Applications by selecting Component Services|Computers|My Computer. Open the SimpleBank application icon and right-click the Roles folder. Select Roles|New and enter **ATMClient** as the role name, as shown in Figure 14.7. Add another role with the name **BankTeller**.

FIGURE 14.7

A role is a symbolic name used to identify a group of users.

After you have created roles, you must assign users to each role. Click the ATMClient icon to show the Users folder. Right-click the Users folder and select New|User. This brings up the Add Users dialog, shown in Figure 14.8. Select a user and click Add. Repeat this for each user you want to add to the role.

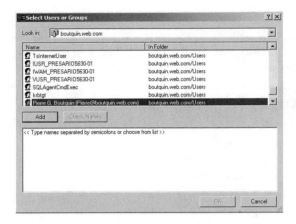

FIGURE 14.8

After you have created a role, you need to assign users to that role.

Repeat this process to add users to the BankTeller role. When you are done, you should see something similar to Figure 14.9.

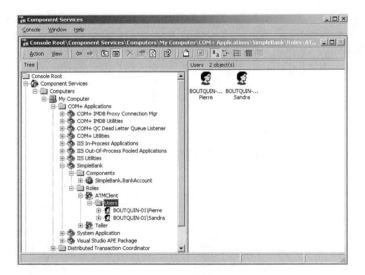

FIGURE 14.9

You can see which users belong to each role in the COM+ Explorer.

> **TIP**
>
> If you will assign the same group of users to roles in more than one application, it may be worthwhile to create an account group containing these users using the Active Directory Users and Computers Explorer (Start|Programs|Administrative Tools|Active Directory Users and Computers).

After you have created the roles and assigned the users to the roles, you need to configure the application security. To do this, right-click the SimpleBank Application icon in the COM+ Explorer and select Properties. Click the Securities tab. Check Enforce Access Checks for This Application and Perform Access Checks at the Process and Component Level. This enables full security checks for all the components in the application.

Now that you have enabled security, you need to set permissions for the components and component methods. Right-click the SimpleBank.BankAccount icon and select Properties; then click the Security tab Check Enforce Component Level Access Checks. This enables security checks for the `BankAccount` class.

Drill down until you get to the methods of the `BankAccount` class: Interfaces|_BankAccount|Methods. Right-click the Balance method and click the Security tab. Allow access for this method to both roles. For the Deposit and Withdraw method, grant access only to the ATMClient role, as shown in Figure 14.10.

FIGURE 14.10
In COM+, you can configure security at the method level.

When a user assigned to the BankTeller role tries to access the Deposit or Withdraw methods, a runtime error occurs, as seen in Figure 14.11.

> **TIP**
>
> You may want to trap the runtime error that occurs when access is denied by COM+. The error number is 70.

FIGURE 14.11
A runtime error occurs when access is denied by COM+.

Building Security-Aware COM+ Components

Programmatic security allows the component writer to make decisions based on the role membership of the user executing the component. As usual, Visual Basic does an excellent job making this as simple as possible. In fact, you need to use only two methods of the SecurityCallContext class: IsSecurityEnabled and IsCallerInRole. The IsSecurityEnabled function allows you to check whether security was enabled for this component. The IsCallerInRole function allows you to check programmatically whether the user calling the component is a member of the specified role. Let's see how this works in practice by adding security awareness to our SimpleBank component.

Open the SimpleBank project in VB. To use the SecurityCallContext class, you need to set a reference to the COM+ Services Type Library, as shown in Figure 14.12.

> **TIP**
>
> If you need your components to remain compatible with Microsoft Transaction Server, you must set a reference to the Microsoft Transaction Server Library (MtxAS.dll). The components using this MTS Library will then run under both MTS and COM+.

You will add a method that returns whether the caller is a member of ATMClient role. Listing 14.3 shows the code that is needed for this.

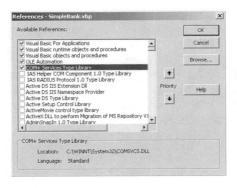

FIGURE 14.12

To build COM+ security-aware components, you need to set a reference to the COM+ Services Type Library.

LISTING 14.3 Adding Security Awareness to the BankAccount Class Is Straightforward

```
Public Property Get IsClient() As Boolean
'*************************************************************************
'* Written By: Pierre G. Boutquin
'* Date:        January 31, 2000
'*
'* Syntax:      IsClient()
'*
'* Parameters:  None.
'*
'* Purpose: This property will return TRUE if the client is a member
'*          of the ATMClient security role.
'*************************************************************************
    Dim oSecurityCallContext As COMSVCSLib.SecurityCallContext

    '--- Get the security context
    Set oSecurityCallContext = COMSVCSLib.GetSecurityCallContext()

    '--- Initialize the return value
    IsClient = False

    '--- Check to see if security is enabled
    If oSecurityCallContext.IsSecurityEnabled() Then
        '--- Check to see if the caller is in the correct role
        '--- Adjust the return value if the caller is in the correct role
        If oSecurityCallContext.IsCallerInRole("ATMClient") Then IsClient = True
    End If
End Property
```

> ### TIP
>
> You may get an access-denied error when trying to compile SimpleBank.DLL. This is because the DLL is still running in the COM+ runtime environment. To shut down the SimpleBank application, open the COM+ Explorer, right-click the application, and select Shut Down. You will also need to make sure that the harness project is not open in another Visual Basic session when trying to compile the DLL.

Because you added a new function to the component, you also need to change the test harness to test this function. Open the `TestBank` project and add the `EnableUI` function shown in Listing 14.4 to the form code. You also need to add the call to `EnableUI` in the `Form_Load` event. That is it. Save and test the project.

LISTING 14.4   The New Test Harness Tests the Security Awareness of the Component

```
Private Sub Form_Load()
   '--- Create the Bank Account object
   Set m_oBankAccount = New SimpleBank.BankAccount
   '--- Enable the User Interface
   EnableUI
   '--- Update the User Interface
   UpdateUI
End Sub

Private Sub EnableUI()
   '--- Check to make sure the account is a client
   If Not m_oBankAccount.IsClient() Then
      '--- The account is not a client, disable the controls
      cmdDeposit.Enabled = False
      cmdWithdraw.Enabled = False
   End If
End Sub
```

Summary

In this chapter, you learned about COM+ and its two security models: declarative security and programmatic security. Declarative security enables programmers not to worry about security during implementation. An administrator can configure security at deployment time. Programmatic security gives a programmer an easy way to selectively allow access without having to use the Windows NT security APIs. In the next chapter, you look at the management and operations of the Certificate Server and how it can be used to issue digital certificates for an organization.

Microsoft Certificate Server

IN THIS CHAPTER

- How Certificate Authorities Work
- Generating a Root Certificate
- Issuing, Managing, and Revoking Certificates

In the first section of this book, you learned how certificates are a key element in the use of encryption. If you haven't guessed by now, certificates are an important part of current security and encryption schemes as a means of identifying people and systems.

If you need to control security for an organization, either for secure authorization purposes or for creating secure communication applications, you may find yourself needing to operate your own Certificate Server. This is easily done using Microsoft's Certificate Server (called Certificate Services in Windows 2000).

How Certificate Authorities Work

Certificate Authorities (CA) are fairly straightforward server applications that basically take in certificate requests, reformat and sign them, and then make the resulting certificate available for retrieval by the requester. The function of a CA is actually a bit more involved than just that; otherwise it would be easy for people to set themselves up as their own CA. The biggest requirement that a CA needs to meet is one of trust. People and applications that receive a certificate issued by a particular CA need to be able to trust that the CA verified that the owner of the certificate is who he or she claims to be. They also need to trust that the CA is who it claims to be.

Certificate Authority Hierarchies

The identity of a CA is established by the CA making its own certificate available to the public. This certificate is the certificate that the CA uses for signing all the certificates that it issues. The CA can issue itself its own certificate, signing it with itself, or the CA can have its certificate issued and signed by another CA. This results in a hierarchy of CAs, most likely culminating in a single CA that is very widely known and trusted, as shown in Figure 15.1.

If the root of the CA hierarchy is a company such as Verisign (www.verisign.com), whose certificate is distributed preinstalled as a root certificate in most Web browsers today, then when someone receives a certificate issued by a lower-level CA, by tracing the hierarchy to Verisign, a chain of trust can be established. If a corporate security department wants to set up its own CA and issue a self-signed certificate as the corporate root certificate, all the employees can choose (or more likely be required) to accept the certificate as a root certificate. When certificates can be traced to an accepted root certificate, that certificate is automatically trusted.

If a CA revokes a certificate issued to another CA, then all the certificates issued by the second CA are now suspect. However, unless users and applications are diligent in checking against updated Certificate Revocation Lists (CRL) issued by the CAs in the hierarchy, the suspect certificates may go unnoticed.

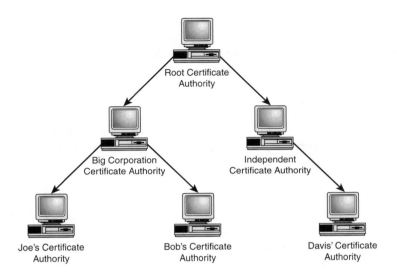

FIGURE 15.1

A Certificate Authority hierarchy.

Requesting and Issuing Certificates

You have already seen the process of requesting and being issued a certificate in Chapter 5, "Requesting and Receiving Certificates." In that chapter, you learned that the process is basically a matter of the client requesting the certificate, generating a public/private key pair, packaging the public key in a certificate request, and sending that request to a CA. The CA then makes the decision of whether to issue the certificate or to reject the request. After the CA has issued the certificate, the client retrieves the certificate from the CA, as shown in Figure 15.2.

What you didn't learn is how the CA makes the decision on whether to issue or reject a particular certificate request. Each certificate request passes through a series of rules and policies that sometimes can automatically decide to issue or reject the certificate. There are times, however, that a certificate request requires human intervention to make the decision.

Depending on the type of certificate that you are requesting, the CA has to perform various degrees of verification of your identity. These range from a simple validation that the email address you provide for inclusion in the certificate is a valid email address, to requiring that you appear in person at a notary public with various forms of identification. For corporations, the requirements are just as wide ranging.

With Microsoft's Certificate Server, you have the ability to define your own rules governing how and when certificates are issued. You even have the ability to build plug-ins in Visual Basic for extending the policy functionality (although this is not covered in this book). Building your own plug-in modules involves using the Certificate Services COM objects, two of which you used in Chapters 5 and 7.

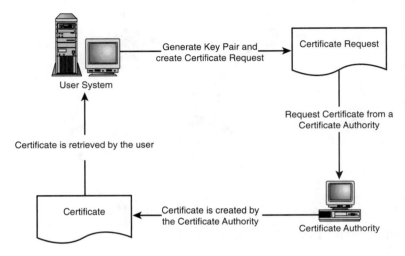

FIGURE 15.2
The Certificate request and issuance process.

Generating a Root Certificate

Installing Certificate Services on a Windows 2000 server is a simple matter of selecting to install it from the `Configure Your Server` utility. Prior to installing Certificate Services, you need decide whether your server will be running as an Active Directory server. Active Directory has to be installed prior to Certificate Services if you are going to be running both on the same machine. If you have installed Active Directory on the server, you have the option of configuring Certificate Services as an Enterprise Certificate Authority. If Active Directory is not running on the server, your Certificate Services are limited to running as a standalone CA.

After you have the Certificate Services installed, you'll be taken through the process of generating the CA certificate. You'll be presented with the Certificate Services Setup Wizard, which will ask you which type of Certificate Authority you want to set up, as shown in Figure 15.3. The options are listed in Table 15.1.

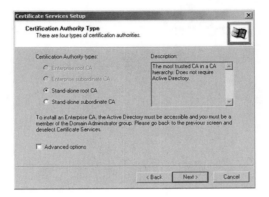

FIGURE 15.3
Choosing the Certificate Authority type.

TABLE 15.1 Possible Certificate Authority Types

Type	Description
Enterprise Root CA	This CA is intended to be the CA for an organization. This CA can issue certificates for use with Active Directory and the Kerberos authentication protocol. This CA has a self-issued certificate and there is no CA above this one.
Enterprise Subordinate CA	This CA is intended to be a CA within an organization. This CA can issue certificates for use with Active Directory and the Kerberos authentication protocol. The certificate for this CA has to be requested and issued by another CA.
Stand-alone Root CA	This CA is intended as a general purpose CA. This CA has a self-issued certificate and there is no CA above this one.
Stand-alone Subordinate CA	This CA is intended as a general purpose CA. The certificate for this CA has to be requested and issued by another CA.

The next step in the process is filling in all the information for the Certificate Authority's certificate, as shown in Figure 15.4. This information includes the name for the Certificate Authority, the corporation or organization name, the name of the unit within the organization, the location, the email address, and a description of the CA.

15

MICROSOFT
CERTIFICATE
SERVER

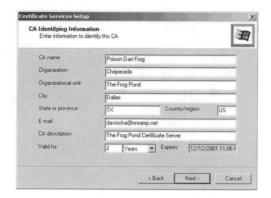

The third step of the Certificate Services Setup process is specifying the location of the certificate database and log, as shown in Figure 15.5.

Finishing up the Certificate Services Setup Wizard, if you are creating a root CA, your CA will be up and running. If you are creating a subordinate CA, you'll end up with a certificate request that you will need to submit to another CA to have a certificate issued. After the certificate is issued, you'll import it into the Certificate Services.

Issuing, Managing, and Revoking Certificates

After you have Certificate Services installed and running on your server, you can start accepting certificate requests and issuing certificates. You perform these tasks through the Certification Authority utility under the Administrative Tools on the Start menu.

Issuing and Denying Certificates

Certificate Services are installed with a Web interface as a default method of accepting certificate requests, issuing certificates, and for downloading Certificate Revocation Lists. This Web interface uses some ActiveX controls that are shipped with Certificate Services to create the certificate request. The primary control used for this purpose is the Certificate Enrollment Control, which you worked with in Chapter 5. This control calls out to the Crypto API to generate a public/private key pair on the requester's computer and packages the public key in a certificate request. The Web interface then automatically submits this certificate request to the Certificate Services through the Internet Information Server (IIS) interface.

After certificate requests have been received by the Certificate Server, you can view them in the Pending Requests folder. From here, you can select a request and choose to issue or deny the request, based on whether the request meets your issuance criteria. To issue a certificate, select the request in the list of pending requests. Right-click the mouse and select All Tasks|Resubmit from the context menu, as shown in Figure 15.6. To reject a request, right-click the mouse and select All Tasks|Deny from the context menu.

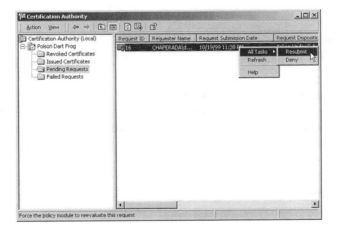

FIGURE 15.6
Issuing (resubmitting) a certificate.

After you have issued a certificate request, you will find the issued certificate in the Issued Certificates folder. The requests you've denied, you'll find in the Failed Requests folder.

Revoking Certificates

No matter how vigilant you might be on which certificate requests you issue or deny, there will be times that you need to revoke a certificate that you've issued. This is a simple two-step process. The first step is selecting the certificate in the Issued Certificates folder. For the next step, right-click the mouse and select All Tasks|Revoke Certificate from the context menu, as shown in Figure 15.7. When you revoke the certificate, you'll have the option of specifying the reason for revoking the certificate.

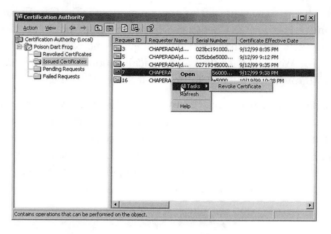

FIGURE 15.7

Revoking a certificate.

After you have revoked the certificate, you need to publish a new Certificate Revocation List (CRL). You can do this by selecting the Revoked Certificates folder, right-clicking the mouse, and selecting All Tasks|Publish from the context menu, as shown in Figure 15.8. At this point, the Certificate Server may present you with a dialog, stating that the current CRL is still valid. You should continue on and publish a new CRL for downloading by users.

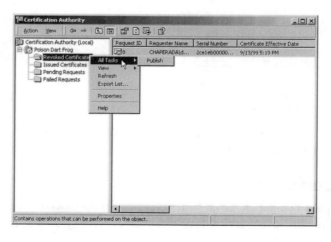

FIGURE 15.8

Publishing a Certificate Revocation List.

Summary

In this chapter, you received a brief overview of the Microsoft Certificate Services that are available for Windows 2000 servers. All the functionality covered in this chapter is also available for the previous versions of Microsoft's Certificate Server. In the preceding few pages, you learned the basics of setting up and running your own certificate server, including how to issue, deny, and revoke certificates.

> **NOTE**
>
> Running a real Certificate Authority is quite a bit more involved than what was covered here. If you need to run your own CA and issue your own certificates, you'll need to spend quite a bit of time on the qualification criteria and set up the appropriate processes for guaranteeing that those criteria are met before each certificate is issued. You'll also need to spend some time understanding how to configure the policies for the CA, and possibly even create your own policies using Visual Basic to create policy plug-ins. Details on creating your own policy plug-ins can be found on the MSDN Web site (www.msdn.microsoft.com) and Library CD.

In the next couple of chapters, you'll learn about some of the security standards in common use today. You'll also learn about some of the legal issues surrounding certificates and encryption. This is an area that is in the midst of change, and so this is, at best, a snapshot of the current legal landscape.

15

MICROSOFT CERTIFICATE SERVER

Security Standards

IN THIS CHAPTER

- **C2 Security**
- **DES and RSA**
- **PGP and Kerberos**
- **Smart Cards and Tokens**
- **Emerging Technologies and Standards**

Today, regular users of the Internet are inundated with products and services that can be purchased over the World Wide Web. The Internet also can be used in several ways for electronic commerce, such as

- **Home banking.** The ability to conduct personal bank transactions from the comfort of your couch. This includes making deposits and transferring funds from your personal accounts.
- **Consumer purchasing via the Internet.** The Internet gives today's users the capability to buy goods and services over the Internet. These services range from photo processing to purchasing automobiles.
- **Electronic funds transfer.** This includes the ability to purchase shares of stock with money transferred from your checking account.

Any one of these ways of electronic commerce is subject to security breaches. The junior high student who just received a computer for his birthday might find it fun to hack into your bank account. A disgruntled employee might seek revenge against your company and use your credit card number to make unauthorized purchases. The possibilities are as numerous as the reasons to commit such acts.

Today's news is filled with horror stories like the preceding scenarios. Some are true and some are designed to scare you into action. Today's Internet is like the Wild West of years ago—a big frontier with lots of potential for profit and very few regulations. Just as the Wild West had sheriffs in each town, today's Internet has many protocols designed to provide secure electronic transactions.

In addition to simply describing what standards exist that are designed to protect you and your data from Internet theft, this chapter highlights the differences between the individual standards and discusses their strengths and weaknesses.

C2 Security

The National Security Agency (NSA) and the National Computer Security Center (NCSC) use a number of different standards to determine and evaluate the level of security that tested hardware and software products provide. These standards are collectively known as the Rainbow series, named after the colors of the cover of each of the publications. These standards are commonly referred to as the Orange Book standards. The Orange Book classifications were designed to provide a standard to determine the level of security in products that hardware and software manufactures were supplying to the Department of Defense. The C2 security rating is one of the Orange Book classifications.

The Orange Book series of classifications is divided into a range of four letters, from "A" to "D," where "A" is the most secure and "D" is the least secure. Within each rating, the classifications are further broken down into classes. The "C" level has two classes, C1 and C2. Of these two classes, the C2 class has the higher security rating. Some of the criteria used to establish these rankings are

- Discretionary access and control (an administrator must be able to determine who has access to which files, and so on)
- Identification and authentication (see Chapters 10 and 11)
- Auditing (an administrator must be able to audit all security events, including users logging on and off, access to secure files, and so on)
- Object reuse (all objects that are allocated in memory must be initialized prior to use to prevent access to any remnants of prior data that were previously held in memory)

The C2 ranking is used as the base-line for any systems to be purchased for use by some branches of the U.S. Government. Because of this policy, the C2 ranking is often touted to show how secure a system is, with the intent that you will then make a purchase based on this information. What is not often publicized is that, to meet the C2 certification, a system must be configured in a specific way that is often not followed in the business world. The necessary configuration for C2 security is considered to be too strict and inconvenient by most business users who aren't interested in following a strict, military-style protocol for accessing files and running applications.

A C2 classification of a product does not necessarily mean that you will be able to unpack the product and immediately enjoy the benefits of the C2-level security. Manufacturers that have obtained a C2 classification have had to submit a very specific configuration to the NCSC to qualify. The certification process for software involves a thorough analysis of the software implementation to determine what ranking all security-related aspects of the software meet.

All of this means that if you use a different version of a software product than was classified, or if you do not perform the required Registry and permission tweaks, you may not have a product that will pass as a C2-certified product. If you truly need C2 classification for a hardware or software product—to support a government agency, for example—you will need to use the exact version and configurations certified to guarantee full certification.

For more information about what is covered in C2 security and what it means, visit the Orange Book site at `http://www.radium.ncsc.mil/tpep/library/rainbow/5200.28-STD.html`. You may also wish to visit the Microsoft C2 security notice at `http://www.microsoft.com/NTServer/security/exec/feature/c2_security.asp`.

DES and RSA

DES and RSA are actually algorithms rather than standards. However, because the vast majority of security standards are based on one or both of these algorithms, they are briefly mentioned here to provide you with a complete understanding of how the standards work. For example, Secure Electronic Transactions (SET), a method for encrypting credit card information, uses DES as its default symmetric key algorithm, and the RSA asymmetric key algorithms for digital signatures and digital envelopes.

DES

DES (Data Encryption Standard) is the default data encryption algorithm used for protecting financial information. Originally published in 1977 by IBM for use by the United States government to protect valuable and sensitive—but unclassified—data, this standard was subsequently adopted by the American National Standards Institute (ANSI) as the Data Encryption Algorithm (DEA).

DES is a block cipher, which means that it encrypts the plain text in blocks of data rather than as a stream of bits. DES has a 64-bit block size and uses a 56-bit key during encryption. DES, which was originally designed for hardware, operates on the text a total of 16 times by these two techniques, as dictated by the key. In communication implementations, both the sender and the receiver must know the same secret key, which is used both to encrypt and decrypt the message. DES can also be used for single-user encryption, such as to store files on a hard disk in encrypted form. Secure key distribution in a multiuser environment can cause security problems; DES provides an ideal solution to this.

DES is used by financial institutions to encrypt Personal Information Numbers (PINs). This type of security is also found in some implementations of Smart Card products.

> **NOTE**
>
> Because of the age of the DES algorithm, it is no longer considered to be as secure as it originally was. Due to this perceived slip in security, several variations on the DES algorithm have been developed in an attempt to make DES a much more secure algorithm. The most well known of these variations is probably the Triple-DES algorithm, where the DES algorithm is applied three times, using a variation of the encryption key.

RSA

The RSA algorithm was invented in 1977 by Ron Rivest, Adi Shamir, and Leonard Adleman. These three MIT professors later formed RSA Data Security, Inc. The name of the company, and the algorithm, is derived from the initials of the last names of the three inventors of the algorithm. RSA Data Security holds the patent for the RSA algorithm and sells encryption software based on it.

Some of the key features of the RSA algorithm are the following:

- The RSA algorithm became the first public-key algorithm that works for encryption and digital signatures.
- The RSA algorithm is easy to understand and implement.
- RSA is the most widely used public-key cryptosystem today and has often been called a de facto standard.
- RSA is a public-key cryptosystem designed to provide both encryption and authentication.

RSA is found in Internet standards and proposed protocols including PEM (Privacy Enhanced Mail), S/MIME, PEM-MIME, S-HTTP, and SSL; it is the PKCS standard for the software industry, as well.

RSA requires a commercial license if you intend to use the algorithm in any product that you make or sell. However, RSA Data Security usually allows free, noncommercial use of RSA, with written permission, for academic or university research purposes. In addition, RSA Data Systems has made available at no charge (in the U.S. and Canada) a collection of cryptographic routines in source code, including the RSA algorithm; it can be used, improved, and redistributed noncommercially. For more information or to download a trial copy of RSA, visit RSA Security's Web page at `http://www.rsasecurity.com`.

NOTE

Although RSA charges a license fee for use of its algorithm, you don't have to pay this fee when using the Crypto API. Because the RSA algorithms are packaged in a Cryptographic Service Provider (CSP), and are not packaged in your application, you are actually using the RSA license owned by the creator of the CSP. For instance, if you are using one of Microsoft's CSPs that implement the RSA algorithms, you are using Microsoft's license for the RSA algorithms. In short, you don't need to pay RSA for the right to use their encryption algorithms in your applications because Microsoft has already paid RSA for you.

PGP and Kerberos

Authentication allows the recipient of a digital signal to have confidence in the integrity of the sender and the message. Authentication protocols can be based on either conventional private-key encryption systems like DES or on public-key systems like RSA. Authentication in public-key systems uses digital signatures.

PGP

Pretty Good Privacy (PGP) is a unique product in that it serves the dual role of a powerful encryption package and a sophisticated authentication package. PGP was written by Phil Zimmerman in 1990, using the RSA algorithm for encryption. Since then, PGP has attained popularity as a powerful encryption program for email and has become the de facto standard. PGP is considered to be strong encryption.

PGP uses a method known as asymmetric cypher, or public-key encryption, where two separate keys are required. In this method, one of the keys is made public and the other is a secret key. Anything encrypted using either of these two keys can only be decrypted using the other key. Usually, the sender encrypts a message using the public key of the message recipient. Only the recipient can decrypt the message using his or her secret key.

This process of using a public key and a secret key effectively provides everyone with the ability to use the standard because the public keys are readily available from public-key servers. This method also creates the rather unique problem of authentication of keys; unless the public key was obtained directly from the owner of the key, authentication is suspect primarily because no methods of verification are in place to validate authenticity.

To provide the necessary authentication of the keys, all keys are signed with a 128-bit unique ID by the owner of the secret key. This ID can then be used to validate the authenticity of the suspect key.

With so many reports of viruses attacking computer systems and destroying files, it can be disheartening to think that your data may inadvertently download the seeds to your server's destruction. PGP to the rescue. PGP can be used to sign digital files just as easily as it can be used to sign a key. This allows you to sign a file and be certain that the integrity of the file or document has not been compromised by a virus. This type of functionality is typically used in email applications to protect the downloading credit card or other personal information from user response forms on Web sites.

Kerberos

Kerberos is a third-party authentication protocol designed for UNIX TCP/IP networks. A Kerberos service, sitting on the network, acts as a trusted arbitrator. Kerberos provides secure network authentication, allowing a person to access different machines on the network. Kerberos is based on symmetric cryptography. It shares a different secret key with every entity on the network. Knowledge of the secret key is proof of identity.

The Kerberos protocol uses a central server that knows everyone's secret key (for a person, this is the person's password, stored in an encrypted form). When one computer wants to connect to another, the server generates session keys for each to identify itself. The server sends each computer the session keys, encrypted with its secret key. The computer will decrypt the session key and use it to send secure communications to the other computer.

The Kerberos authentication service was originally developed at MIT for Project Athena. The UNIX software has been put in the public domain and can be used by anybody.

Although Kerberos provides strong authentication measures, it should not be relied on as the sole means to protect would-be attackers from gaining entrance to a secure system. Kerberos has some important limitations that dictate the need for some type of public-key cryptography. These are some of areas of weakness with Kerberos protocol:

- Denial-of-service attacks. These types of attacks occur when an attacker attempts to prevent a protected application from performing the normal authentication process. In such cases, Kerberos is not able to properly determine a normal error from an attacker-induced error causing a breakdown in security. Although this is not common throughout the Kerberos protocol, weak areas exist where this type of attack can be effective.

- Password guessing or dictionary attacks. These types of attacks are launched when an attacker repeatedly attempts to decrypt the messages obtained in response to the attacker attempting to gain access. These messages could be captured and run through a dictionary until readable plain text is produced.

Smart Cards and Tokens

One of the major problems regarding the purchasing of goods and services on the Internet is ensuring a secure collection of payment. Unsecured card systems pose a great risk to the cardholder. Cybercash systems are not universally accepted and rely on a credit card to start the process. A number of companies and organizations believe that the answer to this problem lies in the Smart Card.

Smart Cards, invented by Roland Moreno in 1972, are physically similar to a credit card, with one significant difference: the capability to store a microprocessor within the card. Over the last two decades, Roland's company, Innovatron Ingenierie, located in France, has been licensing the technology. Today, Smart Cards appear in everyday use around the world, although particularly in Europe. Companies such as Direct TV use Smart Cards as part of the authentication process to descramble the satellite signal. Without this card, the satellite dish is unable to process the Direct TV service.

Two basic types of Smart Cards are intelligent and nonintelligent. The intelligent Smart Cards contain a microprocessor that has the capability to store and process information. This processor can be controlled by the card issuer to make decisions about the use and disbursement of information contained within the memory of the card. For example, a Smart Card could be programmed to automatically add or withdraw money from a user's account, based on information obtained from the controlling application.

The nonintelligent versions of the cards have a stored value and work very much like a typical phone card. As you make a purchase of a service, the value of the card is automatically decremented. This type of card could be used in a typical vending situation to buy retail products, phone services, and so on.

The microprocessors in both types of cards provide protection against damage and theft. This allows Smart Cards to be a much more reliable method of storing information than magnetic stripe cards. Smart Cards provide their security through strong encryption techniques based on a Personal Identification Number (PIN) and Dynamic Data Authentication using the RSA algorithm.

Some of the advantages to using Smart Cards are

- **Convenience.** Smart Cards can be used to pay for anything from phone calls to purchases made using a foreign currency.
- **Safety.** The security measure built in to the Smart Card provides more safety than traditional magnetic swipe cards.
- **Capability to make secure purchase via the Internet**. As the Internet matures into more of a global intercommerce network, the capability to make secure purchases will have an immediate appeal.
- **Multiple currencies on one card**. Smart Cards have the capability to store amounts for up to five different currencies, making them the ideal form of currency for international companies and for individuals who travel abroad.

Some of the disadvantages of using Smart Cards include

- **Potential loss of privacy.** Information stored on a Smart Card is made available to whomever has the proper identification key. This causes great concern among those who believe that Smart Cards could be used by a controlling power to create an Orwellian society, in which only Smart Card holders can purchase goods or services (this disadvantage is counter-balanced by the fact that you have to have possession of the physical card to have access to the information stored on it).
- **Lack of hardware standards.** Smart Cards are very popular in Europe; however, the lack of hardware standards in the free-enterprise system has caused delays in the widespread adoption of Smart Cards in North America and Canada.

Microsoft ships a Smart Card SDK as part of its Platform SDK. You can download the Platform SDK at `http://msdn.microsoft.com/downloads/sdks/platform/platform.asp`.

Emerging Technologies and Standards

Because the Internet is constantly changing, the security protocols used to protect the valuable information stored on the various servers that compose and connect to the Internet also must evolve and change. Two protocols are highlighted in this section. The first, Point-to-Point

Tunneling, is currently undergoing a number of changes and enhancements because the cost to access the Internet and the price of associated support hardware have drastically fallen over the past year. The second protocol is lesser known simply because it provides key enhancements to Secure Sockets without changing the implementation of Secure Sockets in an application.

Point-to-Point Tunneling

Essentially, tunneling is a method of connecting two or more LANs that are physically connected only via an IP or Internet Network. This allows for the capability to create a private virtual network through the use of a standard IP or Internet Network. The IP packets are wrapped inside an IP/UDP and are sent over the Internet. These IP packets are normally encrypted for an added measure of security.

One of the more popular aspects of PPTP is its support for a wide range of communications backbones. Corporations will not have to change their existing network addressing to take advantage of PPTP benefits.

In its effort to create a standard for PPTP, Microsoft founded the PPTP Forum. The PPTP forum was cofounded with the member companies of the PPTP protocol. This forum supports PPTP as an open industry standard. These member companies include those companies previously mentioned. In addition to the strong corporate support offered by the PPTP Forum, a large amount of third-party support exists as well.

The PPTP specification has been continually updated since its inception. Work is currently under way to make the PPTP specification an industry standard. The specification has been submitted to the Internet Engineering Task Forces (IETF) and is now available as an Internet draft. Microsoft has also released sample source code on the Web, to further aid in implementation of the PPTP specification.

PPTP allows you to use the Internet as your own secure virtual private network (VPN). This protocol has been integrated with Remote Access Services (RAS) server, part of Windows NT Server. PPTP gives your users the capability to dial in to a local Internet Service Provider (ISP), connect directly to the Internet, and to access the corporate network just as easily and securely as if they were at their desks.

PPTP Security technology offers the following additional advantages:

- Decreased transmission costs by connecting via the Internet, in contrast to a traditional long-distance phone line.

- Decreased hardware costs through the centralization of computer resources such as modems and network cards.

- Decreased overhead through robust data encryption and a built in compatibility with all network protocols, such as IP, IPX, PPX and NetBUI.

- Support for Windows NT and Windows 98.
- Flexible networking. You can deploy PPTP either at the remote client PC or at the ISP local points of presence.

Although PPTP has its strengths, a few reasons why you may not want to implement the PPTP protocol include the following:

- Network Access Server (NAS, what you dial into when you connect to your ISP using PPP or SLIP) must support PPP and PPTP.
- It does not support ARA and SLIP.
- It is platform dependent, requiring Windows NT Server as the Home Gateway (PPTP server that you connect to).
- It cannot handle multipoint connections.

The biggest reason to use tunneling is for security. On PPTP-enabled networks, remote users can dial in to a local ISP to connect to their corporate network. Through the use of PPTP, this connection is made secure. A tunnel can also accommodate concurrent usage by dial-in users. This makes the process of configuration easier.

Many corporations have IP addresses that do not allow public access via the Internet. To access these addresses from remote locations outside of the company firewall, IP tunneling over the Internet must be used.

> **CAUTION**
>
> Although PPTP is often used to connect from outside a company's firewall to the internal network within that company, you need to be aware of where you are trying to establish a PPTP connection from. If you are at another company's facility, you may not be allowed to make a PPTP connection through that company's firewall. PPTP is intended to enable you to make a connection from a client outside a firewall to a PPTP server on the inside. PPTP is not intended to make a connection from a client inside a firewall to a PPTP server outside the firewall.

The PCT Specification

Private Communication Technology (PCT) is a specification that Microsoft created to provide secure communication between client and server applications. A major part of the specification provides for authentication of the server and optionally the client. The PCT specification is based on the assumption that a stable and reliable transport protocol (TCP/IP) exists for transmitting and receiving data on networks and on the Internet.

The protocol is a security protocol that is designed to provide secure transmissions of data over the Internet. This protocol provides some of the same basic functionality as Secure Socket Layer (SSL), in that it prevents snooping of data involved in the following:

- **Communications security.** The capability to encrypt communications provides protection against anyone eavesdropping on the network.

- **Financial transaction privacy.** Only those sites or individuals authorized to receive data will be able to read it.

- **Authentication.** This can be thought of as ensuring that all communications appearing to be from a single person have actually originated from that person and have not been altered in the transmission process.

The specification, although in the early stages of development, has already gained support from such companies as CyLink Corp, FTP Software, Netmanage, and RSA Data Security, among many others. The specification attempts to solve several of the issues in Secure Sockets Layer (SSL) by using technology developed for Secure Transaction Technology (STT).

The PCT specification is significantly stronger than the current key limitations imposed by the U.S. government. This increased resistance to attacks is derived through the separation of authentication from encryption. Even with this new feature, the new PCT specification is still backward compatible with SSL. This is good news for all those application developers who have created applications designed to use SSL as their security protocol.

Essentially, PCT 1.0 is a Dynamic Link Library (DLL) for MS Internet Information Server running under Windows NT 4.0. Microsoft offers no support for the use of the specification.

Summary

In this chapter you learned about several of the standards being used in the Internet encryption and security arena. These standards range from the security rating of systems to encryption algorithms and authentication methods. In the next chapter you'll learn about the legal landscape surrounding encryption and digital certificates.

Legal Issues of Digital Signatures and Encryption

IN THIS CHAPTER

- The Legal Implications of Digital Signatures: Is a Digital Signature a Legal Signature?
- Using Digital Certificates with Your Application
- Encryption and Export Issues

Although this is largely a "how-to" book dealing with security and cryptography for VB programmers, it is very important to understand how the code you write impacts the real world. Achieving technical security is usually not sufficient for most security applications. This is especially true if those applications will be used outside the corporate boundaries or on the Web.

It is important not only to achieve technical security in your solution, but also to achieve legal and financial security. This chapter addresses the issues you need to understand to design a complete solution. I also talk about how to avoid running afoul of U.S. and international export and import restrictions on encryption products. Ignoring these restrictions and breaking these laws, regardless of whether you do or don't agree with them, might land you in jail.

The Legal Implications of Digital Signatures: Is a Digital Signature a Legal Signature?

It should be clear by now that a digital signature can provide the following technical security properties: authentication, data integrity, and (in some cases) non-repudiation. A digital signature is a security mechanism. Its meaning in the real world is something else entirely.

A digital signature may be used to create a legal signature, but only if proper procedures are followed. For a digital signature to create the effect of a legal signature, the following must be done:

- The signer must view the entire document (or data to be signed).
- The signer must intend to authenticate the document to be signed.
- The document must be digitally signed *in the proper form* by the signer who is named in the corresponding certificate.
- The use of digital signatures as legal signatures must be legal in the jurisdiction(s) of the parties.
- The signed document must be validated at the time of signing.
- The signed document may need to be countersigned by a time-stamping authority or cyber notary if the signature must be relied on past the time of the signer's certificate expiration.

As you can see, the first four requirements are not measurable by software. Yet, if you need a legal signature in support of legal non-repudiation, you must address these requirements.

Additionally and importantly, digital signatures are not specifically recognized in law in most jurisdictions as being valid legal signatures. As of this writing, the United States has no national statute governing digital signatures used for commercial purposes. U.S. state laws either say nothing or apply only to certain transactions, and they often conflict with each other. Internationally, a few countries (Canada, Singapore) have adopted national statutes, and a European Union directive is in place that will lead to national legislation in the E.U. countries over the next few years. An alternative to this quagmire will be discussed in the following section.

When You Want to Use a Legal Signature

Legal signatures are not required of every application that uses digital signatures. However, if the purpose of your application is to record a human being's agreement, acknowledgment, assent, acceptance of information, and so on, then you have a need for a legal digital signature. Put another way, if your application is replacing (or would replace) a paper process that requires an ink signature, you must meet the requirements of legal digital signatures.

Recording Intent

In the United States, commercial law states that a document is signed when it "includes any symbol executed or adopted by a party with present intention to authenticate a writing." How do you know someone intends to authenticate a writing by making a digital signature? You have to ask them.

This could be done by a dialog box that states, "By clicking 'SIGN' below, you intend to be bound by the terms stated above." You should also include a statement of intent in the information to be signed, because your dialog box will not be captured as part of the signed data.

A classic contract states at the bottom something like, "agreed and accepted this 15th day of February, 2000." Your statement of intent needs to be appropriate in the context of the information to be signed. For example, a digitally signed time sheet or expense report might state, "The above information is true to the best of my knowledge and belief." You might need to involve your corporate legal team in these questions.

Recording the Form of the Transaction

For a document to be properly authenticated at a later date, you must be able to prove up the "four corners of the document." In other words, you must be able to prove what the person saw with his or her own eyes when the document was signed.

> **NOTE**
>
> I'm sure we've all seen movies in which one person is tricked into signing a blank piece of paper, only to find later that the paper has been turned into a contract of some sort. If the person who was tricked can prove that the paper was blank when he or she signed it, then the contract is not legal. In this situation, the holder of the contract would be unable to prove that the contract in hand is what the signer saw when he or she signed his or her name to the paper.

Consider typical forms-based applications. The user enters data into the form. The data is sent to a server for data validation. After the data is validated, it is written to a database. I would venture to say that 99% of software applications written do it this way. However, this is legally insufficient. It really did not matter much in the days of enterprise applications. The enterprise was the ruler of the kingdom and, as such, made most of the rules. Now it is the Internet world. This world is governed by statutory and contract law, which includes the laws of many jurisdictions and two dominant legal systems—common law and civil law.

You must record both the form and the content of the document. You must be able to prove what the user saw when he or she signed the document. This includes all data, writings, images, colors, and so on. You must be able to reproduce—from the digitally signed information—what the user saw when he or she signed the information.

This is easier to do with Web-based information and harder to do with hard-coded user interfaces. Here's an example of capturing a legal digital signature in a Web-based transaction:

1. Authenticate the user to the form page using Digital Authentication (SSLv3 client authentication; this step is optional).

2. Have the user enter the data into the form and submit the form using standard HTTP POST processing.

3. Validate the data at the server and record the data in a database.

4. Present a standard HTML page (or XML variant as they are standardized over time) with the complete information to be signed. This is the equivalent of a paper page. Ideally, the page should not have any external references (such as Java source files, IMG files, external style sheets, and so on). What the user saw should be clearly provable from the page source. The page data should include a clear statement of intent.

5. Have the user digitally sign the page using an appropriate mechanism (such as the AlphaTrust.com Web Page Signing Control, available from www.alphatrust.com). The signed data must include the entire Web page from <HTML> through </HTML>.

6. The signed data, including the signing certificate and optionally, the certificate chain, must be posted back to the server. The signed data should be in a standard PKCS#7 or CMS format.

7. The signed data is validated at the server by a Web-based process or COM control (such as the AlphaTrust.com Web Page Validation object, available from www.alphatrust.com). The data validation must include a signature check and a certificate revocation check. Optionally, you may countersign with a time stamp or use a data certification service to "seal" the signed data for historical preservation.

8. The signed data is stored in a database as part of the transaction record.

9. You may optionally send the signed data to the user for the user's records.

The requirement to store the signed data impacts the database size accordingly. There is no way around saving this data, though. At least storage keeps getting cheaper and cheaper.

Using Digital Certificates with Your Application

The choice of digital certificates, or Digital IDs, used in your application matters a great deal. A digital certificate is nothing more than a bag o' bytes. It has no intrinsic meaning. To use a credit card analogy, a digital certificate is the equivalent of a magnetic stripe card. The magnetic stripe card is meaningful only if it can be used for something useful. It's more useful if is says VISA on it than if it says San Jose Public Library or Joe's Office.

Digital IDs generally fall into three classes:

- Digital IDs issued by corporate certificate servers
- Digital IDs issued by public Certification Authorities (such as Verisign, Thawte, CyberTrust, and so on)
- Digital IDs issued by public Authentication Service Providers (such as AlphaTrust.com)

Certificates Issued by an Internal Certificate Server

Digital IDs issued by internal corporate certificate servers, such as Microsoft Certificate Server, may be useful for low-value corporate applications. These certificates are normally only valid for use within the corporation that issued the certificates. These digital signatures made using these Digital IDs have no legal meaning, unless the signature is made in a jurisdiction that permits them for the purpose being used. Check with your lawyer. Proper precautions must be taken to securely implement and protect the CA equipment, and policies and procedures must be developed regarding installation, maintenance and administration.

Properly implemented internal CAs can cost between $500,000 and several million dollars to set up, and they can cost at least $60,000 per month to operate (according to Forrester Research). The cost of an internal CA is related to the value of the data or transactions being protected.

Setting up a production enterprise CA involves integrating PKI (Public-Key Infrastructure) software, validation software, directory services, Web applications, and client software. Then you must be prepared to scale these services, because they demand 24×7×365 uptime with rapid, forward-deployed response to validation requests. No wonder the PKI vendors are making their money on consulting services.

Certificates Issued by a Public CA

Public Certification Authorities, such as Verisign, offer Digital ID issuance and management services on an outsourced basis. This is analogous to the enterprise CA discussed in the preceding section, except that you take advantage of the infrastructure already built out by the public CA. Additionally, if you have your Digital IDs issued inside the public network of the CA, they will be recognized by Web-based applications because the root CA certificates for many of these services are built into the browsers. This was done largely to facilitate SSL server validation by Web browsers.

Typically, certificates from public CAs like Verisign are used for public situations, such as on the Internet. When you go to Amazon.com to buy a book, you need to be able to confirm that the certificate your browser receives when switching to SSL mode was issued to Amazon.com, and not to Joe's Books. By using a certificate issued by a public CA like Verisign, whose root certificate is preinstalled in every Web browser, you can verify the certificate without having to worry about the trustworthiness of the issuing CA.

The downside of this approach is that any Web client will recognize your Digital ID as valid and may rely on signatures made using such Digital IDs. This can lead to large undefined liabilities because you may not have a contract with the other party; they may not be in a jurisdiction that recognizes digital signatures. Also, as a relying party to such Digital IDs, you have no idea how the other party was properly validated, whether they had control of their Digital ID when they made a signature, and what remedies you may have in the event of a breached agreement. In short, legal certainties are low and potential financial liabilities are high.

Most public CAs do not validate the identities of individual users, but rely on delegated enterprise registration agents within companies to validate their own employees. The procedures used to validate users of a public CA's network may, therefore, vary from company to company. Quite often, low cryptographic strength software (to achieve maximum interoperability) is used. The primary use of public CAs has been and continues to be issuing Web server certificates for SSL transactions.

You must also be sure that you have software from the public CA that supports revocation checking and validation checking. Be sure the CA's infrastructure is scaled and responsive to all requests. Many public CAs are essentially outsourced certificate-signing engines and disclaim most all liability for their actions or inaction.

Certificates Issued by a Public Authentication Service Provider

Authentication Service Providers (ASPs) are companies that provide the services of a public CA combined with a complete transaction network that deals with the issues of legalities and risk management. ASPs (such as AlphaTrust.com) serve Internet e-commerce application needs where a robust PKI is required, coupled with defined legal validity of transactions and protection against fraud and loss.

ASPs are used by business-to-business e-commerce hubs, commercial Web sites (especially in the financial, medical, legal, and governmental fields), and enterprises to digitally authenticate users into Web resources and provide legally valid digital signatures and encryption for data privacy. ASPs will strongly validate the identity of all users of the ASP's system and stand behind that validation with a strong warranty.

ASPs typically operate a legal framework to which all users are a party and which provides for the legal validity of digital signatures and recourse for all parties—even across international boundaries. The primary business of ASPs is providing a plug-and-play solution for e-commerce applications that strongly authenticates all users and provides a clearly understood and risk-managed environment for e-commerce transactions.

For example, AlphaTrust.com, the only commercially operating ASP as of this writing, provides three grades of Digital IDs with $2,500, $25,000 and $250,000 of warranty protection, respectively. It operates a robust PKI with certificate-revocation checking using multiple protocols, and digital signatures made using its Digital IDs have legal validity among all users worldwide.

Certificate Formats

Digital certificates conform to a standard developed by the ITU-T (formerly CCITT), called X.509. It is part of the X.500 directory specifications. X.509 certificates are specified in three versions: v1, v2, and v3. The Internet Engineering Task Force has profiled X.509 certificates for use with Internet applications. This is defined in RFC 2459 (available from www.ietf.org). This RFC specifies X.509v3 certificates. V3 certificates contain certificate extensions. Several of these extensions have legal and policy implications. They are designed for automated processing by software, and the software is expected to understand the meaning of these extensions.

Extensions can be marked as critical or not. If an extension is marked critical and the software does not understand the extension, the software must not process or rely on the certificate.

V3 extensions specified in RFC 2459 that can have legal or policy implications include

- Key usage
- Extended key usage
- Certificate policies
- Policy mappings
- Basic constraints
- Name constraints
- Policy constraints

You should consult this specification before using certificates including these extensions.

Single-Purpose Versus Multipurpose Certificates

Two primary purposes for which digital certificates are used are digital signatures and encryption (key encipherment). Many implementations in use on the Internet today use a single certificate for all uses (a multipurpose certificate). Such certificates are issued to an individual and used for digital signatures (in client authentication and secure email (S/Mime)) and encryption (secure email and encrypting file system in Windows 2000). Often, the key usage extension is absent or specifies both digital signature and key encipherment.

Attacks are possible when the same certificate is used for both digital signature and encryption applications. A better design is to use a separate certificate for digital signature and another certificate for encryption. This is accomplished by setting the appropriate key-usage extension in each certificate and setting the extension as critical.

An interoperability issue exists with single-purpose certificates. When used in some applications, such as S/MIME email, the client application ignores the key-usage extension and uses the first certificate it finds for the purpose it needs. This can result in a digital signature certificate being used to encrypt information to an email recipient. The recipient will not be able to decrypt the email because it can't use its digital signature certificate for this purpose.

When deciding on single versus multipurpose certificates, you must consider the environment in which certificates will be used.

Trust Models—Choosing the Right One

Public-Key Infrastructures generally come in three flavors:

- Open PKI
- Closed PKI
- Contractual PKI

These infrastructures differ in their scope and availability. Everyone can take part in an Open PKI, while a Closed PKI is limited to those who are part of a specific group or organization. A Contractual PKI is somewhere in between, being closed to all but those who pay for a membership. Which PKI infrastructure is most appropriate depends on the situation.

Issuing Certificates with an Open PKI

Certificates issued in an open PKI (exemplified by Verisign) are designed to be recognized and relied on by all Internet-based applications. This model was developed to support recognition of SSL server certificates. Both Netscape and Microsoft browsers and email applications have embedded within them "root" certificates of many "public" certification authorities.

All certificates issued within these open systems will be automatically trusted by software, whether the user wants to or not. This makes deployment somewhat easier, but it has the effect of exposing the certificate user and certificate issuer to unlimited liability. This is because the certificate user may have no legal relationship (called privity) with the certificate relier that defines the meaning of the transactions. Reliers could rely, to their detriment, on messages digitally signed by the user and have either no recourse or excessive recourse. Also, in some jurisdictions, there is a rebuttable presumption that if a party receives a digitally signed message, the party can rely on the fact that it was signed by the user (whether it was or not). It is then up to the user to prove that the user did not sign something. It is hard to prove a negative. Open PKIs are convenient, but they can be risky. Legal validity, risk management, and transaction privity are usually not defined at all in an open PKI.

Using the Closed PKI

The closed PKI is designed for a closed community of users. This is exemplified by an enterprise PKI, in which all users are members of the enterprise, or by an extranet PKI, such as the Automotive Network Exchange (ANX). In this model, all users and reliers are controlled by an administrative body. Only users who have a specific need are allowed to use the PKI. This model is useful for small communities for which central administration is possible. It is not intended to scale to large numbers.

The Contractual PKI

The contractual PKI offers the best of both worlds. In a contractual PKI, exemplified by AlphaTrust.com, participation in the PKI is open to almost everyone; however, each participant must apply for membership in the system. In joining the contractual PKI, the user must agree to the usage or member contract. This has the advantage of bringing all users of the system into contractual privity with one another, thereby defining the rights, responsibilities, and risks of participants.

Contractual PKIs are often operated as part of an Authentication Service that provides other benefits, such as legal validity of digital signatures, warranty protection for transactions, online validation of certificates, and value-added services such as time stamping, audit trail, and archiving. Using certificates provided by an ASP are often an excellent choice for Internet applications.

Encryption and Export Issues

Encryption has long been regulated by the U.S. and other governments as a munition, or weapon of war. Exporting software in violation of export regulations could land you in jail. For a long time, the U.S. would not allow any software that used symmetric encryption keys longer than 40 bits or asymmetric encryption keys longer than 512 bits to be exported without a license.

In January 2000, the U.S. issued new export regulations that permit the export of strong encryption retail products to most destinations worldwide. Most Microsoft products are now eligible for export and worldwide download in their strong encryption versions. This includes the Windows operating systems, Internet Explorer, Microsoft Outlook, and Exchange. See http://www.microsoft.com/exporting for complete information.

Strong Versus Export-Grade Encryption

Despite the relaxation in the regulations, most Microsoft and Netscape software programs in service today are the export, or "weak," encryption versions. This is almost 100% true outside the U.S. and Canada, and probably 70% true within the U.S. and Canada, because downloaded software such as browsers were almost always the "weak" encryption versions.

Windows 2000 and Windows Millennium ship only with "strong" encryption because of the change in regulations, but it will be a while before the installed base is upgraded. This means that you must see that your clients are upgraded, if you use strong encryption, or live with weak encryption (that is, 40-bit RC5 and 512-bit RSA). An interim relaxation in regulations occurred in 1998, which upped the 40-bit restricting to 56-bits. This effectively permitted 56-bit DES to be exported. Therefore, you probably will have no idea what your clients can support.

Enabling Strong Encryption on Your Windows Clients

As you know by now, cryptographic operations on Win32 platforms are implemented using cryptographic service providers, or CSPs. All Win32 operating systems come with the Microsoft Base Cryptographic Provider v1.0. This CSP provides symmetric and asymmetric operations using "weak," or export-grade key lengths.

For strong cryptographic operations to be performed, the Microsoft Enhanced Cryptographic Provider v1.0 must be installed. This CSP can be installed by several methods:

- Applying a 128-bit version of any Windows NT Service Pack
- Installing a 128-bit version of Internet Explorer
- Installing the High Encryption Pack update to Internet Explorer
- Installing the 128-bit version of Outlook 98 or 2000

With the Enhanced CSP, you will be able to perform up to 16,384 bit RSA (although there is no need for this—1024- or 2048-bit will do nicely), 1024-bit DSA, 128-bit RC5, and 168-bit triple-DES encryption.

All installations of this CSP require a reboot of the computer. Plan for what you need. Most applications need strong encryption because the weak versions have been broken, and so you must plan to test for and upgrade your clients as needed.

Complying with Export Regulations

If you use Microsoft's cryptographic systems and do not include any cryptographic code in your application, you should not have to seek export clearance for your application. If you export any strong encryption products, such as the upgrades previously described, you may need to seek export clearance. Also, some nations have import restrictions on encryption software. In some jurisdictions, software originating in one country and legally imported into another country may not be re-exported to a third country.

In the U.S., encryption exports are regulated by the Bureau of Export Administration of the U.S. Department of Commerce. See `http://www.bxa.doc.gov/encryption` for more information.

Summary

In this chapter, you received a good look at the current legal state of encryption and digital signatures in the U.S. These laws are not International, so if you need to build encryption applications for use outside the U.S., you might want to check on the laws in the countries where your applications will be used. If you want to find out more about the legal status of digital signatures, you might want to check out some of the following sources: The European Union Electronic Signature Legislations (`http://europa.eu.int/comm/dg15/en/media/sign/index.htm`), the American Bar Association—Digital Signature Guidelines (`http://www.abanet.org/scitech/ec/isc/ dsgfree.html`), and the U.S. and International Legislative Updates (`http://www.bakernet.com/ ecommerce`).

17

LEGAL ISSUES

Cryptographic Service Providers

IN THIS APPENDIX

- **The Cryptographic Service Provider (CSP) Plug-In Architecture**
- **Available CSPs**

One of the advantages of using Microsoft's Crypto API is that you can easily change encryption algorithms and strengths. You do so by plugging in a different Cryptographic Service Provider (CSP).

The Cryptographic Service Provider (CSP) Plug-In Architecture

CSPs use a separate API to plug into the Crypto API and provide cryptographic services to applications that need them. This API, the Crypto SPI (Service Provider Interface), allows applications to select one of many CSPs to perform their encryption needs, based on the specific needs of the applications, as illustrated in Figure A.1.

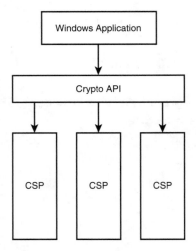

FIGURE A.1
Multiple CSPs can be accessed through the Crypto API.

How the CSP performs the cryptographic functions is up to the creator of the CSP. Several CSPs perform all their functions in software, whereas some CSPs use specialized hardware devices to perform their cryptographic functions. A few Smart Card manufacturers also provide CSPs to access the cryptographic capabilities of their Smart Cards.

Along with performing cryptographic functions, CSPs are also responsible for storing and maintaining encryption keys and certificates. Some, like the Microsoft CSPs, store these keys and certificates in protected areas of the Registry database. Others, like Smart Card CSPs, store certificates in a removable device.

Available CSPs

It is impossible to provide a complete list of the available CSPs, as the list frequently changes. Some companies develop new CSPs and make them available, whereas other companies are bought by companies that either decide to quit offering the CSP or rename the CSP to reflect the new owner's product line. As a result, the list of available CSPs provided here is no more than a snapshot of some of the currently available CSPs at the time I am writing this appendix. This list does not contain all the available CSPs, and those included may have changed by the time you read this book.

> **NOTE**
>
> There is a list of CSP vendors available through the Security section of the Microsoft Web site, but it is hopelessly out of date, and hasn't been updated in several years.

Atalla (Compaq)

www.atalla.com

The Compaq TrustMaster CSP is a hardware encryption card that goes in the PCI bus in your computer. By performing all the encryption processes on a dedicated card, the Atalla cards can offload the processing load from the main computer processor. The Atalla cards also have a "tamper-sensor" that detects whether someone is trying to hack into the protected memory on the card and immediately zeroes out all sensitive data, including passwords, encryption keys, and algorithms. This feature makes the Atalla more secure than a software CSP, which maintains all these sensitive elements in the main computer memory, which is vulnerable to hacking.

Certicom

www.certicom.ca

Certicom offers a couple of CSPs that use elliptic curve encryption algorithms. Elliptic curve algorithms are much smaller and faster than more traditional algorithms. Elliptic curve algorithms are also currently believed to be much stronger than traditional algorithms, and are starting to be accepted as another encryption standard. However, elliptic curve algorithms still have a way to go before they become the dominant form of encryption on the Internet.

Datakey

www.datakey.com

Datakey's SignaSure CSP incorporates Smart Cards into your Crypto API application. The keys are generated on the Smart Card, and all encryption functions are performed on the card.

All sensitive information is therefore kept out of the main computer memory and secured on a portable hardware token that can be moved from computer to computer.

NOTE

Not all Smart Cards perform encryption on the card itself. Some Smart Cards do little more than store public and private encryption keys. These keys are passed into the main computer memory, where the encryption is performed. These Smart Cards, although faster, are not as secure as those that perform the encryption on the card itself.

E-Lock

www.elock.com

E-Lock offers a family of products that provide the entire Public Key infrastructure for a corporation. Its Assured PKI product integrates with Microsoft's Certificate Server and Crypto API to provide the public key services for the corporate infrastructure. As part of this entire package, E-Lock includes its own E-Lock CSP. This CSP enables you to build Crypto API applications that are integrated with the entire corporate Public Key infrastructure.

Gemplus

www.gemplus.com

Gemplus is one of the leaders in the Smart Card arena. This company's GemSafe SDK, for building applications that use its Smart Cards, is available in several formats, including as a Crypto API CSP. Your Crypto API applications therefore can use Gemplus's Smart Cards to perform all your encryption needs, as well as storing your passwords, public and private keys, and certificates. The GemSafe CSP has been included in some of the Windows 2000 beta distributions, so there is a chance it might be included in some of the release versions of Windows 2000.

Microsoft

www.microsoft.com

Microsoft provides several of its own CSPs with Windows and even more that can be downloaded from the Microsoft Web site or purchased from Microsoft. Some of these CSPs have restrictions on them, whereas others don't. All the restrictions on the Microsoft CSPs are because of national and international encryption laws in the various countries where Microsoft Windows is available.

Microsoft Base Cryptographic Provider

The Microsoft Base Cryptographic Provider provides a broad set of basic cryptographic functions, with key lengths and encryption strengths that can be freely exported from the United States. (Some restrictions are placed on their import in other countries.)

Microsoft Strong Cryptographic Provider

WINDOWS **2000** The Microsoft Strong Cryptographic Provider is an extension to the Microsoft Base Cryptographic Provider that is currently available only for Windows 2000. It provides the capabilities of both the Microsoft Base Cryptographic Provider and the Microsoft Enhanced Cryptographic Provider, with much larger keys than are available with the base provider. The smaller key sizes of the base provider are the default key sizes generated and used with this CSP.

Microsoft Enhanced Cryptographic Provider

The Microsoft Enhanced Cryptographic Provider provides the same functionality as the Microsoft Base Cryptographic Provider, except that it uses much larger key sizes. Because of the larger key sizes, this CSP provides much stronger encryption than the base provider but also has more legal restrictions on its distribution and availability.

Microsoft DSS Cryptographic Provider

The Microsoft DSS Cryptographic Provider provides functionality for hashing, signing, and signature verification only. It does not provide any encryption functionality.

Microsoft Base DSS and Diffie-Hellman Cryptographic Provider

The Microsoft Base DSS and Diffie-Hellman Cryptographic Provider provides all the data signing and verification functionality in the Microsoft DSS Cryptographic Provider, along with support for the Diffie-Hellman key exchange and encryption, which is a 40-bit DES derivative.

Microsoft DSS and Diffie-Hellman/SChannel Cryptographic Provider

WINDOWS **2000** The Microsoft DSS and Diffie-Hellman/SChannel Cryptographic Provider builds on the Microsoft Base DSS and Diffie-Hellman Cryptographic Provider by adding support for the SSL3 and TLS1 protocols. This CSP is currently available only for the Windows 2000 platform.

Microsoft RSA/SChannel Cryptographic Provider

WINDOWS **2000** The Microsoft RSA/SChannel Cryptographic Provider supports the RSA algorithms for hashing, data signing, and signature verification. It also provides support for the SSL3 and TLS1 client authentication. It is currently available only for the Windows 2000 platform.

A

CRYPTOGRAPHIC
SERVICE
PROVIDERS

Rainbow ISG

isg.rainbow.com

Rainbow Technologies CryptoSwift is an encryption accelerator card that fits into the PCI bus on your computer. The CryptoSwift CSP offloads all encryption processing to the CryptoSwift accelerator card(s), relieving the main processor of the work and speeding up server performance by up to 90 percent. The CryptoSwift cards are scaleable and can work in parallel; so, as your encryption capacity needs to increase, you can add additional cards to your server and increase your capacity linearly.

Schlumberger

www.schlumberger.com

Schlumberger is another one of the leaders in the Smart Card marketplace. The Schlumberger CSP provides access through the Crypto API to the cryptographic capabilities of Schlumberger Smart Cards, including key generation; key, certificate, and password storage; as well as cryptographic functionality. The Schlumberger CSP has been included on some of the Windows 2000 betas, so chances are good that it might be included with some of the release versions of Windows 2000.

Spyrus

www.spyrus.com

Spyrus CSP provides the capability to use its LINKS Privacy Card to perform encryption using a tamper-resistant hardware encryption card. You can choose from two Spyrus CSPs, depending on which set of encryption algorithms your applications need. All encryption functions are performed on the hardware card, where the private keys are also stored.

INDEX

A

Listing   565

Other Related Titles

MTS Programming with Visual Basic
Scot Hillier
ISBN: 0-672-31425-8
$29.99 US/$44.95 CAN

Doing Objects in Visual Basic 6
1-56276-577-9
Deborah Kurata
$49.99 US/$74.95 CAN

Peter Norton's Guide to Visual Basic 6
0-672-31054-6
Peter Norton
$29.99 US/$42.95 CAN

Dan Appleman's Developing COM/ActiveX Components with Visual Basic 6
1-56276-576-0
Dan Appleman
$49.99 US/$71.95 CAN

Visual Basic 6 Unleashed, Professional Reference Edition
0-672-31508-4
Rob Thayer
$39.99 US/$57.95 CAN

Peter Norton's Complete Guide to Windows 2000 Server
0-672-31777-X
Peter Norton
$39.99 US/$59.95 CAN

The Waite Group's Visual Basic 6 Client/Server How-To
1-57169-154-5
Noel Jerke
$49.99 US/$71.95 CAN

Database Access with Visual Basic
1-56276-567-1
Jeffery McManus
$39.99 US/$56.95 CAN

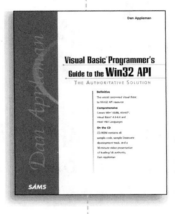

Dan Appleman's Visual Basic Programmer's Guide to the WIN32 API
Dan Appleman
0-672-31590-4
$59.99 US/$89.95 CAN

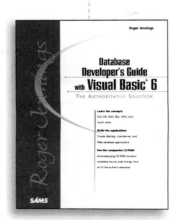

Roger Jenning's Database Developers's Guide with Visual Basic 6
Roger Jennings
0-672-31063-5
$59.95 US/$$89.95 CAN

SAMS

www.samspublishing.com

All prices are subject to change.

The IT site
you asked for...

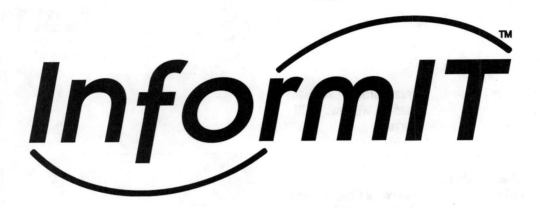

InformIT is a complete online library delivering
information, technology, reference, training, news,
and opinion to IT professionals, students,
and corporate users.

Find IT Solutions Here!

www.informit.com